CHILDREN'S BOOK AWARD HANDBOOK

Diana F. Marks

Illustrations by Susanne Frey

LIBRARIES

U N L I M I T E D

A Member of the Greenwood Publishing Group

Westport, Connecticut • London

Library of Congress Cataloging-in-Publication Data

Marks, Diana F.
  Children's book award handbook / by Diana F. Marks; illustrations by Susanne Frey.
    p. cm.
  Includes bibliographical references and index.
  ISBN 1-59158-304-7 (pbk. : alk. paper)
  1. Children's literature, American—Awards. 2. Young adult literature, American—Awards. 3. Children's literature—Awards. 4. Young adult literature—Awards. 5. Children's literature—Illustrations—Awards. 6. Young adult literature—Illustrations—Awards. I. Title.
  Z1037.A2M37   2006
  810.8'09282079—dc22   2006003720

British Library Cataloguing in Publication Data is available.

Library of Congress Catalog Card Number: 2006003720
ISBN: 1-59158-304-7

First published in 2006

Libraries Unlimited, 88 Post Road West, Westport, CT 06881
A Member of the Greenwood Publishing Group, Inc.
www.lu.com

Printed in the United States of America

The paper used in this book complies with the
Permanent Paper Standard issued by the National
Information Standards Organization (Z39.48–1984).

10 9 8 7 6 5 4 3 2 1

Copyright Acknowledgments

Illustrations of the Newbery Medal, Caldecott Medal, Laura Ingalls Wilder Award have been approved by the American Library Association.

Illustration of the Charlotte Zolotow Award CCBC has been approved by the Cooperative Children's Book Center, University of Wisconsin—Madison School of Education.

Contents

Acknowledgments

I want to thank

- Sharon Coatney, Elizabeth Budd, and Emma Bailey, my editors at Libraries Unlimited. I appreciate their concern for the book and me.

- Heidi Estrin, Library Director, Feldman Children's Library at Congregation B'nai Israel in Boca Raton, Florida, and the 2004–2005 Chair of the Sydney Taylor Book Award Committee of the Association of Jewish Libraries. Heidi provided me with a great amount of information regarding the Sydney Taylor Book Award.

- Robert L. Sibert, President of Bound to Stay Bound Books, Inc., and Susan Roman, former Executive Director of ALSC and currently Dean of Dominican University's Graduate School of Library and Information Science. They both helped me regarding the Robert F. Sibert Informational Award.

- Margaret Mary Kimmel, Ph.D., Professor of Library and Information Science at the University of Pittsburgh. She shared her knowledge regarding the Mildred L. Batchelder Award.

- Sandra Rios Balderrama, Oralia Garza de Cortes, Toni Bissessar, Satia Orange, Melinda Greenblatt, Elizabeth Martinez, and Linda Perkins, members of REFORMA and ALA. They were so helpful regarding the development of the Pura Belpré Award.

- Deborah Pope, Executive Director of the Ezra Jack Keats Foundation. She provided me with so much detail regarding the history of the Ezra Jack Keats New Writer and New Illustrator Award.

- Anne Irish, Executive Director of the Association of Booksellers for Children. She gave me a great deal of information regarding the E. B. White Read Aloud Award.

- Susanne Frey, my illustrator. We make a great team.

- Beth Auwarter, friend and librarian, who first inspired me to tackle this project.

- Betty Minetola, friend and librarian, and Karen Freedman, friend and library assistant, who were always good listeners.

- Shirley Heuchemer, my mother, for chasing down various books for me.

- Peter, my husband, and my sons, Kevin and Colin, for cheering me on.

Introduction

In the spring of 2004, my librarian friend, Beth Auwarter, told me I had to write a book about John Newbery. "All these children," she said, "want the 'gold books.' They want the books with the gold seals on them. They want books that have won awards. They want to know who this guy John Newbery is. But I don't know much about John Newbery, so go write a picture book about him."

Being a good friend and an excellent follower of directions, I researched the life of John Newbery and discovered why no one had written a children's book about the man. Not much information regarding Newbery can be found, and what is out there must be understood in the context of place and time.

So then, I thought I would check out the life of Randolph Caldecott—later period, more information, but not much excitement. I have to admit, though, I got very interested in all the children's awards and their namesakes. First, I wanted to know why two of America's most prestigious children's literature awards were named after British people. Then I found the names of people I had never heard of, names like Michael Printz and Mildred L. Batchelder. I became intrigued not only with the lives of these people but also with how the awards got started. I interviewed friends of Pura Belpré and the son of Robert F. Sibert. I e-mailed the Executive Director of the Ezra Jack Keats Foundation, and I talked to the Executive Director of the Association of Booksellers for Children. I asked the founders of several awards to review my writing. I interviewed American Library Association staff members, and I bothered REFORMA members several times. Finally, I ended up with a head full of knowledge and to me an exciting book proposal.

Libraries Unlimited liked my book proposal, but they wanted more. They wanted me to design activities that librarians, teachers, and parents could immediately use. That has proven to be the hardest part. I am a teacher, but I found it difficult to create worksheets and step-by-step directions for activities that were in my head but not on paper.

So you have in your hands a book that you can use in many ways. I have written a chapter for each of twenty-one children's literature awards and their namesakes. Each chapter has several subsections. For really busy people, I have provided an overview of the award and the person behind the award. For those with more time I have written a biography of the namesake of the award. I have also included a timeline of the person's life. The timeline is actually one of the most interesting features, particularly for the authors. I found it fascinating when authors wrote what books. I have also written a section about the history and criteria for the award. I have organized an easy-to-read list of the award-winning authors, illustrators, or books. In addition, I have assembled a list of easy to do activities regarding each award, its namesake, and the award books or recipients. Last, I have created several handouts and activities that you can immediately use.

I know you have too much to accomplish in too little time. This book can make your life easier. Obviously, you care about children's literature. Good literature continues to fascinate children and the adults who care about them. I hope this book helps you achieve your goals, whatever they may be.

CHAPTER 1

Children's Literature Awards and Their Namesakes

Overview

Children's literature as an entity separate from adult literature is relatively new. Before John Newbery (1713–1767), children (those who could read, that is) read *Gulliver's Travels* or *Robinson Crusoe*. A few more books of interest to children were around, but the pickings were slim. John Newbery felt all children should be educated. He further believed that children could gain that education by reading more. The way to read more, he reasoned, would be to read interesting books. He began publishing children's books in 1744. Other publishers, seeing how successful he was, also began to publish books for children.

Today the children's book market is huge, and children have a plethora of choices as to what books to buy. Children, as well as adults, can also buy books through a variety of venues, including bookstores, the Internet, book clubs, and book fairs.

Organizations such as the American Library Association and the International Board on Books for Young People have long sought to honor good books and good authors and illustrators. The Newbery Medal, established in 1922 by the American Library Association, was the first children's literature award created in the world. The Caldecott Medal followed later, in 1938. Other awards were created until today many awards for children's literature exist. Each of the awards has a unique focus. For example, the Coretta Scott King Award celebrates African American writings and illustrations. The Hans Christian Andersen Award acknowledges lifetime contributions of writers and illustrators around the world. We even have an award for works that are funny, the Sid Fleischman Humor Award.

The field has become so specialized that some awards have been designated for literature for young adults. The Margaret A. Edwards Award and the Michael L. Printz Award for Excellence in Young Adult Literature are two of those awards. Other awards, such as the Edgar Award, have a special category for teenage readers.

Over twenty awards are named after people, most of them writers or illustrators. Some awards have been named after librarians, and one award, the Robert F. Sibert Informational Award, honors Robert F. Sibert, a bookbinder who could spot good children's literature.

Rules exist for each award. For example, children have wondered why J. K. Rowling has not received the Newbery Medal. The rules for that award state that only books originally published in the United States are considered. Therefore, Rowling will not receive the Newbery for her Harry Potter series, first published in Great Britain. Committees of devoted experts decide on the award winners. They spend countless hours reading many books, discussing the merits of a large number of them, and deciding on the ultimate award recipients—the "first-place finishers." Fortunately, most award committees also pick honor books, outstanding works that have great merit, the "second-place finishers." The Charlotte Zolotow Award extends the honors one more category and lists highly commended books, the "third-place finishers."

Award winners reflect the times in which they lived. For example, Hendrik Willem van Loon's book, *The Story of Mankind,* received the 1922 Newbery Medal. Not too many children today would choose to read the book's accurate but disjointed glimpses of historical events. However, the book was probably very desirable then. Other award-winning books, such as Robert McCloskey's *Make Way for Ducklings,* the 1942 Caldecott Medal book, speak for all times and have become classics.

Timeline of Awards

The following timeline gives a good perspective on the history of children's book awards. The John Newbery Medal, as noted earlier, existed for sixteen years before the Randolph Caldecott Medal was created. The Caldecott was followed by the Edgar Award, founded in 1945. Many more awards quickly followed, and by the end of the timeline, we see that a new award was born every year.

Year	Award
1922	John Newbery Medal
1938	Randolph Caldecott Medal
1945	Edgar Award
1953	Jane Addams Book Award
1954	Laura Ingalls Wilder Award
1955	Kate Greenaway Medal
1956	Hans Christian Andersen Award
1966	Mildred L. Batchelder Award
1967	Boston Globe-Horn Book Award
1970	Coretta Scott King Award
1973	Golden Kite Award
1978	Sydney Taylor Book Award
1982	Scott O'Dell Award for Historical Fiction
1986	Ezra Jack Keats New Writer and New Illustrator Award
1988	Margaret A. Edwards Award
1993	Lee Bennett Hopkins Poetry Award
1996	Pura Belpré Award
1998	Charlotte Zolotow Award
2000	Michael L. Printz Award for Excellence in Young Adult Literature
2001	Robert F. Sibert Informational Book Award
2002	Astrid Lindgren Memorial Award
2003	E. B. White Read Aloud Award
2004	Theodor Seuss Geisel Award

Birthdays of Award Namesakes

The following list of birthdays can be very useful. Teachers or librarians could create a "Birthday Bulletin Board" dedicated to the award namesakes. The birth month might be a good time to introduce the awards to children.

Month	Person
January	Edgar Allan Poe (19) Robert F. Sibert (20)
February	Pura Belpré (2) Laura Ingalls Wilder (7)
March	Theodor Seuss Geisel (2) Ezra Jack Keats (11) Kate Greenaway (17) Randolph Caldecott (22)
April	Hans Christian Andersen (2) Lee Bennett Hopkins (13) Coretta Scott King (27)
May	Scott O'Dell (23) Michael L. Printz (27)
June	Charlotte Zolotow (26)
July	E. B. White (11) John Newbery (probably 9; baptized 19)
August	
September	Jane Addams (6) Mildred L. Batchelder (7)
October	Margaret A. Edwards (23) Sydney Taylor (30)
November	Astrid Lindgren (14)
December	

Children's Activities Pertaining to Any Person, Award, or Book

Children should be active learners regarding literature, awards, and their namesakes. To stimulate children to read more, they should be encouraged to:

1. Collect, categorize by award, and read books that have won awards.

2. Read books that won awards some years ago and find out how literature has changed through time. They can also compare and contrast older winners with newer winners.

3. Write letters suggesting possible winners to the award-nominating bodies.

4. Make commercials for their favorite award-winning books.

5. Choose one award-winning book and rewrite a portion from another point of view.

6. Write to living authors/illustrators.

7. Change books into plays and present the results.

8. Make word searches or crossword puzzles regarding award winners.

9. Write a different ending of a particular book with an ending they do not like.

10. Make a book into a comic book.

11. Propose a new award for a group of authors or books not presently recognized and find someone to name it after.

12. Record the books onto audiocassettes.

13. Illustrate a narrative book.

14. Find illustration award-winning books and analyze the styles. Then children could try to imitate the style.

15. Pretend to be the person after whom the award is named. For example, a child could pretend to be John Newbery and could dress as he might have dressed. Then another child could interview the pretender.

16. Create book jackets for award-winning books.

17. Compose and produce music to accompany certain portions of award-winning books.

18. Change the genre of award-winning books. For example, they could change a narrative to a poem.

19. Using a large world map, mark the birthplaces of authors, illustrators, and the namesakes for the awards.

20. Mark a calendar with the birthdays of authors, illustrators, and the namesakes for the awards.

21. Make a diorama of a favorite award-winning book.

22. Interview other children and record their favorite award winners, and then make a bar graph to show the results.

23. Make a board game about an award-winning book or author.

24. Participate in a game show regarding authors, illustrators, and the people for whom the awards are named.

25. Make use of the ever-popular food connection. For example, Gary Soto's book *Chato's Kitchen*, winner of the 1996 Pura Belpré Illustration Award for Susan Guevera, features a menu. Children could make and eat some of the items on the menu.

Conclusion

More children's literature awards are bound to appear, and they should continue to appear; good writing and good illustrating should always be recognized. Librarians, teachers, parents, and children can all use these authors, illustrators, and books as a standard and as a starting point. These awards help answer the child's ever-recurring question, "What good book can I read next?"

CHAPTER 2

Jane Addams and the
Jane Addams Book Award

Overview

The Jane Addams Book Award is presented annually to the best children's picture book and to the best book for older children that espouse Jane Addams's goals. Honor books may also be awarded. Jane Addams was a social activist who created a settlement house for the poor in Chicago in 1889. Throughout her life she promoted world peace, racial equality, and women's suffrage.

Jane Addams was born in 1860 to an affluent family. Always aware of the advantages of her wealth, Jane early on decided to spend her time helping the poor and downtrodden. She also became active in both national and world politics. She tried to keep America out of World War I, and she was the first American woman to win the Nobel Peace Prize. Jane Addams died in 1935.

The Women's International League for Peace and Freedom (WILPF) and the Jane Addams Peace Association administer the Jane Addams Book Award. Until 2002, the award was announced on Jane Addams's birthday, September 6. Beginning in 2003, the winners have been announced on April 28, the date marking the creation of the WILPF. The winners receive their cash prizes and certificates on the third Friday of October.

Jane Addams Biography

Jane Addams has been called the "Mother of the World." She used her inheritance and the royalties from her books to aid immigrants, improve industrial safety, establish child labor laws, fight for women's rights, and promote peace. While the Jane Addams Book Award honors her, she never wrote any children's books.

Laura Jane Addams was born in Cedarville, Illinois, to John Huy Addams and Sarah Weber Addams on September 6, 1860. Her deeply religious parents had come from Pennsylvania to establish a gristmill. Her father was quite successful and served as an Illinois state senator from 1854 to 1870. He was also a stationmaster on the Underground Railroad. Jane and her four older siblings, Mary, Martha, Weber, and Alice, lived very comfortably.

In 1863, Sarah Weber Addams died in childbirth. The baby also died. Several years later, Jane's father married Anna Hostetter Haldeman, a widow with two children. Jane's new stepbrother, George Haldeman, was slightly younger than Jane, but they became constant companions. Both attended the local one-room schoolhouse.

In 1877, Jane was accepted into Smith College, but her father would allow her only to attend Rockford Female Seminary. He was one of the seminary's trustees, and two of Jane's older sisters had gone there. He felt that Jane needed to get married and that the seminary would prepare her for marriage and motherhood.

Reluctantly, Jane packed her bags to go to Rockford Female Seminary, but in the end she found the school to be intellectually stimulating. She learned Greek and Latin, and she traveled to various oratory contests. At one of those contests, she met Ellen Gates Starr, and the two would be great friends for the rest of their lives. Jane finished her schooling at Rockford in 1881. She was the valedictorian out of a class of seventeen.

That same year Jane's father died of appendicitis, and Jane became very depressed. After attending graduation ceremonies at Rockford Female Seminary in 1882, she decided to become a doctor and was accepted into the Women's Medical College of Philadelphia. However, a spinal curvature problem she had had since birth caused her great pain, as a result of which she had to rethink her plans. She had surgery performed to correct the spinal curve, but her six-month recovery was slow and painful.

From 1883 to 1885 and again from 1887 to 1888, Jane toured Europe. It was during these travels that she decided that she wanted to contribute to the lives of others, but she floundered for a method. During her second grand tour of Europe, she visited Toynbee Hall, a settlement house in London, England, where wealthy, educated males helped the poor. At last she had found her way to help others. Upon her return to the United States, she decided to help immigrants by creating a settlement house in Chicago, Illinois.

Ellen Gates Starr and Jane searched Chicago for the right location. At last they discovered a derelict mansion surrounded by slums filled with immigrants. There, in 1889, they founded Hull-House where Jane was to live and work for the rest of her life. By 1893, Hull-House was providing classes, childcare, clubs, and facilities for neighborhood activities. Later the facility added an art gallery, a bookbinding facility, and even a post office so that immigrants could safely and inexpensively send money to loved ones in their home countries.

Jane soon found herself involved with Chicago politics. In 1894, she helped create the Chicago Federation of Settlements. The following year, after complaining bitterly about the poorly run private garbage-collecting companies, she became the garbage inspector for the 19th Ward, near West Side of Chicago.

Soon Jane became involved in politics at the national level. In 1902, she published *Democracy and Social Ethics*, and a year later, she was elected vice president of the National Woman's Trade Union League, an organization that helped women establish unions within their workplaces. From 1905 to 1908, she was a member of the Chicago Board of Education. She published another book, *Newer Ideals of Peace*, in 1907, and in 1909, she helped found the National Association for the Advancement of Colored People. The same year, she was also elected the first woman president of the National Conference of Charities and Corrections (later the National Conference of Social Work).

In 1910, she received honorary degrees from Yale University and Smith College and was the mediator in the Chicago Garment Workers Strike. In that same year, she published *Twenty Years at Hull-House*.

During the next year, Jane Addams became the first vice president of the National American Woman Suffrage Association. She was also the first head of the National Federation of Settlement and Neighborhood Centers. In 1912, she seconded Theodore Roosevelt's nomination at the Progressive Party Convention. She created the Woman's Peace Party in 1915 and was elected its first chair. She vainly hoped that the United States would not enter World War I. Also in 1915, she presided at the International Congress of Women at The Hague, Netherlands.

Jane Addams created the Women's International League for Peace and Freedom (WILPF) in 1919 and served as its president until 1929. Still feeling a need to help minorities, she helped create the American Civil Liberties Union in 1920. Eight years later, she traveled to Hawaii to preside over the Pan-Pacific Women's Union Conference.

In 1931, Jane Addams became the first American woman to receive the Nobel Peace Prize, but she was too ill to attend the ceremony at Oslo. The American ambassador to Norway accepted the prize for her. Her part of the monetary award, $16,000, was given to the WILPF.

Jane Addams died from cancer in Chicago on May 21, 1935. She was buried in Cedarville, Illinois.

The first Jane Addams Book Award was given in 1953 to Eva Knox Evans for her book, *People Are Important*.

Jane Addams Timeline

Date	Event
1860	Born Laura Jane Addams in Cedarville, Illinois, to John Huy Addams and Sarah Weber Addams on September 6
1863	Mother died
1869	Father married Anna Haldeman
1877	Was accepted into Smith College; father made her attend Rockford Female Seminary
1881	Finished schooling at Rockford Female Seminary; father died
1882	Attended graduation ceremony at Rockford; had surgery done to correct spinal curve
1883	Toured Europe until 1885
1887	Toured Europe again
1888	Visited Toynbee Hall in London, England
1889	Founded Hull-House with Ellen Gates Starr
1894	Helped create Chicago Federation of Settlements
1895	Took job of garbage inspector for 19th Ward, near West Side
1902	Published *Democracy and Social Ethics*
1903	Became vice president of National Woman's Trade Union League
1905	Was a member of Chicago Board of Education until 1908
1907	Published *Newer Ideals of Peace*
1909	Helped found National Association for the Advancement of Colored People; elected first woman president of the National Conference of Charities and Corrections (later National Conference of Social Work)
1910	Received honorary degree from Yale; was a mediator in Chicago Garment Workers Strike; published *Twenty Years at Hull-House*
1911	First vice president of National American Woman Suffrage Association; first head of National Federation of Settlement and Neighborhood Centers
1912	Seconded Theodore Roosevelt's nomination at Progressive Party convention
1915	Helped create Woman's Peace Party, elected first chair; presided at International Congress of Women at The Hague, Netherlands
1919	Created Women's International League for Peace and Freedom; was its president until 1929
1920	Helped create American Civil Liberties Union
1928	Presided over conference of Pan-Pacific Women's Union in Hawaii
1931	Became first American woman to receive Nobel Peace Prize
1935	Died in Chicago on May 21 and buried in Cedarville, Illinois
1953	Jane Addams Book Award given for the first time

History and Criteria of Award

Jane Addams worked tirelessly to help the downtrodden, to create child labor laws, to support women's suffrage, and to bring peace to a struggling world. She was the first American woman to win the Nobel Peace Prize. She died in 1935.

The Jane Addams Children's Book Award annually honors books that promote peace, equality for minority groups, world issues, and equality for both men and women. The award was created in 1953. The Women's International League for Peace and Freedom (WILPF) and the Jane Addams Peace Association jointly administer the award. The two groups' regulations regarding the award process are as follows.

1. A national group reviews books published in the previous year.

2. The books may be fiction, nonfiction, or poetry.

3. The books must have been published in the United States, but they may have been published elsewhere as well.

4. The books may have been published in other languages as well as English.

5. Honor books may also be chosen.

The official Jane Addams Book Award guidelines state that the books must answer at least one of the following questions:

How can people settle disputes peaceably but still retain diversity?

How can we begin to think more creatively and humanely about injustice and conflict, past or present, real or fictionalized?

How can young people participate in creative solutions to the problems of war, social injustice, racism, sexism, homophobia, ageism, and the concerns of the physically challenged?

How can people of all races, cultures, nations, and economic systems live peacefully together?

Does the book promote an understanding of the role of women in society, gender roles, and the need to overcome gender stereotypes (e.g., role models of both genders)?

Originally, the Jane Addams Book Award sponsored one category of awards. However, in 1993, the sponsoring groups decided to honor picture books as well as longer books. The winners receive a cash prize and a certificate. Seals may be affixed to the award-winning books.

Award and Honor Books

Year	Award	Title	Author/Illustrator	Publisher
2005	Book for Older Children	*With Courage and Cloth: Winning the Fight for a Woman's Right to Vote*	Ann Bausum	National Geographic Society
	Honor Book	*The Heaven Shop*	Deborah Ellis	Fitzhenry & Whiteside
	Picture Book	*Sélavi, That Is Life: A Haitian Story of Hope*	Youme Landowne	Cinco Puntos Press
	Honor Books	*Hot Day on Abbott Avenue*	Karen English, author Javaka Steptoe, illustrator	Clarion
		Henry and the Kite Dragon	Bruce Edward Hall	Philomel Books/Penguin
		Sequoyah: The Cherokee Man Who Gave His People Writing	James Rumford, author Anna Sixkiller Huckaby, translator	Houghton Mifflin
2004	Book for Older Children	*Out of Bounds: Seven Stories of Conflict and Hope*	Beverley Naidoo	HarperCollins
	Honor Books	*Getting Away with Murder: The True Story of the Emmett Till Case*	Chris Crow	Phyllis Fogelman/Penguin
		Shutting Out the Sky: Life in the Tenements of New York 1880–1924	Deborah Hopkinson	Orchard Books
	Picture Book	*Harvesting Hope: The Story of Cesar Chavez*	Kathleen Krull, author Yuyi Morales, illustrator	Harcourt
	Honor Books	*Girl Wonder: A Baseball Story in Nine Innings*	Deborah Hopkinson, author Terry Widener, illustrator	Atheneum
		Luba: The Angel of Bergen-Belsen	Luba Tryszynska-Frederick, author Ann Marshall, illustrator	Tricycle Press

Year	Award	Title	Author/Illustrator	Publisher
2003	Book for Older Children	*Parvana's Journey*	Deborah Ellis	Groundwood Books/Douglas & McIntyre
	Honor Books	*The Same Stuff as Stars*	Katherine Paterson	Clarion
		When My Name Was Keoko	Linda Sue Park	Clarion
	Picture Book	*Patrol: An American Soldier in Vietnam*	Walter Dean Myers, author Ann Grifalconi, illustrator	HarperCollins
	Honor Books	*Si, Se Puede! Yes, We Can! Janitor Strike in L.A.*	Diana Cohn, author Francisco Delgado, illustrator	Cinco Puntos Press
		The Village That Vanished	Ann Grifalconi, author Kadir Nelson, illustrator	Dial
2002	Book for Older Children	*The Other Side of Truth*	Beverley Naidoo	HarperCollins
		A Group of One	Rachna Gilmore	Henry Holt
		True Believer	Virginia Euwer Wolff	Atheneum
	Picture Book	*Martin's Big Words: The Life of Dr. Martin Luther King, Jr.*	Doreen Rappaport, author Bryan Collier, illustrator	Jump at the Sun/Hyperion
	Honor Book	*Amber Was Brave, Essie Was Smart*	Vera B. Williams	Greenwillow/HarperCollins
2001	Book for Older Children	*Esperanza Rising*	Pam Muñoz	Scholastic
	Honor Books	*The Color of My Words*	Lynn Joseph	Joanna Cotler Book/HarperCollins
		Darkness over Denmark: The Danish Resistance and the Rescue of the Jews	Ellen Levine	Holiday House
		Walking to the Bus-Rider Blues	Harriette Gillem Robinet	Jean Karl Book/Atheneum
	Picture Book	*The Composition*	Antonio Skármeta, author Alfonso Ruano, illustrator	Groundwood Books

Year	Award	Title	Author/Illustrator	Publisher
	Honor Book	*The Yellow Star: The Legend of King Christian X of Denmark*	Carmen Agra Deedy, author Henri Sorensen, illustrator	Peachtree Publishers
2000	Book for Older Children	*Through My Eyes*	Ruby Bridges	Scholastic
	Honor Books	*The Birchbark House*	Louise Erdrich	Hyperion
		Kids on Strike!	Susan Campbell Bartoletti	Houghton Mifflin
	Picture Book	*Molly Bannaky*	Alice McGill, author Chris K. Soentpiet	Houghton Mifflin
	Honor Books	*A Band of Angels: A Story Inspired by the Jubilee Singers*	Deborah Hopkinson, author Raúl Colón, illustrator	Anne Schwartz/Atheneum
		When Sophie Gets Angry—Really, Really Angry ...	Molly Bank	Blue Sky/Scholastic
1999	Book for Older Children	*Bat 6*	Virginia Euwer Wolff	Scholastic
	Honor Books	*The Heart of a Chief*	Joseph Bruchac	Dial
		No More Strangers Now	Tim McKee, author Anne Blackshaw, photography	Melanie Kroupa/ DK Ink
		Restless Spirit: The Life and Work of Dorothea Lange	Elizabeth Partridge	Viking
	Picture Book	*Painted Words: Spoken Memories: Marianthe's Story*	Aliki	Greenwillow
	Honor Books	*Hey, Little Ant*	Phillip and Hannah Hoose, authors Debbie Tilley, illustrator	Tricycle Press
		i see the rhythm	Toyomi Igus, author Michele Wood, illustrator	Children's Book Press
		This Land Is Your Land	Woody Guthrie, author and lyricist Kathy Jakobsen, illustrator	Little, Brown

Year	Award	Title	Author/Illustrator	Publisher
1998	Book for Older Children	*Habibi*	Naomi Shihab Nye	Simon & Schuster
	Honor Books	*The Circuit: Stories from the Life of a Migrant Child*	Francisco Jimenez	University of New Mexico Press
		Seedfolks	Paul Fleischman	HarperCollins
	Picture Book	*Seven Brave Women*	Betsy Hearne, author Bethanne Andersen, illustrator	Greenwillow
	Honor Books	*Celebrating Families*	Rosemarie Hausherr	Scholastic
		Passage to Freedom: The Sugihara Story	Ken Mochizuki, author Dom Lee, illustrator	Lee & Low
1997	Book for Older Children	*Growing Up in Coal Country*	Susan Campbell Bartoletti	Houghton Mifflin
	Honor Books	*Behind the Bedroom Wall*	Laura E. Williams	Milkweed
		Second Daughter: The Story of a Slave Girl	Mildred Pitts Walter	Scholastic
	Picture Book	*Wilma Unlimited*	Kathleen Krull, author David Diaz, illustrator	Harcourt, Brace
	Honor Book	*The Day Gogo Went to Vote*	Elinor Batezat Sisulu, author Sharon Wilson, illustrator	Little, Brown
1996	Book for Older Children	*The Well*	Mildred D. Taylor	Dial
	Honor Books	*From the Notebooks of Melanin Sun*	Jacqueline Woodson	Blue Sky/Scholastic
		On the Wings of Peace: Writers and Illustrators Speak Out for Peace in Memory of Hiroshima and Nagasaki		Clarion
		The Watsons Go to Birmingham—1963	Christopher Paul Curtis	Delacorte
	Picture Book	*No award given*		
	Special Commendation	*The Middle Passage*	Tom Feelings	Dial

Year	Award	Title	Author/Illustrator	Publisher
1995	Book for Older Children	*Kids at Work: Lewis Hine and the Crusade Against Child Labor*	Russell Freedman	Clarion
	Honor Books	*Cezanne Pinto*	Mary Stolz	Knopf
		I Hadn't Meant to Tell You This	Jacqueline Woodson	Delacorte
	Picture Book	*Sitti's Secret*	Naomi Shihab Nye, author Nancy Carpenter, illustrator	Four Winds Press
	Honor Book	*Bein' with You This Way*	W. Nikola-Lisa, author Michael Bryant, illustrator	Lee & Low
1994	Book for Older Children	*Freedom's Children: Young Civil Rights Activists Tell Their Stories*	Ellen Levine	G. P. Putnam's Sons
	Honor Book	*Eleanor Roosevelt: A Life of Discovery*	Russell Freedman	Clarion
	Picture Book	*This Land Is My Land*	George Littlechild	Children's Book Press
	Honor Book	*Soul Looks Back in Wonder*	Tom Feelings	Dial
1993	Book for Older Children	*A Taste of Salt: A Story of Modern Haiti*	Frances Temple	Orchard Books
	Honor Book	*Letters from a Slave Girl: The Story of Harriet Jacobs*	Mary E. Lyons	Scribners
	Picture Book	*Aunt Harriet's Underground Railroad in the Sky*	Faith Ringgold	Crown
	Honor Book	*Mrs. Katz and Tush*	Patricia Polacco	Bantam
1992	Winner	*Journey of the Sparrows*	Fran Leeper Buss, author, with the assistance of Daisy Cubias	Lodestar
	Honor Book	*Now Is Your Time! The African-American Struggle for Freedom*	Walter Dean Myers	HarperCollins

Year	Award	Title	Author/Illustrator	Publisher
1991	Winner	*The Big Book for Peace*	Ann Durrell and Marilyn Sachs, editors	Dutton
	Honor Books	*The Journey: Japanese-Americans, Racism and Renewal*	Sheila Hamanaka	Richard Jackson/Orchard Books
		The Middle of Somewhere: A Story of South Africa	Sheila Gordon	Orchard Books
1990	Winner	*A Long Hard Journey: The Story of the Pullman Porter*	Patricia and Fredrick McKissack	Walker
	Honor Books	*Number the Stars*	Lois Lowry	Houghton Mifflin
		Shades of Gray	Carolyn Reeder	Macmillan
		The Wednesday Surprise	Eve Bunting	Clarion
1989	Winners (Tie)	*Anthony Burns: The Defeat and Triumph of a Fugitive Slave*	Virginia Hamilton	Knopf
		Looking Out	Victoria Boutis	Four Winds Press
	Honor Books	*December Stillness*	Mary Downing Hahn	Clarion
		The Most Beautiful Place in the World	Ann Cameron	Knopf
		Rescue: The Story of How Gentiles Saved Jews in the Holocaust	Milton Meltzer	Harper & Row
1988	Winner	*Waiting for the Rain: A Novel of South Africa*	Sheila Gordon	Orchard Books/Franklin Watts
	Honor Books	*Nicolas, Where Have You Been?*	Leo Lionni	Knopf
		Trouble at the Mines	Doreen Rappaport	Crowell
1987	Winner	*Nobody Wants a Nuclear War*	Judith Vigna	Albert Whitman
	Honor Books	*All in a Day*	Mitsumasa Anno	Philomel

Year	Award	Title	Author/Illustrator	Publisher
		Children of the Maya: A Guatemalan Indian Odyssey	Brent Ashabranner, author Paul Conklin, photographer	Dodd, Mead
1986	Winner	*Ain't Gonna Study War No More: The Story of America's Peace Seekers*	Milton Meltzer	Harper & Row
	Honor Book	*Journey to the Soviet Union*	Samantha Smith	Little, Brown
1985	Winner	*The Short Life of Sophie Scholl*	Hermann Vinke	Harper & Row
	Honor Books	*The Island on Bird Street*	Uri Orlev, author Hillel Halkin, translator	Houghton Mifflin
		Music, Music for Everyone	Vera B. Williams	Greenwillow
1984	Winner	*Rain of Fire*	Marion Dane Bauer	Clarion/Houghton Mifflin
1983	Winner	*Hiroshima No Pika*	Toshi Maruki	Lothrop, Lee & Shepard
	Honor Books	*The Bomb*	Sidney Lenz	Lodestar/Dutton
		If I Had a Paka: Poems in Eleven Languages	Charlotte Pomerantz	Greenwillow
	West Coast Honor Book	*People at the Edge of the World: The Ohlone of Central California*	Betty Morrow	Bacon
	Special Recognition	*All the Colors of the Race*	Arnold Arnoff	Lothrop, Lee & Shepard
		Children as Teachers of Peace	Gerald Jampolsky	Celestial Press
1982	Winner	*A Spirit to Ride the Whirlwind*	Athena V. Lord	Macmillan
	Honor Books	*Let the Circle Be Unbroken*	Mildred D. Taylor	Dial
		Lupita Mañana	Patricia Beatty	Morrow
1981	Winner	*First Woman in Congress: Jeannette Rankin*	Florence Meiman White	Julian Messner
	Honor Books	*Chase Me, Catch Nobody!*	Erik Haugaard	Houghton Mifflin
		Doing Time: A Look at Crime and Prisons	Phyllis Clark and Robert Lehrman	Hastings House

Year	Award	Title	Author/Illustrator	Publisher
		We Are Mesquakie, We Are One	Hadley Irwin	Feminist Press
1980	Winner	*The Road from Home: The Story of an Armenian Girl*	David Kherdian	Greenwillow
	West Coast Honor Book	*Woman from Hiroshima*	Toshio Mori	Isthmus
	Special Recognition	*Natural History*	M. B. Goffstein	Farrar, Straus & Giroux
1979	Winner	*Many Smokes, Many Moons: A Chronology of American Indian History*	Jamake Highwater	Lippincott
	Honor Books	*Escape to Freedom*	Ossie Davis	Viking
		The Great Gilly Hopkins	Katherine Paterson	Crowell
1978	Winner	*Child of the Owl*	Laurence Yep	Harper & Row
	Honor Books	*Alan and Naomi*	Myron Levoy	Harper & Row
		Mischling, Second Degree	Ilse Koehn	Greenwillow
	Special Recognition	*Amifka*	Lucille Clifton	Dutton
		The Wheel of King Asoka	Ashok Davar	Follett
1977	Winner	*Never to Forget: The Jews of the Holocaust*	Milton Meltzer	Harper & Row
	Honor Book	*Roll of Thunder, Hear My Cry*	Mildred D. Taylor	Dial
1976	Winner	*Paul Robeson*	Eloise Greenfield	Crowell
	Honor Books	*Dragonwings*	Laurence Yep	Harper & Row
		Song of the Trees	Mildred D. Taylor	Dial
		Z for Zachariah	Robert C. O'Brien	Atheneum
1975	Winner	*The Princess and the Admiral*	Charlotte Pomerantz	Addison-Wesley
	Honor Books	*The Eye of Conscience*	Milton Meltzer and Bernard Cole	Follett
		My Brother Sam Is Dead	James Lincoln Collier and Christopher Collier	Four Winds

Year	Award	Title	Author/Illustrator	Publisher
		Viva la Raza!	Elizabeth Sutherland Martinez and Enriquetta Longeaux y Vasquez	Doubleday
1974	Winner	*Nilda*	Nicholasa Mohr	Harper & Row
	Honor Books	*A Hero Ain't Nothin' but a Sandwich*	Alice Childress	Coward, McCann & Geoghegan
		Men Against War	Barbara Habenstreit	Doubleday
		A Pocket Full of Seeds	Marilyn Sachs	Doubleday
1973	Winner	*The Riddle of Racism*	S. Carl Hirsch	Viking
	Honor Book	*The Upstairs Room*	Johanna Reiss	Crowell
1972	Winner	*The Tamarack Tree*	Betty Underwood	Houghton Mifflin
1971	Winner	*Jane Addams: Pioneer of Social Justice*	Cornelia Meigs	Little, Brown
1970	Winner	*The Cay*	Theodore Taylor	Doubleday
1969	Winner	*The Endless Steppe*	Esther Hautzig	Crowell
1968	Winner	*The Little Fishes*	Erik Haugaard	Houghton Mifflin
1967	Winner	*Queenie Peavy*	Robert Burch	Viking
1966	Winner	*Berries Goodman*	Emily Cheney Neville	Harper & Row
1965	Winner	*Meeting with a Stranger*	Duane Bradley	Lippincott
1964	Winner	*Profiles in Courage: Young Readers Memorial Edition*	John F. Kennedy	Harper & Row
1963	Winner	*The Monkey and the Wild, Wild Wind*	Ryerson Johnson	Abelard-Schuman
1962	Winner	*The Road to Agra*	Aimee Sommerfelt	Criterion
1961	Winner	*What Then, Raman?*	Shirley L. Arora	Follett
1960	Winner	*Champions of Peace*	Edith Patterson Meyer	Little, Brown
1959	No award given			
1958	Winner	*The Perilous Road*	William O. Steele	Harcourt, Brace

Year	Award	Title	Author/Illustrator	Publisher
1957	Winner	*Blue Mystery*	Margot Benary-Isbert	Harcourt, Brace
1956	Winner	*Story of the Negro*	Arna Bontemps	Knopf
1955	Winner	*Rainbow Round the World*	Elizabeth Yates	Bobbs-Merrill
1954	Winner	*Stick-in-the-Mud*	Jean Ketchum	Cadmus Books, E. M. Hale
1953	Winner	*People Are Important*	Eva Knox Evans	Capital

Activities

1. Jane Addams developed an art gallery at Hull-House. Children could decide why she decided to do that. They could visit: http://www.state.il.us/hpa/lib/edservices/JaneAddams. htm. to read about Hull-House, the art gallery, and the other facilities. They could then find art prints and create their own art gallery.

2. Jane Addams felt that war was not always necessary to achieve peace. Children could find symbols for peace and create a peace poster.

3. Ann Bausum received the Jane Addams Book Award in 2005 for *With Courage and Cloth: Winning the Fight for a Woman's Right to Vote*. Children could visit Ann's Web site at: http://www.annbausum.com/ and read about her research and what she could not include in the book. They could share their findings by giving a speech.

4. Deborah Ellis has received the Jane Addams Book Award twice, first for *Parvana's Journey* in 2003 and then as an honor book for *The Heaven Shop* in 2005. Ellis is Canadian. Children could check out her Web site at: http://www.allen-unwin.com.au/authors/apEllis.asp, and they could find out where she lives and what she does when she is not writing. They could create a "Day in the Life of Deborah Ellis" and share it with their friends.

5. Linda Sue Park's *When My Name Was Keoko* was a Jane Addams Honor Book in 2003. She received the Newbery Medal for *A Single Shard* in 2002. Children could read both books and decide which one is better. They could also compare and contrast the two books by using a Venn diagram. They could visit her Web site at: http://www. lspark.com/.

6. The Jane Addams Book Award has been given since 1953. Children could locate older winning books and newer winning books and compare/contrast them.

7. Jane Addams received the Nobel Peace Prize in 1931. Children could find out the names of other recipients at http://nobelprize.org/search/all_laureates_c.html. They could see if any of the other recipients were the subjects, or the authors, of any Jane Addams Children's Book Award books.

8. Jane Addams helped people in many ways. Children could help people in some way as well. Perhaps they could have a food drive to fill the local food bank. Perhaps they could develop conflict mediation systems. They may want to help new immigrants.

9. Patricia Polacco's *Mrs. Katz and Tush* was a Jane Addams Honor Book in 1993. Children could visit her Web site at: http://www.patriciapolacco.com/ and learn about the book. They could change one segment of the story into a play.

10. Susan Campbell Bartoletti received the Jane Addams Book Award in 1997 for *Growing Up in Coal Country*. Her *Kids on Strike!* was an honor book in 2000. Children could visit her Web site at: http://www.scbartoletti.com/ and look at some of her other books and the awards they have received. Children could also read both *Kids on Strike!* and *Growing Up in Coal Country*. Then they could decide which book had greater impact on them. They could share their thoughts with their friends by creating a commercial for their book choice.

Jane Addams and the Jane Addams Book Award

Student Handout 1—Information

Who Was Jane Addams?

Jane Addams was called the "Mother of the World." She provided support for immigrants, wrote books that promoted peace, and worked hard for the rights of all races and for women.

Jane Addams was born to a fairly rich family on September 6, 1860. Early in her life, she realized she was lucky to have been born into wealth. She decided to devote her life to helping others. She graduated from Rockford Female Seminary in Illinois. Her father wanted her to marry and have children. Jane had other ideas. While traveling in Europe, she visited a settlement house, a place where immigrants could receive aid and support. Jane and a friend, Ellen Gates Starr, founded Hull-House, a settlement house in Chicago, in 1889. The settlement house provided classes for immigrants, childcare facilities, housing assistance, and even an art gallery. Jane lived and worked there the rest of her life.

Soon Jane found herself involved in politics. She helped create the Chicago Federation of Settlements. For a time she was the garbage inspector for part of Chicago. She became active in the National Woman's Trade Union League. She was one of the founders of the National Association for the Advancement of Colored People. In 1915, she created the Woman's Peace Party, and she was elected its first chair.

Jane Addams formed the Women's International League for Peace and Freedom (WILPF) in 1919. She was its president until 1929. Still feeling a need to help minorities, she helped create the American Civil Liberties Union in 1920.

In 1931, Jane Addams became the first American woman to receive the Nobel Peace Prize. Jane was ill and could not attend the ceremony at Oslo. The American ambassador to Norway accepted the prize for her. Her part of the monetary award, $16,000, was given to the WILPF.

Jane Addams died in Chicago on May 21, 1935. She was buried in Cedarville, Illinois.

What Is the Jane Addams Book Award?

The Jane Addams Book Award is presented annually to the best children's picture book and the best book for older children that promote world peace, racial equality, and women's suffrage. Honor books may also be awarded. The Women's International League for Peace and Freedom and the Jane Addams Peace Association administer the Jane Addams Book Award. The winners receive cash prizes and certificates. Seals may be added to both the medal books and the honor books. The books must be published in the United States, but they may also have been published in other countries. The books may be fiction, nonfiction, or poetry. The first Jane Addams Book Award was presented in 1953.

Jane Addams and the Jane Addams Book Award

Student Handout 2—Questions

Name_____ Date_____

Investigate the life of Jane Addams, and find out more about the Jane Addams Book Award. Then answer the following questions.

1. Where and when was Jane Addams born?

2. Why did she decide to spend so much time helping others?

3. How did Jane Addams help immigrants new to Chicago?

4. What civic groups did Jane Addams help found? Are those groups still active today?

5. What major award did Jane Addams receive?

6. Where and when did Jane Addams die?

7. List at least three ways Jane Addams helped people.

8. How would history have been different if Jane Addams had not devoted her life to others?

9. List three facts about the Jane Addams Book Award.

10. Why was Jane Addams called the "Mother of the World?"

From *Children's Book Award Handbook* by Diana F. Marks. Westport, CT: Libraries Unlimited. Copyright © 2006.

Jane Addams and the Jane Addams Book Award

Student Handout 3—Peace Symbols

Name_____ Date_____

Jane Addams devoted her life to helping others. She felt very strongly that peaceful resolution to conflicts was always possible.

In the space below, draw all the peace symbols you can think of.

In the space below, draw a new symbol or a combination of symbols that could stand for peace. Add your new illustration to a bulletin board.

Jane Addams and the Jane Addams Book Award

Student Handout 4—Research and Technology

Name_____ Date_____

In 1931, Jane Addams was the first American woman to win the Nobel Peace Prize. Go to the following site: http://nobelprize.org/search/all_laureates_c.html and find the name of another Nobel Peace Prize winner. Then find out more information regarding that person. After you have found all the information you need, create a poster or slide show about your person. Include the following information about your person. You may not find the answers to all the questions. You may wish to add more information than the following.

1. What person did you choose?

2. Why did you choose this person?

3. Where and when was this person born?

4. What are some interesting facts about his or her childhood?

5. What education did this person achieve?

6. What did this person do to receive the Nobel Peace Prize?

7. What did the person do after receiving the Nobel Peace Prize?

8. Did this person marry or have children?

9. What else is interesting about this person?

10. Where and when did this person die? On the other hand, is he or she still living?

CHAPTER 3

Hans Christian Andersen and the Hans Christian Andersen Award

Overview

The Hans Christian Andersen Award is bestowed every two years to the world's best children's book authors and illustrators. Hans Christian Andersen was a famous storyteller, known for his fairy tales. Hans Christian Andersen was born in 1805 in Odense, Denmark, to a poor couple and received little education. He went to Copenhagen to try to become an actor. However, being ungainly and uneducated, he had little luck. A benefactor paid for his education, and he became a writer. His first book of fairy tales appeared in 1835, and children loved his works. Some of his most famous stories are *Thumbelina*, *The Little Match Girl*, and *The Ugly Duckling*. He never married, but millions of children loved him and his tales. He was given the keys to Odense in 1867. He died in 1875.

The Hans Christian Andersen Award was created by the International Board on Books for Young People (IBBY) in 1956 to honor a children's writer. In 1966, IBBY decided to honor an illustrator every two years as well. The award recognizes not a single work, but an author's or illustrator's entire contribution to literature. American recipients include Virginia Hamilton and Maurice Sendak. Winners from other countries include Astrid Lindgren, Mitsumasa Anno, and Uri Orlev. The awards are announced in the spring of even-numbered years, and the Queen of Denmark presents the awards to the recipients during IBBY's summer conference.

Hans Christian Andersen Biography

Hans Christian Andersen started life with several strikes against him. He was poor, uneducated, awkward, and shy. However, he became one of the most beloved children's writers of all time. His fairy tales, including "The Little Mermaid" and "The Emperor's New Clothes," still enchant children 150 years later. His works have been translated into over 100 languages, and Andersen died a famous and beloved man.

Hans Christian Andersen was born in Odense, Denmark, on April 2, 1805. His father was a shoemaker, and his mother was a washerwoman. The family had little money, and Hans received an inadequate education. When Hans was seven years old, his father took him to see a play. He decided then to become an actor. He made a puppet theater at home, and he preferred to play alone. At age fourteen, he left Odense for Copenhagen in 1819 in hopes of becoming a successful actor. However, he was awkward and uneducated; no one wanted to hire him.

Fortunately, Jonas Collin, a director of the Royal Theatre, felt Hans had potential and sent the young man to school. Hans went back to school to be taught by Dr. Simon Meisling, but Hans was years older than the other children. Moreover, Dr. Meisling terrified him, and he felt out of place among the other students. However, Hans would not give up, and he was able to complete his studies. He published *Youthful Attempts,* a book of short stories, in 1822. In 1829, he passed the entrance examination for the University of Copenhagen. In the same year, he toured Denmark and published *A Walking Tour from Homen's Canal to the Eastern Point of Amager in the Years 1828 and 1829.* He also published a play, *Love in Saint Nicholas Church Tower.*

For the rest of his life Andersen published a major piece just about every year. He also was able to travel to many places. In 1830, he published *Poems*, and in the following year he published *Fantasies and Sketches* and traveled to Germany. In 1833, he traveled to France, Germany, and Italy and also published *Collected Poems.*

In 1835, Andersen published *Fairy Tales, Told to Children*, which included "The Princess and the Pea" and "The Tinderbox." Children loved these stories. In the next six years, he published five more books of tales. In 1837, he traveled to Sweden, and in 1840, he again traveled through Europe, this time visiting Greece. He never visited the United States. As he learned, American publishers were selling many of his works, but they never paid him a royalty.

In 1843, Andersen met Clara Schumann, a famous pianist and composer and wife of the composer Robert Schumann, and he traveled to France and Germany. He met Jenny Lind, the well-known Swedish singer, and he fell in love with her. His love was not requited.

King Christian VIII in 1844 invited Andersen to visit him. In 1845, "The Ugly Duckling" and "The Nightingale" were included in *Nye Eventyr* (*New Fairy Tales*). By then Andersen was truly famous. Two years later, he toured England and Scotland, meeting Charles Dickens and publishing *The True Story of My Life.*

Andersen published *The Two Baronesses* in 1848, *The Fairy Tale of My Life* in 1855, and *To Be, or Not to Be?* in 1857. From 1858 to 1870, he published eleven more books of tales. In 1859, he received the Maximilian Order of Art and Science from King Maximilian II of Bavaria.

Andersen visited the World Exposition in Paris in 1867, and he received keys to the city of Odense on December 6 of that year. The year after, he visited Holland, Germany, France, and Switzerland. In 1870, he published his last book, *Lucky Peer.* In 1873, he was able to travel to Switzerland. He never married.

Hans Christian Andersen died in Copenhagen, Denmark, on August 4, 1875. His funeral was held on August 11. In tribute, a statue of the Little Mermaid stands in the harbor of Copenhagen.

The International Board on Books for Young People (IBBY) was created in 1953, and the group presented the first Hans Christian Andersen Award for writing in 1956. In 1966, IBBY bestowed the first Hans Christian Andersen Award for illustration.

In 2005, the Danish government celebrated Andersen's two hundredth birthday.

Hans Christian Andersen Timeline

Date	Event
1805	Born in Odense, Denmark, on April 2
1819	Left Odense for Copenhagen
1822	Went back to school taught by Dr. Meisling; published *Youthful Attempts*
1829	Passed entrance exam for the University of Copenhagen
1829	Toured Denmark; published *A Walking Tour from Homen's Canal to the Eastern Point of Amager in the Years 1828 and 1829*; published play *Love in Saint Nicholas Church Tower*
1830	Published *Poems*
1831	Published *Fantasies and Sketches;* traveled to Germany
1833	Traveled to France, Germany, and Italy; published *Collected Poems*
1835	Published *Fairy Tales, Told to Children*
1835–1841	Published five more books of tales
1836	Published *O. T.*
1837	Published *Only a Fiddler;* traveled to Sweden
1839	Published *Picture Book without Pictures*
1840	Published *The Mulatto; The Moorish Maid;* toured Europe again, including trip to Greece
1842	Published *A Poet's Bazaar*
1843	Met Clara Schumann; traveled to France and Germany; met Jenny Lind and fell in love with her
1843–1848	Published five more books of tales
1844	Was invited by King Christian VIII to visit him
1847	Traveled to England and Scotland, met Charles Dickens; published *The True Story of My Life*
1848	Published *The Two Baronesses*
1852–1853	Published two more books of tales
1855	Published *The Fairy Tale of My Life*
1857	Published *To Be, or Not to Be?*
1858–1870	Published eleven more books of tales
1859	Received the Maximilian Order of Art and Science from King Maximilian II of Bavaria
1867	Visited the World Exposition in Paris; received keys to the city of Odense on December 6
1868	Traveled to Holland, Germany, France, and Switzerland
1870	Published *Lucky Peer*
1873	Traveled to Switzerland
1875	Died in Copenhagen, Denmark, on August 4; funeral held August 11
1953	The International Board on Books for Young People created
1956	First Hans Christian Andersen Award for writing presented
1966	First Hans Christian Andersen Award for illustration presented

History and Criteria of Award

The Hans Christian Andersen Award is an international award given every two years to the best authors and illustrators of children's books. The award does not recognize one book but rather a lifetime of literary contributions. The International Board on Books for Young People (IBBY), founded in Zurich, Switzerland, in 1953, sponsors the Hans Christian Andersen Award. A nonprofit group, IBBY is "committed to bringing books and children together." During World War II, many libraries were destroyed or damaged, children's book production virtually stopped, and the facilities produced other materials. In addition, movies and television were becoming more and more popular to the detriment of reading. Members of IBBY felt that a children's literature award might motivate children to read more. Accordingly, it created the Hans Christian Andersen Award to recognize authors and illustrators who have made a "lasting contribution to children's literature."

IBBY created the Rules for the Conferment of the International Hans Christian Andersen Award, as follows.

1. The award will be given every two years.

2. The author or illustrator must be living at the time of nomination.

3. IBBY is composed of at least fifty National Sections. Each section represents a country. An individual can be nominated only by his or her National Section.

4. For the first three awards, the award was presented to a book published in the previous two years. Thus, in 1956 Eleanor Farjeon won the award for *The Little Bookroom*; Astrid Lindgren in 1958 received the award for *Rasmus pD luffen* (*Rasmus on the Road*, or *Rasmus and the Vagabond*); and Erich Kästner won the award in 1960 for *Als ich ein kleiner Jung war* (*When I Was a Little Boy*). In 1962, the group changed the rules and based the award on an author's body of work.

5. IBBY decided to add another medal for the best illustrator in 1966.

6. A jury of ten voting members and three nonvoting ex-officio members sit on the jury. One of the ex-officio members is the jury leader.

7. A portfolio of the nominee's work must be compiled. It must include a biography (preferably an autobiography), a bibliography, a collection of at least five but not more than ten books by the author or illustrator, and books in original languages and in foreign languages if possible. Each portfolio is carefully constructed, and attention to detail is evident. Even the covers of the portfolios are works of art.

8. IBBY also publishes an "Honor List" every two years.

The Hans Christian Andersen Award has been called the Little Nobel Prize. The Queen of Denmark bestows a gold medal (depicting Hans Christian Andersen in profile) and a diploma to each of the winners.

Fairy Tales Written by Hans Christian Andersen

Note: These titles have been translated from Danish, and variations in titles exist.

"A-B-C Book, The"
"Angel, The"
"Anne Lisbeth"
"Aunty Toothache"
"Beauty of Form and Beauty of Mind"
"Beetle Who Went on His Travels, The"
"Bell, The"
"Bell-Deep, The"
"Bird of Popular Song, The"
"Bishop of Borglum and His Warriors"
"Bottle Neck, The"
"Buckwheat, The"
"Brave Tin Soldier, The"
"Butterfly, The"
"By the Almshouse Window"
"Candles, The"
"Cheerful Temper"
"Child in the Grave, The"
"Children's Prattle"
"Comet, The"
"Conceited Apple-Branch"
"Court Cards, The"
"Cripple, The"
"Croak"
"Daisy, The"
"Dance, Dance, Doll of Mine!"
"Danish Popular Legends"
"Darning-Needle, The"
"Days of the Week, The"
"Delaying Is Not Forgetting"
"Drop of Water, The"
"Dryad, The"
"Dumb Book, The"
"Elf of the Rose, The"
"Elfin Hill, The"
"Emperor's New Clothes, The"
"Everything in the Right Place"
"Farm-Yard Cock and the Weather-Cock, The"
"Fir Tree, The"
"Flax, The"
"Flea and the Professor, The"
"Flying Trunk, The"
"Folks Say—"
"Garden of Paradise, The"
"Gardener and the Manor, The"
"Gate Key, The"

"Girl Who Trod on the Loaf, The"
"Goblin and the Huckster, The"
"Goblin and the Woman, The"
"God Can Never Die"
"Godfather's Picture Book"
"Golden Treasure, The"
"Goloshes of Fortune, The"
"Grandmother"
"Great-Grandfather"
"Great Grief, A"
"Great Sea-Serpent, The"
"Happy Family, The"
"Holger Danske"
"Ib and Little Christina"
"Ice Maiden, The"
"In a Thousand Years"
"In the Nursery"
"In the Uttermost Parts of the Sea"
"Jack the Dullard"
"Jewish Maiden, The"
"Jumper, The"
"Last Dream of the Old Oak, The"
"Last Pearl, The"
"Leaf from Heaven, A"
"Little Claus and Big Claus"
"Little Elder Tree Mother, The"
"Little Green Ones, The"
"Little Ida's Flowers"
"Little Match-Seller, The"
"Little Mermaid, The"
"Little Turk"
"Loveliest Rose in the World, The"
"Luck May Lie in a Pin"
"Lucky Peer"
"Mail-Coach Passengers, The"
"Marsh King's Daughter, The"
"Metal Pig, The"
"Money Box, The"
"Most Incredible Thing, The"
"Moving Day"
"Neighboring Families, The"
"New Century's Goddess, The"
"Nightingale, The"
"Old Bachelor's Nightcap, The"
"Old Church Bell, The"
"Old Grave-Stone, The"
"Old House, The"

"Old Street Lamp, The"
"Ole-Luk-Oie, the Dream-God"
"Ole the Tower-Keeper"
"On Judgment Day"
"Our Aunt"
"Pea Blossom, The"
"Peiter, Peter and Peer"
"Pen and the Inkstand, The"
"Penman, The"
"Philosopher's Stone, The"
"Phoenix Bird, The"
"Pigs, The"
"Poor Woman and the Little Canary Bird, The"
"Porter's Son, The"
"Portuguese Duck, The"
"Poultry Meg's Family"
"Princess and the Pea, The"
"Psyche, The"
"Puppet-Show Man, The"
"Races, The"
"Rags, The"
"Red Shoes, The"
"Rose from Homer's Grave"
"Saucy Boy, The"
"Shadow, The"
"She Was Good for Nothing"
"Shepherdess and the Sweep, The"
"Shepherd's Story of the Bond of Friendship, The"
"Shirt-Collar, The"
"Silver Shilling, The"
"Snail and the Rose-Tree, The"
"Snowdrops, The"
"Snow Man, The"
"Snow Queen, The"
"Something"
"Soup from a Sausage Skewer"
"Storks, The"

"Storm Shakes the Shield, The"
"Story, A"
"Story from the Sand-Hills, A"
"Story of a Mother, The"
"Story of the Wind, The"
"Story of the Year, The"
"String of Pearls, A"
"Sunbeam and the Captive, The"
"Sunshine Stories"
"Swan's Nest, The"
"Swineherd, The"
"Talisman"
"Teapot, The"
"Tinder-Box, The"
"There Is No Doubt about It"
"This Fable Is Intended for You"
"Thistle's Experiences, The"
"Thorny Road of Honor, The"
"Thumbelina"
"Toad, The"
"Top and Ball, The"
"Two Brothers"
"Two Maidens"
"Ugly Ducking, The"
"Under the Willow Tree"
"Urbanus"
"VFnr and GlFnr"
"What Old Johanne Told"
"What One Can Invent"
"What the Moon Saw"
"What the Old Man Does Is Always Right"
"What the Whole Family Said"
"Which Is the Happiest?"
"Wicked Prince, The"
"Wild Swans, The"
" 'Will-o-the-Wisp Is in the Town,' Says the Moor-Woman, The"
"Windmill, The"

Award Recipients

Year	Award	Author/Illustrator	Country
2004	Writing	Martin Waddell	Ireland
	Illustration	Max Velthuijs	Netherlands
2002	Writing	Aidan Chambers	United Kingdom
	Illustration	Quentin Blake	United Kingdom
2000	Writing	Ana Maria Machado	Brazil
	Illustration	Anthony Browne	United Kingdom
1998	Writing	Katherine Paterson	United States
	Illustration	Tomi Ungerer	France
1996	Writing	Uri Orlev	Israel
	Illustration	Klaus Ensikat	Germany
1994	Writing	Michio Mado	Japan
	Illustration	Jörg Müller	Switzerland
1992	Writing	Virginia Hamilton	United States
	Illustration	Kveta Pacovská	Czech Republic
1990	Writing	Tormod Haugen	Norway
	Illustration	Lisbeth Zwerger	Austria
1988	Writing	Annie M. G. Schmidt	Netherlands
	Illustration	Dusan Kállay	Czechoslovakia
1986	Writing	Patricia Wrightson	Australia
	Illustration	Robert Ingpen	Australia
1984	Writing	Christine Nöstlinger	Austria
	Illustration	Mitsumasa Anno	Japan
1982	Writing	Lygia Bojunga Nunes	Brazil
	Illustration	Zbigniew Rychlicki	Poland
1980	Writing	Bohumil Riha	Czechoslovakia
	Illustration	Suekichi Akaba	Japan
1978	Writing	Paula Fox	United States
	Illustration	Svend Otto S.	Denmark
1976	Writing	Cecil Brdker	Denmark
	Illustration	Tatjana Mawrina	USSR
1974	Writing	Maria Gripe	Sweden
	Illustration	Farshid Mesghali	Iran
1972	Writing	Scott O'Dell	United States
	Illustration	Ib Spang Olsen	Denmark

Year	Award	Author/Illustrator	Country
1970	Writing	Gianni Rodari	Italy
	Illustration	Maurice Sendak	United States
1968	Writing	James Krüss	Germany
	Writing	José Maria Sanchez-Silva	Spain
	Illustration	Jiri Trnka	Czechoslovakia
1966	Writing	Tove Jansson	Finland
	Illustration	Alois Carigiet	Switzerland
1964	Writing	René Guillot	France
1962	Writing	Meindert DeJong	United States
1960	Writing	Erich Kästner	Germany
1958	Writing	Astrid Lindgren	Sweden
1956	Writing	Eleanor Farjeon	United Kingdom

Activities

1. Andersen lived in Denmark. Children could research the country and create a large map of Denmark. They could mark major cities and natural features, such as rivers and lakes.

2. Andersen wrote many fairy tales. Some children have assumed his works have been around for several hundred years. Children could make a list of fairy tales they know and then find out if Andersen wrote them.

3. When he was young, Andersen created a puppet theater. He loved to put on plays. Children could transform one of his fairy tales into a puppet play, make the puppets, and present the play.

4. Andersen enjoyed telling his stories to children. As he told the stories, he would often cut paper to add to the experience. Children could view one of his paper cuttings at: http://www.kb.dk/kultur/expo/klenod/hca.htm. Then they could try some paper cutting.

5. Children could read some of his fairy tales at: http://hca.gilead.org.il/. Then they could read their favorite fairy tale to a group of friends.

6. Children could examine a list of the award recipients. Then they could make a frequency table of the winners' countries. Which country has been represented the most?

7. Robert Ingpen is an Australian illustrator. Children could read his biography and glimpse his illustrative works at: http://www.alumni.rmit.edu.au/fame/fame_profile.asp?id=223. Ingpen has also painted murals and designed stamps. Students could design a stamp for a recipient of the Hans Christian Andersen Award.

8. Martin Waddell received the Hans Christian Andersen Award in 2004 for illustration. Children could read an interview with him at: http://www.ulst.ac.uk/thisisland/modules/myplaceyourplace/person3.html. They could find out what other pen name he uses (Catherine Sefton). They could make a list of Martin Waddell books, and then they could make a list of Catherine Sefton books.

9. Eleanor Farjeon was the first winner of the Hans Christian Andersen Award. Children could visit the Web site at: http://www.eldrbarry.net/rabb/farj/farj.htm and read some of her works. The children could see if children's literature topics have changed over time.

10. Astrid Lindgren won the Hans Christian Andersen Award in 1958. Now an Astrid Lindgren Memorial Award exists. Children could compare and contrast the two awards by making a Venn diagram.

Hans Christian Andersen and the Hans Christian Andersen Award

Student Handout 1—Information

Who Was Hans Christian Andersen?

Hans Christian Andersen was born in Odense, Denmark, on April 2, 1805. His father was a shoemaker, and his mother was a washerwoman. The family was poor, and Hans received little education. When Hans was seven years old, his father took him to see a play. He decided then to become an actor. He made a puppet theater at home, and he preferred to play alone. At age fourteen, he left Odense for Copenhagen in 1819. He thought he could become a successful actor, but he was awkward and uneducated. No one wanted to hire him.

Fortunately, a wealthy man paid for Hans to attend school. The teacher terrified him, and the students were much younger. However, he stuck it out and finished school. He started to write plays and books for adults, and he was somewhat successful.

He started to write stories for children. He became very successful and wealthy. From about 1830 until 1870, he published about a book a year. In 1835, he published *Fairy Tales, Told to Children.* The book included "The Princess and the Pea" and "The Tinderbox." He also traveled throughout Europe. He never visited the United States. He discovered that American publishers were selling many of his books, but they never paid him a royalty.

King Christian VIII in 1844 invited Andersen to visit him. In 1845, "The Ugly Duckling" and "The Nightingale" were included in *Nye Eventyr* (*New Fairy Tales*). By then Andersen was truly famous. Two years later, Andersen toured England and Scotland. He met Charles Dickens and published *The True Story of My Life.*

Andersen visited the World Exposition in Paris and received keys to the city of Odense on December 6, 1867. The year after, he visited Holland, Germany, France, and Switzerland. In 1870, he published his last book, *Lucky Peer.*

Hans Christian Andersen died in Copenhagen, Denmark, on August 4, 1875.

What Is the Hans Christian Andersen Award?

The Hans Christian Andersen Award is an international award given every two years to the best authors and illustrators of children's books. The award does not recognize one book but a lifetime of literary contributions. The International Board on Books for Young People (IBBY), founded in Zurich, Switzerland, in 1953, sponsors the Hans Christian Andersen Award. A nonprofit group, IBBY is "committed to bringing books and children together." IBBY created the Hans Christian Andersen Award to recognize authors and illustrators who have made a "lasting contribution to children's literature." IBBY also publishes an Honor List every two years.

IBBY is composed of at least fifty National Sections. Each section represents a country. An individual can be nominated only by his or her National Section. A portfolio of the nominee's work must be compiled. It must include a biography (preferably an autobiography), a bibliography, a collection of at least five but not more than ten books by the author or illustrator, books in original languages and in foreign languages if possible. Each portfolio is carefully constructed, and attention to detail is evident. Even the covers of the portfolios are works of art.

The Hans Christian Andersen Award has been called the Little Nobel Prize. The Queen of Denmark bestows a gold medal (depicting Hans Christian Andersen in profile) and a diploma to each of the winners.

Hans Christian Andersen and the Hans Christian Andersen Award

Student Handout 2—Questions

Name_____ Date_____

Investigate the life of Hans Christian Andersen and find out more about the Hans Christian Andersen Award. Then answer the following questions.

1. Where and when was Hans Christian Andersen born?

2. What was his childhood like?

3. What was school like?

4. Was he successful as an actor?

5. What type of story made Hans famous and wealthy?

6. How do we know that people adored Hans Christian Andersen?

7. Where and when did Hans Christian Andersen die?

8. When was the Hans Christian Andersen Award first presented?

9. How is the Hans Christian Andersen Award different from the John Newbery Medal?

10. Why do you think the Hans Christian Andersen Award is called the Little Nobel Prize?

Hans Christian Andersen

Student Handout 3—Did He Write It?

Name_____ Date_____

Hans Christian Andersen wrote many fairy tales. However, others, including the Grimm Brothers and Charles Perrault, wrote or recorded them as well. Below is a list of fairy tales. Can you pick out the Hans Christian Andersen fairy tales?

Name of Fairy Tale	Who Wrote It?
1. Cinderella	
2. Hansel and Gretel	
3. The Little Mermaid	
4. The Ugly Duckling	
5. Rumpelstiltskin	
6. Little Red Riding Hood	
7. Sleeping Beauty	
8. The Snow Queen	
9. Rapunzel	
10. Thumbelina	
11. The Princess and the Pea	
12. The Bremen Town Musicians	

Hans Christian Andersen

Student Handout 3—Did He Write It? Answers

Name_____ Date_____

Hans Christian Andersen wrote many fairy tales. However, others, including the Grimm Brothers and Charles Perrault, wrote or recorded them as well. Below is a list of fairy tales. Can you pick out the Hans Christian Andersen fairy tales?

Name of Fairy Tale	Who Wrote It?
1. Cinderella	Charles Perrault
2. Hansel and Gretel	Grimm Brothers
3. The Little Mermaid	Hans Christian Andersen
4. The Ugly Duckling	Hans Christian Andersen
5. Rumpelstiltskin	Grimm Brothers
6. Little Red Riding Hood	Charles Perrault
7. Sleeping Beauty	Charles Perrault
8. The Snow Queen	Hans Christian Andersen
9. Rapunzel	Grimm Brothers
10. Thumbelina	Hans Christian Andersen
11. The Princess and the Pea	Hans Christian Andersen
12. The Bremen Town Musicians	Grimm Brothers

Hans Christian Andersen

Student Handout 4—Paper Cutting

Name_____ Date_____

Hans Christian Andersen wrote many fairy tales. He often entertained children by sharing his stories with them. While he spoke, he often cut paper to "illustrate" his words. You will make a paper cutting. You might want to view one of his paper cuttings at: http://www.kb.dk/kultur/expo/klenod/hca.htm.

You will need plain paper, a pencil, scissors, art supplies, and a source of inspiration.

1. Find some inspiration for a scene or object. Perhaps you might read a Han Christian Andersen fairy tale. On the other hand, you could read a book by a Hans Christian Andersen Award winner.

2. Fold the plain paper in half.

3. Sketch half of a scene along the fold.

4. Cut out the scene.

5. Unfold the paper and see if you like your creation.

6. You can refold if you want and make more cuts.

7. When you are happy, you might want to add detail using paints, colored pencils, or other art supplies.

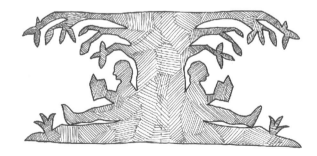

CHAPTER 4

Mildred L. Batchelder and the
Mildred L. Batchelder Award

Overview

The Mildred L. Batchelder Award was established in 1965 after Mildred gave her last speech as executive secretary of the Children's Services Division and Young Adult Services Division. American Library Association (ALA) officials wanted to honor Mildred. They also wanted to recognize American publishers who translate and then publish those translations of foreign books for children. Batchelder was a librarian who felt strongly that American children should read literature from other countries.

Mildred L. Batchelder began her career as a school librarian in Omaha, Nebraska. She was a librarian for a few more years before she took a position at ALA. She worked there for thirty years, working tirelessly for children's librarians and libraries. She had a particular interest in foreign books and their importance in multicultural understandings. Of even greater interest to her were English translations of children's books published in other countries.

The Mildred L. Batchelder Award recognizes publishers of foreign books for children and was first presented in 1968. Members of the Association for Library Service to Children (ALSC) serve on a committee that reviews books and decides on the winners. The names of the winners are announced at the midwinter meeting of the ALA, and the awards are presented to the publishers during ALA's summer conference.

Mildred L. Batchelder Biography

Mildred L. Batchelder was described as petite but a powerhouse. She had a way of motivating and empowering people. Often depending on crutches or canes, Mildred would enter a meeting and stir up the waters. Although not terribly organized, she was a prolific letter writer. She took a particular interest in children's books from other countries that promoted international understanding. The Mildred L. Batchelder Award honors both her contribution to children's literature and the American publishers who translate and print excellent books from other countries. Much of the following information comes from Dorothy Jean Anderson's doctoral thesis, *Mildred L. Batchelder: A Study in Leadership*, published in 1981.

Born in Lynn, Massachusetts, on September 7, 1901, Mildred Leona Batchelder loved to read. She also enjoyed exploring the outdoors. Her parents, George Prescott Batchelder and Blanche Ranger Tuttle Batchelder, gave Mildred and her two sisters, Ruth and Lois, a great deal of freedom. The family particularly enjoyed their summer camp. The children especially liked to meander through low-tide waters and marshes.

Mildred attended Mount Holyoke College, but she felt unsophisticated compared to her peers. She graduated in 1922 with no particular plans for her future. In 1923, she decided to become a librarian and enrolled in the New York State Library School. During the summer she did "practice work" at the Cleveland Public Library in Cleveland, Ohio. Unable to find a job, she returned to the New York State Library School and graduated in 1924. She moved to Omaha, Nebraska, and became head of the children's department of the public library system.

In 1927, Mildred resigned from the Omaha job and became the Children's Librarian at the Minnesota State Teachers College in St. Cloud. Tension developed between Mildred and her superior, however, and a year later she was fired. She then took a position as librarian at Haven Intermediate School in Evanston, Illinois. The school library became the public library after the children left for the day. She took a real interest in the role of the school librarian. She also began to publish articles, and she taught summer library courses at the University of Indiana.

Mildred was the hospitality chairperson at the American Library Association conference in 1933. Held in Chicago at the site of the World's Fair, the conference opened up new areas of interest for Mildred. She became a part of the executive committee of the school libraries section of the association. On January 27, 1936, she was hired as school library specialist within ALA and worked for the association in various capacities until she resigned in 1966.

Mildred held several titles while employed by the ALA. From 1936 until 1951, she worked tirelessly for school librarians, meeting with National Education Association officials, corporate executives, and anyone else who could assist her in helping school librarians. She also began the Latin American Project, a collection of books from the region that promoted understanding of different cultures. She attended a White House conference on rural education in 1944. After World War II, she collected books for libraries destroyed in the war. She also talked the State Department into donating unused audiovisual equipment to public libraries.

The American Association of School Librarians (AASL), was part of the ALA's Division of Libraries for Children and Young People (DLCYP). In 1951, the AASL decided to break away from the rest of the division, and fired Mildred, who had been their executive secretary. This action both bewildered and surprised her. However, she stayed on in ALA, becoming Executive Secretary, DLCYP, and Special Assistant to the ALA Executive Secretary for Special Membership Promotion. In 1957, the committees regrouped, and Mildred was named Executive Secretary, Children's Services Division and Young Adult Services Division.

In 1961, Mildred created a library of over 2000 foreign children's books for the Seattle World's Fair. She also toured Europe, but this was not a vacation. Maintaining a formidable schedule, she met with many librarians, authors, and editors. She continued to focus on the importance of children's books published in other countries. Mildred also coaxed and cajoled librarians into collecting and maintaining audiovisual materials.

During this period, Mildred experienced some health problems. In 1962, one hip joint had to be replaced, and in the next year, the other hip joint was replaced. However, even when she was in the hospital, she continued to meet with staff members and other professionals. She became healthy enough to get around with crutches or canes. Occasionally she would use a wheel chair. She was able to tour Europe again in 1964, repeating the frenetic pace of the previous trip.

Mildred retired from the ALA on April 30, 1966. In her farewell speech, given in July of 1965, she stressed the positives of books published in other countries. Soon after, ALA dignitaries created the Mildred Batchelder Award, honoring American publishers who translate and print books by foreign authors. The first Mildred L. Batchelder Award was given on International Children's Book Day, April 2, 1968 to Alfred A. Knopf for publishing Erich Kästner's *The Little Man*. James Kirkup was the translator.

Even in retirement, Mildred was very busy. She received the Alumnae Association's Centennial Award from Mount Holyoke in 1972. In 1976, she was injured in an automobile accident in Georgia. Although she was in the hospital for a month, she still corresponded with others. In 1979, she became an honorary member of the board of the International Youth Library, and in 1985, she was awarded the Chicago Children's Reading Round Table Award. Mildred was instrumental in developing the May Massee Collection. May Massee was a book editor whose book projects are housed at Emporia State College in Kansas.

Mildred also became very involved with the Kerlan Collection, a center for research regarding children's books, at the University of Minnesota. The center collected both original and translated versions of Batchelder Award-winning books, as well as various editions of Newbery and Caldecott books. Others, including writers and translators, added to the works. Through the Kerlan Collection, researchers could trace the path from original foreign books through translation to printing in English.

Mildred moved to the Swedish Retirement Association in Evanston, Illinois, and died on August 25, 1998.

Mildred L. Batchelder Timeline

Date	Event
1901	Born September 7 in Lynn, Massachusetts, to George Prescott Batchelder and Blanche Ranger Tuttle Batchelder
1904	Sister Ruth born
1910	Sister Lois born
1922	Graduated from Mount Holyoke College
1923	Attended New York State Library School; did "practice work" in Cleveland Public Library
1924	Obtained a Bachelor of Library Science degree from New York State Library School; on September 1 became head of children's department of the Omaha Public Library
1925	Published first *Library Notes*
1927	Resigned from Omaha Public Library on June 28 and took position as Children's Librarian at St. Cloud, Minnesota State Teachers College
1928	Was fired from St. Cloud job; took position as librarian at Haven Intermediate School, Evanston, Illinois (also public library after school day)
1932–1933	Taught summer library courses at University of Indiana
1933	Was Hospitality Chairperson at 1933 ALA conference in Chicago (World's Fair)
1934	Was appointed to executive committee of school libraries section of ALA; taught summer library course at Syracuse
1935	Applied for School Library Specialist position in U.S. Office of Education; did not get job
1936	Began career on January 27 at ALA as school library specialist; taught summer library course at Columbia University
1937	Began Latin American Project to collect translations of books written from the region
1938	Was Chief, School and Children's Library Division and School and Children's Library Specialist until 1947
1943	Began constructing lists of books promoting international understanding
1944	Attended conference on rural education at White House on October 5
Post WWII	Persuaded State Department to donate unused audiovisual equipment to public libraries; began project to collect books for European libraries destroyed in war
1947	Was Chief, Department of Information and Advisory Services and Executive Secretary, DLCYP
1948	Participated in Institute on Professional Education for Librarianship at University of Chicago; helped establish International Youth Library in Munich
1949	Was Chief, School and Children's Library Office, and Executive Secretary, DLCYP
1950	Invited by President Truman to attend Mid-Century White House Conference on Children and Youth, December 3–7; AASL decided to form its own unit in ALA
1951	Was fired from AASL; was asked to stay on half time until February; resigned; took job still within ALA as Executive Secretary, DLCYP, and Special Assistant to ALA Executive Secretary for Special Membership Promotion
1953	Wrote article regarding public libraries for Doubleday Company Parents' Encyclopedia

Date	Event
1954	Was executive secretary, DLCYP
1956	DLCYP disbanded, and new groups formed in ALA
1957	Was executive secretary, Children's Services Division and Young Adult Services Division
1961	Created library of more than 2,000 foreign children's books for Seattle World's Fair; took European trip to visit libraries and meet with authors and editors
1962	Had one hip joint replaced
1963	Had other hip joint replaced
1964	Toured Europe again to visit libraries and meet with authors and editors; fell in Stockholm; returned December 21
1966	Retired on April 30; created Batchelder Award; received Grolier Award from ALA
1969	First Mildred L. Batchelder Award given
1972	Was given Alumnae Association's Centennial Award at Mount Holyoke
1976	Was in car accident in Georgia and was hospitalized for a month
1979	Became honorary member of board for International Youth Library
1985	Was awarded Chicago Children's Reading Round Table Award
1998	Died August 25 in Evanston, Illinois

History and Criteria of Award

In July 1965 at the ALA convention in Detroit, Michigan, Mildred L. Batchelder gave her last speech as Executive Secretary, Children's Services Division and Young Adult Services Division. She was retiring after working for ALA for thirty years.

Throughout her working career, Mildred emphasized the importance of translating and publishing foreign books. She visited the International Youth Library in Munich, Germany, and she traveled to Europe to meet with librarians, writers, and publishers. In her farewell speech, "Learning about Children's Books in Translation," she spoke of the importance of good translations. She also stressed the relationships between American publishers and foreign publishers, the criteria of book selection, and the role of literary agents.

At the end of the speech, ALA members suggested that a foreign literature award should be created and that it should be named after Mildred Batchelder. A Children's Services Division committee developed the terms of the award, which the ALA executive board approved in 1966.

The terms of the award are simple.

1. The award honors American publishers who translate and publish children's books from other countries.

2. Books that appeal to children up to age fourteen will be considered.

3. The books must have meritorious literary value.

4. A foreign publisher must publish the book first before an American publisher can translate and publish it.

5. Folk literature will not be judged.

6. The committee will not consider any book that was first published in English.

7. Finally, the award will be given to books published in the year before the award. For example, the 1988 award was given to a book published in 1987.

On International Children's Book Day, April 2, 1968, CSD President Augusta Baker presented the first Mildred L. Batchelder Award to Alfred A. Knopf for its translation of Erich Kästner's *The Little Man*. James Kirkup was the translator.

The 1975 award was presented on International Children's Book Day at the Kerlan Collection at the University of Minnesota. There students read both the original text and the translated text.

Mildred spoke at the tenth anniversary of the Batchelder Award, held at the Skokie, Illinois, Public Library.

More than fifty awards have been distributed. Mildred L. Batchelder's goal of rewarding American publishers who translate and publish foreign books has been realized.

Award and Honor Books

Year	Award	Publisher	Title	Author	Translator
2006	Winner	Arthur A. Levin Books (Scholastic)	*An Innocent Soldier*	Josef Holub	Translated from German by Michael Hofmann
	Honor Books	Phaidon Press Limited	*Nicholas*	René Goscinny	Translated from French by Anthea Bell
		Bloomsbury Children's Books	*When I Was a Soldier*	Valéry Zenatti	Translated from French by Adriana Hunter
2005	Winner	Delacorte Press/Random House Children's Books	*The Shadows of Ghadames*	Joëlle Stolz	Translated from French by Catherine Temerson
	Honor Books	Farrar, Straus & Giroux	*The Crow-Girl: The Children of Crow Cove*	Bodil Bredsdorff	Translated from Danish by Faith Ingwersen
		Richard Jackson Books/Simon & Schuster's Atheneum Division	*Daniel Half Human and the Good Nazi*	David Chotjewitz	Translated from German by Doris Orgel
2004	Winner	Walter Lorraine Books/Houghton Mifflin Company	*Run, Boy, Run*	Uri Orlev	Translated from Hebrew by Hillel Halkin
	Honor Book	Chronicle Books	*The Man Who Went to the Far Side of the Moon: The Story of Apollo 11 Astronaut Michael Collins*	Bea Uusma Schyffert	Translated from Swedish by Emi Guner
2003	Winner	The Chicken House/Scholastic	*The Thief Lord*	Cornelia Funke	Translated from German by Oliver Latsch
	Honor Book	David R. Godine	*Henrietta and the Golden Eggs*	Hanna Johansen, author Käthi Bhend, illustrator	Translated from German by John Barrett
2002	Winner	Cricket Books/Carus Publishing	*How I Became an American*	Karen Gündisch	Translated by James Skofield
	Honor Book	Viking	*A Book of Coupons*	Susie Morgenstern, author Serge Bloch, illustrator	Translated from French by Gil Rosner

Year	Award	Publisher	Title	Author	Translator
2001	Winner	Arthur A. Levine/Scholastic	*Samir and Yonatan*	Daniella Carmi	Translated from Hebrew by Yael Lotan
	Honor Book	David R. Godine	*Ultimate Game*	Christian Lehmann	Translated from French by William Rodarmor
2000	Winner	Walker & Co.	*The Baboon King*	Anton Quintana	Translated from Dutch by John Nieuwenhuizen
	Honor Books	Farrar, Straus & Giroux	*Collector of Moments*	Quint Buchholz	Translated from German by Peter F. Neumeyer
		R&S Books	*Vendela in Venice*	Christina Bjork, author Inga-Karen Eriksson, illustrator	Translated from Swedish by Patricia Crampton
		Front Street	*Asphalt Angels*	Ineke Holtwijk	Translated from Dutch by Wanda Boeke
1999	Winner	Dial	*Thanks to My Mother*	Schoschana Rabinovici	Translated from German by James Skofield
	Honor Book	Viking	*Secret Letters from 0 to 10*	Susie Morgenstern	Translated from French by Gil Rosner
1998	Winner	Henry Holt	*The Robber and Me*	Josef Holub, author Mark Aronson, editor	Translated from German by Elizabeth D. Crawford
	Honor Books	Scholastic	*Hostage to War: A True Story*	Tatjana Wassiljews	Translated from German by Anna Trenter
		Viking	*Nero Corleone: A Cat's Story*	Elke Heidenrich	Translated from German by Doris Orgel
1997	Winner	Farrar, Straus & Giroux	*The Friends*	Kazumi Yumoto	Translated from Japanese by Cathy Hirano
1996	Winner	Houghton Mifflin	*The Lady with the Hat*	Uri Orlev	Translated from Hebrew by Hillel Halkin
	Honor Books	Henry Holt & Co.	*Damned Strong Love: The True Story of Willi G. and Stephan K.*	Lutz Van Dijk	Translated from German by Elizabeth D. Crawford

Year	Award	Publisher	Title	Author	Translator
		Walker & Co.	*Star of Fear, Star of Hope*	Jo Hoestlandt	Translated from French by Mark Polizzotti
1995	Winner	Dutton	*The Boys from St. Petri*	Bjarne Reuter	Translated from Danish by Anthea Bell
	Honor Book	Lothrop, Lee & Shepard	*Sister Shako and Kolo the Goat: Memories of My Childhood in Turkey*	Vedat Dalokay	Translated from Turkish by Güner Ener
1994	Winner	Farrar, Straus & Giroux	*The Apprentice*	Pilar Molina Llorente	Translated from Spanish by Robin Longshaw
	Honor Books	Farrar, Straus & Giroux	*The Princess in the Kitchen Garden*	Annemie and Margriet Heymans	Translated from Dutch by Johanna H. Prins and Johanna W. Prins
		Viking	*Anne Frank Beyond the Diary: A Photographic Remembrance*	Ruud van der Rol and Rian Verhoeven, in association with the Anne Frank House	Translated from Dutch by Tony Langham and Plym Peters
1993	No award given				
1992	Winner	Houghton Mifflin	*The Man from the Other Side*	Uri Orlev	Translated from Hebrew by Hillel Halkin
1991	Winner	Dutton	*A Hand Full of Stars*	Rafik Schami	Translated from German by Rika Lesser
1990	Winner	Dutton	*Buster's World*	Bjarne Reuter	Translated from Danish by Anthea Bell
1989	Winner	Lothrop, Lee & Shepard	*Crutches*	Peter Härtling	Translated from German by Elizabeth D. Crawford
1988	Winner	McElderry Books	*If You Didn't Have Me*	Ulf Nilsson	Translated from Swedish by Lone Thygesen Clecher and George Blecher
1987	Winner	Lothrop, Lee & Shepard	*No Hero for the Kaiser*	Rudolph Frank	Translated from German by Patricia Crampton

Year	Award	Publisher	Title	Author	Translator
1986	Winner	Creative Education	*Rose Blanche*	Christophe Gallaz and Robert Innocenti	Translated from Italian by Martha Coventry and Richard Craglia
1985	Winner	Houghton Mifflin	*The Island on Bird Street*	Uri Orlev	Translated from Hebrew by Hillel Halkin
1984	Winner	Viking Press	*Ronia, the Robber's Daughter*	Astrid Lindgren	Translated from Swedish by Patricia Crampton
1983	Winner	Lothrop, Lee & Shepard	*Hiroshima No Pika*	Toshi Maruki	Translated from Japanese through Kurita-Bando Literary Agency
1982	Winner	Bradbury Press	*The Battle Horse*	Harry Kullman	Translated from Swedish by Lone Thygesen Clecher and George Blecher
1981	Winner	William Morrow & Co.	*The Winter When Time Was Frozen*	Els Pelgrom	Translated from Dutch by Maryka and Rahael Rudnik
1980	Winner	Dutton	*The Sound of the Dragon's Feet*	Aliki Zei	Translated from Greek by Edward Fenton
1979	Winners	Harcourt, Brace & Jovanovich, Inc.	*Rabbit Island*	Jörg Steiner	Translated from German by Anne Conrad Lammers
		Franklin Watts	*Konrad*	Christine Nöstlinger	Translated from German by Anthea Bell
1978	No award given				
1977	Winner	Atheneum	*The Leopard*	Cecil Brdkar	Translated from Danish by Gunnar Poulsen
1976	Winner	Henry Z. Walck	*The Cat and Mouse Who Shared a House*	Ruth Hürlimann	Translated from German by Anthea Bell
1975	Winner	Crown	*An Old Tale Carved Out of Stone*	A. Linevski	Translated from Russian by Maria Polushkin

Year	Award	Publisher	Title	Author	Translator
1974	Winner	Dutton	*Petros' War*	Aliki Zei	Translated from Greek by Edward Fenton
1973	Winner	William Morrow & Co.	*Pulga*	S. R. Van Iterson	Translated from Dutch by Alexander and Alison Gode
1972	Winner	Holt, Rinehart & Winston	*Friedrich*	Hans Peter Richter	Translated from German by Edite Kroll
1971	Winner	Pantheon Books	*In the Land of Ur, the Discovery of Ancient Mesopotamia*	Hans Baumann	Translated from German by Stella Humphries
1970	Winner	Holt, Rinehart & Winston	*Wildcat Under Glass*	Aliki Zei	Translated from Greek by Edward Fenton
1969	Winner	Charles Scribner's Sons	*Don't Take Teddy*	Babbis Friis-Baastad	Translated from Norwegian by Lise Srmme McKinnon
1968	Winner	Alfred A. Knopf	*The Little Man*	Erich Kästner	Translated from German by James Kirkup

Activities

1. The award-winning books were originally published in other languages. Children could choose a language and translate some common English words. A good Web site for translation is: http://world.altavista.com/. They could make a poster with the English words next to the translations.

2. Mildred Batchelder was born in Massachusetts, attended library school in New York, worked in Minnesota and Nebraska, and became an ALA employee in Illinois. Children could find a large U.S. map and mark the states. They could add information regarding state birds, flowers, and so on.

3. Mildred Batchelder attended two White House conferences, one on rural education and the second on children and youth. She was able to share her ideas with the president at each conference. Children could write a persuasive letter to the president and state their views on libraries, books, reading, or other topics.

4. Mildred Batchelder twice toured Europe. She visited libraries and publishers. Children could plan a trip to Europe. They could choose a reason for their trip, the countries they would visit, and their daily itinerary. They could present all that information in the form of a log.

5. The Mildred L. Batchelder Award is given to American publishers who translate and print a book from another country. Children could make a frequency table of the publishers and find out which publisher has been given the most Batchelder Awards.

6. Children could make a frequency table of the original languages of the books. They could find out which language has been translated the most from the award-winning books.

7. The Chicken House/Scholastic Publishing received the 2003 Mildred L. Batchelder Award for Cornelia Funke's *The Thief Lord.* Children could check out Cornelia Funke's top ten bedtime stories at: http://books.guardian.co.uk/top10s/top10/0,6109,1063558, 00.html. They could find out how many of her favorite stories have American authors. Then they could make up their own top ten favorite bedtime stories.

8. Houghton Mifflin has received the Mildred L. Batchelder Award four times for translating the works of Uri Orlev. Students could visit the author's site at: http://www. ithl.org.il/author_info.asp?id=192. They could create a poster about his life and his works.

9. Viking Press received the 1984 Mildred L. Batchelder Award for *Ronia, the Robber's Daughter,* written by Astrid Lindgren. The Astrid Lindgren Memorial Award was created in 2002. Children could compare and contrast the two awards by making a Venn diagram.

10. The award-winning books were originally published in other languages. Children could invite a person who speaks other languages to work with them. They could find out how easy or hard it is to learn English or another language.

Mildred L. Batchelder and the Mildred L. Batchelder Award

Student Handout—Information

Who Was Mildred L. Batchelder?

Mildred Leona Batchelder was born in Lynn, Massachusetts, on September 7, 1901. She loved to read and participate in outdoor activities. She graduated from Mount Holyoke College in 1922 with no particular career in mind. She decided to become a librarian and enrolled in the New York State Library School. She graduated in 1924 and moved to Omaha, Nebraska, where she was head of the children's department of the public library system. After several years there, she moved to Minnesota and then to Illinois where she was a school librarian. She became active in the American Library Association (ALA) and finally became Executive Secretary of an ALA division.

Mildred became very interested in foreign books. In 1961, she created a library of over 2000 foreign children's books for the Seattle World's Fair. She toured Europe, meeting librarians, educators, and publishers. Mildred retired from ALA on April 30, 1966. In her farewell speech, given in July of 1965, she stressed the positives of books published in other countries.

Mildred L. Batchelder died on August 25, 1998.

What Is the Mildred L. Batchelder Award?

The Mildred L. Batchelder Award is given every year to American publishers who translate and then publish foreign books for children. The Mildred L. Batchelder Award was first presented in 1968. Members of the Association for Library Service to Children, a division of the ALA, serve on a committee that reviews books and decides on the winners. The names of the winners are announced at the midwinter meeting of the ALA, and the awards are presented to the publishers during ALA's summer conference.

Mildred L. Batchelder and the Mildred L. Batchelder Award

Student Handout 2—Questions

Name_____ Date_____

Investigate the life of Mildred L. Batchelder and find out more about the Mildred L. Batchelder Award. Then answer the following questions.

1. Where and when was Mildred L. Batchelder born?

2. What training did she receive to become a librarian?

3. Where did she work as a librarian?

4. Why do you think she began to work for the American Library Association?

5. Ask your librarian if he or she belongs to the American Library Association. What are the benefits and what are the disadvantages of belonging to the group?

6. In what kind of books did Mildred develop a strong interest?

7. When did Mildred L. Batchelder die?

8. List three facts about the Mildred L. Batchelder Award.

9. Books published in foreign countries have to be translated. Find out how a person becomes a translator.

10. Why do translators have to be careful when they change foreign text to English?

From *Children's Book Award Handbook* by Diana F. Marks. Westport, CT: Libraries Unlimited. Copyright © 2006.

Mildred L. Batchelder and the Mildred L. Batchelder Award

Student Handout 3—Hello!

Name_____ Date_____

Mildred L. Batchelder felt that American children should learn about other cultures by reading books published in foreign countries. The Mildred L. Batchelder Award honors American publishers who translate and publish foreign books for children.

Let's find out how good your foreign language skills are. Below is a list of "Hello" phrases in different languages. Write down what language you think the expression is. Then do some research and see if you are right.

Phrase	What Language Do You Think It Is?	What Language Is It?
1. Example: Bonjour		French
2. Kalimera		
3. Buon giorno		
4. Jambo		
5. Annyong ha shimnikka		
6. Konichiwa		
7. Merhaba		
8. Guten Tag		
9. Szia		
10. Zdravstvuite		
11. Al salaam a'alaykum		
12. Shalom		
13. Bore da		
14. Hola		
15. Ni hao		

Mildred L. Batchelder and the Mildred L. Batchelder Award

Student Handout 3—Hello!—Answers

Name_____ Date_____

Mildred L. Batchelder felt that American children should learn about other cultures by reading books published in foreign countries. The Mildred L. Batchelder Award honors American publishers who translate and then publish those translations of foreign books for children.

Let's find out how good your foreign language skills are. Below is a list of "Hello" phrases in different languages. Write down what language you think the expression is. Then do some research and see if you are right.

Phrase	What Language Do You Think It Is?	What Language Is It?
1. Bonjour		French
2. Kalimera		Greek
3. Buon giorno		Italian
4. Jambo		Swahili
5. Annyong ha shimnikka		Korean
6. Konichiwa		Japanese
7. Merhaba		Turkish
8. Guten Tag		German
9. Szia		Hungarian
10. Zdravstvuite		Russian
11. Al salaam a'alaykum		Arabic
12. Shalom		Hebrew
13. Bore da		Welsh
14. Hola		Spanish
15. Ni hao		Chinese

From *Children's Book Award Handbook* by Diana F. Marks. Westport, CT: Libraries Unlimited. Copyright © 2006.

Mildred L. Batchelder and the Mildred L. Batchelder Award

Student Handout 4—The World

Name_____ Date_____

Mildred L. Batchelder was a librarian and a leader in the American Library Association for many years. She became very interested in foreign books for children. She felt that American children should broaden their knowledge of the world. Foreign books would provide that knowledge. The Mildred L. Batchelder Award is given to the American publisher that translates and publishes the best foreign book for children.

Color in the attached bookmark. Then find a Mildred L. Batchelder Award Book or Honor Book. On the other hand, find another great book. The library has many excellent books. Use your bookmark to mark your spot in the book.

My Bookmark

My Name _____

I have read these books:

_____

_____

_____

_____

_____

_____

_____

_____

_____

_____

_____

_____

_____

_____

_____

CHAPTER 5

Pura Belpré and the Pura Belpré Award

Overview

The Pura Belpré Award is given every two years to the best Latina/Latino children's writers and illustrators. Pura Belpré was a librarian, writer, puppeteer, champion of good children's literature, and advocate for superb literature for Latina/Latino children.

Born in Puerto Rico, Pura Belpré came to the United States in 1920. She became a librarian for the New York Public Library system. As time went by, she developed her writing and storytelling techniques. She wrote and published a number of Puerto Rican folktales. She enjoyed creating elaborate puppets and presenting puppet shows, often in Spanish, to community groups. She translated into Spanish a number of children's books, including Munro Leaf's *The Story of Ferdinand*. She constantly shared good literature with children.

The Pura Belpré Award was first presented in 1996. Members of the Association for Library Service to Children (ALSC) and REFORMA (National Association to Promote Library and Information Services to Latinos and the Spanish-Speaking) serve on a jury that reviews books and decides on the winners. The names of the winners are announced at the midwinter meeting of the American Library Association (ALA), and the awards are presented to the authors and illustrators during ALA's summer conference.

Pura Belpré Biography

Pura Belpré was an author, storyteller, librarian, puppeteer, advocate for Latino children, and voice for all children where literature was concerned. The Pura Belpré Award is a testimony to her many years of service to children and literature.

Several dates have been proposed for the date of her birth. However, the one most often cited is February 2, 1899. Other suggested dates are December 2, 1901, and February 2, 1903. She was born in Cidra, Puerto Rico, and baptized in Juana Diaz. Cidra, located in the interior of Puerto Rico, is about an hour away from San Juan. Her father was of French background. He was a contractor, and he often moved the family around the island to where he worked. He enjoyed telling stories, and he had a fine sense of humor.

Pura liked all the places where she lived, and she especially loved the outdoors. In an interview, she stated: "I was a lover of nature. As a child I lived almost a pastoral existence. I wandered through pathways and fields dotted with color and drenched with morning dew, listening to the wind and watching the awakening of the living creatures. All this storing of beauty and feelings, preserved since childhood, found its way into my writing many years later. It added freshness and richness to the folklore I retold children."

Pura graduated from Central High School in Santurce in 1919, and in 1920 she started her college education at the University at Rio Piedras. However, she left school to attend her sister's wedding in New York City and never returned to the University at Rio Piedras.

New York City intrigued her, and she started working in the garment industry. A librarian named Ernestine Rose, thinking that the library at 135th Street served a Spanish-speaking community, asked Pura's sister, Elisa, to be her assistant. Elisa, who had been a teacher in Puerto Rico for ten years, turned down the job but recommended her sister. Pura fell in love with the job. She became the first Puerto Rican librarian in the New York Public Library. In 1926, she attended the New York Public Library School.

One of Pura's instructors was the storyteller Mary Gould Davis, who one class day suggested that the class write stories. Pura decided to share one of her favorite childhood stories, *Perez and Martina*, a romance between a cockroach and a mouse. The well-received story was first published in 1932. She decided to write down other tales she remembered, and she often spent her vacations doing just that. She also decided to become a children's librarian.

The library at 135th Street served more of an African American culture than a Hispanic culture. However, Pura said she soaked up the "black renaissance of art and literature, and the upsurge of poets, novelists, dramatists, and musicians."

Pura transferred to the Seward Park branch in Lower Manhattan, immersing herself in the Jewish community, where storytelling was very important. During her two-year stay there, she continued to write down the stories of her childhood.

Again she was transferred, this time to the 115th Street branch in a truly Hispanic neighborhood. The library's first Feast of the Three Kings was celebrated during which the children received presents. Pura wrote down the story in "The Three Magi," and it was included in *The Animals' Christmas* compiled by Anne Eaton and published by Viking Press. A puppet theater was also a first, and plays were presented in both Spanish and English. The shows traveled to schools, hospitals, and summer park venues. She became actively involved with civic groups such as La Liga Puertorriquena e Hispana and made the library vital to the community.

Pura was transferred to other library branches, where she repeated her success formula. Eventually, she moved to the Aguilar branch at 170 East 110th Street, known as "El Barrio." She was so successful that she was asked to speak at the 1942 American Library Association meeting in Cincinnati, Ohio. Her paper was about her work with the Spanish-speaking reader in the New York Public Library. There she met Dr. Clarence Cameron White, an African American concert violinist and composer who had come to Cincinnati to conduct the June Festival of Music. They fell in love and were married on December 26, 1943. Pura resigned her librarian position in 1945 so that she could tour with her husband. While they traveled often, their home was always in Harlem. She also dedicated herself to writing. One of her books published during this period was *The Tiger and the Rabbit and Other Tales*.

Clarence Cameron White was about nineteen years older than Pura and died of cancer in 1960. In 1961, Pura took on the job of Spanish Children's Specialist in the Office of Children's Services. That job led to another, the Children's Specialist at the South Bronx Library Project. Although she retired in March 1969, she continued to work on a per diem basis. One of her chief responsibilities was overseeing the extremely popular puppet shows that traveled to different parts of New York City. She made the puppets out of papier-mache and sewed the costumes. She gave workshops on puppetry and storytelling at places such as the Museum of Natural History and New York University.

Pura Belpré became a highly respected individual. She was honored by New York City School District #7 with a Citation of Merit, and Brooklyn's School District #16 named their first bookmobile for preschoolers the Pura Belpré Children's Caravan. In 1970, she received the annual award from El Instituto de Puerto Rico. Her peers called her DoZa Pura.

She wrote at least nine books. She also translated a number of English-language books into Spanish, including *The Story of Ferdinand* by Munro Leaf and *Danny and the Dinosaur* by Sid Hoff.

Pura Belpré died on July 1, 1982. Her book *Firefly Summer*, which several experts believe to be largely autobiographical, was published posthumously in 1996. The first Pura Belpré Award was given in 1996, and awards have been given every two years since. Her *Perez and Martina* was re-released in 2004.

Pura Belpré Timeline

Date	Event
1899	Born in Cidra, Puerto Rico, probably on February 2
1919	Graduated from Central High School, Santurce, Puerto Rico
1920	Entered the University at Rio Piedras but left to attend sister's wedding in New York City; decided to live in United States
1921	Took a job at 135th Street Library; became first Puerto Rican librarian in New York Public Library
1926	Studied at Library School of the New York Public Library
1929	Transferred to 115 Street Branch of New York Public Library
1932	Published *Perez and Martina: A Portorican Folk Tale*
1942	Spoke at ALA Conference in Cincinnati, Ohio; met future husband, Clarence Cameron White
1943	Married Clarence Cameron White on December 26, 1943
1944	Published "The Three Magi" as part of anthology *The Animals' Christmas*
1945	Resigned from New York Public Library to travel with her husband
1946	Published *The Tiger and the Rabbit and Other Tales*
1960	Following Clarence Cameron White's death, returned to work part-time in library as Spanish Children's Specialist
1962	Published *Juan Bobo and the Queen's Necklace: A Puerto Rican Folk Tale*
1968	Retired but worked for newly created South Bronx Library Project
1969	Published *Oté: A Puerto Rican Folk Tale* and *Santiago*; translated *I Can Read Books* from English to Spanish
1970	Received an award from El Instituto de Puerto Rico
1971	Published *Libros en Espanol: An Annotated List of Children's Books in Spanish*; translated *Easy Book Readers* from English to Spanish
1972	Published *Dance of the Animals: A Puerto Rican Folk Tale*
1973	Published *Once in Puerto Rico: Six Tales from Puerto Rico*
1978	Published *The Rainbow-Colored Horse*
1982	Died on July 1
1996	*Firefly Summer* published posthumously; First Pura Belpré Award given
2004	*Perez and Martina* re-released

History and Criteria of Award

Pura Belpré died in 1982, but the first Pura Belpré Awards were given in 1996. What happened between 1982 and 1996? How did the Pura Belpré Award become reality?

Much of the following information is a result of conversations conducted on November 4, 2004, and February 28, 2005, with Sandra Rios Balderrama, office manager for the REFORMA (National Association to Promote Library and Information Services to Latinos and the Spanish-Speaking) national office. Around 1991 or 1992, Oralia Garza de Cortes, then librarian for the Austin Public Library, and Sandra Rios Balderrama, then Supervising Librarian of Branch Services of the Oakland Public Library, met. Sandra also served on the Children's Services Committee of REFORMA. They lamented the lack of children's materials for Latino children. What was available was old and stereotypical, good for historical or archival purposes but little else. They wanted to provide today's Latinos with contemporary and relevant materials, and so they continued to meet and talk. Eventually they decided to use REFORMA as a base. REFORMA was formed in 1971 as an affiliate of the American Library Association (ALA). A small, volunteer organization with about twenty-five chapters, REFORMA seeks to provide library services that are bilingual and bicultural. The group believed that one vehicle that could provide such services was an award for excellent writing about the culture.

Oralia, Sandra, and others decided that the best way to develop the award was to create a joint award with REFORMA and the Association for Library Service to Children (ALSC), a division of ALA. As a model, they adopted the framework of the Coretta Scott King Award. At that time, the Coretta Scott King Award was part of the Social Responsibilities Round Table (SRRT) of ALA.

Proposals began to go back and forth between ALSC and REFORMA. Committees from both groups looked at the documentation. While in New Orleans in 1994 at the annual ALA conference, Sandra and others compiled a list of names for the award. This list included names of Latinas/Latinos, such as Cesar Chavez. but they wanted names with a greater connection to literature and libraries. Toni Bissassar, Senior Librarian for the Youth Room at the Oakland Public Library and an acquaintance of Pura, thought of Pura Belpré.

Toni Bissessar and Oralia Garza de Cortes continued to get approvals in small steps. REFORMA was excited over the idea, but ALSC was not sure about a joint award. Mario Gonzales, then president of REFORMA, felt that the proposal was great and observed that he got the "chills" just thinking about it. They drafted a proposal that included the following requirements:

1.   One award would be given to an author, and one award would be given to an illustrator.

2.   Honor books could also be awarded.

3.   The books had to be published in the United States or Puerto Rico.

4.   The award winners must be citizens of the United States or Puerto Rico.

5.   Other procedures and rules were outlined.

Linda Perkins, president of ALSC at the time, became essential. A strong proponent of multiculturalism, she gave a boost of energy and credibility to the project. She also knew the "ropes" of how to make the award a reality. A historic meeting took place when she came to REFORMA. The two groups decided to go forward and would have equal voices in all decisions. They decided that the chair would be from ALSC one year and from REFORMA the next. Then they decided who should sit on the jury.

REFORMA wanted to give a monetary award, but ALSC felt it went against past practices. Finally, it was decided that the prize would be awarded every two years. Elizabeth Martinez, executive director of ALA from 1994 to 1997, was a big influence and created the Pura Belpré Endowment. She and Melinda Greenblatt, Senior Program Officer, Library Power, New Visions for Public Schools, were responsible for the stamp face and design. Satia Orange from the ALA OLOS (Office of Literacy Outreach Services) arranged for press conferences after the winners were announced. She was also a key person in getting posters of the winning books created.

The first Pura Belpré award jury met and generated a list of candidates. The first awards were given at the first REFORMA conference in Austin, Texas. The first narrative award was given in 1996 to Judith Ortiz Cofer for her book, *An Island Like You: Stories of the Barrio*. The first illustration award was given to Susan Guevara for her artwork in *Chato's Kitchen*. Since then, the Pura Belpré Award Board has biennially rewarded exceptional works for Latino children.

Works by Pura Belpré

Books

Dance of the Animals: A Puerto Rican Folk Tale. New York: Frederick Warne, 1972.

Firefly Summer. Houston, TX: Pinata Books, 1996. (published posthumously)

Juan Bobo and the Queen's Necklace: A Puerto Rican Folk Tale. New York: Frederick Warne, 1962.

Once in Puerto Rico: Six Tales from Puerto Rico. New York: Frederick Warne, 1973.

Oté: A Puerto Rican Folk Tale. New York: Pantheon Books, 1969.

Oté: Un cuento folklorico puertoriqueno. New York: Pantheon Books, 1969.

Perez and Martina: A Portorican Folk Tale. New York: Frederick Warne, 1932. 2nd ed., New York: Frederick Warne, 1961. *(Note*: In 2004 *Perez and Martina: A Portorican Folk Tale* was re-released and published by BookSurge.)

Perez y Martina: Un cuento folklorico puertoriqueno. New York: Frederick Warne, 1966.

The Rainbow-Colored Horse. New York: Frederick Warne, 1978.

Santiago. New York: Frederick Warne, 1969.

Santiago. New York: Frederick Warne, 1971. Spanish translation.

The Tiger and the Rabbit and Other Tales. Boston: Houghton Mifflin Co., 1946.

The Tiger and the Rabbit and Other Tales. 2nd ed. Philadelphia: Lippincott, 1965.

Contribution to Anthology

"The Three Magi" in *The Animals' Christmas* (Anne Thaxter Eaton, editor). New York: Viking Press, 1944.

Translations into Spanish

Bonsall, Crosby. *Dejen que papá duerma. Easy Book Reader.* New York: Grosset & Dunlap, 1971.

Bonsall, Crosby. *El caso del forastero hambriento (The Case of the Hungry Stranger). I Can Read Book.* New York: Harper Row, 1969.

De Paola, Tomie. *Nuestra SeZora de Guadalupe (The Lady of Guadalupe).* New York: Holiday House, 1980.

Greene, Carla. *Los camioneros: ¿qué hacen? (Truck Drivers: What Do They Do?). I Can Read Book.* New York: Harper & Row, 1969.

Hoban, Russell. *Carlitos el vagabundo (Charlie the Tramp).* New York: Scholastic Book Service, 1966.

Hoff, Syd. *Danielito v el dinosauro (Danny and the Dinosaur). I Can Read Book.* New York: Harper & Row, 1969.

Kessler, Leonard. *Aquí viene el ponchado (Here Comes the Strikeout). I Can Read Book.* New York: Harper & Row, 1969.

Leaf, Munro. *El cuento de Ferdinando (The Story of Ferdinand)*. New York: Viking Press, 1962.

Lucky Book Club. *El hombre de pan de jengibre (The Gingerbread Man)*. New York: Scholastic Book Service, 1975.

McNulty, Faith. *Arturito el astuto (Arty the Smarty)*. *Easy Book Reader*. New York: Grosset & Dunlap, 1971.

Minarik, Elsa. *Osito (Little Bear)*. *I Can Read Book*. New York: Harper & Row, 1969.

Newell, Hope. *Date prisa cachazudo*. *Easy Book Reader*. New York: Grosset & Dunlap, 1971.

Newman, Paul. *Ningún lugar para jugar (No Place to Play)*. *Easy Book Reader*. New York: Grosset & Dunlap, 1971.

Selsam, Millicent E. *Teresita y las orugas (Teresita and the Caterpillars)*. *I Can Read Book*. New York: Harper & Row, 1969.

Suba, Susan. *¿Vendrás a mi fiesta? Easy Book Reader*. New York: Grosset & Dunlap, 1971.

Thayer, Jane. *El perrito que deseaba un niZo (The Puppy Who Wanted a Boy)*. New York: William Morrow, 1970.

Tresselt, Alvin R. *El viejo y el tigre (The Old Man and the Tiger)*. *Easy Book Reader*. New York: Grosset & Dunlap, 1971.

Nonprint Materials

Adaptation of "Juan Bobo" from *The Tiger and the Rabbit and Other Tales* [filmstrip].

Ashanti to Zulu; African Traditions. Weston, CT: Weston Woods Studios, 1977.

Oté. [filmstrip]. Weston, CT: Weston Woods Studios, 1977.

Oté. [sound recording] del libro Oté por Pura Belpré. Weston, CT: Weston Woods Studios, 1976.

Pérez and Martina. [sound recording retold by Pura Belpré]. CMS Records, 1966.

Profiles in Literature: Maurice Sendak and Pura Belpré. [video recording]. Norristown, PA: 1974–1977.

Award and Honor Books

Year	Award	Author/Illustrator	Title	Publisher/Year of Publication
2006	Narrative Medal Book	Viola Canales	*The Tequila Worm*	Wendy Lamb Books, 2005
		Carmen T. Benier-Grand	*Cesar: ¡Si, Se Puede! Yes We Can!*	Marshall Cavendish, 2005
		Pat Mora	*Doña Flor: A Tall-Tale About a Giant Woman with a Big Heart*	Alfred A. Knopf, 2005
		Pam Muñoz Ryan	*Becoming Naomi León*	Scholastic, 2004
	Illustration Medal Book	Paul Colón	*Doña Flor: A Tall-Tale About a Giant Woman with a Big Heart*	Alfred A. Knopf, 2005
	Illustration Honor Book	Lulu Delacre	*Arrorró, Mi Niño: Latino Lullabies and Gentle Games*	Lee & Low, 2004
		David Diaz	*Cesar: ¡Si, Se Puede! Yes We Can!*	Marshall Cavendish, 2005
		Rafael López	*My Name Is Celia/Me Llamo Celia: La Vida de Celia Cruz/The Life of Celia Cruz*	Luna Rising, 2004
2004	Narrative Medal Book	Julia Alvarez	*Before We Were Free*	Alfred A. Knopf, 2002
	Narrative Honor Books	Nancy Osa	*Cuba 15*	Delacorte Press, 2003
		Amada Irma Pérez	*My Diary from Here to There/Mi Diario de Aquí Hasta Allá*	Children's Book Press, 2002
	Illustration Medal Book	Yuyi Morales	*Just a Minute: A Trickster Tale and Counting Book*	Chronicle Books, 2003
	Illustration Honor Books	Robert Casilla, Illustrator. Written by L. King Pérez	*First Day in Grapes*	Lee & Low, 2002
		David Diaz, Illustrator. Written by Nancy Andrews-Goebel	*The Pot That Juan Built*	Lee & Low, 2002
		Yuyi Morales, Illustrator. Written by Kathleen Krull	*Harvesting Hope: The Story of Cesar Chavez*	Harcourt, 2003
2002	Narrative Medal Book	Pam Muñoz Ryan	*Esperanza Rising*	Scholastic Press, 2000
	Narrative Honor Book	Francisco Jimenez	*Breaking Through*	Houghton Mifflin, 2001

Year	Award	Author/Illustrator	Title	Publisher/Year of Publication
		Francisco X. Alarcon	*Iguanas in the Snow*	Children's Book Press, 2001
	Illustration Medal Book	Susan Guevara, illustrator. Written by Gary Soto	*Chato and the Party Animals*	Putnam's, 2000
	Illustration Honor Book	Joe Cepeda, illustrator. Retold by Marisa Montes	*Juan Bobo Goes to Work*	HarperCollins, 2000
2000	Narrative Medal Book	Alma Flor Ada	*Under the Royal Palms: A Childhood in Cuba*	Atheneum Books, 1998
	Narrative Honor Books	Francisco X. Alarcon, author. Illustrated by Maya Christina Gonzalez	*From the Bellybutton of the Moon and Other Summer Poems/Del Ombligo de a Luna y Otro Poemas de Verano*	Children's Book Press, 1998
		Juan Felipe Herrera, author. Illustrated by Karen Barbour	*Laughing out Loud, I Fly: Poems in English and Spanish*	HarperCollins, 1998
	Illustration Medal Book	Carmen Lomas Garza	*Magic Windows*	Children's Book Press, 1999
	Illustration Honor Books	George Ancona	*Barrio: Jose's Neighborhood*	Harcourt, Brace, 1998
		Felipe Davalos, illustrator. Text by Joseph Slate	*The Secret Stars*	Marshall Cavendish, 1998
		Amelia Lau Carling	*Mama & Papa Have a Store*	Dial Books, 1998
1998	Narrative Medal Book	Victor Martinez	*Parrot in the Oven: mi vida*	Joanna Cotler/HarperCollins, 1996
	Narrative Honor Books	Francisco X. Alarcon, author. Illustrated by Maya Christina Gonzalez	*Laughing Tomatoes and Other Spring Poems/Jitomates Risuenos y otros poemas de primavera*	Children's Book Press, 1997
		Floyd Martinez	*Spirits of the High Mesa*	Arte Publico Press, 1997
	Illustration Medal Book	Stephanie Garcia, illustrator. Text by Gary Soto	*Snapshots from the Wedding*	Putnam's, 1997
	Illustration Honor Books	Carmen Lomas Garza	*In My Family/En mi familia*	Children's Book Press, 1996
		Enrique O. Sanchez, illustrator. Text by Nina Jaffe	*The Golden Flower: A Taino Myth from Puerto Rico*	Simon & Schuster, 1996

Year	Award	Author/Illustrator	Title	Publisher/Year of Publication
		Simon Silva, illustrator. Text by Alma Flor Ada; English translation by Rosa Zubizarreta	*Gathering the Sun: an Alphabet in Spanish and English*	Lothrop, 1997
1996	Narrative Medal Book	Judith Ortiz Cofer	*An Island Like You: Stories of the Barrio*	Melanie Kroupa/Orchard Books, 1995
	Narrative Honor Books	Lucia Gonzalez, author. Illustrated by Lulu Delacre	*The Bossy Gallito/El Gallo de Bodas: A Traditional Cuban Folktale*	Scholastic, 1994
		Gary Soto	*Baseball in April, and Other Stories*	Harcourt, 1994
	Illustration Medal Book	Susan Guevara, illustrator. Text by Gary Soto	*Chato's Kitchen*	Putnam's, 1995
	Illustration Honor Books	George Ancona	*Pablo Remembers: The Fiesta of the Day of the Dead*	Lothrop, 1993
		Lulu Delacre, illustrator. Retold by Lucia Gonzalez	*The Bossy Gallito/El Gallo de Bodas: A Traditional Cuban Folktale*	Scholastic, 1994
		Carmen Lomas Garza. Spanish language text by Rosalma Zubizaretta	*Family Pictures/Cuadros de Familia*	Children's Book Press, 1990

Activities

1. Pura Belpré wrote a number of books. These books concentrate primarily on Puerto Rican folktales. Children could read some of those books and then write down what they have learned about Puerto Rico from reading the books.

2. Pura Belpré translated a number of children's books from English to Spanish. The English versions and the Spanish versions could be shared with children.

3. Pura Belpré loved to make puppets and present puppet shows. Children could choose one of the Pura Belpré Award books and present the book as a puppet show.

4. Pura Belpré was born in Puerto Rico. Children could draw a map of the island of Puerto Rico. They could mark San Juan, Cidra, and other places on the map. They could also calculate the distance from Puerto Rico to New York City. A great Web site with great sounds is http://welcome.topuertorico.org/.

5. Pura Belpré was born in Puerto Rico, but she lived almost all of her adult life in New York City. Children could make two collages, one of her childhood and one of her adult life.

6. Pura Belpré translated a number of books from English to Spanish. Children could make an English-Spanish picture dictionary. A good Web site is: http://www.wordreference.com/.

7. Students could locate and mark on a world map the countries that today are predominantly Spanish-speaking.

8. Pura Belpré married Clarence Cameron White, a composer and concert violinist. Children could compose and perform a piece of original music to honor Pura Belpré.

9. Pura Belpré wrote a story about Juan Bobo, *Juan Bobo and the Queen's Necklace: A Puerto Rican Folk Tale*. One 2002 illustration honor book was *Juan Bobo Goes to Work*. Children could find out if there are any more Juan Bobo books or stories to read. The Internet is a good source of stories. Try: http://p2001.health.org/Ctw15/storypm.htm.

10. David Diaz illustrated the 2004 honor book, *The Pot That Juan Built*. For some excellent information about him, see Houghton Mifflin's Web site at: http://www.eduplace.com/kids/hmr/mtai/diaz.html. Children could make some simple air-dry clay pots.

11. Alma Flor Ada won the 2000 narrative award for *Under the Royal Palms: A Childhood in Cuba*. Her book *Gathering the Sun: an Alphabet in Spanish and English* received the 1998 honor book for illustration. Children could read those books and others by her. Children could also explore her Web site at: http://www.almaada.com/. Another good Web site regarding her work is Houghton Mifflin's Web site at: http://www.eduplace.com/kids/hmr/mtai/ada.html

12. An ELL teacher could speak to children about his or her job.

13. Pura Belpré spoke both English and Spanish. A person who speaks other languages could present information to children.

14. Pura Belpré was a librarian as well as a writer and puppeteer. A librarian could speak to children regarding the job and the education necessary to become a librarian.

15.   Francisco X. Alarcon, a Pura Belpré Award winner, writes poetry. Children could read an interview with him at: http://www.dcn.davis.ca.us/go/gizmo/1997/alarcon.html. Then they could write letters to him.

17.   Yuyi Morales (http://www.yuyimorales.com/) and Lulu Delacre (http://www.luludelacre.com/) are both award-winning authors and illustrators. Children could check out their books and their Web sites and see how their artistic styles are different. They could try to mimic one of the styles.

18.   Pam Munoz Ryan (http://www.pammunozryan.com/) won the Pura Belpré Award and the Jane Addams Award for *Esperanza Rising*, the Robert F. Sibert Informational Book Award for *When Marian Sang*, and other awards for other books. Children could compare and contrast her works by creating a Venn diagram.

Pura Belpré and the Pura Belpré Award

Student Handout 1—Information

Who Was Pura Belpré?

Pura Belpré was born in Puerto Rico probably on February 2, 1899. Her childhood was pleasant and filled with love. In 1920, she came to New York City to be at her sister's wedding. She never permanently lived in Puerto Rio again. A librarian asked Pura's sister to take a job at the library. The sister turned down the job but suggested Pura's name. Pura accepted the offer and became a librarian for the New York Public Library system. She took courses in librarianship, and one of her teachers encouraged her to write down some of her childhood stories. Pura Belpré thus became a writer. She also enjoyed making elaborate puppets and sets for her touring shows. Some of the puppet shows were in Spanish.

Pura Belpré married Clarence Cameron White, a composer and concert violinist. She quit her job to be with him in his travels. She also published a number of books during those years. After Clarence Cameron White died in 1960, Pura returned to her librarian job. She also translated into Spanish a number of well-known books, including *Danny and the Dinosaur*. She was such a respected member of New York City and so important a figure in Latina/Latino literature that she was given the title DoZa Pura.

Pura Belpré died on July 1, 1982.

What Is the Pura Belpré Award?

The Pura Belpré Award is given to the best Latino/Latina writer and the best Latino/Latina illustrator of children's books. Members of the Association for Library Service to Children (ALSC) and REFORMA (National Association to Promote Library and Information Services to Latinos and the Spanish-Speaking) serve on a committee that reviews books. It presents the awards every two years, and honor books may be named. The winners receive a medal, and seals are added to both the medal books and the honor books. The first Pura Belpré Award was given in 1996. The books must be published in the United States or Puerto Rico, and the recipients must be residents or citizens of the United States or Puerto Rico.

Pura Belpré and the Pura Belpré Award

Student Handout 2—Questions

Name_____ Date_____

Investigate the life of Pura Belpré, and find out more about the Pura Belpré Award. Then answer the following questions.

1. Where and when was Pura Belpré born?

2. Pura Belpré came to New York City in 1920. Would she have taken a plane or a boat? How do you know?

3. How did Pura Belpré become a librarian?

4. How did Pura Belpré become a writer?

5. How do we know that many people loved and respected her?

6. When did Pura Belpré die?

7. List at least three ways Pura Belpré helped children.

8. How is Pura Belpré like you?

9. How is Pura Belpré different from you?

10. Ask your librarian how he or she came to that job. Was it a different path than the one Pura Belpré took?

11. List three facts about the Pura Belpré Award.

12. How do you think the award committee finds books to consider?

From *Children's Book Award Handbook* by Diana F. Marks. Westport, CT: Libraries Unlimited. Copyright © 2006.

Pura Belpré and the Pura Belpré Award

Student Handout 3—Research Puerto Rico!

Name_____ Date_____

Pura Belpré was born in Puerto Rico, but she moved to New York City. Use an atlas and encyclopedias to answer the following questions.

1. Where is Puerto Rico located?

2. List some of Puerto Rico's neighbors.

3. What is the capital of Puerto Rico?

4. What does the phrase "Puerto Rico" mean?

5. Puerto Rico belongs to the United States, but it is not a state. What is it?

6. How did the United States obtain Puerto Rico?

7. How big is Puerto Rico?

8. How many people live there?

9. What is the climate like?

10. What crops are grown in Puerto Rico?

11. Who are some famous Puerto Ricans?

12. Which is bigger, New York City or Puerto Rico?

13. Would you rather live in New York City or in Puerto Rico?

14. Draw the Puerto Rican flag on the back of this worksheet.

From *Children's Book Award Handbook* by Diana F. Marks. Westport, CT: Libraries Unlimited. Copyright © 2006.

Pura Belpré and the Pura Belpré Award

Student Handout 4—Puppet Activity

The Pura Belpré Award honors Latina/Latino writers and illustrators. The award, first given in 1986, is presented every two years. Pura Belpré was a librarian and a writer. One of her favorite activities was to make puppets and present puppet shows. So let's make puppets and present a puppet show!

For each puppet, you will need:

    2 paper plates

    clear tape

    scissors

    decorative items such as paints, markers, glitter, construction paper and googly eyes

To make the basic head of a puppet:

1. Fold both paper plates in half so that the bottom of the plate is inside the fold.

2. Cut one of the paper plates along the fold.

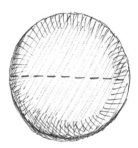

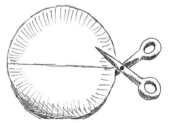

3. Keep the other paper plate folded. Place one of the halves on top of the folded plate. The plate inside should meet the folded plate inside.

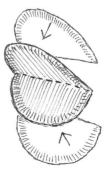

4. Line up the plate edges and tape.

5. Turn the folded paper plate over and tape the other half to the folded portion.

6. You have created a bottom pocket for your thumb and a top pocket for your four fingers.

7. You have made the mouth of the puppet.

8. Your arm will become the body of the puppet.

9. Decorate your puppet with all kinds of detail. Add eyes and paint on a mouth.

10. Decide on a puppet play to present. Perhaps you could find a Pura Belpré Award book and present it. Create the script, practice, and stage. Have a great time!

CHAPTER 6

Randolph Caldecott and the Randolph Caldecott Medal

Overview

The Randolph Caldecott Medal yearly honors the finest illustrators of children's books published in the United States. Randolph Caldecott was a British illustrator who lived from 1849 to 1886. While he illustrated newspaper articles and books for adults, he is most noted for his illustrations of children's books.

Caldecott was born in Chester, England, and as an adult, he moved to Manchester to work in a bank. However, once he had enough monetary funds, he moved to London to be an artist. He worked for newspapers, and he illustrated travel books. He also illustrated two books by Washington Irving. Caldecott made a deal with publisher Edmund Evans to illustrate two children's books a year. However, he wanted a royalty rather than the standard fee. He had become very successful, but his frequent bouts of gastritis made work difficult. In late 1885, he and his wife decided to travel to the United States in hopes of helping him regain his health. Instead, he became more and more ill, and he died in Florida in 1886.

The Randolph Caldecott Medal has been awarded every year since 1938. At least one honor book has been recognized every year as well. The Association for Library Service to Children (ALSC), a division of the American Library Association (ALA), administers the award. Winners are announced at the midwinter ALA meeting, and the awards are presented at the ALA summer conference.

Randolph Caldecott Biography

People acquainted with literature know that the Caldecott Award honors illustrators of children's books, and they may even know that Randolph Caldecott was a British illustrator. Some, however, mistakenly believe that John Newbery and Randolph Caldecott were peers and may have actually collaborated. Actually, Caldecott was born in 1846, about eighty years after Newbery died. Caldecott created lively and humorous illustrations that graced Victorian books for children.

Randolph Caldecott was born to John Caldecott and Mary Dinah on March 22, 1846, in Chester, England. His father was an accountant. From his early years Randolph was frail, and he would battle many medical conditions throughout his relatively short life. He enjoyed being outside, and he knew early on that he liked to draw. His mother died in August 1852. Randolph attended King Henry

VII School, where he was elected head boy. He took a job as a bank clerk in 1861 in the Whitchurch Ellesmere Bank in Whitchurch, Shropshire. He also tried to sell life insurance, but he was not very successful. His art became a hobby, though he was able to sell an illustration of a fire to the *Illustrated London News.*

In late 1866, Randolph met William Langton, who hired him to work for the Manchester and Salford Bank in Manchester. Randolph had never lived in such a large city, but he enjoyed sketching scenes about busy city life. He also attended evening classes at the Manchester School of Art. He could make friends easily, and in 1867, he joined the Brasenose Club, a group that promoted artistic expression. He also began exhibiting his artwork, including a piece entitled "At the Wrong End of the Wood."

In 1870, Randolph was given the opportunity to show his portfolio to Thomas Armstrong, a successful artist who had moved from Manchester to London. Armstrong felt Randolph had potential. Randolph also sold an oil and watercolor painting. Now with enough financial reserves to quit his bank job, he moved to London and became an artist. He moved to London in 1872 and attended Slade School, an art institute. He started to paint some decorative panels in Bank House, and he sold some illustrations to Henry Blackburn, the owner of *London Society* magazine. Caldecott was commissioned by Henry Blackburn to travel through the Harz Mountains to gather some impressions for illustrations. The next year his illustrations appeared in Blackburn's *Harz Mountains: A Tour of Toy Country.* Some of the illustrations were re-printed in New York's *Harpers New Monthly Magazine.*

Even though he was not healthy, Randolph took jobs from 1873 to 1875 with various London newspapers as a "special reporter." Since photographs were not common in newspapers, newspaper publishers hired artists to produce black and white sketches of current happenings. These were then inserted into the newspaper text. Randolph also met Jules Dalou, a French artist and art instructor. Jules's English was less than perfect, and Randolph wanted to learn how to sculpt clay, so they bartered English lessons for art lessons.

In 1873, Caldecott accompanied Blackburn to the Universal Exhibition of Arts and Industry in Vienna. While the trip was relatively unimportant, the illustrations were monumental. Caldecott's impressions of the trip were among the first illustrations to be reproduced by photolithography. This meant that woodcuts were not necessary. Photolithography made illustration faster and easier. The photolithography illustrations were often more finely detailed than woodcut illustrations.

Randolph's big break came in 1875 when *Old Christmas,* written by Washington Irving, was published with his illustrations. The next year *Bracebridge Hall,* again by Washington Irving, was published with Caldecott's illustrations. Just after the publication of *Bracebridge Hall,* Caldecott met Walter Crane, an illustrator and a competitor. Although Caldecott's health forced him to move to the French Riviera in January 1877, he was still able to produce works that could be published.

Caldecott arranged a business deal in early 1878 with Edmund Evans, a publisher and bookseller, to illustrate two children's books a year. Instead of the standard commission from the publisher, he requested a royalty, a very unusual arrangement back then. Together they published *The Diverting History of John Gilpin* and *The House that Jack Built* that year. Both books were tremendously successful. Toward the end of that year, Caldecott met Kate Greenaway, a fellow illustrator and a competitor who also worked with Edmund Evans. Some of their friends hoped the two might become romantically involved. A romance never developed between them, but they did remain close friends.

In 1879, Caldecott was elected a member of the Manchester Academy of Fine Arts, and he illustrated two more books for Evans, *Elegy on the Death of a Mad Dog* and *The Babes in the Woods.* Caldecott also met the writer Juliana Horatio Ewing, and later he would illustrate a few of her books.

In the fall of 1879, Caldecott moved to a small house, Wybournes, Kemsing, near Sevenoaks, Kent. There he set up a workshop and busily used local folk for his illustration models. On March 18, 1880, Caldecott married Marian Harriet Brind. In that same year, he illustrated two more children's books, *Sing a Song of Sixpence* and *Three Jovial Huntsmen.* He also illustrated Blackburn's travel book, *Breton Folk: An Artistic Tour of Brittany.* He was elected member of the Manchester Academy of Fine Arts in 1879.

Over the next five years, Caldecott illustrated at least two children's books per year, including *Hey Diddle Diddle* and *Bye, Baby Bunting*. His illustrations were detailed and eye-catching, and they were filled with activity and action. Perhaps what best defined his illustrations was humor. His characters were honest folk trying to do the best they could. However, sometimes fate overtook the event, and all one could do was laugh.

Caldecott's poor health continued to hamper his work and hobbies. He and Marian decided to take an extended trip through the United States. They planned to arrive in New York, travel down the East Coast, journey west through the South to California, and then return to New York. They sold their house in October 1885 and traveled across the Atlantic. But even the ocean voyage to New York was exhausting. They started their trip down the East Coast, but his gastritis flared up. The further down the coast they traveled, the sicker he became.

Randolph Caldecott died in St. Augustine, Florida, on February 13, 1886. He was buried there. Today Randolph Caldecott Societies are active in both the United Kingdom and the United States.

Randolph Caldecott Timeline

Date	Event
1846	Born on March 22 in Chester, England, to John Caldecott and Mary Dinah
1852	Mother Mary Dinah died of fever in August
1861	Began to work as a bank clerk in Whitchurch, Shropshire; sold first illustration (of a fire) to a newspaper, the *Illustrated London News*
1867	Moved to Manchester and worked for Manchester and Salford Bank; attended evening classes at Manchester School of Art
1869	Became a member of Brasenose Club; exhibited first work, "At the Wrong End of the Wood"
1870	Showed portfolio to Thomas Armstrong, artist in London
1872	Sold oil and water color painting; moved to London, attended Slade School; sold illustrations to Henry Blackburn (*London Society Magazine*); started to paint decorative panels in Bank House; traveled through Harz Mountains (in preparation for book contract)
1873	Finished painting the decorative panels in Bank House; met George Routledge and Edmund Evans; *Harz Mountains: A Tour of Toy Country* published with his illustrations; portions of book and illustrations reprinted in *Harpers New Monthly Magazine*; met Jules Dalou and bartered English lessons for modeling clay lessons; became "special reporter" for various London newspapers
1875	Published *Old Christmas*
1876 1877	Published *Bracebridge Hall*; met Walter Crane; moved to French Riviera for health reasons
1878	Made deal with Edmund Evans to illustrate two children's books a year; wanted royalties instead of a commission; published *The Diverting History of John Gilpin* and *The House that Jack Built*; met Kate Greenaway
1879	Met Juliana Horatio Ewing; elected member of Manchester Academy of Fine Arts; published *Elegy on the Death of a Mad Dog* and *The Babes in the Woods*
1880	Married Marian Harriet Brind on March 18; published *Sing a Song of Sixpence*, *Three Jovial Huntsmen* and *Breton Folk: An Artistic Tour of Brittany*
1881	Published *The Farmer's Boy* and *The Queen of Hearts*
1882	Published *The Milkmaid*, *Hey Diddle Diddle* and *Bye, Baby Bunting*
1883	Published *A Frog he would a-wooing go*, *The Fox Jumps over the Parson's Gate*, *Aesop's Fables* and *A Sketchbook of R. Caldecott*
1884	Published *Daddy Darwin's Dovecote*, *Jackanapes*, *Come Lasses and Lads*, *Ride a Cock Horse to Banbury Cross* and *A Farmer went Trotting upon his Grey Mare*
1885	Published *Lob Lie-by-the-Fire*, *An Elegy on the Glory of Her Sex, Mrs. Mary Blaize* and *The Great Panjandrum Himself*; sold house and traveled to the United States
1886	Died in St. Augustine, Florida, on February 13
1938	First Caldecott Medal awarded

History and Criteria of Medal

The American Library Association (ALA) awarded its first John Newbery Medal in 1922. Around 1937 members of ALA felt that illustrators of children's picture books also deserved recognition. Frederic G. Melcher, the originator of the John Newbery Award, suggested the creation of a second medal, rewarding children's book illustrators. He also suggested that the award be named after Randolph J. Caldecott, a nineteenth-century illustrator of children's books. Caldecott, like Newbery, was English.

The Section for Library Work with Children and the School Libraries Section created a joint committee to delineate rules and procedures. The ALA Executive Board approved their document, and the first Randolph Caldecott Award was issued in 1938. Since 1937, the ALA group responsible for the Caldecott Award has changed several times. Today the Association for Library Service to Children (ALSC), part of ALA, monitors the award.

René Paul Chambellan, an American sculptor, drafted the Caldecott Medal, and he also designed the Newbery Medal. The front of the Caldecott Medal is one of Caldecott's illustrations from *The Diverting Story of John Gilpin.* John Gilpin is trying to control his galloping horse while geese, dogs, and people scurry to get out of the way. The winner's name and date are engraved on the back.

The Caldecott has been awarded every year since 1932. The committee could also note other books of great merit. These books were called "runners up." However, in 1971 the committee changed the title "runners up" to "honor books." At least one honor book has been noted every year since 1932.

The Randolph Caldecott Committee examines many books over the course of a year. The illustrator must reside in the United States, and the book must be published in America. The text must be in English. The book must be independent of other media, for example, video. The award may be given to co-illustrators, and the medal may be awarded posthumously. The award is given to books published in the previous year. The committee may look at the overall text and features of the book as well as the illustrations.

Children's Books Illustrated by Randolph Caldecott

Babes in the Wood, The. London: George Routledge & Sons, 1879.

Bye, Baby Bunting. London: George Routledge & Sons, 1882.

Come Lasses and Lads. London: George Routledge & Sons, 1884.

Daddy Darwin's Dovecote. A Country Tale by Juliana Horatia Ewing. London: Society for Promoting Christian Knowledge, 1884.

Diverting History of John Gilpin. London: George Routledge & Sons, 1878.

Elegy on the Death of a Mad Dog. London: George Routledge & Sons, 1879.

An Elegy on the Glory of Her Sex, Mrs. Mary Blaize. London: George Routledge & Sons, 1885.

Farmer Went Trotting upon his Grey Mare, A. London: George Routledge & Sons, 1884.

Farmer's Boy, The. London: George Routledge & Sons, 1881.

Fox Jumps over the Parson's Gate, The. London: George Routledge & Sons, 1878.

Frog he would a-wooing go. London: George Routledge & Sons, 1883.

Great Panjandrum, The. London: George Routledge & Sons, 1885.

Hey Diddle Diddle. London: George Routledge & Sons, 1882.

House that Jack Built, The. London: George Routledge & Sons, 1878.

Jackanapes by Juliana Horatia Ewing. London: Society for Promoting Christian Knowledge, 1883 or 1884.

Lob Lie-by-the-Fire, or The Luck of Lingborough by Juliana Horatia Ewing. London: Society for Promoting Christian Knowledge, 1885.

Milkmaid, The. London: George Routledge & Sons, 1882.

Queen of Hearts, The. London: George Routledge & Sons, 1881.

Ride a Cock Horse to Banbury Cross. London: George Routledge & Sons, 1884.

Sing a Song for Sixpence. London: George Routledge & Sons, 1880.

Three Jovial Huntsmen. London: George Routledge & Sons, 1880.

Medal and Honor Books

Year	Award	Illustrator	Title	Publisher
2006	Medal Winner	Chris Raschka	*The Hello, Goodbye Window*	Di Capua/Farrar, Straus & Giroux
	Honor Books	Bryan Collier	*Rosa*	Henry Holt
		Jon J. Muth	*Zen Shorts*	Scholastic
		Marjorie Priceman	*Hot Air: The (Mostly) True Story of the First Hot-Air Balloon Ride*	Anne Schwartz Book (Atheneum)
		Beckie Prange	*Song of the Water Boatman and Other Pond Poems*	Houghton Mifflin
2005	Medal Winner	Kevin Henkes	*Kitten's First Full Moon*	Greenwillow
	Honor Books	Barbara Lehman	*The Red Book*	Houghton Mifflin
		E. B. Lewis	*Coming on Home Soon*	G. P. Putnam's Sons
		Mo Willems	*Knuffle Bunny: A Cautionary Tale*	Hyperion
2004	Medal Winner	Mordicai Gerstein	*The Man Who Walked Between the Towers*	Roaring Brook Press/Millbrook Press
	Honor Books	Margaret Chodos-Irvine	*Ella Sarah Gets Dressed*	Harcourt
		Steve Jenkins and Robin Page	*What Do You Do with a Tail Like This?*	Houghton Mifflin
		Mo Willems	*Don't Let the Pigeon Drive the Bus*	Hyperion
2003	Medal Winner	Eric Rohmann	*My Friend Rabbit*	Roaring Brook Press/Millbrook Press
	Honor Books	Tony DiTerlizzi	*The Spider and the Fly*	Simon & Schuster
		Peter McCarty	*Hondo & Fabian*	Henry Holt & Co.
		Jerry Pinkney	*Noah's Ark*	SeaStar Books, a division of North-South Books, Inc.
2002	Medal Winner	David Wiesner	*The Three Pigs*	Clarion/Houghton Mifflin
	Honor Books	Brian Selznick	*The Dinosaurs of Waterhouse Hawkins*	Scholastic
		Bryan Collier	*Martin's Big Words: The Life of Dr. Martin Luther King, Jr.*	Jump at the Sun/Hyperion
		Marc Simont	*The Stray Dog*	HarperCollins
2001	Medal Winner	David Small	*So You Want to Be President?*	Philomel
	Honor Books	Christopher Bing	*Casey at the Bat*	Handprint

Year	Award	Illustrator	Title	Publisher
		Betsy Lewin	*Click, Clack, Moo: Cows that Type*	Simon & Schuster
		Ian Falconer	*Olivia*	Atheneum
2000	Medal Winner	Simms Taback	*Joseph Had a Little Overcoat*	Viking
	Honor Books	Trina Schart Hyman	*A Child's Calendar*	Holiday House
		David Wiesner	*Sector 7*	Clarion Books
		Molly Bank	*When Sophie Gets Angry-Really Really Angry …*	Scholastic
		Jerry Pinkney	*The Ugly Duckling*	Morrow
1999	Medal Winner	Mary Azarian	*Snowflake Bentley*	Houghton
	Honor Books	Brian Pinkney	*Duke Ellington: The Piano Prince and His Orchestra*	Hyperion
		David Shannon	*No, David!*	Scholastic
		Uri Shulevitz	*Snow*	Farrar, Straus & Giroux
		Peter Sis	*Tibet Through the Red Box*	Frances Foster Books
1998	Medal Winner	Paul O. Zelinsky	*Rapunzel*	Dutton
	Honor Books	David Small	*The Gardener*	Farrar, Straus & Giroux
		Christopher Myers	*Harlem*	Scholastic
		Simms Taback	*There Was an Old Lady Who Swallowed a Fly*	Viking
1997	Medal Winner	David Wisniewski	*Golem*	Clarion
	Honor Books	Holly Meade	*Hush! A Thai Lullaby*	Melanie Kroupa/Orchard Books
		David Pelletier	*The Graphic Alphabet*	Orchard Books
		Dav Pilkey	*The Paperboy*	Richard Jackson/Orchard Books
		Peter Sis	*Starry Messenger*	Frances Foster Books Farrar, Straus & Giroux
1996	Medal Winner	Peggy Rathmann	*Officer Buckle and Gloria*	G. P. Putnam
	Honor Books	Stephen T. Johnson	*Alphabet City*	Viking
		Marjorie Priceman	*Zin! Zin! Zin! A Violin*	Simon & Schuster
		Brian Pinkney	*The Faithful Friend*	Simon & Schuster
		Janet Stevens	*Tops & Bottoms*	Harcourt
1995	Medal Winner	David Diaz	*Smoky Night*	Harcourt

Year	Award	Illustrator	Title	Publisher
	Honor Books	Jerry Pinkney	*John Henry*	Dial
		Paul O. Zelinsky	*Swamp Angel*	Dutton
		Eric Rohmann	*Time Flies*	Crown
1994	Medal Winner	Allen Say	*Grandfather's Journey*	Houghton
	Honor Books	Ted Lewin	*Peppe the Lamplighter*	Lothrop
		Denise Fleming	*In the Small, Small Pond*	Holt
		Gerald McDermott	*Raven: A Trickster Tale from the Pacific Northwest*	Harcourt
		Kevin Henkes	*Owen*	Greenwillow
		Chris Raschka	*Yo! Yes?*	Orchard
1993	Medal Winner	Emily Arnold McCully	*Mirette on the High Wire*	G. P. Putnam's Sons
	Honor Books	Lane Smith	*The Stinky Cheese Man and Other Fairly Stupid Tales*	Viking
		Ed Young	*Seven Blind Mice*	Philomel
		Carole Byard	*Working Cotton*	Harcourt
1992	Medal Winner	David Wiesner	*Tuesday*	Clarion
	Honor Book	Faith Ringgold	*Tar Beach*	Crown
1991	Medal Winner	David Macaulay	*Black and White*	Houghton
	Honor Books	Fred Marcellino	*Puss in Boots*	Di Capua/Farrar, Straus & Giroux
		Vera B. Williams	*"More More More," Said the Baby: Three Love Stories*	Greenwillow
1990	Medal Winner	Ed Young	*Lon Po Po: A Red-Riding Hood Story from China*	Philomel
	Honor Books	Bill Peet	*Bill Peet: An Autobiography*	Houghton
		Lois Ehlert	*Color Zoo*	Lippincott
		Jerry Pinkney	*The Talking Eggs: A Folktale from the American South*	Dial
		Trina Schart Hyman	*Hershel and the Hanukkah Goblins*	Holiday House
1989	Medal Winner	Stephen Gammell	*Song and Dance Man*	Knopf
	Honor Books	Allen Say	*The Boy of the Three-Year Nap*	Houghton
		David Wiesner	*Free Fall*	Lothrop

Year	Award	Illustrator	Title	Publisher
		James Marshall	*Goldilocks and the Three Bears*	Dial
		Jerry Pinkney	*Mirandy and Brother Wind*	Knopf
1988	Medal Winner	John Schoenherr	*Owl Moon*	Philomel
	Honor Book	John Steptoe	*Mufaro's Beautiful Daughters: An African Tale*	Lothrop
1987	Medal Winner	Richard Egielski	*Hey, Al*	Farrar, Straus & Giroux
	Honor Books	Ann Garifalconi	*The Village of Round and Square Houses*	Little, Brown
		Suse MacDonald	*Alphabatics*	Bradbury
		Paul O. Zelinsky	*Rumpelstiltskin*	Dutton
1986	Medal Winner	Chris Van Allsburg	*The Polar Express*	Houghton
	Honor Books	Stephen Gammell	*The Relatives Came*	Bradbury
		Don Wood	*King Bidgood's in the Bathtub*	Harcourt
1985	Medal Winner	Trina Schart Hyman	*Saint George and the Dragon*	Little, Brown
	Honor Books	Paul O. Zelinsky	*Hansel and Gretel*	Dodd
		Nancy Trufari	*Have You Seen My Duckling?*	Greenwillow
		John Steptoe	*The Legend of Jumping Mouse: A Native American Legend*	Lothrop
1984	Medal Winner	Alice and Martin Provensen	*The Glorious Flight: Across the Channel with Louis Bleriot*	Viking
	Honor Books	Trina Schart Hyman	*Little Red Riding Hood*	Holiday
		Molly Bang	*Ten, Nine, Eight*	Greenwillow
1983	Medal Winner	Marcia Brown	*Shadow*	Scribner
	Honor Books	Vera B. Williams	*A Chair for My Mother*	Greenwillow
		Diane Goode	*When I Was Young in the Mountains*	Dutton
1982	Medal Winner	Chris Van Allsburg	*Jumanji*	Houghton
	Honor Books	Stephen Gammell	*Where the Buffaloes Begin*	Warne
		Anita Lobel	*On Market Street*	Greenwillow
		Maurice Sendak	*Outside Over There*	Harper

Year	Award	Illustrator	Title	Publisher
		Alice and Martin Provensen	*A Visit to William Blake's Inn: Poems for Innocent and Experienced Travelers*	Harcourt
1981	Medal Winner	Arnold Lobel	*Fables*	Harper
	Honor Books	Ilse Plume	*The Bremen-Town Musicians*	Doubleday
		Molly Bang	*The Grey Lady and the Strawberry Snatcher*	Four Winds
		Joseph Low	*Mice Twice*	McElderry/Atheneum
		Donald Crews	*Truck*	Greenwillow
1980	Medal Winner	Barbara Cooney	*Ox-Cart Man*	Viking
	Honor Books	Rachel Isadora	*Ben's Trumpet*	Greenwillow
		Chris Van Allsburg	*The Garden of Abdul Gasazi*	Houghton
		Uri Shulevitz	*The Treasure*	Farrar, Straus & Giroux
1979	Medal Winner	Paul Goble	*The Girl Who Loved Wild Horses*	Bradbury
	Honor Books	Donald Crews	*Freight Train*	Greenwillow
		Peter Parnall	*The Way to Start a Day*	Scribner
1978	Medal Winner	Peter Spier	*Noah's Ark*	Doubleday
	Honor Books	David Macaulay	*Castle*	Houghton
		Margot Zemach	*It Could Always Be Worse*	Farrar, Straus & Giroux
1977	Medal Winner	Leo and Diane Dillon	*Ashanti to Zulu: African Traditions*	Dial
	Honor Books	William Steig	*The Amazing Bone*	Farrar, Straus & Giroux
		Nonny Hogrogian	*The Contest*	Greenwillow
		M. B. Goffstein	*Fish for Supper*	Dial
		Beverly Brodsky	*The Golem: A Jewish Legend*	Lippincott
		Peter Parnall	*Hawk, I'm Your Brother*	Scribner
1976	Medal Winner	Leo and Diane Dillon	*Why Mosquitoes Buzz in People's Ears*	Dial
	Honor Books	Peter Parnall	*The Desert Is Theirs*	Scribner
		Tomie dePaola	*Strega Nona*	Prentice-Hall
1975	Medal Winner	Gerald McDermott	*Arrow to the Sun*	Viking
	Honor Book	Tom Feelings	*Jambo Means Hello: A Swahili Alphabet Book*	Dial
1974	Medal Winner	Margot Zemach	*Duffy and the Devil*	Farrar, Straus & Giroux

Year	Award	Illustrator	Title	Publisher
	Honor Books	Susan Jeffers	*Three Jovial Huntsmen*	Bradbury
		David Macaulay	*Cathedral*	Houghton
1973	Medal Winner	Blair Lent	*The Funny Little Woman*	Dutton
	Honor Books	Gerald McDermott	*Anansi the Spider: A Tale from the Ashanti*	Holt
		Leonard Baskin	*Hosie's Alphabet*	Viking
		Nancy Ekholm Burkert	*Snow-White and the Seven Dwarfs*	Farrar, Straus & Giroux
		Tom Bahti	*When Clay Sings*	Scribner
1972	Medal Winner	Nonny Hogrogian	*One Fine Day*	Macmillan
	Honor Books	Arnold Lobel	*Hildilid's Night*	Macmillan
		Janina Domanska	*If All the Seas Were One Sea*	Macmillan
		Tom Feelings	*Moja Means One: Swahili Counting Book*	Dial
1971	Medal Winner	Gail E. Haley	*A Story A Story*	Atheneum
	Honor Books	Blair Lent	*The Angry Moon*	Atlantic
		Arnold Lobel	*Frog and Toad Are Friends*	Harper
		Maurice Sendak	*In the Night Kitchen*	Harper
1970	Medal Winner	William Steig	*Sylvester and the Magic Pebble*	Windmill Books
	Honor Books	Ezra Jack Keats	*Goggles!*	Macmillan
		Leo Lionni	*Alexander and the Wind-Up Mouse*	Pantheon
		Robert Andrew Parker	*Pop Corn and Ma Goodness*	Viking
		Brinton Turkle	*Thy Friend, Obadiah*	Viking
		Margot Zemach	*The Judge: An Untrue Tale*	Farrar, Straus & Giroux
1969	Medal Winner	Uri Shulevitz	*The Fool of the World and the Flying Ship*	Farrar, Straus & Giroux
	Honor Book	Blair Lent	*Why the Sun and the Moon Live in the Sky*	Houghton
1968	Medal Winner	Ed Emberley	*Drummer Hoff*	Prentice-Hall
	Honor Books	Leo Lionni	*Frederick*	Patheon
		Taro Yashima	*Seashore Story*	Viking
		Ed Young	*The Emperor and the Kite*	World

Year	Award	Illustrator	Title	Publisher
1967	Medal Winner	Evaline Ness	*Sam, Bangs, & Moonshine*	Holt
	Honor Book	Ed Emberley	*One Wide River to Cross*	Prentice-Hall
1966	Medal Winner	Nonny Hogrogian	*Always Room for One More*	Holt
	Honor Books	Roger Duvoisin	*Hide and Seek Fog*	Lothrop
		Marie Hall Ets	*Just Me*	Viking
		Evaline Ness	*Tom Tit Tot*	Scribner
1965	Medal Winner	Beni Montresor	*May I Bring a Friend?*	Atheneum
	Honor Books	Marvin Bileck	*Rain Makes Applesauce*	Holiday
		Blair Lent	*The Wave*	Houghton
		Evaline Ness	*A Pocketful of Cricket*	Holt
1964	Medal Winner	Maurice Sendak	*Where the Wild Things Are*	Harper
	Honor Books	Leo Lionni	*Swimmy*	Pantheon
		Evaline Ness	*All in the Morning Early*	Holt
		Philip Reed	*Mother Goose and Nursery Rhymes*	Atheneum
1963	Medal Winner	Ezra Jack Keats	*The Snowy Day*	Viking
	Honor Books	Bernarda Bryson	*The Sun Is a Golden Earring*	Holt
		Maurice Sendak	*Mr. Rabbit and the Lovely Present*	Harper
1962	Medal Winner	Marcia Brown	*Once a Mouse*	Scribner
	Honor Books	Peter Spier	*Fox Went out on a Chilly Night: An Old Song*	Doubleday
		Maurice Sendak	*Little Bear's Visit*	Harper
		Adrienne Adams	*The Day We Saw the Sun Come Up*	Scribner
1961	Medal Winner	Nicolas Sidjakov	*Baboushka and the Three Kings*	Parnassus
	Honor Book	Leo Lionni	*Inch by Inch*	Obolensky
1960	Medal Winner	Marie Hall Ets	*Nine Days to Christmas*	Viking
	Honor Books	Adrienne Adams	*Houses from the Sea*	Scribner
		Maurice Sendak	*The Moon Jumpers*	Harper
1959	Medal Winner	Barbara Cooney	*Chanticleer and the Fox*	Crowell
	Honor Books	Antonio Frasconi	*The House that Jack Built: La Maison Que Jacques A Batie*	Harcourt

Year	Award	Illustrator	Title	Publisher
		Maurice Sendak	*What Do You Say, Dear?*	W. R. Scott
		Taro Yashima	*Umbrella*	Viking
1958	Medal Winner	Robert McCloskey	*Time of Wonder*	Viking
	Honor Books	Don Freeman	*Fly High, Fly Low*	Viking
		Paul Galdone	*Anatole and the Cat*	McGraw-Hill
1957	Medal Winner	Marc Simont	*A Tree Is Nice*	Harper
	Honor Books	Marie Hall Ets	*Mr. Penny's Race Horse*	Viking
		Tasha Tudor	*1 Is One*	Walck
		Paul Galdone	*Anatole*	McGraw-Hill
		James Daugherty	*Gillespe and the Guards*	Viking
		William Pène du Bois	*Lion*	Viking
1956	Medal Winner	Feodor Rojankovsky	*Frog Went A-Courtin'*	Harcourt
	Honor Books	Marie Hall Ets	*Play with Me*	Viking
		Taro Yashima	*Crow Boy*	Viking
1955	Medal Winner	Marcia Brown	*Cinderella, or the Little Glass Slipper*	Scribner
	Honor Books	Marguerite de Angeli	*Book of Nursery and Mother Goose Rhymes*	Doubleday
		Tibor Gergely	*Wheel on the Chimney*	Lippincott
		Helen Sewell	*The Thanksgiving Story*	Scribner
1954	Medal Winner	Ludwig Bemelmans	*Madeline's Rescue*	Viking
	Honor Books	Robert McCloskey	*Journey Cake, Ho!*	Viking
		Jean Charlot	*When Will the World Be Mine?*	W. R. Scott
		Marcia Brown	*The Steadfast Tin Soldier*	Scribner
		Maurice Sendak	*A Very Special House*	Harper
		A. Birnbaum	*Green Eyes*	Capitol
1953	Medal Winner	Lynd Ward	*The Biggest Bear*	Houghton
	Honor Books	Marcia Brown	*Puss in Boots*	Scribner
		Robert McCloskey	*One Morning in Maine*	Viking
		Fritz Eichenberg	*Ape in a Cape: An Alphabet of Odd Animals*	Harcourt
		Margaret Bloy Graham	*The Storm Book*	Harper

Year	Award	Illustrator	Title	Publisher
		Juliet Kepes	*Five Little Monkeys*	Houghton
1952	Medal Winner	Nicolas, pseud. (Nicolas Mordvinoff)	*Finders Keepers*	Harcourt
	Honor Books	Marie Hall Ets	*Mr. T. W. Anthony Woo*	Viking
		Marcia Brown	*Skipper John's Cook*	Scribner
		Margaret Bloy Graham	*All Falling Down*	Harper
		William Pène du Bois	*Bear Party*	Viking
		Elizabeth Olds	*Feather Mountain*	Houghton
1951	Medal Winner	Katherine Milhous	*The Egg Tree*	Scribner
	Honor Books	Nicolas, pseud. (Nicolas Mordvinoff)	*The Two Reds*	Harcourt
		Marcia Brown	*Dick Whittington and his Cat*	Scribner
		Dr. Seuss	*If I Ran the Zoo*	Random House
		Helen Stone	*The Most Wonderful Doll in the World*	Lippincott
		Clare Turlay Newberry	*T-Bone the Baby Sitter*	Harper
1950	Medal Winner	Leo Politi	*Song of the Swallows*	Scribner
	Honor Books	Lynd Ward	*America's Ethan Allen*	Houghton
		Hildegard Woodward	*The Wild Birthday Cake*	Doubleday
		Marc Simont	*The Happy Day*	Harper
		Dr. Seuss	*Bartholomew and the Oobleck*	Random House
		Marcia Brown	*Henry-Fisherman*	Atheneum
1949	Medal Winner	Berta and Elmer Hader	*The Big Snow*	Macmillan
	Honor Books	Robert McCloskey	*Blueberries for Sal*	Viking
		Helen Stone	*All Around the Town*	Lippincott
		Leo Politi	*Juanita*	Scribner
		Kurt Weise	*Fish in the Air*	Viking
1948	Medal Winner	Roger Duvoisin	*White Snow, Bright Snow*	Lothrop
	Honor Books	Marcia Brown	*Stone Soup*	Scribner
		Dr. Seuss	*McElligot's Pool*	Random House

Year	Award	Illustrator	Title	Publisher
		Hildegard Woodward	*Roger and the Fox*	Doubleday
		Virginia Lee Burton	*Song of Robin Hood*	Houghton
		Georges Schreiber	*Bambino the Clown*	Viking
1947	Medal Winner	Leonard Weisgard	*The Little Island*	Doubleday
	Honor Books	Leonard Weisgard	*Rain Drop Splash*	Lothrop
		Jay Hyde Barnum	*Boats on the River*	Viking
		Tony Palazzo	*Timothy Turtle*	Welch
		Leo Politi	*Pedro, The Angel of Olvera Street*	Scribner
		Marjorie Torrey	*Sing in Praise: A Collection of the Best Loved Hymns*	Dutton
1946	Medal Winner	Maude and Miska Petersham	*The Rooster Crows*	Macmillan
	Honor Books	Leonard Weisgard	*Little Lost Lamb*	Doubleday
		Marjorie Torrey	*Sing Mother Goose*	Dutton
		Ruth Gannett	*My Mother Is the Most Beautiful Woman in the World*	Lothrop
		Kurt Weise	*You Can Write Chinese*	Viking
1945	Medal Winner	Elizabeth Orton Jones	*Prayer for a Child*	Macmillan
	Honor Books	Tasha Tudor	*Mother Goose*	Oxford University Press
		Marie Hall Ets	*In the Forest*	Viking
		Marguerite de Angeli	*Yonie Wondernose*	Doubleday
		Kate Seredy	*The Christmas Anna Angel*	Viking
1944	Medal Winner	Louis Slobodkin	*Many Moons*	Harcourt
	Honor Books	Elizabeth Orton Jones	*Small Rain: Verses from the Bible*	Viking
		Arnold E. Bare	*Pierre Pidgeon*	Houghton
		Berta and Elmer Hader	*The Mighty Hunter*	Macmillan
		Jean Charlot	*A Child's Good Night Book*	W. R. Scott
		Plato Chan	*Good-Luck Horse*	Whittlesey

Year	Award	Illustrator	Title	Publisher
1943	Medal Winner	Virginia Lee Burton	*The Little House*	Houghton
	Honor Books	Mary and Conrad Buff	*Dash and Dart*	Viking
		Clare Turlay Newberry	*Marshmallow*	Harper
1942	Medal Winner	Robert McCloskey	*Make Way for Ducklings*	Viking
	Honor Books	Maude and Miska Petersham	*An American ABC*	Macmillan
		Velino Herrera	*In My Mother's House*	Viking
		Holling C. Holling	*Paddle-to-the-Sea*	Houghton
		Wanda Gág	*Nothing At All*	Coward
1941	Medal Winner	Robert Lawson	*They Were Strong and Good*	Viking
	Honor Book	Clare Turlay Newberry	*April's Kittens*	Harper
1940	Medal Winner	Ingri and Edgar Parin d'Aulaire	*Abraham Lincoln*	Doubleday
	Honor Books	Berta and Elmer Hader	*Cock-a-Doodle-Doo*	Macmillan
		Ludwig Bemelmans	*Madeline*	Viking
		Lauren Ford	*The Ageless Story*	Dodd
1939	Medal Winner	Thomas Handforth	*Mei Li*	Doubleday
	Honor Books	James Daugherty	*Andy and the Lion*	Viking
		Clare Turlay Newberry	*Barkis*	Harper
		Laura Adams Armer	*The Forest Pool*	Longmans
		Wanda Gág	*Snow White and the Seven Dwarfs*	Coward
		Robert Lawson	*Wee Gillis*	Viking
1938	Medal Winner	Dorothy P. Lathrop	*Animals of the Bible, A Picture Book*	Lippincott
	Honor Books	Robert Lawson	*Four and Twenty Blackbirds*	Stokes
		Boris Artzybasheff	*Seven Simeons: A Russian Tale*	Viking

Activities

1. Randolph Caldecott drew illustrations for newspapers. These pictures depicted current happenings. Children could find out why the newspapers used illustrators and not photographers.

2. Randolph Caldecott died in Florida. Children could find out more about Florida and make a collage of items grown or made in Florida.

3. Children could visit the American Randolph Caldecott Society at: http://www.rcsamerica.com/ and read a biography of Randolph Caldecott. They could also research the purposes of the Randolph Caldecott Society.

4. Both Randolph Caldecott and John Newbery lived in the United Kingdom, but they lived during different centuries. Children could research some world events and find out which of the two would have known about the event.

5. Caldecott drew his pictures using primarily pen and ink. Children could also experiment with pen and ink drawings.

6. Caldecott drew his illustrations. Then some of the drawings were transferred to woodcuts. Older children could visit: http://www.cbbag.ca/BookArtsWeb/WoodEngraving.html and find out how woodcuts are made. Children could make their own "woodcuts" using pieces of potato or apple.

7. Mo Willems received the Newbery Honor Award in both 2004 and 2005. Children could visit his Web site at: http://www.mowillems.com/ and check out the sketch of the week. There they could also read his essays and see how he won six Emmys.

8. Kevin Henkes (http://www.kevinhenkes.com/) has won both a Newbery Medal and a Caldecott Medal. Children could vote to see who likes his illustrations better than his writing or vice versa.

9. Children could gather some Caldecott Award–winning books from different decades. They could create a history of children's illustrating styles.

10. Students could make a frequency table of Medal Winners and see which illustrator has won the most Caldecott Awards.

Randolph Caldecott and the Randolph Caldecott Medal

Student Handout 1—Information

Who Was Randolph Caldecott?

Randolph Caldecott was a famous English illustrator. He drew pictures for children's books. Randolph was born in England on March 22, 1846. He was often sick, even as a child. His father worked as an accountant, and his mother died when he was about six years old. When he grew up, he worked in a bank. His hobby was drawing. He moved to a big city and worked for a bigger bank. He kept drawing. Finally, he quit his bank job and began drawing pictures for books.

Randolph became famous for his drawings. He drew pictures for two children's books every year. One book he illustrated was *The House that Jack Built.* His illustrations were often funny, and they were full of action. Children liked to look at the small details in his pictures. He began to feel sick again. He and his wife decided to come to the United States for a long trip. The boat trip to America was hard for him. He died in Florida on February 13, 1886.

What Is the Randolph Caldecott Medal?

The Randolph Caldecott Medal is given every year to the best illustrations. The book must be published in the United States, and the words must be in English. The award was first given in 1932, and honor books may also be chosen.

From *Children's Book Award Handbook* by Diana F. Marks. Westport, CT: Libraries Unlimited. Copyright © 2006.

Randolph Caldecott and the Randolph Caldecott Medal

Student Handout 2—Questions

Name_____ Date_____

Learn about the life of Randolph Caldecott, and find out more about the Randolph Caldecott Medal. Then answer the following questions.

1. Who was Randolph Caldecott?

2. Where and when was Randolph Caldecott born?

3. Where did Randolph work before he became an illustrator?

4. Why did children like to look at his pictures?

5. Where and when did he die?

6. What is the Randolph Caldecott Medal?

7. When was it first given?

Randolph Caldecott and the Randolph Caldecott Medal

Student Handout 3—Would He Have Used It?

Name_____ Date_____

Randolph Caldecott lived from 1846 to 1886. He was only forty years old when he died. Below is a list of inventions. Decide if the invention was available to Caldecott during his lifetime. In other words, would he have used it?

Invention	Would He Have Used It? (Yes or No)	Year of Invention
Telephone		
Magnetic Compass		
Slinky		
Thermometer		
Fountain Pen		
Stapler		
Handheld Calculator		
Piano		
Candy Cane		
Golf Balls		
Morse Code		
Geiger Counter		
Crayons		
Safety Pin		
Pasteurization		
Helicopter		
Bifocals		
Cotton Gin		
Daguerreotype Camera		
Pocket Watch		

From *Children's Book Award Handbook* by Diana F. Marks. Westport, CT: Libraries Unlimited. Copyright © 2006.

Randolph Caldecott and the Randolph Caldecott Medal

Student Handout 3—Would He Have Used It?—Answers

Name_____ Date_____

Randolph Caldecott lived from 1846 to 1886. He was only forty years old when he died. Below is a list of inventions. Decide if the invention was available to Caldecott during his lifetime. In other words, would he have used it?

Invention	Would He Have Used It?	Your Estimate as to Year of Invention
Telephone	Yes	1876
Magnetic Compass	Yes	1182
Slinky	No	1943
Thermometer	Yes	1724
Fountain Pen	Yes	1884
Stapler	Yes	1841
Handheld Calculator	No	1967
Piano	Yes	1709
Candy Cane	Yes	1670
Golf Balls	Yes	1400
Morse Code	Yes	1838
Geiger Counter	No	1908
Crayons	No	1903
Safety Pin	Yes	1849
Pasteurization	Yes	1856
Helicopter	No	1939
Bifocals	Yes	1780
Cotton Gin	Yes	1794
Daguerreotype Camera	Yes	1839
Pocket Watch	Yes	1675

Randolph Caldecott and the Randolph Caldecott Medal

Student Handout 4—Cooperative Illustration Project

Name_____ Date_____

Randolph Caldecott was an English illustrator who lived from 1846 to 1886. His illustrations for children's books were filled with humor, action, and detail. The Randolph Caldecott Medal is given every year to the best-illustrated children's book just published in the United States. Today you are going to be both author and illustrator, but you will not illustrate your own writing. You will need:

- a friend or classmate
- 2 pieces of unlined paper
- 2 pencils
- 2 rulers
- art supplies like crayons, paints, or colored pencils
- creative ideas

Now let's get started.

1. Use the ruler and pencil to draw a few lines toward the bottom of the paper. Your friend will do the same with his or her paper.

2. Write a sentence or two on the lines that tell a story or a part of a story. Your friend will do the same with his or her paper.

3. Give your paper to your friend or classmate. Your friend will give his or her paper to you.

4. Your classmate or friend will use the art supplies to illustrate your story. You will use the art supplies to illustrate his or her story.

5. Look at the finished products. Do you like writing or illustrating better?

CHAPTER 7

Margaret Alexander Edwards and the Margaret A. Edwards Award

Overview

The Margaret A. Edwards Award is awarded every year to an author whose body of work has best contributed to young adult literature. Margaret Alexander Edwards was a librarian who dedicated her life to libraries, adolescents, and the dissemination of young adult literature.

Born in 1902, Margaret Alexander Edwards grew up in rural Texas. Early in her career, she taught English and Latin in Texas and Maryland. She became a librarian at the Enoch Pratt Free Library in Baltimore, Maryland, remaining there until 1962. She was very active in the American Library Association, and she wrote numerous articles. During the rationing periods of World War II, she rented a horse and wagon, filled the wagon with books, and drove the wagon to various Baltimore neighborhoods. Thus, she brought the library to its patrons. Her book, *The Fair Garden and the Swarm of Beasts: The Library and the Young Adult,* discusses her philosophy about working with young adults. The book is still in print.

The Margaret A. Edwards Award was first presented in 1988. The Young Adult Library Services Association (YALSA), a division of the American Library Association (ALA), administers the award, and *School Library Journal* sponsors the award. A jury of five members reviews suggestions from librarians and young adults. The winner is announced at the ALA midwinter meeting, and the winner receives the citation and $2,000 at the ALA summer conference.

Margaret A. Edwards Biography

Margaret Alexander Edwards was a hard-working, hard-driving librarian who advocated for young adult readers. She worked at the Enoch Pratt Free Library in Baltimore, Maryland, for thirty years. She was active in the American Library Association, and she wrote numerous articles.

Margaret Alexander was born on October 23, 1902, on a cotton farm near Childress, Texas. Her parents, Claude and Hadena Crews Alexander, were religious and hard-working farmers. Margaret and her sister Helen rebelled against much of the religious doctrine her parents, former teachers, taught them. Since the family barely made ends meet, few books were available in the home. The Bible, Dickens, Milton, and a few other classics were well used. The two girls often visited the local library, but again the selection was small. They read Horatio Alger and *Anne of Green Gables.* An honor student, Margaret graduated from Childress High School. She then attended Trinity College in Waxachie (now San Antonio), Texas, where she was a library assistant. She graduated in 1922 summa cum laude.

Margaret taught for five years, earning about $1,250 a year in two small towns in Texas. She went to New York City in 1927 and earned a Master's degree in Latin from Columbia University in 1928, after which she started teaching Latin in a high school in Towson, Maryland. However, she was fired in 1932 when she tried to give unwanted advice to her superior.

At age thirty and in the middle of the Great Depression, Margaret was unemployed. As she began her search for work, she saw a posting on the door of the Enoch Pratt Free Library in Baltimore, Maryland. The library was giving examinations for a librarian-in-training program.

Joseph L. Wheeler, the director of the library, hired Margaret, sensing that what she lacked in training she made up in energy and intelligence. At first, she worked in the reference department. However, at the beginning of the school year, Wheeler transferred her to the Popular Library, working for Pauline McCauley. The Popular Library featured fiction and nonfiction for adults and a small section for young adults. In becoming a librarian for young people, Margaret had at last found her calling. Aware that she knew little about the books in her library, every night she took home numerous books and read them. She also realized she needed more than her own opinions about the various books; she therefore asked advice from library patrons as to level of interest and the appropriateness of certain books.

In 1935, Margaret was offered the position of secretary of the Young People's Reading Roundtable of the American Library Association, but both Wheeler and McCauley felt she was not ready for the position. When the rebellious Margaret talked about leaving and returning to Columbia for a degree in librarianship, the three compromised: Margaret would remain at Enoch Pratt and take on the ALA role. She also would take summer classes at Columbia University for librarianship. In 1937, she became the young people's librarian at Enoch Pratt Free Library, and she received a raise. A year later, she published "Introducing Books to Young Readers" in the *ALA Bulletin*. She also chaired a committee that created the yearly list of books for young people for *Booklist*. In spring 1940, she completed a project to create young adult collections in library branches. She also became the chairperson of the Young People's Reading Roundtable.

In 1941, Margaret earned a library degree from Columbia University, having taken classes for four summers to receive the degree. By the early 1940s, World War II had become a part of everyone's life, and one of its many profound effects was the rationing of gasoline and tires. Margaret published an article in the May 1, 1943, issue of *Library Journal* suggesting that librarians fill horse-drawn wagons with books and drive the wagons through neighborhoods. In essence, the library would come to the patrons. A year later, she became the secretary of the Division of Libraries for Children and Young People. Putting her ideas into practice, she rented a horse and wagon, filled the wagon with a variety of books, and drove it through Baltimore neighborhoods during the summers of 1943 through 1945. The Pratt Library Book Wagon was very popular.

During the war years, Margaret met Dr. Philip H. Edwards, the principal of Baltimore City College, an all-male Baltimore high school. He was tall and intelligent, with a Ph.D. in Latin. They were married in 1945. Two years later, they moved to a large farm in Harford County, Maryland. She no longer had the time to drive the Pratt Library Book Wagon.

By now, Margaret was busily engaged in speaking to groups, coaxing teenagers to read, working with the ALA, and writing articles. She also became a role model for her staff. Each employee was required to have an individualized reading list of at least 300 books. Numerous meetings concentrated on these books and on methods to bring the books to teenagers. Margaret began giving book talks in local high schools, and at the same time publishers were printing more and better young adult books. In 1947, she was elected to the ALA Council. She sponsored *You're the Critic* in 1948, and she became vice president of the Maryland Library Association in 1949. A year later, she became president of the organization. She also published a handbook, *Work with Young People* and was appointed the library's Coordinator of Work with Young People.

In 1951, Margaret helped the Baltimore City Public Schools create book fairs. Six years later, she served as ALA representative to the National Council of Teachers of English to compile *Books for You.* In 1957, she received the Grolier Award for her energizing work with librarians and her dedication to young people. Three years later, she again helped the National Council of Teachers of English compile *Books for You* and became a member of the ALA Committee on Standards for Work with Young Adults in Public Libraries. In 1961, she headed a committee that selected the information to be included in *Top of the News.* The next year Margaret Alexander Edwards retired from Enoch Pratt Free Library. Her friends, knowing how much she loved her farm, gave her a Hereford bull calf, and the librarians gave her bales of hay. In retirement, she kept very busy, providing workshops and becoming active in the League of Women Voters.

In 1969, Margaret published her most famous book, *The Fair Garden and the Swarm of Beasts: The Library and the Young Adult.* The book, advocating for young adult readers, is still in print. Today's librarians still find the book helpful.

On April 19, 1988, Margaret Alexander Edwards died. Her will bequeathed the majority of her estate to a trust to "further the personal reading of young adults." The Margaret Alexander Edwards Trust was created in 1989. The trust provides grants to librarians who "further the personal reading of young adults." The first Margaret A. Edwards Award, administered by YALSA and sponsored by *School Library Journal,* was presented in 1988.

Margaret A. Edwards Timeline

Date	Event
1902	Born Margaret Alexander on October 23 on a cotton farm near Childress, Texas, to Claude and Hadena Crews Alexander
?	Graduated from Childress High School
1922	Graduated from Trinity College in Waxachie (now San Antonio) Texas
?	Taught in Texas for five years
1928	Earned a master's degree in Latin from Columbia University; started teaching Latin in a high school in Towson, Maryland
1932	Was fired from her teaching job; applied for a training class at Enoch Pratt Free Library in Baltimore, Maryland
1935	Offered position as secretary of the Young People's Reading Roundtable of the American Library Association; supervisors felt she should not take position
1937	Received raise and an appointment to the job as young people's librarian
1938	Published in the *ALA Bulletin*, "Introducing Books to Young Readers"; chaired committee that created the yearly list of books for young people for *Booklist*
1940	Completed project to create young adult collections in library branches (sponsored by Kellogg Foundation); became chairperson of the Young People's Reading Roundtable
1941	Earned library degree from Columbia University; published an article in the May 1 issue of *Library Journal*, suggesting that horse-drawn wagons be filled with books and driven through neighborhoods
1942	Was secretary of the Division of Libraries for Children and Young People
1943	Rented, filled, and drove the wagons through the neighborhoods during the summers of 1943 through 1945
1944	Hired an assistant on January 1
1945	Married Dr. Philip H. Edwards, principal of Baltimore City College, an all-male high school
1947	Moved to a farm in Harford County, Maryland; was elected to the ALA Council
1948	Sponsored *You're the Critic*
1949	Became vice president of Maryland Library Association
1950	Became president of Maryland Library Association; published the handbook, *Work with Young People*; appointed Coordinator of Work with Young People
1951	Worked with Baltimore City Public Schools to create book fairs
1957	Helped as ALA representative to the National Council of Teachers of English to compile *Books for You*; received the Grolier Award
1960	Again helped the National Council of Teachers of English compile *Books for You*; became a member of the ALA Committee on Standards for Work with Young Adults in Public Libraries
1961	Headed a committee that decided information to be included in *Top of the News*
1962	Retired from Enoch Pratt Free Library
1969	Published *The Fair Garden and the Swarm of Beasts: The Library and the Young Adult*
1988	Died on April 19; her will bequeathed the majority of her estate to a trust to "further the personal reading young adults"
1989	Margaret Alexander Edwards Trust created
1998	Margaret A. Edwards Award created; first award given

History and Criteria of Award

Margaret Alexander Edwards worked tirelessly for young adult readers. She served as an excellent role model for other librarians, and she was very active in the American Library Association. She was one of the first librarians who believed that young adult readers should be noticed and encouraged.

Neff A. Perlman, publisher of *School Library Journal*, suggested to Lillian N. Gerhardt, editor-in-chief of the periodical, that an award should be created to honor the lifetime achievements of authors who write for young adults. Gerhardt felt that *School Library Journal* should sponsor it but that the American Library Association should give the award. She asked the Young Adult Services Division (YASD), now YALSA, to develop the award. In 1986, the School Library Journal Young Adult Author Award/Selected and Administered by the American Library Association's Young Adult Services Division was founded.

Joan Atkinson, Vivian Wynn, and Marian Hargrove, then officers of YASD, worked with a committee to develop the criteria. The group decided that the award would be presented to people for a lifetime of contributions to young adult literature.

1. The award jury would examine books that help adolescents learn about themselves and the world around them.

2. The winning books had to possess good literary qualities.

3. The winning books had to help young adults develop their own philosophies.

4. Young adults had to like these books, and the books had to be appealing to people all over the country.

5. The award would be presented every two years.

Eventually two changes were made. First, the title of the award, the School Library Journal Young Adult Author Award/Selected and Administered by the American Library Association's Young Adult Services Division, was changed to the Margaret A. Edwards Award. Second, the award would be presented every year instead of every two years.

Present juries use the following rules:

1. The books must be written with young adults in mind.

2. The books must be in print at the time of nomination.

3. The author must be living.

4. If coauthors are honored, at least one of the coauthors must be living.

5. An award winner will be considered for another award in the future but not more than once every six years.

6. The books must have been published in the United States.

7. The books must have been published at least five years prior to nomination. This five-year time period allows young adult readers to find and critique the books.

School Library Journal funds the award and any administrative costs the committee incurs. The award winner receives a citation and a cash prize of $2,000. The winner accepts the award at the ALA annual conference and gives a short speech.

Award Recipients

Year	Author/Illustrator
2006	Jacqueline Woodson
2005	Francesca Lia Block
2004	Ursula K. Le Guin
2003	Nancy Garden
2002	Paul Zindel
2001	Robert Lipsyte
2000	Chris Crutcher
1999	Ann McCaffrey
1998	Madeleine L'Engle
1997	Gary Paulsen
1996	Judy Blume
1995	Cynthia Voigt
1994	Walter Dean Myers
1993	M. E. Kerr
1992	Lois Duncan
1991	Robert Cormier
1990	Richard Peck
1988	S. E. Hinton

Activities

1. Margaret Alexander Edwards grew up in Texas, but she worked most of her life in Maryland. Children could identify those states on a large map and figure out how the states are alike and different. A Venn diagram would be a useful tool for this activity.

2. Margaret Alexander Edwards taught Latin for a time. Students could learn some Latin by visiting: http://languages.4status.net/latin/. They could create a small Latin dictionary.

3. Margaret Alexander Edwards specialized in librarianship with young adults. Young adults could list the important parts of young adult literature that make it different from children's literature and adult literature.

4. Margaret Alexander Edwards earned two Master's degrees, one in Latin and one in library science. A counselor could discuss with students how a person obtains a Master's degree.

5. S. E. Hinton, in 1988, was the first person to receive the Margaret A. Edwards Award. Students could visit Hinton's Web site at: http://www.sehinton.com/. They could find out where she currently lives. They could create a brochure about S. E. Hinton and Tulsa, Oklahoma.

6. Robert Cormier received the Margaret A. Edwards Award in 1991. He died in 2000. However, an excellent interview with him exists at: http://www.ipl.org/div/kidspace/askauthor/Cormier.html. Young adults could find out which authors were his heroes. Then each student could create list of his or her author heroes.

7. Gary Paulsen was the recipient of the 1997 Margaret A. Edwards Award. He has written a number of well-known books, including *Hatchet* and *Nightjohn*. Young adults could explore a Web site at: http://www.randomhouse.com/features/garypaulsen/. They could play the White Fox Survival Game.

8. Francesca Lia Block was the 2005 recipient of the Margaret A. Edwards Award. Young adults could visit her Web site at: http://www.francescaliablock.com/. They could then list all her books and take a poll as to the best.

9. Madeleine L'Engle received the 1998 Award. Young adults could visit her unusual Web site at: http://www.madeleinelengle.com/. There they could try out the Madeleine L'Engle Workshop.

10. Paul Zindel received the 2002 Margaret A. Edwards Award. Charlotte Zolotow suggested he be a writer. She was also his editor. Young adults could visit: http://www.charlottezolotow.com/paul_zindel.htm. There they could read about how Paul and Charlotte worked together. Then they could list the ways Charlotte helped Paul.

Margaret Alexander Edwards and the Margaret A. Edwards Award

Student Handout 1—Information

Who Was Margaret Alexander Edwards?

Margaret Alexander was born on October 23, 1902, on a cotton farm near Childress, Texas. Her parents were religious and hard-working farmers. Margaret and her sister rebelled against much of the religious doctrine her parents, former teachers, taught them. Since the family barely made ends meet, few books were available in the home. The two girls often visited the local library, but the selection was small. An honor student, Margaret graduated from Childress High School. She then attended Trinity College in Waxachie (now San Antonio), Texas, where she was a library assistant. She graduated in 1922 summa cum laude.

Margaret taught for five years in two small towns in Texas. She went to New York City and earned a master's degree in Latin from Columbia University in 1928. She taught Latin in Towson, Maryland. However, she was fired in 1932 when she gave advice to her superior.

At age thirty and in the middle of the Great Depression, Margaret was unemployed. The Enoch Pratt Free Library in Baltimore, Maryland, was giving examinations for a librarian-in-training program. The director of the library hired her. Margaret found her calling when she became a librarian for young people. She found that she knew little about the books in her library, so every night she took home numerous books and read them.

In 1935, Margaret was offered the position as secretary of the Young People's Reading Roundtable of the American Library Association (ALA). In 1941, she earned a library degree from Columbia University. She had taken classes for four summers to receive the degree. World War II became a part of everyone's life, and gasoline and tires were rationed. Many people were unable to visit the library. Margaret rented a horse and wagon, filled the wagon with a variety of books, and drove it through Baltimore neighborhoods during the summers of 1943 through 1945. The Pratt Library Book Wagon was very popular.

Margaret met Dr. Philip H. Edwards, a principal with a Ph.D. in Latin. They were married in 1945. Two years later, they moved to a large farm in Harford County, Maryland. By now, Margaret was busy with many activities. She was speaking to groups, coaxing teenagers to read, working with ALA, and writing articles. She gave book talks in local high schools, and publishers printed more and better young adult books.

In 1957 and in 1960, she helped the National Council of Teachers of English compile *Books for You*. She received the 1957 Grolier Award for her energizing work with librarians and her dedication to young people. She became a member of the ALA Committee on Standards for Work with Young Adults in Public Libraries. In 1962, Margaret Alexander Edwards retired. Her friends gave her a Hereford bull calf, and the librarians gave her bales of hay. In 1969, she published her most famous book, *The Fair Garden and the Swarm of Beasts: The Library and the Young Adult.* The book, advocating for young adult readers, is still in print.

On April 19, 1988, Margaret Alexander Edwards died.

What Is the Margaret A. Edwards Award?

The Margaret A. Edwards Award is awarded every year to an author whose body of work has best contributed to young adult literature. The Margaret A. Edwards Award was first presented in 1988. The Young Adult Library Services Association (YALSA), a division of the American Library Association, administers the award, and *School Library Journal* sponsors the award. A jury of five members reviews suggestions from librarians and young adults. The winner is announced at the ALA midwinter meeting, and the winner receives the citation and $2,000 at the ALA summer conference.

Margaret Alexander Edwards and the Margaret A. Edwards Award

Student Handout 2—Questions

Name_____ Date_____

Investigate the life of Margaret Alexander Edwards, and find out more about the Margaret A. Edwards Award. Then answer the following questions.

1. Where and when was Margaret Alexander Edwards born?

2. What was her job before she became a librarian?

3. How did she become a librarian?

4. What did she do to entice teenagers to read more?

5. What offices did she hold in the American Library Association?

6. What was the Pratt Library Book Wagon?

7. When did she die?

8. What is the Margaret A. Edwards Award?

9. Who decides the award recipients?

10. How does a young adult book differ from a children's book?

Margaret Alexander Edwards and the Margaret A. Edwards Award

Student Handout 3—Texas and Maryland

Name_____ Date_____

Margaret Edward Alexander was born and raised in Texas. However, she lived and worked in Maryland for most of her adult life. Let's see what you know about Texas and Maryland. See if you can answer the following questions. Use some references to find the answers you do not know.

1. Which state is bigger?

2. Which state has been a state longer?

3. Which state has the larger population?

4. Which state has more states bordering it?

5. Which state has the lower point in altitude?

6. Which state has the higher point in altitude?

7. Which state is the birthplace of more presidents?

8. Which state has more U.S. senators?

9. Which state has a state mammal as a symbol?

10. Which state is the home to the National Aquarium?

Margaret Alexander Edwards and the Margaret A. Edwards Award

Student Handout 3—Texas and Maryland—Answers

Name_____ Date_____

Margaret Edward Alexander was born and raised in Texas. However, she lived and worked in Maryland for most of her adult life. Let's see what you know about Texas and Maryland. See if you can answer the following questions. Use some references to find the answers you do not know.

1. Which state is bigger? Texas (268,601 square miles)

2. Which state has been a state longer? Maryland (April 28, 1788)

3. Which state has the larger population? Texas (20,851,820 people)

4. Which state has more states bordering it? Trick question—they both have four bordering states.

5. Which state has the lower point in altitude? Maryland—Bloody Point Hole is 174 feet below sea level.

6. Which state has the higher point in altitude? Texas—Guadalupe Peak is 8,749 feet high.

7. Which state is the birthplace of more presidents? Texas—Two presidents Eisenhower and Lyndon Baines Johnson. Maryland, surprisingly, no presidents

8. Which state has more U.S. senators? Trick question—they both send two senators to Washington, D.C.

9. Which state has a state mammal as a symbol? Texas—the armadillo

10. Which state is the home to the National Aquarium? Maryland in the city of Baltimore

From *Children's Book Award Handbook* by Diana F. Marks. Westport, CT: Libraries Unlimited. Copyright © 2006.

Margaret Alexander Edwards and the Margaret A. Edwards Award

Student Handout 4—Authors Game

Name_____ Date_____

The Margaret A. Edwards Award honors the lifetime achievements of excellent writers for young adults. You can learn about some of these authors and their books and have a good time as well. You are going to make an "authors" type of game.

You will need forty index cards and some markers.

1. Choose ten of the authors who have won the Margaret A. Edwards Award.

2. Locate the names of four books by each of the authors.

3. Make a "book" of four cards for each author and his or her four books. Write down the author's name at the top of the card in one color marker. Write down the four titles in another color marker. With a third marker, circle a different title on each card.

4. The rules are the same as "Go Fish."

5. Shuffle the cards, play the game, and have a good time!

CHAPTER 8

Theodor Seuss Geisel and the Theodor Seuss Geisel Award

Overview

The Theodor Seuss Geisel Award is given yearly to the author(s) and illustrator(s) of the best beginning reader book published in the previous year. Theodor Seuss Geisel, also known as Dr. Seuss, has enriched the lives of young readers since the publication of his first book in 1937, *And to Think That I Saw It on Mulberry Street.*

Theodor Seuss Geisel, born in 1904 in Springfield, Massachusetts, wrote at least forty-nine books that both delighted parents and inspired children to become better readers. Several of his books were made into movies or television shows. He wrote such classics as *The Cat in the Hat* and *How the Grinch Stole Christmas!* He did not like to speak to audiences, and he wrote and rewrote his books for months before they were published. He died in 1991.

The Theodor Seuss Geisel Award was presented for the first time in 2006. Members of the Association for Library Service to Children (ALSC) serve on a jury that reviews books and decides on the winners. The names of the winners are announced at the midwinter meeting of the American Library Association (ALA), and the awards are presented to the authors and illustrators during ALA's summer conference.

Theodor Seuss Geisel Biography

Theodor Seuss Geisel is better known as Dr. Seuss. Dr. Seuss has become an icon in children's literature. His works have been translated into at least fifteen languages, and more than 200 million copies of his books have been sold. His characters are famous around the world. Movies and television specials have featured his books.

Dr. Seuss was born Theodor Seuss Geisel on March 2, 1904, in Springfield, Massachusetts. His parents, Henrietta Seuss and Theodor Robert Geisel, were the offspring of German immigrants. Henrietta had spent a great deal of time in her parents' bakery, and Theodor had learned the brewery business from his parents. An older sister by two years, Marnie, welcomed the baby. Ted, as he was known to everyone, grew up in a neighborhood filled with relatives and close friends. His mother often recited rhymes she had made to keep track of the bakery offerings.

Ted went to elementary school and then on to high school. The Geisel family went through a period of tough times when the United States entered World War I. Some members of the community were not kind to Ted's family because of their German heritage. In addition, once Prohibition came into effect on January 16, 1920, the family's brewery business had to close. Ted's father found a job as superintendent of the local zoo.

Ted entered Dartmouth College in the fall of 1921. He enjoyed his years there and for a time was the editor of *Jack O'Lantern*, the college's humor periodical. However, when he and some of his friends hosted a party on campus during Prohibition, the college removed him from the position. He continued to submit entries to the periodical under the name Seuss. As graduation approached, he told his father that he had received a fellowship to attend the University of Oxford. His father proudly announced Ted's accomplishment to the community, but in actual fact, Ted had applied for the fellowship but had not received it. Not wanting to be embarrassed, his father gathered up the money and sent him to Oxford. Ted left for England in August of 1924.

At Oxford, Ted planned to gain the skills needed to become a professor of English. Although he attended classes, he dedicated little time to his studies. Instead, he began to draw more and more cartoons. Another American student, Helen Palmer, noticed his work and was so impressed that she advised him to forget Oxford and become an artist. He decided he would not finish his studies and took a lengthy trip through Europe.

Eventually, in 1927, he returned to America. His first cartoon appeared that year in the *Saturday Evening Post*. Others began to notice his work, and he was hired by the magazine *Judge* in 1927. In November of that same year he married Helen Palmer. He published more and more cartoons, one of which featured an insect repellent called Flit. In 1931, the company that manufactured the repellent contacted him, and he created most of their advertising for several years. Unlike most people, he and Helen were able to live fairly comfortably during the Depression.

In 1936, the two took a cruise, and to relieve the monotony of the ship's motors, which had begun to get on his nerves, Ted began writing a children's book to pass the time. Upon his return home, he went to twenty-seven publishers to see if they would print his book, *And to Think That I Saw It on Mulberry Street*. They all rejected his work. He ran into an old Dartmouth friend who worked for Vanguard Press, which agreed to publish the book. The book received only moderate success. Undeterred, he began writing other books for children, including *Horton Hatches the Egg*.

Shortly after the bombing of Pearl Harbor, Ted joined the army. Because he was thirty-eight years old, he was not sent to the front. Instead, he went to Hollywood and produced informational movies for the soldiers and documentaries for the war effort. There he worked with the well-known Hollywood animator, Chuck Jones. Ted left military service on January 13, 1946.

In 1948, Ted and Helen felt somewhat comfortable financially, and they bought an observation tower in La Jolla, California, converting it into a home. In that same year, he earned his first Caldecott Honor Award for *McElligot's Pool*. A year later, he published *Bartholomew and the Oobleck*. In 1950, he published *If I Ran the Zoo* and received another Caldecott Honor Award for *Bartholomew and the Oobleck*. The following year he won an Academy Award for Best Cartoon for *Gerald McBoing-Boing* and another Caldecott Honor Award for *If I Ran the Zoo*.

By now, Ted was becoming very well known, but his fame escalated to an entirely new height in 1957 with the publication of *The Cat in the Hat* and *How the Grinch Stole Christmas!* The next year he and Helen teamed up with Random House to publish Beginner Books, books that would promote reading instruction and still appeal to children. Sometimes he wrote the manuscript, and others created the illustrations. Sometimes he used other pseudonyms, including Rosetta Stone and Theo. LeSieg.

Over the next few years he published at least one book a year and sometimes as many as three. A friend and Random House publisher, Bennett Cerf, had bet Ted that he could not write a good children's book using a vocabulary of less than fifty words. Ted accepted the challenge and published the now legendary *Green Eggs and Ham* in 1960.

In 1967 Helen, who had also become a successful children's author, died, and Ted was distraught. However, he fell in love with an old friend, Audrey Stone Dimond, who divorced her husband and married Ted in 1968. Her two daughters became an important part of the household. Ted continued to write, publishing "big books," the ones he developed on his own. He also continued to publish Beginner Books in conjunction with Random House. In addition, he developed another type of book series, Bright & Early Books, for the pre-reader. Some of his books, such as *The Lorax,* published in 1971, took more of a political stance. In 1980, he received the Laura Ingalls Wilder Award for his lifetime contributions to children's literature. In 1984, he published one of his most controversial books, *The Butter Battle Book.* This book, written during the Cold War, is a satire. In the book, two cultures become involved in a destructive arms race over the issue of how to butter a slice of toast. In that same year, he received a Pulitzer Prize.

In the mid-1980s, Ted's health began to fail; he suffered a heart attack, and he also underwent treatment for cancer. Even so, he continued to work. *You're Only Old Once!* appeared in 1986. His *Oh, the Places You'll Go!* was published to rave reviews in 1990, and the book continues to show strong sales around graduation dates. He died on September 24, 1991, at his house in La Jolla, California.

Ted worked from about 10:00 A.M. to 6:00 P.M. just about every workday of his life. His creative process remained pretty much a secret. It is known, however, that he was meticulous and particular, and that for the most part, he resisted editors' suggested changes. A very wealthy writer, Ted was generous, sending hundreds of books to early reading programs and sponsoring many other programs that rewarded creativity and the arts. He was an extremely private person, avoiding public speeches and interviews. He rarely opened his studio to reporters or writers. When he was out with the public, the question he hated the most was "Where do you get your ideas?"

Since Dr. Seuss's death, several of his books have been published posthumously. One of his books, *My Many Colored Days*, was written in 1973 but was not published until 1996. It was illustrated by Steve Johnson and Lou Fancher. *Hooray for Diffendoofer Day!* was published in 1998. Two movies, *The Grinch* and *The Cat in the Hat*, were released, respectively, in 2001 and 2003.

In 2004, the American Library Association announced the creation of the Theodor Seuss Geisel Award, recognizing the best writers and illustrators of beginning reader books.

Theodor Seuss Geisel Timeline

Date	Event
1904	Born Theodor Seuss Geisel to Henrietta Seuss and Theodor Robert Geisel in Springfield, Massachusetts, on March 2
1906	Sister Henrietta born; died 18 months later
1908	Entered kindergarten
1920	Prohibition began on January 16; father's brewery was shut down; father took job as local zoo superintendent
1921	Entered Dartmouth College in September
1925	Graduated from Dartmouth on June 23; left for England on August 24 to attend Oxford
1927	Left Europe on February 13; first cartoon appeared in *Saturday Evening Post*; was hired by *Judge*; married Helen Palmer on November 29
1931	Worked in advertising for an insect repellent company, Flit; mother died
1937	Published *And to Think That I Saw It on Mulberry Street*
1938	Published *The 500 Hats of Bartholomew Cubbins*
1939	Published *The King's Stilts*; quit working for Flit
1940	Published *The Seven Lady Godivas* and *Horton Hatches the Egg*
1943	Was inducted into the army on January 7; joined the "Hollywood front"
1945	Sister Marnie died in September
1946	Left military active duty as lieutenant colonel on January 13
1947	Published *McElligot's Pool*
1948	Published *Thidwick, the Big-Hearted Moose*; purchased observation tower in La Jolla, California, and converted it into residence; received Caldecott Honor Award for *McElligot's Pool*
1949	Published *Bartholomew and the Oobleck*
1950	Published *If I Ran the Zoo*; received Caldecott Honor Award for *Bartholomew and the Oobleck*
1951	Won Academy Award for Best Cartoon for *Gerald McBoing-Boing*; received Caldecott Honor Award for *If I Ran the Zoo*
1953	Published *Scrambled Eggs Super!*; created a live-actor movie *The 5,000 Fingers of Dr. T.*
1954	Published *Horton Hears a Who!*
1955	Received honorary doctorate from Yale in May; published *On Beyond Zebra!*
1956	Published *If I Ran the Circus*
1957	Published *The Cat in the Hat* and *How the Grinch Stole Christmas!*
1958	Began working for Random House and its Beginner Books Division; published *Yertle the Turtle and Other Stories* and *The Cat in the Hat Comes Back*
1959	Published *Happy Birthday to You!*
1960	Published *One Fish, Two Fish, Red Fish, Blue Fish* and *Green Eggs and Ham*
1961	Published *The Sneetches and Other Stories* and *Ten Apples up on Top!*
1962	Published *Dr. Seuss's Sleep Book*

Date	Event
1963	Published *Dr. Seuss's ABC: An Amazing Alphabet Book* and *Hop on Pop*
1965	Published *Fox in Socks* and *I Wish that I Had Duck Feet* and *I Had Trouble in Getting to Solla Sollew*
1966	Published *Come Over to My House*; *How the Grinch Stole Christmas!* premiered on television
1967	Published *The Cat in the Hat Songbook*; Helen died on October 23
1968	Published *The Foot Book* and *The Hat Book*; married Audrey Stone Dimond on June 21; father died on December 9
1969	Published *I Can Lick 30 Tigers Today! And Other Stories* and *My Book about Me*
1970	Published *I Can Draw It Myself by Me, Myself* and *Mr. Brown Can Moo! Can You?*
1971	Published *The Lorax* and *I Can Write! A Book by Me, Myself*; received a Peabody for animated *How the Grinch Stole Christmas!* and *Horton Hears a Who!*
1972	Published *In a People House* and *Marvin K. Mooney, Will You Please Go Now!*
1973	Published *Did I Ever Tell You How Lucky You Are?* and *Shape of Me and Other Stuff* and *The Pop-up Mice of Mr. Brice*
1974	Published *Wacky Wednesday* and *There's a Wocket in My Pocket!* and *Great Day for Up!*
1975	Published *Oh, the Thinks You Can Think!* and *Would You Rather Be a Bullfrog?* and *Because a Little Bug Went Ka-choo!*
1976	Published *The Cat's Quizzer: Are You Smarter than the Cat in the Hat?* and *Hooper Humperdink ...? Not Him!*
1977	Published *Please Try to Remember the First of Octember!*; won Emmy for Best Children's Special for *Halloween Is Grinch Night*
1978	Published *I Can Read with My Eyes Shut!*
1979	Published *Oh, Say Can You Say?*
1980	Published *Maybe You Should Fly a Jet! Maybe You Should Be a Vet*; received Laura Ingalls Wilder Award
1981	Published *The Tooth Book*
1982	Published *Hunches in Bunches*; won Emmy for Best Children's Special for *The Grinch Grinches the Cat*
1983	Underwent surgery for cancer
1984	Published *The Butter Battle Book*; received Pulitzer Prize
1986	Published *You're Only Old Once!*; received New York Library Literary Lion
1987	Published *I Am Not Going to Get Up Today!* (illustrated by James Stevenson)
1990	Published *Oh, the Places You'll Go!*
1991	Died in La Jolla, California, on September 24
1995	Published posthumously *Daisy-Head Mayzie*
1996	Published posthumously *My Many Colored Days* (written in 1973)
1998	Published posthumously *Hooray for Diffendoofer Day!*
2001	*The Grinch* (movie) premiered; *Seussical* (Broadway production) opened
2002	Dr. Seuss National Memorial opened in Springfield, Massachusetts, in May
2003	*The Cat in the Hat* (movie) premiered
2004	Theodor Seuss Geisel Award created to honor writers and illustrators of beginning reader books

History and Criteria of Award

Theodor Seuss Geisel, better known as Dr. Seuss, won many awards in his lifetime. The Theodor Seuss Geisel Award is given yearly to the author(s) and illustrator(s) of the best beginning reader book published in the year previous to the award. The Association for Library Science to Children (ALSC), a division of the American Library Association (ALA), administers the award. The award was created in 2004, and the first books to be evaluated were published in 2005.

ALSC has set some specific rules regarding the award.

1. The author(s) and illustrator(s) must be citizens or residents of the United States.

2. The book must have been published originally in the United States.

3. There may be co-authors and co-illustrators.

4. The award may be given posthumously.

5. The committee will examine all types of writing, fiction, nonfiction, or poetry.

6. The book must be written with pre-kindergarten to second grade readers as an audience.

7. Honor books may be named.

8. The book must feature illustrations, and these illustrations must contribute to the story.

9. The book must contain a minimum of twenty-four pages and a maximum of ninety-six pages.

10. Short chapters are allowed.

11. The book must motivate children to read.

12. The sentences should be short.

13. New words should be repeated to make sure children understand and retain them.

Works by Theodor Seuss Geisel

And to Think That I Saw It on Mulberry Street. New York: Vanguard Press, 1937.

Bartholomew & the Oobleck. New York: Random House, 1949.

The Butter Battle Book. New York: Random House, 1984.

Cat in the Hat. New York: Random House, 1957.

Cat in the Hat Comes Back. New York: Random House, 1958.

Cat in the Hat Songbook. New York: Random House, 1993.

The Cat's Quizzer. New York: Random House, 1993.

Daisy-Head Mayzie. New York: Random House, 1995.

Did I Ever Tell You How Lucky You Are? New York: Random House, 1973.

Dr. Seuss's ABC. New York: Random House, 1963.

Dr. Seuss's Sleep Book. New York: Random House, 1962.

The Five Hundred Hats of Bartholomew Cubbins. New York: Random House, 1938.

Foot Book. New York: Random House, 1968.

Fox in Socks. New York: Random House, 1965.

Great Day for Up! New York: Random House, 1974.

Green Eggs and Ham. New York: Random House, 1960.

Happy Birthday to You. New York: Random House, 1959.

Hop on Pop. New York: Random House, 1963.

Horton Hatches the Egg. New York: Random House, 1940.

Horton Hears a Who. New York: Random House, 1954.

How the Grinch Stole Christmas! New York: Random House, 1957.

Hunches in Bunches. New York: Random House, 1982.

I Am Not Going to Get up Today! New York: Random House, 1987.

I Can Draw It Myself: By Me, Myself with a Little Help from My Friend Dr. Seuss. New York: Random House, 1970.

I Can Lick Thirty Tigers Today & Other Stories. New York: Random House, 1969.

I Can Read with My Eyes Shut! New York: Random House, 1978.

I Had Trouble in Getting to Solla Sollew. New York: Random House, 1992.

If I Ran the Circus. New York: Random House, 1956.

If I Ran the Zoo. New York: Random House, 1950.

King's Stilts. New York: Random House, 1939.

Lorax, The. New York: Random House, 1971.

McElligot's Pool. New York: Random House, 1947.

Marvin K. Mooney, Will You Please Go Now? New York: Random House, 1972.

Mister Brown Can Moo, Can You? New York: Random House, 1970.

My Book About Me. New York: Random House, 1969.

Oh, Say Can You Say? New York: Random House, 1979.

Oh, the Places You'll Go! New York: Random House, 1990.

Oh! The Thinks You Can Think! New York: Random House, 1975.

On Beyond Zebra. New York: Random House, 1955.

One Fish, Two Fish, Red Fish, Blue Fish. New York: Random House, 1960.

Scrambled Eggs Super! New York: Random House, 1953.

The Seven Lady Godivas. New York: Random House, 1987.

Shape of Me & Other Stuff. New York: Random House, 1973.

Sneetches & Other Stories. New York: Random House, 1969.

There's a Wocket in My Pocket! New York: Random House, 1974.

Thidwick, the Big-Hearted Moose. New York: Random House, 1948.

Yertle the Turtle & Other Stories. New York: Random House, 1958.

You're Only Old Once! New York: Random House, 1986.

Medal and Honor Books

Year	Award	Author/Illustrator	Title	Publisher
2005	Medal Book	Cynthia Rylant, author, and Suçie Stevenson	*Henry and Mudge and the Great Grandparents*	Simon & Schuster
	Honor Books	Tedd Arnold, author, and illustrator	*Hi! Fly Guy*	Cartwheel Books (Scholastic)
		Suzanne Bloom, author and illustrator	*A Splendid Friend, Indeed*	Boyds Mills Press
		Erica Silverman, author, and Betsy Lewin, illustrator	*Cowgirl Kate and Cocoa*	Harcourt
		Jean Van Leeuwen, author, and Ann Schweninger, illustrator	*Amanda Pig and the Really Hot Day*	Dial

Activities

1. Theodor Seuss Geisel was born in Massachusetts. He lived in New York City for a time, and then he moved to California. Children could locate these states on a large map. They could find information on the population of each state. A good Web site regarding population is: http://home.cfl.rr.com/usainfo/. They could find out which state has the greater population. They could project the population for each state over the next twenty years.

2. *Bartholomew and the Oobleck* was a 1950 Caldecott Honor Book. Children could read the book and then make some "Oobleck" out of school glue and liquid starch.

3. *Green Eggs and Ham* was published in 1960. Children could scramble some eggs, add a bit of green food coloring, and cook the eggs. Then they could eat the eggs and read the book.

4. Dr. Seuss got many of his ideas from doodling. Children could create some doodles and then make them into recognizable things.

5. Children could make a parody of *The Cat in the Hat*. Perhaps the parody could be called *The Ants in the Pants*.

6. Children could participate in the Read Across America program that happens annually on March 2, Theodor Seuss Geisel's birthday. Children could check the following Web site for support: http://www.nea.org/readacross/index.html.

7. Theodor Seuss Geisel enjoyed making up words. Lorax, wocket, sneetches, Diffendoofer are just a few of his original words. Children could read some of his books and create a dictionary of his words. They could also make up some words.

8. Dr. Seuss created several political cartoons regarding World War II. Children can view one at: http://orpheus.ucsd.edu/speccoll/dspolitic/pm/10716cs.jpg. They can view another at: http://orpheus.ucsd.edu/speccoll/dspolitic/pm/1942/20321cs.jpg. Children could look at some current political cartoons. Then children could then create their own political cartoons.

9. Dr. Seuss created many new characters. Children could create an ABC book of his characters.

10. Dr. Seuss received a Special Award and Citation from the Pulitzer Organization in 1984 for his contribution to children's literature. Children could explore the Pulitzer Prize Web site at: http://www.pulitzer.org/. They could find out who Joseph Pulitzer was and how the Pulitzer Prizes came to exist. They could summarize their findings in a short report.

Theodor Seuss Geisel and the Theodor Seuss Geisel Award

Student Handout 1—Information

Who Was Theodor Seuss Geisel?

Theodor Seuss Geisel is better known as Dr. Seuss. He wrote close to fifty books, and those books have been translated into many languages. His works have inspired television specials and movies.

Theodor Seuss Geisel was born in 1904 in Springfield, Massachusetts. His parents were the offspring of German immigrants. Ted, as he was known to his family and friends, enjoyed his childhood. However, during World War I, some community members were not kind to him because of his German background. Ted graduated from Dartmouth College in 1924. He told his parents he had received a fellowship to attend the University of Oxford in England. His father announced this accomplishment to the entire community. However, Ted had applied for the fellowship but had been turned down. His father did not want to be embarrassed, so he scraped up the money. Ted went to England.

There Ted met Helen Palmer. They were married in 1927 after they had returned from England. For several years he earned money by designing advertisements for a bug repellent and by publishing cartoons in magazines. His first children's book, *And to Think That I Saw it on Mulberry Street,* was rejected by many publishers before Vanguard agreed to print it.

The United States entered World War II, and Ted enlisted. However, he was thirty-eight years old. He did not fight, but he did create movies for soldiers and for the war effort. After World War II, he went back to writing children's books.

Before long, he was writing and illustrating very successful children's books, including *Bartholomew and the Oobleck, The Cat in the Hat,* and *How the Grinch Stole Christmas!* He also began writing Easy Reader Books, published by Random House. Helen died in 1967. He continued to write, and in 1968 he married Audrey Stone Dimond. He worked every day for about eight hours. He had a heart attack, and he had cancer. A wealthy man, Ted gave away many copies of his books, and he sponsored many literacy and arts programs.

Ted was very shy, and he did not like to speak before large groups. Theodor Seuss Geisel died on September 24, 1991, at his house in La Jolla, California.

What Is the Theodor Seuss Geisel Award?

The Theodor Seuss Geisel Award is given every year to the author(s) and illustrator(s) of the best beginning reader book published in the year previous to the award. The Association for Library Science to Children (ALSC), a division of the American Library Association (ALA), decides which books will win the award. The award was created in 2004, and the first books to be evaluated will have been published in 2005. The winners will receive their awards in 2006.

Several award rules exist. The books should be written for children up to about grade two. The book's sentences should be short, and words should be repeated. The books must have illustrations, and any type of writing (fiction, nonfiction, and poetry) can receive the award.

Theodor Seuss Geisel and the Theodor Seuss Geisel Award

Student Handout 2—Questions

Name_____ Date_____

Investigate the life of Theodor Seuss Geisel, and find out more about the Theodor Seuss Geisel Award. Then answer the following questions.

1. Where and when was Theodor Seuss Geisel born?

2. Where did he attend college?

3. What were his jobs after he returned to the United States from England?

4. What did he do during World War II?

5. What are the names of some of his books?

6. How are you like Theodor Seuss Geisel?

7. How are you different from Theodor Seuss Geisel?

8. Did Dr. Seuss like to give speeches?

9. When was the Theodor Seuss Geisel Award created?

10. List three facts about the Theodor Seuss Geisel Award.

From *Children's Book Award Handbook* by Diana F. Marks. Westport, CT: Libraries Unlimited. Copyright © 2006.

Theodor Seuss Geisel and the Theodor Seuss Geisel Award

Student Handout 3—Dr. Seuss Favorites

Name_____ Date_____

Dr. Seuss's real name was Theodor Seuss Geisel. Dr. Seuss wrote more than forty books for children. Below are the names of some of his most famous books. Ask your classmates to tell you which is their favorite Dr. Seuss book. Write each child's name next to his/her favorite.

Name of Dr. Seuss Book	Names of People Who Believe This Book Is Their Favorite Dr. Seuss Book
And to Think That I Saw It on Mulberry Street	
Bartholomew & the Oobleck	
Cat in the Hat	
Green Eggs and Ham	
Horton Hears a Who	
How the Grinch Stole Christmas	
If I Ran the Circus	
One Fish, Two Fish, Red Fish, Blue Fish	
Thidwick, the Big-Hearted Moose	
Yertle the Turtle & Other Stories	

Theodor Seuss Geisel and the Theodor Seuss Geisel Award

Student Handout 4—Oobleck

Name_____ Date_____

Theodor Seuss Geisel, also known as Dr. Seuss, wrote *Bartholomew & the Oobleck*. In the book, a goopy stuff called oobleck falls from the sky and covers everything. Let's make some oobleck.

You will need:

    ½ cup white school glue

    ¼ cup liquid starch

    food coloring (optional)

    small, disposable container

    disposable spoon

    wax paper

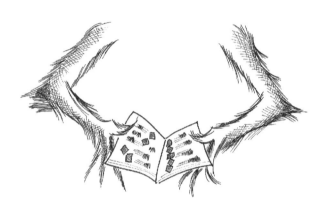

Here's how:

1. Mix the white school glue and the liquid starch in the disposable container.

2. Add food coloring if you want. However, food coloring can stain clothing and skins. So be careful!

3. Lift the oobleck out of the container and let it squish through your fingers.

4. Knead it on the wax paper until it is smooth.

5. If it is too sticky, add a bit more liquid starch.

6. If it does not flow, add a bit more white glue.

7. This oobleck does not last long. Use it the day you make it.

    Note: Do not pour this down a sink or drain. It will clog the drain. Dispose of it in the trash.

CHAPTER 9

Kate Greenaway and the Kate Greenaway Medal

Overview

The Kate Greenaway Medal is given annually to the best illustrator of children's literature published in Great Britain. Kate Greenaway was one of the three most important illustrators of nineteenth-century Great Britain.

Kate Greenaway was born in 1846. She received little formal education, but she did attend several art schools. She designed greeting cards before she received a commission to illustrate the book, *Infant Amusements, or How to Make a Nursery Happy.* The success of the book led to other jobs. Eventually she wrote and illustrated *Under the Window, with Coloured Pictures and Rhymes for Children,* a very popular book. She continued to illustrate the works of others, but she also wrote and illustrated at least one book a year from 1880 to 1896. She died in 1901. Her illustrations of happy and whimsical children are still popular today.

The Library Association of Great Britain established the Kate Greenaway Medal in 1955. Today it is administered by the Youth Libraries Group, a division of the Chartered Institute of Library and Information Professionals (CILIP). The short list of candidates is announced in March or April. Readers can shadow the decision-making process and express their preferences via the Internet. The winning book is announced at an award ceremony in July.

Kate Greenaway Biography

Kate Greenaway was one of the three most famous illustrators of children's work in nineteenth-century England. Randolph Caldecott and Walter Crane were her competitors. She depicted children dressed in clothes that were old-fashioned even for that time. Her subjects had a sort of dreamy, idealistic nature. While the children were busy and happy, they never seemed to get dirty, or even worse, get in trouble.

Kate Greenaway was born in Hoxton, London, England, on March 17, 1846. Her parents, John and Elizabeth (Jones) Greenaway, intended that their baby's name be "Kate." However, officials entered the name "Catherine" on the birth certificate; Kate seldom used this name. Kate's father worked as an engraver for a publisher. A year after Kate was born, the family moved to a large farm owned by a great aunt in Rolleston. Kate was happy there, playing in the gardens. However, the publishing house went bankrupt in 1850, and the family moved to Islington. There, Elizabeth opened a very successful dress and millinery shop. Kate spent more time by herself, but she was happiest when she could play in a garden behind the shop. She enjoyed creating an imaginary world. Kate did not have much formal education; she was taught at home, and her teachers were often not very educated themselves. Even when she was with her teachers, she seemed distracted.

In 1857, Kate had to accompany a cousin, Marion, to an art school. Marion grew tired of the art lessons, but Kate flourished. She drew a series of pictures of people surviving and fleeing an uprising in India. She held her first exhibition of work at the Dudley Gallery, Egyptian Hall, Piccadilly, England. She attended the Female School of Art in 1865.

Two years later, Kate's first published illustration appeared, the frontispiece of *Infant Amusements, or How to Make a Nursery Happy,* by William Kingston. The piece brought her recognition, as a result of which she had relatively constant work. She designed greeting cards for Marcus Ward, painted portraits of wealthy people's children, and illustrated children's books. In 1870, she was commissioned to illustrate *Madame D'Aulnoy's Fairy Tales.* This book made her a popular and respected illustrator. She enrolled in London's Slade School of Art around 1872. Randolph Caldecott also attended the school around the same time. Five years later, she held an exhibition of her work at the Royal Academy.

The year 1878 was very important to her. John Greenaway introduced Kate to printer and publisher Edmund Evans, who was quite impressed with her delicate drawings. They published her *Under the Window, with Coloured Pictures and Rhymes for Children.* The book sold out of its first run and had to be printed again and again. Within her lifetime, 100,000 copies of the book were sold. Kate made a very smart decision early in her career. While she sold the rights to copy her illustrations, she retained ownership of the original work. In that same year, she met Randolph Caldecott, the illustrator. He also worked with Edmund Evans, as did Walter Crane. Some people felt that Kate and Randolph might become romantically linked, but that did not come to pass. However, they remained good friends and amicable competitors.

Kate took advantage of her popularity and in 1880 published *Kate Greenaway's Birthday Book for Children.* At this time, she also met John Ruskin, the very famous and influential art critic, and began a friendship that would last twenty years. Kate may have been deeply in love with him, despite his being twenty-five years older than she. They exchanged many letters in which he at times praised her work and at others seemed extremely critical.

By now, Kate Greenaway's illustration style had become very popular. She illustrated many books by other authors. In addition, from 1880 to 1894 she wrote and illustrated under her name at least one book a year, including *Kate Greenaway's Alphabet, A Apple Pie,* and *Kate Greenaway's Painting Book.* However, none of the books was as popular as *Under the Window, with Coloured Pictures and Rhymes for Children.* She also published almanacs every year that featured monthly calendars with sayings and illustrations. Her style was copied by many artists, and books purportedly illustrated by her abounded. She became angry and frustrated when she found imitation Greenaway items such as dolls and wallpaper patterns.

In 1885, Kate moved to Frognal, a London suburb, where she had had a house designed and built for her family and herself. She continued to be somewhat popular. John Greenaway died on August 26, 1890, and Kate entered a period of depression, made worse by the fact that she had overextended herself with the house and its furnishings. She held an exhibition at the Gallery of Fine Art Society in London, whose sales produced enough money for her to keep the house. Elizabeth Greenaway died on February 2, 1894, and Kate became very despondent. Two years later and then again in 1898 she held an exhibit at the same place. By this time, she felt her illustrations had gone out of style. Having sold just about all the original artwork she had created through the years, she tried to produce income by painting portraits.

Kate published her last book, *Kate Greenaway's Almanack and Diary for 1897,* in 1896. In November of 1899, she learned she had breast cancer. With the death of John Ruskin in January 20, 1900, she became even more depressed and had difficulty being creative and original. Kate, having sought medical treatment for breast cancer too late, died in Frognal on November 6, 1901.

The Library Association (Great Britain) created the Kate Greenaway Medal in 1955. The medal honors the best illustrators of children's books in Great Britain. Today reprints of Kate Greenaway books and miscellaneous items abound. Some children and parents like the innocence and happiness portrayed in her works. Kate Greenaway has left a legacy of the ideal childhood.

Kate Greenaway Timeline

Date	Event
1846	Born Catherine Greenaway in Hoxton, London, England, to John and Elizabeth (Jones) Greenaway on March 17
1847	Family moved to a large farm in Rolleston, England; stayed there until 1850
1850	Father's publisher went broke, and father moved family to Islington; mother opened up a shop.
1857	Accompanied cousin Marion to art school; became interested in art after drawing a series of pictures of people surviving and fleeing an uprising in India
1858	Held first exhibition of work at the Dudley Gallery, Egyptian Hall, Piccadilly, England
1865	Enrolled in Female School of Art
1867	Published first illustration, frontispiece of *Infant Amusements, or How to Make a Nursery Happy*
1869	Began designing greeting cards and illustrating children's books
1870	Was commissioned to illustrate an edition of *Madame D'Aulnoy's Fairy Tales*
ca. 1872	Enrolled in Slade School of Art
1877	Held exhibition of work at Royal Academy
1878	Began working relationship with printer and publisher Edmund Evans; met Randolph Caldecott; self-published *Under the Window, with Coloured Pictures and Rhymes for Children*
1880	Published *Kate Greenaway's Birthday Book for Children*; began a twenty-year friendship with John Ruskin
1881	Published *Mother Goose, or The Old Nursery Rhymes*
1882	Published *Almanack for 1883*
1883	Published *Almanack for 1884*
1884	Published *A Painting Book* and *Almanack for 1885*
1885	Moved to Frognal, London, with her family to a house built for her; published *Marigold Garden*, *Kate Greenaway's Alphabet*, and *Almanack for 1886*
1886	Published *A Apple Pie* and *Almanack for 1887*
1887	Published *Almanack for 1888*
1888	Published *Kate Greenaway's Painting Book*, *The Pied Piper of Hamelin* and *Almanack for 1889*
1889	Published *Kate Greenaway's Book of Games* and *Almanack for 1890*
1890	Death of father on August 26; published *Kate Greenaway's Almanack for 1891*
1891	Held exhibition at Gallery of Fine Art Society, London, England; published *Kate Greenaway's Almanack for 1892*
1892	Published *Kate Greenaway's Almanack for 1893*
1893	Held exhibition at Gallery of Fine Art Society, London, England; published *Kate Greenaway's Almanack for 1894*
1894	Mother died on February 2; published *Kate Greenaway's Almanack for 1895*
1896	Published *Kate Greenaway's Almanack and Diary for 1897*
1898	Held exhibition at Gallery of Fine Art Society, London, England
1899	Learned in November that she had breast cancer
1900	John Ruskin died on January 20
1901	Died in Frognal, Hampstead, London, England, on November 6
1955	Kate Greenaway Medal created by the Library Association (Great Britain)

History and Criteria of Medal

The Kate Greenaway Medal was created by the Library Association in 1955 in Great Britain. It is Great Britain's highest honor that can be bestowed on an illustrator of children's literature.

The award winner receives a gold medal and £500 worth of books to be donated to a library of his or her choice. Since 2000, the winner has also received the Colin Mears Award, £5,000. Colin Mears was a children's book collector. His will stipulated that his estate would provide the Kate Greenaway winner with a prize of £5,000.

In April 2002, the Library Association and the Institute of Information Scientists combined to form a new group, the Chartered Institute of Library and Information Professionals (CILIP). CILIP now administers the award.

All types of illustrated children's books are considered for the award. The book must be published in the United Kingdom, but it may have been published elsewhere as well. The book illustrations are evaluated on a combination of originality, interest, artistic merit, connection to text, and overall book appearance.

The selection process starts with the Youth Libraries Group, a division of CILIP. Twelve librarians are selected from the 3,000–member group. Until February, the panel reads the books submitted. The books had to have been published in the previous year. In March or April, the group narrows the list of potential winners to a shortlist. The list is announced, and readers can now evaluate the books. They may read and debate the merits of each book and give their opinions, via the Internet, to the panel. Although the panel does not have to vote the way readers would like them to vote, they certainly consider the messages sent by the readers. The panel meets and decides on the medal recipient. The winner is announced at the awards ceremony in July.

Works Written and Illustrated by Kate Greenaway (all published by Routledge, London, unless otherwise noted)

A Apple Pie, 1886.

Almanack for 1883, 1882.

Almanack for 1884, 1883.

Almanack for 1885, 1884.

Almanack for 1886, 1885.

Almanack for 1887, 1886.

Almanack for 1888, 1887.

Almanack for 1889, 1888.

Almanack for 1890, 1889.

Kate Greenaway's Almanack for 1891, London: J. M. Dent, 1890.

Kate Greenaway's Almanack for 1892, 1891.

Kate Greenaway's Almanack for 1893, 1892.

Kate Greenaway's Almanack for 1894, 1893.

Kate Greenaway's Almanack for 1895, 1894.

Kate Greenaway's Almanack and Diary for 1897, 1896.

Kate Greenaway's Alphabet, 1885.

Kate Greenaway's Birthday Book for Children, 1880.

Kate Greenaway's Book of Games, 1889.

Kate Greenaway's Painting Book, 1888.

Marigold Garden, 1885.

Mother Goose, or The Old Nursery Rhymes, 1881.

Painting Book, A, 1884.

Pied Piper of Hamelin, The, 1888.

Under the Window, with Coloured Pictures and Rhymes for Children, 1878.

Medal Books

Year	Author	Title	Publisher
2005	Chris Riddell	*Jonathan Swift's "Gulliver"*	Walker Books
2004	Shirley Hughes	*Ella's Big Chance*	The Bodley Head
2003	Bob Graham	*Jethro Byrde—Fairy Child*	Walker Books
2002	Chris Riddell	*Pirate Diary*	Walker Books
2001	Lauren Child	*I Will Not Ever Never Eat a Tomato*	Orchard Books
2000	Helen Oxenbury	*Alice's Adventures in Wonderland*	Walker Books
1999	Helen Cooper	*Pumpkin Soup*	Doubleday
1998	P. J. Lynch	*When Jessie Came Across the Sea*	Walker Books
1997	Helen Cooper	*The Baby Who Wouldn't Go to Bed*	Doubleday
1996	P. J. Lynch	*The Christmas Miracle of Jonathan Toomey*	Walker Books
1995	Gregory Rogers	*Way Home*	Andersen Press
1994	Alan Lee	*Black Ships Before Troy*	Frances Lincoln
1993	Anthony Browne	*Zoo*	Julia MacRae
1992	Janet Ahlberg	*The Jolly Christmas Postman*	Heinemann
1991	Gary Blythe	*The Whales' Song*	Hutchinson
1990	Michael Foreman	*War Boy: A Country Childhood*	Pavilion
1989	Barbara Firth	*Can't You Sleep Little Bear?*	Walker Books
1988	Adrienne Kennaway	*Crafty Chameleon*	Hodder & Stoughton
1987	Fiona French	*Snow White in New York*	Oxford University Press
1986	Juan Wijngaard	*Sir Gawain and the Loathly Lady*	Walker Books
1985	Errol Le Cain	*Hiawatha's Childhood*	Faber
1984	Anthony Browne	*Gorilla*	Julia MacRae
1983	Michael Foreman	*Long Neck and Thunder Foot and Sleeping Beauty and Other Favourite Fairy Tales*	Kestrel and Gollancz
1982	Charles Keeping	*The Highwayman*	Oxford University Press
1981	Quentin Blake	*Mr. Magnolia*	Cape
1980	Jan Pienkowski	*The Haunted House*	Heinemann
1979	Janet Ahlberg	*Each Peach Pear Plum*	Kestrel
1978	Shirley Hughes	*Dogger*	The Bodley Head
1977	Gail E. Haley	*The Post Office Cat*	The Bodley Head
1976	Victor Ambrus	*Horses in Battle and Mishka*	Oxford University Press
1975	Pat Hutchins	*The Wind Blew*	The Bodley Head
1974	Raymond Briggs	*Father Christmas*	H. Hamilton

Year	Author	Title	Publisher
1973	Krystyna Turska	*The Woodcutter's Duck*	H. Hamilton
1972	Jan Pienkowski	*The Kingdom under the Sea*	Cape
1971	John Burmingham	*Mr. Grumpy's Outing*	Cape
1970	Helen Oxenbury	*The Quangle Wangle's Hat and the Dragon of an Ordinary Family*	Heinemann
1969	Pauline Baynes	*Dictionary of Chivalry*	Longman
1968	Charles Keeping	*Charlotte and the Golden Canary*	Oxford University Press
1967	Raymond Briggs	*Mother Goose Treasury*	H. Hamilton
1966	Victor Ambrus	*The Three Poor Tailors*	Oxford University Press
1965	C. W. Hodges	*Shakespeare's Theatre*	Oxford University Press
1964	John Burmingham	*Borka: The Adventures of a Goose with No Feathers*	Cape
1963	Brian Wildsmith	*A.B.C.*	Oxford University Press
1962	Antony Maitland	*Mrs. Cockle's Cat*	Constable
1961	Gerald Rose	*Old Winkle and the Seagulls*	Faber
1960	William Stobbs	*Kashtanka and a Bundle of Ballads*	Oxford University Press
1959	No award given		
1958	V. H. Drummond	*Mrs. Easter and the Storks*	Faber
1957	Edward Ardizzone	*Tim All Alone*	Oxford University Press
1956	No award given		

Activities

1. Kate Greenaway is famous for her illustrations. Her competitors were Walter Crane and Randolph Caldecott. Children could view her illustrations at: http://www.iupui.edu/~engwft/greenaway.htm. Then they could view some of Caldecott's illustrations at: http://www.iupui.edu/~engwft/caldecott.htm. Finally, they could examine Crane's works at: http://www.iupui.edu/~engwft/crane.htm. Then they could discuss how the illustrations are similar and how they are different. They could create a Venn diagram to help them organize their thoughts.

2. Kate Greenaway lived in England, and the British do like their tea. The children could host a tea party.

3. Kate Greenaway published a number of almanacks (English spelling). Children could find a reproduction of one of her almanacks and contrast it to an American almanac. They could share their findings by creating a list of attributes for each book type.

4. Kate attended several art schools. Perhaps the art teacher could come in and discuss the workings of an art school.

5. Children could make a frequency table of the Kate Greenaway Medal recipients and see who won the award most often.

6. P. J. Lynch received the Kate Greenaway Medal in 1996 and again in 1998. Children could visit his Web site at: http://www.walkerbooks.co.uk/P.-J.-Lynch and find the name of his hero. Then each student could create a list of his or her heroes.

7. Shirley Hughes received the Kate Greenaway Medal in 1978 and again in 2004. Children could view some of her illustrations and read her biography at: http://www.liverpoolmuseums.org.uk/walker/exhibitions/shirley/intro.asp. They could find out what Shirley Hughes means by the term *narrative painting*. They could create their own narrative paintings.

8. Helen Oxenbury has received the Kate Greenaway Medal twice, once in 1970 and again 2000. Children could read her article about winning the award at: http://www.cilip.org.uk/groups/ylg/ylr/helen.html. They could write letters to her and discuss whether they, too, had ever become frustrated with a project.

9. Children could find some older books that have received the medal and some newer books that have received the medal. They could see if illustration styles have changed over the years. They could share their opinions by creating a slide show.

10. Charles Keeping also received the Kate Greenaway Medal twice. Children could examine some of his illustrations at: http://www.answers.com/topic/charles-keeping. They could find out what other jobs he has had. They could make a timeline of his life.

Kate Greenaway and the Kate Greenaway Medal

Student Handout 1—Information

Who Was Kate Greenaway?

Kate Greenaway was an author and illustrator. She developed a style of drawing showing children in old-fashioned clothing participating in old-fashioned activities. At one time, she was very popular. However, by the end of her life, her illustrations had gone out of fashion.

Kate Greenaway was born in Hoxton, London, England, on March 17, 1846. Kate's father worked as an engraver for a publisher. However, the publishing house went bankrupt in 1850, and the family moved to Islington. There, Kate's mother opened a very successful dress shop. Kate spent more time by herself, but she was most happy when she could play in a garden behind the shop. She enjoyed creating an imaginary world. Kate did not have much formal education. She was taught at home, and her teachers were often not very educated themselves.

In 1857, Kate had to accompany a cousin to an art school. While the cousin grew tired of the art lessons, Kate loved them. She drew a series of pictures of people surviving and fleeing an uprising in India. She held her first exhibition of work at the Dudley Gallery, Egyptian Hall, Piccadilly, England. She attended the Female School of Art in 1865.

Two years later, Kate's first published illustration appeared, the frontispiece of *Infant Amusements, or How to Make a Nursery Happy,* by William Kingston. The piece brought her recognition. Kate had constant work, designing greeting cards, painting portraits of wealthy people's children, and illustrating children's books. In 1870, she illustrated *Madame D'Aulnoy's Fairy Tales.* This book made her a popular and respected illustrator. She enrolled in London's Slade School of Art around 1872.

In 1878, John Greenaway introduced Kate to printer and publisher Edmund Evans, who was quite impressed with her delicate drawings. He published her *Under the Window, with Coloured Pictures and Rhymes for Children.* The book sold out of its first run and had to be printed again and again. Within her lifetime, 100,000 copies of the books were sold.

Kate's illustration style had become very popular. She illustrated many books by other authors. She wrote and illustrated under her name at least one book a year from 1880 to 1894. Some of those books were *Kate Greenaway's Alphabet, A Apple Pie,* and *Kate Greenaway's Painting Book.* However, none of the books was as successful as *Under the Window, with Coloured Pictures and Rhymes for Children.* She published almanacs, featuring monthly calendars with sayings and illustrations every year. Her style was copied by many artists. She became angry and frustrated when she found imitation Greenaway items such as dolls and wallpaper patterns.

In 1885, Kate moved to Frognal, a London suburb, where she had had a house designed and built for her family and herself. However, Kate's parents died, and Kate discovered that she could not afford to live in the house. She sold some of her work, but she found that her style of illustrating was no longer popular.

Kate died in Frognal, England, on November 6, 1901.

What Is the Kate Greenaway Medal?

The Kate Greenaway Medal, given every year, was created by the Library Association in 1955 in Great Britain. It is Great Britain's highest honor that can be given to an illustrator of children's literature. The award winner receives a gold medal and £500 of books to be donated to a library of his or her choice. Since 2000, the winner has also received the Colin Mears Award of £5,000. Colin Mears was a children's book collector. His will stipulated that his estate would provide the Kate Greenaway winner with a prize of £5,000.

From *Children's Book Award Handbook* by Diana F. Marks. Westport, CT: Libraries Unlimited. Copyright © 2006.

Kate Greenaway and the Kate Greenaway Medal

Student Handout 2—Questions

Name_____ Date_____

Investigate the life of Kate Greenaway, and find out more about the Kate Greenaway Medal. Then answer the following questions.

1. Where and when was Kate Greenaway born?

2. Describe her education.

3. How did she become interested in art?

4. What was the name of her most popular book?

5. Why do you think other artists copied her style?

6. How is Kate Greenaway like you?

7. Who or what does the Kate Greenaway Medal honor?

8. What group decides on the medal winner?

9. What does the medal winner receive?

10. Could an illustrator win both the Kate Greenaway Medal and the Newbery Medal?

From Children's Book Award Handbook by Diana F. Marks. Westport, CT: Libraries Unlimited. Copyright © 2006.

Kate Greenaway and the Kate Greenaway Medal

Student Handout 3—Homemade Paints

Name_____ Date_____

Kate Greenaway was both an author and an illustrator. She often used pastel-colored paints. Paint is a combination of a pigment (color) and a binder (a substance to make the pigment stick to the surface). You can make paints!

This paint makes great finger paint, but it also is a good poster paint. This recipe makes four ½-cup containers of paint.

You will need:

    2 cups liquid starch

    1 cup each of 4 shades of dry tempera paint

    mixing spoons

    4 small, airtight containers with lids

    paintbrush

    paper

Here's how to make the paint:

1. Pour about ½ cup liquid starch into each of the four containers.

2. Add the dry paints, a different color to each container.

3. Blend the ingredients until smooth.

4. Paint away!

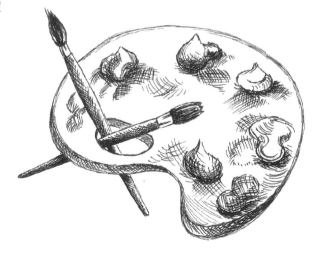

Kate Greenaway and the Kate Greenaway Medal

Student Handout 4—United Kingdom

Name_____ Date_____

Kate Greenaway was born in England. England is part of the United Kingdom. What do you know about the United Kingdom? See if you can answer the questions below. If you do not know some of the answers, research the topic.

1. What four home nations make up the United Kingdom?

2. What is the capital of the United Kingdom?

3. Compare the area of the United Kingdom to some of the states in the United States. Is it closer to the size of New Jersey, Oregon, California or Alaska?

4. What is the United Kingdom's currency?

5. What is the approximate population of the United Kingdom?

6. What are some of the bodies of water surrounding the United Kingdom?

7. Name several sports that were created in the United Kingdom.

8. How far is it from England to France?

9. Do the British really drink all that much tea?

10. What country borders the United Kingdom?

Kate Greenaway and the Kate Greenaway Medal

Student Handout 4—United Kingdom—Answers

Name_____ Date_____

Kate Greenaway was born in England. England is part of the United Kingdom. What do you know about the United Kingdom? See if you can answer the questions below. If you do not know some of the answers, research the topic.

1. What four home nations make up the United Kingdom? England, Scotland, Wales, and Northern Ireland

2. What is the capital of the United Kingdom? London

3. Compare the area of the United Kingdom to some of the states in the United States. Is it closer to the size of New Jersey, Oregon, California, or Alaska? It is a bit smaller than Oregon.

4. What is the United Kingdom's currency? The British Pound

5. What is the approximate population of the United Kingdom? Around 60,500,000 people

6. What are some of the bodies of water surrounding the United Kingdom? The North Sea, the Celtic Sea, the English Channel, the Irish Sea and the Atlantic Ocean

7. Name several sports that were created in the United Kingdom. Soccer, billiards, golf, cricket, squash, and rugby

8. How far is it from England to France? About 35 kilometers, or 21.7 miles

9. Do the British really drink all that much tea? Yes, the United Kingdom is the largest consumer of tea in the world. Each person in the country uses more than five pounds of tea leaves a year to make tea.

10. What country borders the United Kingdom? Ireland

CHAPTER 10

Lee Bennett Hopkins and the Lee Bennett Hopkins Poetry Award

Overview

Lee Bennett Hopkins created the Lee Bennett Hopkins Poetry Award in 1993. The award yearly honors a poet or anthologist who published a book of children's poetry. The award is given for a book published the year before. Honor books may also be recognized. The award is administered by Pennsylvania State University. Lee Bennett Hopkins was a writer, primarily of poetry.

Lee Bennett Hopkins was born in 1938. He became a teacher in 1960, and soon began to incorporate poetry into many of his lessons. He changed careers to become a consultant for Scholastic in 1968. However, he still espoused the powers of poetry. In 1976, he became a full-time writer and anthologist. As of 2005 he had published more than 100 books, the great majority of them poetry.

Lee Bennett Hopkins Biography

Lee Bennett Hopkins could be called "Mr. Poetry." He was a teacher when he discovered the educational properties of poetry. He began writing his own poems, and he has published numerous poetry anthologies about a variety of topics.

Lee Bennett Hopkins was born on April 13, 1938, to Leon Hopkins and Gertrude (Thomas) Hopkins in Scranton, Pennsylvania. Hopkins was named after Lee Bennett, a singer in Jan Garber's band. Hopkins's parents loved to listen to Bennett and the band on the radio. At the time of his birth, Scranton was suffering from the Great Depression and from the closing of area coal mines. About 40 percent of the labor population had no jobs, and many people were forced to move to other areas in search of work. Leon found work as a police officer. Lee spent much of his spare time with his maternal grandmother, an apartment superintendent, and his grandfather, a coal miner. A brother, Donald, was born on August 9, 1941, and a sister, Donna Lea, was born on July 16, 1947.

Lee was young when the United States entered World War II. The war had little impact on his family, other than they were on rations. However, after the war Scranton experienced another economic decline. The Hopkins family became one of the many who moved away seeking employment. They moved to Newark, New Jersey, in 1948. At first they lived with Lee's aunt and her family. Soon they were able to move to a rather dreary basement apartment. Leon and Gertrude were superintendents of the building. Later they moved to a railroad flat, and Leon worked in construction.

Life for the Hopkins family did not become any easier in New Jersey. Leon and Gertrude were fighting on an almost constant basis. Gertrude was an alcoholic and Leon worked long hours, so Lee became responsible for the care of his siblings and the apartment. One day Lee came home and found the apartment totally empty of furniture and possessions. His father was also gone. Several days later Lee looked in the window of a furniture store and saw their furniture. Their father had sold their possessions and left. Lee, his siblings, and his mother moved back in with his aunt. However, living in very close quarters with so many people was not easy. His mother was finally able to find an apartment in the projects. Although the apartment was small, the surrounding neighborhood was filled with people from many backgrounds. Lee absorbed the sights and sounds around him.

Gertrude worked long hours to provide for her children, and as a result, Lee became even more responsible for his siblings. Few rules existed in their household. He himself had no set bedtime, and his mother did not even insist that he attend school. Few books existed in his house, and he did not enjoy reading. His school attendance was sporadic. He felt school had little value, and his academic skills slipped. However, one school teacher shared her love of theater with him, and when he had some money, he went into New York City to see plays. She also encouraged him to read, and she showed him the value of reading classics. She inspired him to become a teacher.

Even though Lee had to work on weekends and after school, he graduated from high school in 1956. He decided to attend Newark State Teachers College (now Kean University). He spent the first two years trying to learn all the facts and skills he should have learned in high school. In addition, he had to work to pay for tuition. However, he found the college teaching courses to be fascinating and useful. He graduated from Newark State Teachers College in 1960 and found a job as a sixth grade teacher in Fair Lawn, New Jersey.

Hopkins truly enjoyed teaching. Within several years he became the resource teacher, sharing all kinds of materials and techniques with his peers. Also, he began to see the value of using poetry. The book he found most valuable was Myra Cohn Livingston's *Whispers and Other Poems*. Soon his principal, Mrs. Haenechen, suggested that he obtain a master's degree from Bank Street College of Education. When he did the math, however, he realized that he could not afford the tuition and pay his other bills, including his sister's parochial school tuition bills. So he declined the offer. The next day the principal told him that he really could attend the Bank Street College of Education. Later, Lee found out that she had arranged for him to get a full scholarship. He obtained his master's degree in 1964, and he worked for Bank Street's "Searchlight on Intelligence," a learning resource center in Harlem. He helped African American students to further their education. One of his techniques to help them was to use poetry, especially the works of Langston Hughes.

Around 1967 Lee published his first book, *Let Them Be Themselves: Language Arts Enrichment for Disadvantaged Children in Elementary Schools*. In 1968, Scholastic hired him as a curriculum and editorial specialist. While at Scholastic, he interviewed authors such as Dr. Seuss, Charlotte Zolotow, Ezra Jack Keats, Pura Belpré, Myra Cohn Livingston, Sydney Taylor, and Beverly Cleary. Those interviews became the basis of *Books Are by People*, published in 1969. Interestingly, some children's literature awards have been named after some of those authors. He also published his first poetry book, *This Street's for Me!*, in 1970. The book's poems were about his years in Harlem.

In 1972, Newark State Teachers College gave Lee the Outstanding Alumnus of the Arts Award, and that year he published another poetry book, *Charlie's World*. He published an additional book of author interviews, *More Books by More People*, in 1974.

Hopkins, having decided to become a full-time writer and anthologist, quit his job in 1976 and moved to Westchester County, New York. The country feeling of Westchester County was far different from the hubbub of New York City. He published his own works, and he created anthologies built around topics of interest to children. In 1977, he published a young adult novel, *Mama*, an account of his childhood. *Wonder Wheels*, another young adult novel, again about his own life, followed in 1979. Kean University bestowed an honorary doctor of laws degree on him in 1980. A year later he published a sequel to *Mama* called *Mama and Her Boys*.

In 1985, Hopkins and his sister were reunited with their father. Over the years Leon had tried to find his children, but the family's frequent moves had made it difficult to trace them. Leon was aware of his son's successes and bragged to all who would listen. Leon died about four years later.

By 1989, Hopkins had become famous for his original poetry and his poetry anthologies. He was awarded the University of Southern Mississippi Medallion and the Keystone State Author of the Year Award. His anthologies are about a variety of subjects, including dinosaurs, baseball, pets, and space.

Hopkins wanted to encourage others to become poets. The first Lee Bennett Hopkins Poetry Award was presented in 1993 to Ashley Bryan for the book *Sing to the Sun*. In 1995 another award, the Lee Bennett Hopkins /International Reading Association Promising Poet Award, was presented for the first time to Deborah Chandra for her *Rich Lizard and Other Poems*.

Hopkins continues to inspire children. In 1996, he won the Christopher Award for his *Been to Yesterdays: Poems of a Life*. He has published more than one hundred books, and he has no plans to stop writing.

Lee Bennett Hopkins Timeline

Date	Event
1938	Born to Leon Hopkins and Gertrude (Thomas) Hopkins in Scranton, Pennsylvania, on April 13
1941	Brother Donald born on August 9
1947	Sister Donna Lea born on July 16
1948	Moved with family to Newark, New Jersey
1956	Graduated from high school and attended Newark State Teachers College (now Kean University)
1960	Graduated from Newark State Teachers College; started teaching sixth grade in Fair Lawn, New Jersey
1964	Obtained master's degree from Bank Street College of Education
ca. 1967	Published *Let Them Be Themselves: Language Arts Enrichment for Disadvantaged Children in Elementary Schools*
1968	Hired as a curriculum and editorial specialist for Scholastic
1969	Published *Books Are by People*
1970	Published *This Street's for Me!*
1972	Newark State Teachers College gave him the Outstanding Alumnus of the Arts Award; published *Charlie's World*
1974	Published *More Books by More People*
1976	Moved to Westchester County, New York, to become a full-time writer
1977	Published *Mama*
1979	Published *Wonder Wheels*
1980	Received honorary doctor of laws degree from Kean University
1981	Published *Mama and Her Boys*
1985	Reunited with his father
1989	Awarded University of Southern Mississippi Medallion and Keystone State Author of the Year Award
1993	First Lee Bennett Hopkins Poetry Award presented
1995	First Lee Bennett Hopkins/International Reading Association Promising Poet Award presented
1996	Won Christopher Award for *Been to Yesterdays*

History and Criteria of Award

Lee Bennett Hopkins has always been active in both education and publishing. From 1975 to 1978, he was a member of the Board of Directors of the National Council of Teachers of English (NCTE). From 1982 to 1985, he was a member of the NCTE Commission on Literature. He was active in the NCTE Children's Literature Assembly from 1984 to 1987. Twice he was chair of the NCTE Poetry Award Committee.

Hopkins wanted to emphasize the importance of poetry written for children. He created the Lee Bennett Hopkins Poetry Award in 1993. In the beginning, the Children's Literature Council of Pennsylvania, based in Hopkins's hometown of Scranton, Pennsylvania, oversaw the award. Pennsylvania State University took over administration of the award in 1999.

The Lee Bennett Hopkins Poetry Award yearly honors a poet or anthologist who published a book of children's poetry. The award is given for a book published the year before. Honor books may also be recognized.

A committee of educators, librarians, and poets evaluates possible award-winning books. Hopkins does not participate in the process, but he does donate the $500 honorarium. The winner also receives a plaque.

The Lee Bennett Hopkins Poetry Award seal that can be affixed to the winning books features an illustration by Jessie Willcox Smith (1863–1935). On the seal, Mother Goose envelops a child under each wing. The words "Lee Bennett Hopkins Poetry Award" circle the seal.

The first Lee Bennett Hopkins Poetry Award was given in 1993 to Ashley Bryan for *Sing to the Sun*.

Selected Works by Lee Bennett Hopkins

All God's Children: A Book of Prayers. New York: Harcourt, Brace, 1998.

Alphathoughts: Alphabet Poems from A to Z. Honesdale, PA: Boyds Mills Press, 2003.

And God Bless Me: Poems Selected by Lee Bennett Hopkins. New York: Alfred A. Knopf, 1982.

Animals from Mother Goose/Lift the Flap. New York: Harcourt, Brace & Company, 1989.

April Bubbles Chocolate: An ABC of Poetry. New York: Simon & Schuster, 1994.

Baseball Poems. New York: Harcourt, Brace, 1993.

Been to Yesterdays: Poems of a Life. Honesdale, PA: Boyds Mills Press, 1995.

Best Friends. New York: Harper & Row, 1986.

The Best of "Book Bonanza". New York: Holt, Rinehart & Winston, c1980.

Blast Off! Poems about Space. New York: HarperCollins, 1995.

By Myself: Poems. New York: T. Y. Crowell, 1980.

A Chorus of Culture: Developing Literacy. By Alma Flor Ada, Violet J. Harris and Lee Bennett Hopkins. Carmel, CA: Hampton Brown, 1994.

Circus! Circus!: Poems. New York: Alfred A. Knopf, 1982.

Click, Rumble, Roar: Poems about Machines. New York: T. Y. Crowell, 1987.

Climb into My Lap: First Poems to Read Together. New York: Simon & Schuster, 1998.

Creatures: Poems. New York: Harcourt, Brace & Jovanovich, 1985.

Crickets and Bullfrogs and Whispers of Thunder: Poems and Pictures. By Harry Behn. Poems selected by Lee Bennett Hopkins. New York: Harcourt, Brace & Jovanovich, 1984.

Dino-Roars. New York: Golden Books, 1999.

Dinosaurs. New York: Harcourt, Brace, 1987.

A Dog's Life: Poems. New York: Harcourt, Brace & Jovanovich, 1983.

Easter Buds Are Springing: Poems for Easter. Honesdale, PA: Boyds Mills Press, 1993.

Elves, Fairies & Gnomes: Poems. New York: Alfred A. Knopf, 1980.

Extra Innings: Baseball Poems. New York: Harcourt, Brace & Jovanovich, 1993.

Flit, Flutter, Fly!: Poems about Bugs and Other Crawly Creatures. New York: Doubleday, 1992.

Go to Bed: A Book of Bedtime Poems. New York: Alfred A. Knopf, 1979.

Good Books, Good Times! New York: HarperCollins, 1990.

Good Morning to You, Valentine. Honesdale, PA: Boyds Mills Press, 1993.

Good Rhymes, Good Times; Original Poems. New York: HarperCollins, 1995.

Hand in Hand: An American History Through Poetry. New York: Simon & Schuster, 1994.

Hanukkah Lights: Holiday Poetry. New York: HarperCollins, 2004.

Happy Birthday. New York: Simon & Schuster, 1991.

Home—to Me: Poems Selected by Lee Bennett Hopkins. New York: Orchard Books, 2002.

Hoofbeats, Claws, and Rippled Fins: Creature Poems. Edited by Lee Bennett Hopkins. New York: HarperCollins, 2002.

How Do You Make an Elephant Float? and Other Delicious Riddles. Chicago: A. Whitman, 1983.

I Am the Cat: Poems. New York: Harcourt, Brace & Jovanovich, 1981.

It's about Time: Poems. New York: Simon & Schuster, 1993.

Kits, Cats, Lions, and Tigers: Stories, Poems, and Verse. Chicago: A. Whitman, 1979.

Let Them Be Themselves. New York: HarperCollins, 1992.

Lives: Poems about Famous Americans. New York: HarperCollins, 1999.

Mama. New York: Simon & Schuster, 1977.

Mama & Her Boys. New York: Simon & Schuster, 1981.

Marvelous Math: A Book of Poems. Edited by Rebecca Davis. New York: Simon & Schuster, 1997.

Merely Players: An Anthology of Life Poems. New York: Elsevier/Nelson, 1979.

Merrily Comes Our Harves In: Poems for Thanksgiving. Edited by Ben Shecter. Honesdale, PA: Boyds Mills, 1993.

Moments. New York: Harcourt, Brace & Jovanovich, 1980.

More Surprises. New York: Harper & Row, 1987.

Morning, Noon, and Nighttime, Too: Poems. New York: Harper & Row, 1980.

Munching: Poems about Eating. Boston: Little, Brown, 1985.

My America: A Poetry Atlas of the United States. Selected by Lee Bennett Hopkins. New York: Simon & Schuster, 2000.

My Mane Catches the Wind: Poems about Horses. New York: Harcourt, Brace & Jovanovich, 1979.

Oh, No! Where Are My Pants? and Other Disaster Poems. New York: HarperCollins, 2005.

On the Farm. Boston: Little, Brown, 1991.

Opening Days: Sports Poems. New York: Harcourt, Brace & Jovanovich, 1996.

Partners in Learning: A Child Centered Approach to Teaching the Social Studies. By Lee Bennett Hopkins and Misha Arenstein. Milpitas, CA: Citation Press, 1971.

Pass the Poetry, Please! New York: HarperCollins, 1998.

Pauses: Autobiographical Reflections of 101 Creators of Children's Books. Edited by Lee Bennett Hopkins. New York: HarperCollins, 1995.

People from Mother Goose/Lift the Flap. New York: Harcourt, Brace & Jovanovich, 1989.

Pterodactyls and Pizza: A Trumpet Club Book of Poetry. Illustrated by Nadine Bernard Westcott. New York: Trumpet Club, 1992.

Pups, Dogs, Foxes, and Wolves: Stories, Poems and Verse. Chicago: A. Whitman, 1979.

Questions: Poems. New York: HarperCollins, 1992.

Ragged Shadows: Poems of Halloween Night. Boston: Little, Brown, 1993.

Rainbows Are Made: Poems by Carl Sandburg. New York: Harcourt, Brace, 1982.

Ring Out, Wild Bells: Poems about Holidays. New York: Harcourt, Brace & Jovanovich, 1992.

School Supplies: A Book of Poems. New York: Simon & Schuster, 1996

The Sea Is Calling Me: Poems. New York: Harcourt, Brace & Jovanovich, 1986.

Side by Side. New York: Simon & Schuster, 1988.

The Sky Is Full of Song. New York: Harper & Row, 1983.

Small Talk: A Book of Short Poems. New York: Harcourt, Brace & Jovanovich, 1995.

Song and Dance: Poems. New York: Simon & Schuster, 1997.

A Song in Stone: City Poems. New York: T. Y. Crowell, 1983.

Spectacular Science: A Book of Poems. New York: Simon & Schuster, 1999.

Sports! Sports! Sports!: A Poetry Collection. New York: HarperCollins, 1999.

Still As a Star: A Book of Nighttime Poems. Boston: Little, Brown, 1989.

Surprises. New York: Harper Trophy. 1986.

These Great United States. New York: Simon & Schuster, 1999.

Through Our Eyes: Poems and Pictures About Growing Up. Boston: Little, Brown, 1992.

To the Zoo: Animal Poems. Boston: Little, Brown, 1992.

Voyages: Poetry by Walt Whitman. Selected by Lee Bennett Hopkins. New York: Harcourt, Brace & Jovanovich, 1992.

Weather: Poems. New York: HarperCollins, 1994.

Wonder Wheels: A Novel. New York: Alfred A. Knopf, 1979.

Yummy: Eating Through a Day. New York: Simon & Schuster, 1990.

Award and Honor Books

Year	Award	Author	Title	Publisher
2005	Award Winner	Walter Dean Myers	*Here in Harlem*	Holiday House
	Honor Awards	Naomi Shihab Nye	*Is This Forever, or What?: Poems and Paintings from Texas*	Greenwillow
		Marilyn Singer	*Creature Carnival*	Hyperion
2004	Award Winner	Stephen Mitchell	*The Wishing Bone and Other Poems*	Candlewick Press
	Honor Awards	Diane Ackerman	*Animal Sense*	Knopf
		Walter Dean Myers	*Blues Journey*	Holiday House
		Samuel Jay Keyser	*The Pond God and Other Stories*	Front Street
		Hope Anita Smith	*The Way a Door Closes*	Henry Holt
2003	Award Winner	Constance Levy	*Splash! Poems of Our Watery World*	Orchard Books
	Honor Awards	April Halprin Wayland	*Girl Coming in for a Landing—A Novel in Poems*	Knopf
		Maria Testa	*Becoming Joe DiMaggio*	Candlewick Press
		Jaime Adoff	*The Song Shoots Out of My Mouth*	Dutton Children's Books
2002	Award Winner	Anna Grossnickle Hines	*Pieces: A Year in Poems and Quilts*	Greenwillow
	Honor Awards	Linda Oatman High	*A Humble Life: Plain Poems*	Wm. B. Eerdmans
		Paul Janeczko	*A Poke in the I: A Collection of Concrete Poems*	Candlewick Press
		Charles R. Smith, Jr.	*Short Takes: Fast-break Basketball Poetry*	Dutton Books
2001	Award Winner	Liz Rosenberg	*Light-Gathering Poems*	Henry Holt
	Honor Award	Paul Janeczko	*Stone Bench in an Empty Park*	Orchard Books
2000	Award Winner	Naomi Shihab Nye	*What Have You Lost?*	Greenwillow
	Honor Awards	Tony Johnston	*An Old Shell: Poems of the Galapagos*	Farrar, Straus & Giroux
		Janet S. Wong	*The Rainbow Hand: Poems about Mothers and Children*	M. K. McElderry Books
1999	Award Winner	Angela Johnson	*The Other Side*	Orchard Books

Year	Award	Author	Title	Publisher
1998	Award Winner	Kristine O'Connell George	*The Great Frog Race and Other Poems*	Clarion Books
1997	Award Winner	David Bouchard	*Voices from the Wild*	Chronicle Books
1996	Award Winner	Barbara Juster Esbensen	*Dance with Me*	HarperCollins
1995	Award Winner	Douglas Florian	*Beast Feast*	Harcourt Brace
1994	Award Winner	Nancy Wood	*Spirit Walker*	Doubleday
1993	Award Winner	Ashley Bryan	*Sing to the Sun*	HarperCollins

Activities

1. Lee Bennett Hopkins was born in Scranton, Pennsylvania. Children could find out more about the state. They could locate Scranton and other major cities on a map. Then they could eat soft pretzels, a popular treat in Pennsylvania.

2. Lee Bennett Hopkins was a teacher before he was a poet. Children could interview a teacher to find out how a person becomes an educator. Each child could then write an essay about whether he or she would like to become a teacher.

3. Children could examine both poetry and prose. They could decide how the two are different. They could decide which they like to read more and which they like to write more. A Venn diagram could help them organize their thoughts.

4. Diane Ackerman's *Animal Sense* was a 2004 honor book. Children could visit her Web site at: http://www.dianeackerman.com/ and research her other accomplishments. They could find out what a dianeackerone is. They could talk to the science teacher and find out what a molecule is. They could create some molecules from toothpicks and small marshmallows.

5. Naomi Shihab Nye's book, *Is This Forever, or What?: Poems and Paintings from Texas*, was a 2005 honor book. Her *What Have You Lost?* received the Lee Bennett Hopkins Poetry Award in 2000. Children could have an interview with her at: http://www.pifmagazine.com/SID/240/. They could learn about her mother and her grandmother.

6. Children could interview their parents and find out who their favorite poets are. They could see if any of those poets had won the Lee Bennett Hopkins Poetry Award.

7. Children could hear a poem and then react to it through art, music, or dance.

8. Children could visit a Web site that helps students write different types of poetry: http://ettcweb.lr.k12.nj.us/forms/newpoem.htm. Then they could have some fun!

9. Students could write some shape poems, poems in the shape of the subject. Children could see some concrete poetry at: http://oregonstate.edu/~smithc/vita/concrpoe.html.

10. Tony Johnston's *An Old Shell: Poems of the Galapagos* was a 2000 honor book. Children could read about her and her books at: http://www.childrenslit.com/f_tonyjohnston.html. Then they could locate the Galapagos Islands on a map.

Lee Bennett Hopkins and the Lee Bennett Hopkins Poetry Award

Student Handout 1—Information

Who Was Lee Bennett Hopkins?

Lee Bennett Hopkins could be called "Mr. Poetry." He has published over 100 books and poetry anthologies. He was born on April 13, 1938, in Scranton, Pennsylvania. The city was suffering from the Great Depression and the closing of area coal mines. Lee's father was a police officer. Lee spent much of his spare time with his grandmother, an apartment superintendent, and his grandfather, a coal miner.

The Hopkins family moved to Newark, New Jersey, in 1948. They lived in a rather dreary basement apartment. Lee's parents were superintendents of the building, but they were not getting along well. One day Lee's father sold all their furniture and left. His mother found an apartment in the projects. Although the apartment was small, the surrounding neighborhood was filled with people from many backgrounds. Lee absorbed the sights and sounds around him.

Few rules existed in the Hopkins household. He had no set bedtime; his mother did not even insist that he attend school. They had few books, and he did not enjoy reading. However, one junior school teacher shared her love of theater with him, and he, when he had some money, went into New York City to see plays. She also encouraged him to read, and she showed him the value of reading classics. She inspired him to become a teacher.

Even though Hopkins had to work on weekends and after school, he graduated from high school in 1956. He decided to attend Newark State Teachers College (now Kean University). He graduated in 1960 and became a sixth grade teacher in Fair Lawn, New Jersey. Hopkins truly enjoyed teaching. In addition, he began to see the value of using poetry. He obtained his master's degree in 1964, and he worked for Bank Street's "Searchlight on Intelligence," a learning resource center in Harlem. He helped African American students to further their education. One of his techniques to help them was to use poetry, especially the works of Langston Hughes.

Around 1967 he published his first book, *Let Them Be Themselves: Language Arts Enrichment for Disadvantaged Children in Elementary Schools*. In 1968, Scholastic hired him as a curriculum and editorial specialist. He interviewed authors, including Dr. Seuss, Charlotte Zolotow, Ezra Jack Keats, Pura Belpré, Sydney Taylor, and Beverly Cleary. Those interviews were included in *Books Are by People*, published in 1969. He also published his first poetry book, *This Street's for Me!,* in 1970. The book's poems were about his years in Harlem.

In 1972, Newark State Teachers College gave him the Outstanding Alumnus of the Arts Award; and he published another poetry book, *Charlie's World*. He published an additional book of author interviews, *More Books by More People,* in 1974. Hopkins decided to become a full-time writer and anthologist. He quit his job in 1976 and moved to Westchester County, New York. In 1977, he published a young adult novel, *Mama*, an account of his childhood. Kean University gave him an honorary doctor of laws degree in 1980. A year later he published a sequel to *Mama* called *Mama and Her Boys*. He was awarded the University of Southern Mississippi Medallion and the Keystone State Author of the Year Award.

What Is the Lee Bennett Hopkins Poetry Award?

Hopkins created the Lee Bennett Hopkins Poetry Award in 1993, which yearly honors a poet or anthologist who published a book of children's poetry. The award is given for a book published the year before. Honor books may also be recognized. Pennsylvania State University administers the award. A committee of educators, librarians, and poets evaluates possible award-winning books. Hopkins does not participate in the process. However, he does donate the $500 honorarium. The winner also receives a plaque.

From *Children's Book Award Handbook* by Diana F. Marks. Westport, CT: Libraries Unlimited. Copyright © 2006.

Lee Bennett Hopkins and the Lee Bennett Hopkins Poetry Award

Student Handout 2—Questions

Name_____ Date_____

Investigate the life of Lee Bennett Hopkins, and find out more about the Lee Bennett Hopkins Poetry Award. Then answer the following questions.

1. Where and when was Lee Bennett Hopkins born?

2. Describe his childhood.

3. Did he enjoy school?

4. Are you surprised that he became a teacher?

5. List three famous authors he interviewed.

6. Why do you think he likes poetry so much?

7. What is a poetry anthology? How do you think Lee Bennett Hopkins gets other authors to add their poems to his books?

8. What is the Lee Bennett Hopkins Poetry Award?

9. How are the winners chosen?

10. Do you like poetry or prose better? Why?

Lee Bennett Hopkins and the Lee Bennett Hopkins Poetry Award

Student Handout 3—Shape Poetry

Name_____ Date_____

Lee Bennett Hopkins could be known as "Mr. Poetry." He has written many books of poems, and he has assembled many poetry anthologies.

One type of poem is a shape poem. A shape poem is written in the shape of the subject. For example, a shape poem about a cat would be written so that the words create a picture of a cat. Here is a shape poem:

The Road
```
                        The
                      road
                   takes you
              where you
               want to go,
                      twisting,
                          turning,
                   climbing high hills,
              snaking through valleys
         speeding sometimes,
         c-r-e-e-p-i-n-g other times,
                      but before you know it,
                          you are where you want to be!
```

Now it is your turn to write a shape poem!

1. Pick a subject. Choose a simple subject, like the moon or a fish.

2. On another piece of paper, write your subject and then list words, phrases, or sentences about your subject.

3. Move the words, phrases, or sentences about your subject around until they form the shape of your subject.

4. Make a good copy of your poem. Make sure you include the title and your name.

5. Add artistic touches, such as color, background, or small drawings, if you want.

6. Share your shape poem with your friends.

From *Children's Book Award Handbook* by Diana F. Marks. Westport, CT: Libraries Unlimited. Copyright © 2006.

Lee Bennett Hopkins and the Lee Bennett Hopkins Poetry Award

Student Handout 4—What Do You Know about Poetry?

Name_____ Date_____

Lee Bennett Hopkins loves poetry. He has written many poetry books, and he has assembled many poetry anthologies. He, of course, knows many poets. Let's find out what you know about poetry and poems.

1. In the space below, write down all the names of poets that you can think of.

2. In the space below, write down all the types of poetry (for example, haiku) that you can think of.

3. Now look at many poetry books. See if you can add more names of poets to question 1 and types of poems to question 2.

4. In the space below, write down the name of your favorite poet and your favorite type of poem.

CHAPTER 11

Ezra Jack Keats and the Ezra Jack Keats New Writer and New Illustrator Award

Overview

The Ezra Jack Keats New Writer and New Illustrator Award honors new authors and illustrators of children's book. Ezra Jack Keats was first an illustrator and then both an author and illustrator of children's books.

Ezra Jack Keats was born in Brooklyn, New York, in 1916 to Jewish immigrants from Poland. He experienced first hand the trials of the Great Depression, and he served in the army during World War II. He lived in Paris for about a year before returning to New York. He illustrated Elizabeth Hubbard Lansing's *Jubilant for Sure*, published in 1954. The success of that book led to steady work in book and magazine illustration. He received a Caldecott Medal in 1963 for *The Snowy Day*. He created the Ezra Jack Keats Foundation in 1964. He wrote and illustrated many children's books, and he illustrated even more books for children. He died in 1983.

The Ezra Jack Keats New Writer and New Illustrator Award was first given in 1983. The winning authors and illustrators can have published no more than five books. The books must espouse cultural diversity and reward peaceful conflict resolutions. The award is provided jointly by the Ezra Jack Keats Foundation and the New York Public Library. The award winners receive their medallions at a ceremony in a branch of the New Your Public Library usually in April.

Past award winners include Faith Ringgold and Angela Johnson.

Ezra Jack Keats Biography

Even as a child, Ezra Jack Keats knew that he wanted to be an artist. He illustrated many books by famous authors. Over the course of his career he also wrote and illustrated many books for children. He experimented with various artistic media, until he found collage. Collage became his favorite method of artistic endeavor.

Jacob (Jack) Ezra Katz was born on March 11, 1916, in Brooklyn, New York, to Augusta Podgainy and Benjamin Katz. Benjamin and Augusta (Gussie) were Jewish immigrants from Poland, and Jack was their third child. A son, Willie, and a daughter, Mae, were glad to have another sibling. Jack showed artistic talent at an early age, sometimes painting on tabletops and other places his parents would have preferred he had left alone. Very little money was to be found in the Katz household. Benjamin was a waiter at a coffee shop, and during the Great Depression, he lost that job.

The family faced some tough times, but young Jack helped out. He worked for a fruit vendor, hauling heavy loads of watermelon. He traded some of his paintings for groceries. His father discouraged him from becoming an artist because he felt that being an artist was difficult and financially unrewarding. Even so, his father took him to art museums, and Jack enjoyed the experiences.

Jack was able to study art at Thomas Jefferson High School. His subjects were people surviving the Great Depression as best they could. His teacher forwarded some photos of Jack's work to Max Weber, a Russian immigrant famous for his modernist works. Jack was invited to the artist's studio where Weber critiqued and encouraged Jack's work. In 1934, Jack represented Thomas Jefferson School in the National Scholastic Art Competition, and he won first prize. His painting, *Shantytown*, portrayed several out-of-work men warming themselves around a fire.

Jack had planned to attend an art school after high school; he even had three scholarships to help pay the bills. However, his father died in January 1935, just two days before Jack's high school graduation. It was Jack who had to identify his father's body. In his father's wallet, he found newspaper clippings of Jack's artistic accomplishments, and for the first time he realized that his father was proud of his creative endeavors. However, not much money could be found in the wallet. Jack, now the support of his mother and sister, could not attend Art Students League.

In 1937, he began working for the WPA (Works Progress Administration), creating murals for public buildings. In 1939, after the WPA was disbanded, Jack became an inker for Five-Star Comics. He was paid $18.50 a week, and most of the money went to his mother. In 1942, he was hired by Fawcett Publications to illustrate background for Captain Marvel comics.

Jack joined the army on April 13, 1943, and here again he used his artistic talent. The army, in the throes of World War II, had him design camouflage patterns that would hide museums and other important buildings. Katz was discharged from the army in 1945 at the conclusion of the war.

While Jack had many talents, few people would hire him because he was Jewish. On February 8, 1948, tired of fighting anti-Semitism, he changed his name to Ezra Jack Keats. Restless, in 1949 he decided to move to Paris. He felt he had enough money to stay several months, but in addition he was able to sell some of his works. He thrived in Paris, absorbing the sights, sounds, and smells of the City of Lights. He stayed almost a year.

Back in New York, Keats sold his Paris paintings. When a friend suggested he become a book illustrator, Jack took samples of his work to many publishing houses, but no one took an interest. Even though he was frugal, his money had become dangerously low. He was very discouraged until he received an assignment to illustrate Elizabeth Hubbard Lansing's *Jubilant for Sure*. Lansing's book was about her nursing experiences helping the poor in Tennessee's Smoky Mountains. Several days later, he was hitchhiking through the region, sketching the sights and the people. *Jubilant for Sure* was published to rave reviews in 1954.

Jubilant for Sure enabled Keats to find other work. Soon he had constant income, illustrating books and magazine stories and covers. In 1960, with Pat Cherr he published his first children's book, *My Dog Is Lost!* In the book Juanito's dog is lost, and the little boy searches through various New York City neighborhoods, looking for his pet.

The year after that he began working on *The Snowy Day*. The protagonist was a small African American boy named Peter, and the story was from Keats's childhood memories. Keats drew inspiration for Peter from a photo he had cut out of a *Life* magazine years before. *The Snowy Day* was published in 1962, and he received the Caldecott Medal for the book in 1963.

Keats was now famous. Children wrote to him, and he appeared at schools. His books were translated into several foreign languages, including Arabic. He created the Ezra Jack Keats Foundation in 1964, and he published *Whistle for Willy* in the same year. In 1965, the Library of Congress named *In a Spring Garden*, a book he illustrated, Book of the Year. From 1965 to 1982, he illustrated at least one book per year. Titles included *Peter's Chair*, *God Is in the Mountain*, and *Regards to the Man in the Moon*. He continued to draw inspiration for some of his books from his childhood memories. He published six more books with Peter as the main character.

UNICEF asked Keats to design greeting cards. His work netted the organization a half million dollars.

In 1983, Keats began a different type of project regarding a musical version of his book, *The Trip:* he was asked to design the scenery and costumes. In April , however, he experienced severe chest pain, and he entered a hospital. During his long hospital stay, he played a recording of the music of *The Trip* over and over. He died on May 6, 1983, after a heart attack, in New York City. *The Trip* was performed for the first time two days later and won critical acclaim.

Keats illustrated at least eighty-five books for children, and he wrote and illustrated at least twenty-four children's books. In 1986, the New York Public Library created the Ezra Jack Keats New Writers Award. Later, the award was expanded to honor new illustrators as well.

Ezra Jack Keats Timeline

Date	Event
1916	Born Jacob (Jack) Ezra Katz on March 11 in Brooklyn, New York, to Benjamin and Augusta Podgainy Katz
1929	Started junior high school
1934	Represented Thomas Jefferson School in the National Scholastic Art Competition; took first prize
1935	Father died two days before Jack's graduation; graduated from high school; obtained a scholarship to Art Students League (Manhattan); could not attend because he had to support his mother and sister
1937	Began working for WPA
1939	End of work with WPA
1943	Joined army on April 13
1945	Discharged from army
1948	Changed his name on February 8 to Ezra Jack Keats
1949	Sailed to France
?	Returned to United States
1954	Illustrated Elizabeth Hubbard Lansing's *Jubilant for Sure*
1960	Published with Pat Cherr *My Dog Is Lost!*
1961	Began working on *The Snowy Day*
1962	Published *The Snowy Day*
1963	Received Caldecott Medal for *The Snowy Day*
1964	Created Ezra Jack Keats Foundation; published *Whistle for Willie*
1965	Published *John Henry, An American Legend*; Library of Congress named *In a Spring Garden*, a book he illustrated, Book of the Year
1966	Published *Jennie's Hat* and *God Is in the Mountain*
1967	Published *Peter's Chair*
1968	Published *A Letter to Amy* and *One Red Sun: A Counting Book*
1969	Published *Goggles!*
1970	Published *Hi, Cat!*; received Caldecott Honor Book Award for *Goggles!*
1971	Published *Apt. 3*
1972	Published *Pet Show!*
1973	Published *Pssst! Doggie* and *Skates*
1974	Published *Dreams* and *Kitten for a Day*
1975	Published *Louie*
1978	Published *The Trip*
1979	Published *Maggie and the Pirate*
1980	Published *Louie's Search*
1981	Published *Regards to the Man in the Moon*
1982	Published *Clementina's Cactus*
?	Asked by UNICEF to design greeting cards
1983	Died May 6 in New York City
1986	New York Public Library created Ezra Jack Keats New Writers Award
1998	Brooklyn School (PS 253) renamed Ezra Jack Keats International School
2001	Award renamed the "Ezra Jack Keats New Writer and New Illustrator Award"

History and Criteria of Award

Ezra Jack Keats created the Ezra Jack Keats Foundation. He died in 1983, and his will stipulated that his book royalties would be given to the Foundation, which was to fund programs designed to foster creativity, inspire learning, and help humanity. The Foundation, originally led by Keats's good friends, Dr. Martin Pope and Dr. Lillie Pope, followed his instructions. The Foundation, now led by Executive Director Dr. Deborah Pope, provides mini-grants to public libraries, fellowships for study at the deGrummond Collection, and storytelling and author workshops at the New York Public Library, to name a few of the projects.

Meanwhile, Hannah Nuba, librarian at the Leroy Branch of the New York Public Library, developed the idea of the Ezra Jack Keats New Writer Award. She had created the Early Childhood Reading and Information Center (ECRIC) at her library. In 1984, Ms. Nuba contacted the Ezra Jack Keats Foundation and suggested that the Ezra Jack Keats New Writer Award be created to honor Keats and reward new writers. The Foundation agreed, and the parameters of the award were determined.

At first, only a best new children's writer award was given. The writer could have published not more than five children's books, and the winning book should celebrate diversity and support peaceful conflict resolution. In 2001, the Ezra Jack Keats New Writer Award committee created a new children's illustrator award as well.

The first chair of the jury was Beatrice Cullinan, professor of early education at New York University. In 1986, she and her peers selected *The Patchwork Quilt* by Valerie Flournoy to be the first winner of the Ezra Jack Keats New Writer Award.

Ms. Nuba continued to administer the award until 2000 when she retired due to ill health. Julie Cummins, head of Children's Services at the New York Public Library, assumed the award responsibilities. Margaret Tice then took over the duties.

The award winners receive a brass medallion. On one side is an image of Keats, and on the other is a picture of Peter, the young boy in *The Snowy Day*. A cash award of $1,000 is also given to the award winners. Finally, the winning books can have Ezra Jack Keats New Writer and New Illustrator Award stickers on the covers.

Works by Ezra Jack Keats

Books Written and Illustrated by Ezra Jack Keats

A Letter to Amy. 1968.

Apt. 3. New York: New York: Macmillan, 1971.

Clementina's Cactus. 1982.

Dreams. New York: Macmillan, 1974.

God Is in the Mountain. New York: Holt, Rinehart & Winston, 1966.

Goggles! New York: New York: Macmillan, 1969.

Hi, Cat! New York: Viking, 1970.

Jennie's Hat. New York: HarperCollins, 1966.

John Henry. An American Legend. New York: Pantheon Books, 1965.

Kitten for a Day. New York: Franklin Watts, 1974.

Letter to Amy. New York: Harper & Row, 1968.

Louie. New York: Four Winds, 1975.

Louie's Search. New York: Four Winds, 1980.

Maggie and the Pirate. 1979.

My Dog Is Lost! (with Pat Cherr) *Mi Perro Se Ha Perdido.* 1960.

One Red Sun: A Counting Book. 1968.

Pet Show! New York: Viking, 1972.

Peter's Chair. 1967.

Pssst! Doggie. 1973.

Regards to the Man in the Moon. New York: Four Winds, 1981.

Skates! F. Watts. 1973.

The Snowy Day. New York: Viking, 1962.

The Trip. Greenwillow, 1978.

Whistle for Willie. New York: 1962.

Partial List of Books Illustrated by Ezra Jack Keats

The Chinese Knew, T. S. Pine and J. Levine. New York: McGraw, 1958.

The Egyptians Knew, T.S. Pine and J. Levine. New York: McGraw-Hill, 1964.

The Eskimos Knew, T. S. Pine and J. Levine. Whittlesey House, 1962.

The Flying Cow, Ruth P. Collins. Walck, 1963.

How to Be a Nature Detective, Millicent E. Selsam. Revised edition. New York: Harper, 1966.

In a Spring Garden, Richard Lewis, editor. New York: Dial, 1965.

In the Park: An Excursion in Four Languages, Esther R. Hautzig. New York: Macmillan, 1968.

Indian Two Feet and His Horse, Margaret Friskey. Scholastic, 1964.

Jim Can Swim, Helen D. Olds. New York: Alfred P. Knopf, 1963.

King's Fountain, The, Lloyd Alexander. New York: E. P. Dutton, 1971.

Little Drummer Boy, The, Katherine Davis, Henry Ohorati and Harry Simeone. New York: Macmillan, 1968.

Naughty Boy, The: A Poem, John Keats. New York: Viking, 1965.

Our Rice Village in Cambodia, R. Tooze. New York: Viking, 1963.

Over in the Meadow, Olive A. Wadsworth. Four Winds Press, 1971.

Penny Tunes and Princesses, Myron Levoy. New York: Harper, 1972.

Speedy Digs Downside Up, Maxine W. Kumin. New York: Putnam, 1964.

Tia Maria's Garden, Ann Nolan Clark. New York: Viking, 1963.

Two Tickets to Freedom: The True Story of Ellen and William Craft, Fugitive Slaves, Florence B. Freedman. New York: Simon & Schuster, 1971.

Zoo, Where Are You? Ann McGovern. New York: Harper, 1964.

Awards

Year	Award	Author/Illustrator	Title	Publisher
2005	New Writer	Janice N. Harrington	*Going North*	Farrar, Straus & Giroux
	New Illustrator	Ana Juan	*The Night Eater*	Scholastic
2004	New Writer	Jeron Ashford Frame	*Yesterday I Had the Blues*	Tricycle Press
	New Illustrator	Gabi Swiatowska	*My Name Is Yoon*	Farrar, Straus & Giroux
2003	New Writer	Shirim Yim Bridges	*Ruby's Wish*	Chronicle
	New Illustrator	Sophie Blackall	*Ruby's Wish*	Chronicle
2002	New Writer	Deborah Wiles	*Freedom Summer*	Simon & Schuster
	New Illustrator	James Lagarrigue	*Freedom Summer*	Simon & Schuster
2001	New Writer	D. B. Johnson	*Henry Hikes to Fitchburg*	Houghton
	New Illustrator	Bryan Collier	*Uptown*	Holt
2000	New Writer	Soyung Pak	*Dear Juno*	Viking
1999	New Writer	Stephanie Stuve-Bodeen	*Elizabeti's Doll*	Lee & Low
1997	New Writer	Juan Felipe Herrera	*Calling the Doves*	Children's Book Press
1995	New Writer	Carl Best	*Taxi! Taxi!*	Little, Brown
1993	New Writer	Faith Ringgold	*Tar Beach*	Crown
1991	New Writer	Angela Johnson	*Tell Me a Story, Mama*	Orchard
1989	New Writer	Yoriko Tsutsui	*Anne's Special Present*	Viking
1987	New Writer	Juanita Havill	*Jamaica's Find*	Houghton
1986	New Writer	Valerie Flournoy	*The Patchwork Quilt*	Dial

Activities

1. Ezra Jack Keats was born in Brooklyn, New York. Children could find out which other awards are named after people who lived in or around New York City. They could make a list of those awards.

2. Ezra Jack Keats received a Caldecott Award for *The Snowy Day*. Children could read the book, still in print. Then, if the weather permits, go out and play in the snow.

3. Ezra Jack Keats used collage in his artwork. Children could make collages.

4. Ezra Jack Keats knew at an early age that he wanted to be an artist. An adult could read one of his books out loud. However, that person would not show the children Keats's illustrations. Then children could create their artistic impressions of his words.

5. Ezra Jack Keats lived in Paris for a time. Children could find out if the Eiffel Tower was in Paris when Jack lived there. They could create a poster of the tower and include facts about the structure.

6. Faith Ringgold was the 1993 recipient of the Ezra Jack Keats New Writer Award. She is now famous. Children could visit her Web site at: http://www.faithringgold.com/ to see what else she has created. Ringgold is also an artist. Children could debate whether she is a better artist or author.

7. Valerie Flournoy received the first Ezra Jack Keats New Writer Award in 1986. She is still writing, and children could visit her Web site at: http://www.eduplace.com/kids/hmr/mtai/flournoy.html. They can learn what is special about Valerie and her sister.

8. Bryan Collier received the 2001 Award for New Illustrator. His biography mirrors that of Ezra Jack Keats. Children could read his biography and see his art at: http://www.bryancollier.com/. Then they could compare and contrast the two men.

9. Deborah Wiles and James Lagarrigue received the 2002 Awards for *Freedom Summer*. Children could go to: http://www.deborahwiles.com/freedom.htm where they can find out how and why the book was written and illustrated.

10. Ezra Jack Keats designed greeting cards for UNICEF. Children could design their own greeting cards. They could send them to one of the Ezra Jack Keats New Writer and New Illustrator Award recipients.

Ezra Jack Keats and the Ezra Jack Keats New Writer and New Illustrator Award

Student Handout 1—Information

Who Was Ezra Jack Keats?

Jacob (Jack) Ezra Katz was born on March 11, 1916, in Brooklyn, New York, to Jewish immigrants from Poland. From an early age he knew he wanted to be an artist. The family had little money. He had planned to go to college, but his father died several days before his high school graduation. He had to work to support his mother and sister. During the Depression he designed murals for the Works Progress Administration. During World War II he designed camouflage for buildings so that the buildings would not be bombed. After the war, he changed his name to Ezra Jack Keats and became an artist in Paris for about a year. He returned to the United States and struggled to find artistic work.

Ezra illustrated a book, *Jubilant for Sure*, and the book was very successful. Then he was able to illustrate many more books and magazine articles. In 1962, he published his most famous book, *The Snowy Day*. It won the Caldecott Medal in 1963. Then he became famous. He created the Ezra Jack Keats Foundation in 1964. Keats illustrated at least eighty-five books for children, and he wrote and illustrated at least twenty-four children's books.

Ezra Jack Keats died on May 6, 1983, after suffering a heart attack, in New York City.

What Is the Ezra Jack Keats New Writer and New Illustrator Award for New Writers and New Illustrators?

The Ezra Jack Keats New Writer and New Illustrator Award honors exceptional new writers and illustrators. Nominees can have published no more than five books. Also, the winning books should celebrate diversity and support peaceful conflict resolution. The winners receive a brass medallion. An image of Keats is on one side. On the other is a picture of Peter, the young boy in *The Snowy Day*. A cash award of $1,000 is also given to the award winners. The winning books can have Ezra Jack Keats New Writer and New Illustrator Award stickers on the covers. Ezra Jack Keats created the Ezra Jack Keats Foundation in 1964. Hannah Nuba, a librarian at the Leroy Branch of the New York Public Library, felt that an award should be created in Ezra's name. In 1984, she contacted the Ezra Jack Keats Foundation, and eventually the award became a real thing. The first award, for writing only, was presented in 1986. In 2001, the award was expanded to include new illustrators.

Ezra Jack Keats and the Ezra Jack Keats New Writer and New Illustrator Award

Student Handout 2—Questions

Name_____ Date_____

Investigate the life of Ezra Jack Keats, and find out more about the Ezra Jack Keats New Writer and New Illustrator Award. Then answer the following questions.

1. Where and when was Ezra Jack Keats born?

2. What was the name he was given at birth? Why do you think he changed his name?

3. How did he use his artistic talents during World War II?

4. What book made him a successful children's book illustrator?

5. What book made him famous?

6. Where and when did Ezra Jack Keats die?

7. How is Ezra Jack Keats like you?

8. List two rules that help the committee decide which books will receive the awards.

9. List at least three other facts about the Ezra Jack Keats Book New Writer and New Illustrator Award.

10. Ask your art teacher how he or she got the job. How was his or her career path different from the career path of Ezra Jack Keats?

11. Do you think it is harder to be a writer or an illustrator? Why?

Ezra Jack Keats and the Ezra Jack Keats New Writer and New Illustrator Award

Student Handout 3—Collage Activity

Name_____ Date_____

Ezra Jack Keats illustrated many books by other authors. He also wrote and illustrated at least twenty books. Ezra Jack Keats's most famous book is probably *The Snowy Day*, published in 1962. In the book, Peter, the main character, explores the outside world after a big snowstorm. Ezra Jack Keats illustrated the book using collage. Collage is a mixture of different types of fabric, paper, and other materials glued onto the background.

Keats cut pieces from linen sheets to make Peter's bed. Other fabrics became Peter's pajamas and snowsuit. Keats created red walls in Peter's room by gluing on pieces of red fabric. He made snowflakes by carving erasers, dipping the ends in different paints, and then pressing the ends on the illustration.

You can make your own collage. You might take inspiration from one of Keats's books or from a winner of an Ezra Jack Keats New Writer and New Illustrator Award.

1. Decide on your scene.

2. Find a sturdy piece of paper or canvas to serve as the background.

3. Lightly sketch with a pencil the scene you want to make.

4. Collect all kinds of materials, fabric, papers, fur, feathers, leaves, bark, beads, and newspaper or magazine pages.

5. Decide which materials you want to use.

6. Cut or tear the different materials.

7. Arrange them on your background.

8. Glue the different materials on the background.

9. Consider adding details with ink or paint.

10. Let the work dry before putting it up for display.

Ezra Jack Keats and the Ezra Jack Keats New Writer and New Illustrator Award

Student Handout 4—Researching Pseudonyms and Adopted Names

Name_____ Date_____

Ezra Jack Keats was born with the name Jacob (Jack) Ezra Katz. He changed his name when he was about thirty-two years old. Many authors, actors, musicians, athletes, and leaders have changed their names and taken pseudonyms or adopted names. Below is a list of the original names of some famous people. See if you can find their pseudonyms or adopted names.

Pseudonym and Adopted Names	Real Name
1. Samuel Langhorne Clemens	
2. Norma Jean Baker	
3. Dana Owens	
4. Edson Arantes do Nascimento	
5. Dwayne Douglas Johnson	
6. Theodore Geisel	
7. Archibald Alexander Leach	
8. Daniel Handler	
9. Richard Starkey	
10. Steveland Morris	
11. William Sydney Porter	
12. Caryn Johnson	
13. Agnes Gonxha Bojaxhiu	
14. Marion Michael Morrison	
15. Joseph Ratzinger	

Ezra Jack Keats and the Ezra Jack Keats New Writer and New Illustrator Award

Student Handout 4—Researching Pseudonyms and Adopted Names—Answers

Name_____ Date_____

Ezra Jack Keats was born with the name Jacob (Jack) Ezra Katz. He changed his name when he was about thirty-two years old. Many authors, actors, musicians, athletes, and leaders have changed their names and taken pseudonyms or adopted names. Below is a list of the original names of some famous people. See if you can find their pseudonyms or adopted names.

Pseudonym or Adopted Name	Real Name
1. Samuel Langhorne Clemens	Mark Twain
2. Norma Jean Baker	Marilyn Monroe
3. Dana Owens	Queen Latifah
4. Edson Arantes do Nascimento	Pelé
5. Dwayne Douglas Johnson	The Rock
6. Theodore Geisel	Dr. Seuss
7. Archibald Alexander Leach	Cary Grant
8. Daniel Handler	Lemony Snicket
9. Richard Starkey	Ringo Starr
10. Steveland Morris	Stevie Wonder
11. William Sydney Porter	O. Henry
12. Caryn Johnson	Whoopi Goldberg
13. Agnes Gonxha Bojaxhiu	Mother Teresa of Calcutta
14. Marion Michael Morrison	John Wayne
15. Joseph Ratzinger	Pope Benedict XVI

From *Children's Book Award Handbook* by Diana F. Marks. Westport, CT: Libraries Unlimited. Copyright © 2006.

CHAPTER 12

Coretta Scott King and the Coretta Scott King Award

Overview

The Coretta Scott King Award is given every year to the best African American children's writers and illustrators. Coretta Scott King, the widow of Martin Luther King, Jr., was a champion of human rights and a model for all children.

Born in 1927 near Marion, Alabama, Coretta Scott walked several miles a day to a one-room schoolhouse. Meanwhile, white children were transported by bus to a much closer and far better equipped school. She graduated from Antioch College and enrolled in the New England Conservatory of Music in Boston. There in 1953 she met and married Martin Luther King, Jr. They both became crucial to the civil rights movement. They had four children before he was assassinated in 1968. After his death, Coretta Scott King continued to be active in the civil rights movement and in the preservation of her husband's legacy. She died on January 30, 2006.

The Coretta Scott King Award was first presented in 1970 to Lillie Paterson for her biography, *Dr. Martin Luther King, Jr.: Man of Peace*. The first illustrator award was given to George Ford for his artistic expressions in the biography *Ray Charles*.

The Coretta Scott King Award is a responsibility of the American Library Association (ALA) and its committees. The Coretta Scott King Committee of the Ethnic Multicultural Information Exchange Round Table (EMIERT) decides on the winning books and the honor books. The names of the winners are announced at the midwinter meeting of the American Library Association, and the awards are presented to the authors and illustrators during ALA's summer conference.

Coretta Scott King Biography

Coretta Scott King wanted to be a professional singer but gave up any aspirations for a musical career when she married one of the most visible civil rights activists, Martin Luther King, Jr. After his assassination in 1968, she raised their four children, continued to fight for the rights of others, and created a fitting memorial to her husband.

Coretta Scott was born on April 27, 1927, to Obedia Leonard Scott and Bernice (McMurray) Scott in Heiberger, near Marion, Alabama. She had a sister, Edythe, and a brother, Obie. Young Coretta experienced the devastating effects of both the Great Depression and segregation. At one point, the children had to pick cotton to add to the family income. Obedia was a farmer, and eventually his farm became very successful. When the family's house was burned in 1942, the family wondered if disgruntled white townsfolk had started the fire.

Coretta attended Lincoln High School, a private school for African Americans. There she learned to play the trumpet and the piano, and she also sang at school recitals. She graduated at the top of her class in 1945. She followed her sister Edythe and enrolled in Antioch College, in Yellow Springs, Ohio. Edythe had been the first African American to attend Antioch full time. Coretta appeared in her first concert as a soloist in 1948 at the Second Baptist Church in Springfield, Ohio. When the time came for Coretta to student teach, local schools refused to take her. Although she protested, Antioch College did little about it. She, therefore, became a student teacher at the Demonstration School at Antioch College. Coretta graduated from Antioch College in 1951 with a B.A. in music and elementary education.

Coretta decided she would rather sing professionally than teach and enrolled in the New England Conservatory of Music in Boston. She had enough money to pay for tuition, but little funds were left for living. For a while, she lived on peanut butter and crackers. In Boston, she met Martin Luther King, Jr., who was completing his degree in theology. After they both obtained their degrees, they traveled to Marion, Alabama, where they were married on June 18, 1953.

The young couple moved to Montgomery, Alabama, and they became the pastor and the pastor's wife of the Dexter Avenue Baptist Church. Coretta gave birth to their first daughter, Yolanda Denise King, on November 17, 1955. Just a few days later, Rosa Parks was arrested for refusing to give up her seat on a Montgomery bus. The Kings were among the organizers of the Montgomery bus boycott from December 5, 1955, to December 21, 1956. In 1956, their house was bombed. The next year Coretta went with her husband to Ghana to witness its independence. Their son Martin Luther King III was born on October 23, 1957.

Two years later the couple traveled to India, making a pilgrimage to the tomb of Mahatma Gandhi. Coretta sang spirituals whenever Martin spoke.

In 1960, the King family moved to Atlanta, Georgia. There, Martin was arrested when he participated in a sit-in at a restaurant. He was sentenced to four months in jail. Coretta appealed to John F. Kennedy, then a presidential candidate, for help. Kennedy used his influence to free Martin.

Dexter Scott King was born on January 30, 1961. The next year Coretta traveled to Geneva, Switzerland, as a Women's Strike for Peace delegate at the Disarmament Conference. On March 28, 1963, their daughter Bernice Albertine King was born. During this period, Coretta performed at "freedom concerts," and all profits went to the Southern Christian Leadership Conference.

The Kings traveled to Oslo, Norway, in 1964 where Martin Luther King, Jr. received the Nobel Peace Prize. As he received more and more demands as a civil rights speaker and activist and made too many commitments, Coretta would speak in his place.

After Martin Luther King, Jr. was assassinated in Memphis, Tennessee, on April 4, 1968, Coretta carried on in his place. Just a few days after his funeral she led a march in Memphis to aid sanitation workers. She also took his place at an anti-Vietnam War rally in New York City.

Coretta mourned the loss of her husband and to honor his memory she continued many of his programs and goals. In 1961, she began to gather support for the Martin Luther King, Jr., Center for Non-Violent Change. The center, located near the Ebenezer Baptist Church where Martin and his father were co-pastors, finally opened in Atlanta, Georgia, in 1981. Earlier, in 1969, she published *My Life with Martin Luther King, Jr.*

Coretta continued to fight for human rights. In 1985, she and three of her children were arrested at the South African embassy in Washington, D.C. where they were protesting South Africa's apartheid policies. Her actions paid off when in 1994 she was able to witness Nelson Mandela being sworn in as president of South Africa.

From the time of her husband's assassination, Coretta campaigned heavily to make Martin Luther King's birthday a national holiday. Martin Luther King's birthday, January 15, was celebrated for the first time as a national holiday in 1986.

In 1993, President Bill Clinton asked Coretta Scott King to witness the meeting between Israel's Prime Minister Yitzak Rabin and Palestine's Chairman Yassir Arafat to sign the Middle East Peace Accords. In 1995, Coretta Scott King stepped down as leader of the Martin Luther King, Jr., Center for Non-Violent Change. Her son, Dexter Scott King, took over the position. Coretta's health began to fail in 2005. She died on January 30, 2006, in Baja California, Mexico.

The first Coretta Scott King Award for writing was given in 1970, and the first Coretta Scott King Award for illustration was presented in 1974.

Coretta Scott King Timeline

Date	Event
1927	Born Coretta Scott on April 27, in Heiberger, near Marion, Alabama, to Obedia Scott and Bernice (McMurray) Scott
1945	Graduated from Lincoln High School and enrolled in Antioch College in Ohio
1951	Graduated from Antioch College and enrolled in the New England Conservatory of Music in Boston
1953	Married Martin Luther King, Jr., on June 18
1954	Moved to Montgomery, Alabama, where her husband became pastor of Dexter Avenue Baptist Church
1955	Daughter Yolanda born on November 17; became involved in Montgomery bus boycott from December 5, 1955 to December 21, 1956
1956	King house bombed
1957	Went with husband to Ghana to witness its independence; son Martin Luther King III born on October 23
1959	Went to India to honor Gandhi
1961	Son Dexter Scott King born on January 30
1962	Was Women's Strike for Peace delegate at the Disarmament Conference in Geneva, Switzerland
1963	Daughter Bernice Albertine King born on March 28
1964	Martin Luther King, Jr., awarded Nobel Peace Prize
1968	Martin Luther King, Jr., assassinated in Memphis, Tennessee, on April 4
1969	Wrote *My Life with Martin Luther King, Jr.*
1970	First Coretta Scott King Award for writing given
1974	First Coretta Scott King Award for illustration given
1981	Martin Luther King, Jr., Center for Non-Violent Change opened its doors in Atlanta, Georgia
1986	Martin Luther King's birthday celebrated for the first time as a national holiday
1993	Asked by President Clinton to witness meeting between Israel's Prime Minister Yitzak Rabin and Palestine's Chairman Yassir Arafat to sign Middle East Peace Accords
1995	Stepped down as leader of Martin Luther King, Jr., Center for Non-Violent Change; son Dexter Scott King took position
2006	Died January 30 in Baja California, Mexico

History and Criteria of Award

In 1969, Glyndon Greer, a school librarian, met Mabel McKissack, also a school librarian, at a booth at the American Library Association meeting in New Jersey. They were both trying to obtain a poster of Dr. Martin Luther King, Jr. Glyndon suggested that an award be created to honor African American writers.

In 1970, Greer took her proposal one step further and created an annual event at the New Jersey Library Association. The first award was presented to Lillie Patterson for her biography, *Dr. Martin Luther King, Jr.: Man of Peace*. The Johnson Publishing Company provided an honorarium.

The American Library Association (ALA) decided to incorporate the award within its boundaries. ALA decided to name the award the Coretta Scott King Award, out of respect for her "courage and determination in continuing the work for peace and brotherhood" and honoring the life of her husband, Martin Luther King, Jr. Greer continued to be very instrumental in the award and the award ceremony until her death in 1981. Lev Mills, from the art department of the University of Atlanta, created the seal and it was adopted in 1982.

In 1974, the award was expanded to include an illustrator. The first illustrator to win that award was George Ford. He illustrated the biography *Ray Charles*, written by Sharon Bell Mathis.

Effie Lee Morris took over responsibility for the award when Greer died. She and Jean Coleman, Director for ALA's Office for Literacy and Outreach Services, created the award criteria. Then ALA Councilor E. J. Josey felt that a special committee should oversee the award. The Coretta Scott King Task Force of the Social Responsibilities Round Table (SRRT) was formed in 1982. In 1993, the SRRT suggested adding a new award, one that acknowledged new writers. Originally, it was called the Genesis Award, but in 1998 the name was changed to the New Talent Award. The name was changed yet again to the John Steptoe Award for New Talent. As of 2005, the Coretta Scott King Committee of the Ethnic Multicultural Information Exchange Round Table administers the awards.

In 1980, the award winners were given encyclopedias from Encyclopaedia Britannica and World Book. In 2005, the author winner was also presented a plaque and $1,000 donated by Johnson Publications as well as a set of encyclopedias donated by Britannica. The illustrator winner receives a plaque and $1,000 donated by Book Wholesalers and a set of encyclopedias donated by World Book.

The award criteria are well defined:

1. The book must portray some portion of African American life.

2. The book must be well written/illustrated and must motivate children to seek their own identity and yet still be responsible citizens.

3. The creator must be African American.

4. The book must be published in the United States in the year before the award is given.

5. The book must be written for children, including preschool to grade 4, grades 5 through 8, or high school.

Award and Honor Books

Year	Award	Author/Illustrator	Title	Publisher
2006	Author Award	Julius Lester	*Days of Tears: A Novel in Dialogue*	Jump at the Sun/Hyperion
	Author Honor Books	Tonya Bolden	*Maritcha: A Nineteenth-Century American Girl*	Henry N. Abrams
		Nikki Grimes	*Dark Sons*	Jump at the Sun/Hyperion
		Marilyn Nelson	*A Wreath for Emmett Till*	Houghton Mifflin
	Illustrator Award	Bryan Collier	*Rosa*	Henry Holt
	Illustrator Honor Book	R. Gregory Christie	*Brothers in Hope: The Story of the Lost Boys of Sudan*	Lee & Low
2005	Author Award	Toni Morrison	*Remember: The Journey to School Integration*	Houghton Mifflin
	Author Honor Books	Shelia P. Moses	*The Legend of Buddy Bush*	Margaret K. McEderrry Books
		Sharon G. Flake	*Who Am I without Him?: Short Stories about Girls and the Boys in Their Lives*	Jump at the Sun/Hyperion
		Marilyn Nelson	*Fortune's Bones: The Manumission Requiem*	Front Street
	Illustrator Award	Kadir Nelson	*Ellington Was Not a Street*	Simon & Schuster
	Illustrator Honor Books	Jerry Pinkney	*God Bless the Child*	Amistad/HarperCollins
		Leo and Diane Dillon	*The People Could Fly: The Picture Book*	Alfred A. Knopf
2004	Author Award	Angela Johnson	*The First Part Last*	Simon & Schuster
	Author Honor Books	Patricia C. and Fredrick L. McKissack	*Days of Jubilee: The End of Slavery in the United States*	Scholastic
		Jacqueline Woodson	*Locomotion*	Grosset & Dunlap
		Sharon Draper	*The Battle of Jericho*	Atheneum
	Illustrator Award	Ashley Bryan	*Beautiful Blackbird*	Atheneum
	Illustrator Honor Books	Colin Bootman	*Almost to Freedom*	Carolrhoda Books
		Kadir Nelson	*Thunder Rose*	Silver Whistle
2003	Author Award	Nikki Grimes	*Bronx Masquerade*	Dial

Year	Award	Author/Illustrator	Title	Publisher
	Author Honor Books	Brenda Woods	*The Red Rose Box*	G. P. Putnam's Sons
		Nikki Grimes	*Talkin' About Bessie: The Story of Aviator Elizabeth Coleman*	Orchard Books/Scholastic
	Illustrator Award	E. B. Lewis	*Talkin' About Bessie: The Story of Aviator Elizabeth Coleman*	Orchard Books/Scholastic
	Illustrator Honor Books	Leo and Diane Dillon	*Rap a Tap Tap: Here's Bojangles-Think of That*	Blue Sky Press/Scholastic
		Bryan Collier	*Visiting Langston*	Henry Holt
2002	Author Award	Mildred Taylor	*The Land*	Phyllis Fogelman Books/Penguin Putnam
	Author Honor Books	Sharon G. Flake	*Money-Hungry*	Jump at the Sun/Hyperion
		Marilyn Nelson	*Carver: A Life in Poems*	Front Street
	Illustrator Award	Jerry Pinkney	*Goin' Someplace Special*	Anne Schwartz/Atheneum
	Illustrator Honor Book	Bryan Collier	*Martin's Big Words*	Jump at the Sun/Hyperion
2001	Author Award	Jacqueline Woodson	*Miracle's Boys*	G. P. Putnam's Sons
	Author Honor Book	Andrea Davis Pinkney	*Let It Shine! Stories of Black Women Freedom Fighters*	Gulliver Books/Harcourt
	Illustrator Award	Bryan Collier	*Uptown*	Henry Holt
	Illustrator Honor Books	Bryan Collier	*Freedom River*	Jump at the Sun/Hyperion
		R. Gregory Christie	*Only Passing Through: The Story of Sojourner Truth*	Random House
		E. B. Lewis	*Virgie Goes to School with Us Boys*	Simon & Schuster
2000	Author Award	Christopher Paul Curtis	*Bud, Not Buddy*	Delacorte
	Author Honor Books	Karen English	*Francie*	Farrar, Straus & Giroux
		Patricia C. and Fredrick L. McKissack	*Black Hands, White Sails: The Story of African-American Whalers*	Scholastic
		Walter Dean Myers	*Monster*	HarperCollins
	Illustrator Award	Brian Pinkney	*In the Time of the Drums*	Jump at the Sun/Hyperion

Year	Award	Author/Illustrator	Title	Publisher
	Illustrator Honor Books	E. B. Lewis	*My Rows and Piles of Coins*	Clarion
		Christopher Myers	*Black Cat*	Scholastic
1999	Author Award	Angela Johnson	*Heaven*	Simon & Schuster
	Author Honor Books	Nikki Grimes	*Jazmin's Notebook*	Dial
		Joyce Hansen and Gary McGowen	*Breaking Ground, Breaking Silence: The Story of New York's African Burial Ground*	Henry Holt
		Angela Johnson	*Heaven*	Orchard Books
	Illustrator Award	Michele Wood	*i see the rhythm*	Children's Book Press
	Illustrator Honor Books	Floyd Cooper	*I Have Heard of a Land*	Joanna Cotler Books/HarperCollins
		E. B. Lewis	*The Bat Boy and His Violin*	Simon & Schuster
		Brian Pinkney	*Duke Ellington: The Piano Prince and His Orchestra*	Hyperion
1998	Author Award	Sharon M. Draper	*Forged by Fire*	Atheneum
	Author Honor Books	James Haskins	*Bayard Rustin: Behind the Scenes of the Civil Rights Movement*	Hyperion
		Joyce Hansen	*I Thought My Soul Would Rise and Fly: The Diary of Patsy, a Freed Girl*	Scholastic
	Illustrator Award	Javaka Steptoe	*In Daddy's Arms I Am Tall: African Americans Celebrating Fathers*	Lee & Low
	Illustrator Honor Books	Ashley Bryan	*Ashley Bryan's ABC of African American Poetry*	Jean Karl/Atheneum
		Christopher Myers	*Harlem*	Scholastic
		Baba Wagué Diakité	*The Hunterman and the Crocodile*	Scholastic
1997	Author Award	Walter Dean Myers	*Slam*	Scholastic
	Author Honor Book	Patricia C. and Fredrick L. McKissack	*Rebels Against Slavery: American Slave Revolts*	Scholastic
	Illustrator Award	Jerry Pinkney	*Minty: A Story of Young Harriet Tubman*	Dial
	Illustrator Honor Books	Gregory Christie	*The Palm of My Heart: Poetry of African American Children*	Lee & Low

Year	Award	Author/Illustrator	Title	Publisher
		Reynold Ruffins	*Running the Road to ABC*	Simon & Schuster
		Synthia Saint James	*Neeny Coming, Neeny Going*	BridgeWater Books
1996	Author Award	Virginia Hamilton	*Her Stories*	Blue Sky Press/Scholastic
	Author Honor Books	Christopher Paul Curtis	*The Watsons Go to Birmingham—1963*	Delacorte
		Rita Williams-Garcia	*Like Sisters on the Homefront*	Delacorte
		Jacqueline Woodson	*From the Notebooks of Melanin Sun*	Blue Sky Press/Scholastic
	Illustrator Award	Tom Feelings	*The Middle Passage: White Ships/Black Cargo*	Dial
	Illustrator Honor Books	Leo and Diane Dillon	*Her Stories*	Blue Sky Press/Scholastic
		Brian Pinkney	*The Faithful Friend*	Simon & Schuster
1995	Author Award	Patricia C. and Fredrick L. McKissack	*Christmas in the Big House, Christmas in the Quarters*	Scholastic
	Author Honor Books	Joyce Hansen	*The Captive*	Scholastic
		Jacqueline Woodson	*I Hadn't Meant to Tell You This*	Delacorte
		Patricia C. and Fredrick L. McKissack	*Black Diamond: Story of the Negro Baseball League*	Scholastic
	Illustrator Award	James Ransome	*The Creation*	Holiday House
	Illustrator Honor Books	Terea Shaffer	*The Singing Man*	Holiday House
		Floyd Cooper	*Meet Danitra Brown*	Lothrop, Lee & Shepard
1994	Author Award	Angela Johnson	*Toning the Sweep*	Orchard
	Author Honor Books	Joyce Carol Thomas	*Brown Honey in Broom Wheat Tea*	HarperCollins
		Walter Dean Myers	*Malcolm X: By Any Means Necessary*	Scholastic
	Illustrator Award	Tom Feelings	*Soul Looks Back in Wonder*	Dial
	Illustrator Honor Books	Floyd Cooper	*Brown Honey in Broom Wheat Tea*	HarperCollins
		James Ransome	*Uncle Jed's Barbershop*	Simon & Schuster
1993	Author Award	Patricia McKissack	*The Dark Thirty: Southern Tales of the Supernatural*	Knopf

Year	Award	Author/Illustrator	Title	Publisher
	Author Honor Books	Mildred Pitts Walter	*Mississippi Challenge*	Bradbury
		Patricia C. and Fredrick L. McKissack	*Sojourner Truth: Ain't I a Woman?*	Scholastic
		Walter Dean Myers	*Somewhere in the Darkness*	Scholastic
	Illustrator Award	Kathleen Atkins Wilson	*The Origin of Life on Earth: An African Creation Myth*	Sights
	Illustrator Honor Books	Wil Clay	*Little Eight John*	Lodestar
		Brian Pinkney	*Sukey and the Mermaid*	Four Winds
		Carole Byard	*Working Cotton*	Harcourt
1992	Author Award	Walter Dean Myers	*Now Is Your Time!: The African-American Struggle for Freedom*	HarperCollins
	Author Honor Book	Eloise Greenfield	*Night on Neighborhood Street*	Dial
	Illustrator Award	Faith Ringgold	*Tar Beach*	Crown
	Illustrator Honor Books	Ashley Bryan	*All Night, All Day: A Child's First Book of African American Spirituals*	Atheneum
		Jan Spivey Gilchrist	*Night on Neighborhood Street*	Dial
1991	Author Award	Mildred D. Taylor	*The Road to Memphis*	Dial
	Author Honor Books	James Haskins	*Black Dance in America: A History Through Its People*	Crowell
		Angela Johnson	*When I Am Old with You*	Orchard
	Illustrator Award	Leo and Diane Dillon	*Aida*	Harcourt
1990	Author Award	Patricia C. and Fredrick L. McKissack	*A Long Hard Journey: The Story of the Pullman Porter*	Walker
	Author Honor Books	Eloise Greenfield	*Nathaniel Talking*	Black Butterfly
		Virginia Hamilton	*The Bells of Christmas*	Harcourt
		Lillie Patterson	*Martin Luther King, Jr., and the Freedom Movement*	Facts on File
	Illustrator Award	Jan Spivey Gilchrist	*Nathaniel Talking*	Black Butterfly

Year	Award	Author/Illustrator	Title	Publisher
	Illustrator Honor Book	Jerry Pinkney	*The Talking Eggs*	Dial
1989	Author Award	Walter Dean Myers	*Fallen Angels*	Scholastic
	Author Honor Books	James Berry	*A Thief in the Village and Other Stories*	Orchard
		Virginia Hamilton	*Anthony Burns: The Defeat and Triumph of a Fugitive Slave*	Knopf
	Illustrator Award	Jerry Pinkney	*Mirandy and Brother Wind*	Knopf
	Illustrator Honor Books	Amos Ferguson	*Under the Sunday Tree*	Harper
		Pat Cummings	*Storm in the Night*	Harper
1988	Author Award	Mildred D. Taylor	*The Friendship*	Dial
	Author Honor Books	Alexis De Veaux	*An Enchanted Hair Tale*	Harper
		Julius Lester	*The Tales of Uncle Remus: The Adventures of Brer Rabbit*	Dial
	Illustrator Award	John Steptoe	*Mufaro's Beautiful Daughters: An African Tale*	Lothrop
	Illustrator Honor Books	Ashley Bryan	*What a Morning! The Christmas Story in Black Spirituals*	Macmillan
		Joe Sam	*The Invisible Hunters: A Legend from the Miskito Indians of Nicaragua*	Children's Press
1987	Author Award	Mildred Pitts Walter	*Justin and the Best Biscuits in the World*	Lothrop
	Author Honor Books	Ashley Bryan	*Lion and the Ostrich Chicks and Other African Folk Tales*	Atheneum
		Joyce Hansen	*Which Way Freedom*	Walker
	Illustrator Award	Jerry Pinkney	*Half a Moon and One Whole Star*	Macmillan
	Illustrator Honor Books	Ashley Bryan	*Lion and the Ostrich Chicks and Other African Folk Tales*	Atheneum
		Pat Cummings	*C.L.O.U.D.S.*	Lothrop
1986	Author Award	Virginia Hamilton	*The People Could Fly: American Black Folktales*	Knopf
	Author Honor Books	Virginia Hamilton	*Junius over Far*	Harper

Year	Award	Author/Illustrator	Title	Publisher
		Mildred Pitts Walter	*Trouble's Child*	Lothrop
	Illustrator Award	Jerry Pinkney	*The Patchwork Quilt*	Dial
	Illustrator Honor Book	Leo and Diane Dillon	*The People Could Fly: American Black Folktales*	Knopf
1985	Author Award	Walter Dean Myers	*Motown and Didi*	Viking
	Author Honor Books	Candy Dawson Boyd	*Circle of Gold*	Apple/Scholastic
		Virginia Hamilton	*A Little Love*	Philomel
	Illustrator Award	No award given		
1984	Author Award	Lucille Clifton	*Everett Anderson's Good-bye*	Holt
	Special Citation	Coretta Scott King	*The Words of Martin Luther King, Jr.*	Newmarket Press
	Author Honor Books	Virginia Hamilton	*The Magical Adventures of Pretty Pearl*	Harper
		James Haskins	*Lena Horne*	Coward-MacCann
		Joyce Carol Thomas	*Bright Shadow*	Avon
		Mildred Pitts Walter	*Because We Are*	Lothrop, Lee & Shepard
	Illustrator Award	Pat Cummings	*My Mama Needs Me*	Morrow
1983	Author Award	Virginia Hamilton	*Sweet Whispers, Brother Rush*	Philomel
	Author Honor Book	Julius Lester	*This Strange New Feeling*	Dial
	Illustrator Award	Peter Mugabane	*Black Child*	Knopf
	Illustrator Honor Books	John Steptoe	*All the Colors of the Race*	Lothrop
		Ashley Bryan	*I'm Going to Sing: Black American Spirituals*	Atheneum
		Pat Cummings	*Just Us Women*	Harper
1982	Author Award	Mildred D. Taylor	*Let the Circle Be Unbroken*	Dial
	Author Honor Books	Alice Childress	*Rainbow Jordan*	Coward-MacCann
		Kristin Hunter	*Lou in the Limelight*	Scribner
		Mary E. Mebane	*Mary: An Autobiography*	Viking

Year	Award	Author/Illustrator	Title	Publisher
	Illustrator Award	John Steptoe	*Mother Crocodile: An Uncle Amadou Tale from Sengal*	Delacorte
	Illustrator Honor Book	Tom Feelings	*Daydreamers*	Dial
1981	Author Award	Sidney Poitier	*This Life*	Knopf
	Author Honor Book	Alexis De Veaux	*Don't Explain: A Song of Billie Holiday*	Harper
	Illustrator Award	Ashley Bryan	*Beat the Drum, Pum-Pum*	Atheneum
	Illustrator Honor Books	Carole Byard	*Grandmama's Joy*	Collins
		Jerry Pinkney	*Count on Your Fingers African Style*	Crowell
1980	Author Award	Walter Dean Myers	*The Young Landlords*	Viking
	Author Honor Books	Berry Gordy	*Movin' Up*	Harper
		Eloise Greenfield and Lessie Jones Little	*Childtimes: A Three-Generation Memoir*	Harper
		James Haskins	*Andrew Young: Young Man with a Mission*	Lothrop
		James Haskins	*James Van Der Zee: The Picture Takin' Man*	Dodd
		Ellease Southerland	*Let the Lion Eat Straw*	Scribner
	Illustrator Award	Carole Byard	*Cornrows*	Coward-MacCann
1979	Author Award	Ossie Davis	*Escape to Freedom*	Viking
	Author Honor Books	Lillie Patterson	*Benjamin Banneker*	Abingdon
		Jeanne W. Peterson	*I Have a Sister, My Sister Is Deaf*	Harper
		Carol Fenner	*Skates of Uncle Richard*	Random
	Illustrator Award	Tom Feelings	*Something on My Mind*	Dial
1978	Author Award	Eloise Greenfield	*Africa Dream*	Crowell
	Author Honor Books	William J. Faulkner	*The Days When the Animals Talked: Black Folk Tales and How They Came to Be*	Follett
		Frankcina Glass	*Marvin and Tige*	St. Martin's
		Eloise Greenfield	*Mary McCleod Bethune*	Crowell
		James Haskins	*Barbara Jordan*	Dial

Year	Award	Author/Illustrator	Title	Publisher
		Lillie Patterson	*Coretta Scott King*	Garrard
		Ruth Ann Stewart	*Portia: The Life of Portia Washington Pittman, the Daughter of Booker T. Washington*	Doubleday
	Illustrator Award	Carole Byard	*Africa Dream*	Crowell
1977	Author Award	James Haskins	*The Story of Stevie Wonder*	Lothrop
	Illustrator Award	No award given		
1976	Author Award	Pearl Bailey	*Duey's Tale*	Harcourt
	Illustrator Award	No award given		
1975	Author Award	Dorothy Robinson	*The Legend of Africana*	Johnson Publishing
	Illustrator Award	No award given		
1974	Author Award	Sharon Bell Mathis	*Ray Charles*	Crowell
	Illustrator Award	George Ford	*Ray Charles*	Crowell
1973	Author Award	Jackie Robinson as told to Alfred Duckett	*I Never Had It Made: The Autobiography of Jackie Robinson*	Putnam
1972	Author Award	Elton C. Fax	*17 Black Artists*	Dodd
1971	Author Award	Charlemae Robbins	*Black Troubador: Langston Hughes*	Rand McNally
1970	Author Award	Lillie Patterson	*Martin Luther King, Jr: A Man of Peace*	Garrard

Activities

1. Coretta Scott King was born in Alabama. Children could research the state, make a make a large map, and fill it with facts they have learned.

2. Coretta Scott King is an accomplished musician. She loved to sing. Perhaps the music teacher or a private vocal teacher could talk to the students or work with a small group of children.

3. Coretta Scott King grew up in cotton country. Children could learn about the history of cotton at: http://www.cotton.org/pubs/cottoncounts/story/index.cfm. They could find out how cotton goes from seed to fabric. They could make a flowchart of the process.

4. Coretta Scott King was a driving force behind the Martin Luther King, Jr., Center for Non-Violent Change. Students could visit the Internet site at: http://www.thekingcenter. org/ and participate in some of the activities.

5. Coretta Scott King and her husband championed civil rights. Children could visit: http://www.cr.nps.gov/nr/travel/civilrights/. The National Parks Service site shows visitors a number of important civil rights locations. Children could mark those locations on a large map of the United States.

6. Walter Dean Myers has received a number of Coretta Scott King Awards. Children could read about him at: http://www.scils.rutgers.edu/~kvander/myers.html. They could also view his bibliography and choose several of his books to compare and contrast. A Venn diagram could be a useful tool in this process.

7. Patricia C. and Fredrick L. McKissack have also been awarded several Coretta Scott King Awards. Children could visit their site at: http://www.childrenslit.com/f_mckissack.html. They could vote on their favorite books by these authors.

8. Virginia Hamilton has received several Coretta Scott King Awards. In 1986 alone, her *The People Could Fly: American Black Folktales* won the award, and her *Junius over Far* was an honor book. Children could visit her Web site at: http://www.virginiahamilton. com/. They could find out a great deal about Hamilton, and they could read some new frog jokes.

9. Children could make a frequency table to find out which authors and illustrators have won the largest number of Coretta Scott King Awards.

10. Mildred Taylor has earned several Coretta Scott King Awards. She also served in the Peace Corps in Ethiopia for two years. Students can learn more about her at: http://www. olemiss.edu/mwp/dir/taylor_mildred/. They can read about the Peace Corps at: http://www.peacecorps.gov/kids/index.html. Perhaps a former Peace Corps volunteer could speak to the children.

Coretta Scott King and the Coretta Scott King Award

Student Handout 1—Information

Who Was Coretta Scott King?

Coretta Scott King was the widow of Martin Luther King, Jr. She continued his work and supported civil rights and human rights around the world.

Coretta Scott was born on April 27, 1927, near Marion, Alabama. Her parents were farmers, and for a time the family struggled to survive. Eventually, however, the truck farm became successful. Coretta experienced segregation during her elementary school years. She walked several miles a day to a one-room schoolhouse. Meanwhile, white children were transported by bus to a much closer and far better equipped school. Coretta attended a private high school for African Americans and graduated at the top of her class. She played the trumpet and the piano, and she loved to sing. She attended Antioch College in Ohio and earned a teaching degree.

Coretta decided she would like to sing professionally. She attended the New England Conservatory of Music in Boston, and there she met Martin Luther King, Jr. They were married in 1953 and moved to Montgomery, Alabama, where he became pastor of the Dexter Avenue Baptist Church. They had four children, and both Martin and Coretta became very active in the civil rights movement. Martin Luther King, Jr. was assassinated in Memphis, Tennessee, on April 4, 1968. She carried on in his place. Just a few days after his funeral she led a march in Memphis to aid sanitation workers, and she soon took his place at an anti-Vietnam rally in New York City.

Coretta mourned the loss of her husband, but she continued many of his programs and goals. In 1961, she began to gather support for the Martin Luther King, Jr., Center for Non-Violent Change. The center, located near the Ebenezer Baptist Church where Martin and his father were co-pastors, opened in Atlanta, Georgia, in 1981. She published *My Life with Martin Luther King, Jr.* in 1969. She stepped down as leader of the Martin Luther King, Jr., Center for Non-Violent Change, in 1995. Her son, Dexter Scott King, took over the position. Coretta Scott King never retired, however. She continued to fight for the rights of minority groups until her death on January 30, 2006.

What Is the Coretta Scott King Award?

The Coretta Scott King Award is presented every year to the best African American writers and illustrators of children's literature. The award also honors the memory of Martin Luther King, Jr. and the contributions Coretta Scott King has made to American society. In 1969, two African American librarians, Glyndon Greer and Mabel McKissack, created the idea of an award to honor African American writers. The first Coretta Scott King Award was presented to a writer only in 1970. In 1974, an award for illustration was added. Presently, the Coretta Scott King Committee of the Ethnic Multicultural Information Exchange Round Table, a part of the American Library Association (ALA), administers the awards. As of 2005, the author winner receives an award of a plaque and $1,000 donated by Johnson Publications and a set of encyclopedias donated by Britannica. The illustrator winner receives a plaque and $1000 donated by Book Wholesalers as well as a set of encyclopedias donated by World Book.

From *Children's Book Award Handbook* by Diana F. Marks. Westport, CT: Libraries Unlimited. Copyright © 2006.

Coretta Scott King and the Coretta Scott King Award

Student Handout 2—Questions

Name_____ Date_____

Investigate the life of Coretta Scott King, and find out more about the Coretta Scott King Award. Then answer the following questions.

1. Where and when was Coretta Scott born?

2. Give two facts about her childhood.

3. What instruments did she play? Did she enjoy singing?

4. Why did she attend the New England Conservatory of Music in Boston?

5. When did she marry Martin Luther King, Jr.?

6. How did Coretta's life change after Martin Luther King, Jr. was assassinated?

7. Why did Coretta create the Martin Luther King, Jr., Center for Non-Violent Change?

8. How was the Coretta Scott King Award created?

9. What do the Coretta Scott King Award winners receive?

10. Why do you think Coretta's name was chosen for the award? Why not name it after Martin Luther King, Jr.?

11. When did Coretta Scott King die?

Coretta Scott King and the Coretta Scott King Award

Student Handout 3—Critical Thinking Activity

Name_____ Date_____

The Coretta Scott King Award honors Coretta Scott King and her fight for the rights of minorities. The award is given to outstanding African American writers and illustrators. Some of the award-winning books have been about African Americans, including Bessie Coleman, Langston Hughes, George Washington Carver, and Sojourner Truth. Below is a list of African Americans who have contributed greatly to society. Organize the following thirty African Americans into exactly six groups with exactly five people in each group. The hard part is that the group names have not been given to you. You must decide how to group them. For example, one group might be athletes. You may need to use some references. Remember to label each group.

Henry Aaron	Aretha Franklin	Charlie Parker
Marian Anderson	Althea Gibson	Rosa Parks
Maya Angelou	Alex Hailey	Colin Powell
Arthur Ashe	Langston Hughes	Leontyne Price
Benjamin Banneker	Mae C. Jemison	Jackie Robinson
Gwendolyn Brooks	Scott Joplin	Wilma Rudolph
Yvonne Braithwaite Burke	Barbara Jordan	Sojourner Truth
George Washington Carver	Martin Luther King, Jr.	Harriet Tubman
Shirley Chisholm	Thurgood Marshall	Alice Walker
Frederick Douglass	Garrett A. Morgan	Granville T. Woods

Coretta Scott King and the Coretta Scott King Award

Student Handout 3—Critical Thinking Activity—Answers

Name_____ Date_____

The Coretta Scott King Award honors Coretta Scott King and her fight for the rights of minorities. The award is given to outstanding African American writers and illustrators. Some of the award-winning books have been about African Americans, including Bessie Coleman, Langston Hughes, George Washington Carver, and Sojourner Truth. Below is a list of African Americans who have contributed greatly to society. Organize the following thirty African Americans into exactly six groups with exactly five people in each group. The hard part is that the group names have not been given to you. You must decide how to group them. For example, one group might be athletes. You may need to use some references. Remember to label each group.

Freedom Fighters

Frederick Douglass
Martin Luther King, Jr.
Rosa Parks
Sojourner Truth
Harriet Tubman

Writers

Maya Angelou
Gwendolyn Brooks
Alex Hailey
Langston Hughes
Alice Walker

Musicians

Marian Anderson
Aretha Franklin
Scott Joplin
Charlie Parker
Leontyne Price

Scientists

Benjamin Banneker
George Washington Carver
Mae C. Jemison
Garrett A. Morgan
Granville T. Woods

Athletes

Henry Aaron
Arthur Ashe
Althea Gibson
Jackie Robinson
Wilma Rudolph

Law and Government

Yvonne Braithwaite Burke
Shirley Chisholm
Barbara Jordan
Thurgood Marshall
Colin Powell

Coretta Scott King and the Coretta Scott King Award

Student Handout 4—Creative Activity

Name_____ Date_____

Coretta Scott King loved music. She learned to play the trumpet and the piano. She planned to become a professional singer until she married Martin Luther King, Jr. The Coretta Scott King Award honors African American writers and illustrators.

Let's combine Coretta's love of music and some of the Coretta Scott King Award-winning books. You are going to create a song about one Coretta Scott King Award book. Then you are going to make some simple musical instruments. Finally, you will sing your new song and play your new instruments at the same time.

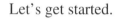

Let's get started.

1. Choose a Coretta Scott King Award Book or Honor Book. Read it and create a simple song or jingle about the book.

2. Make an instrument.

   You could make a tambourine:

   Place a paper plate on a table. Pour about ¼ cup dried beans, uncooked pasta, or beads into the plate. Cover the paper plate with another paper plate so that the edges touch. Staple the set of plates shut. Completely seal the edges together with tape. Decorate the tambourine if you wish. Shake or hit the tambourine to make music.

   You could make a kazoo:

   Place a small piece of wax paper over the end of a paper towel tube. Fasten the two together with a rubber band. With a pencil point, make a small hole about 2 inches from the other end of the kazoo. To play, hum through the open end of the kazoo.

   You could make a drum:

   An empty oatmeal carton or coffee can with a lid can make a great drum. Wrap enough masking tape around one end of a pencil to make a drumstick. Decorate the drum if you wish. To play, hit the drum with the drumstick.

3. Practice singing your new song and playing your instrument. Perhaps some of your friends could accompany you.

4. Perform your new song before your friends and have a good time!

From Children's Book Award Handbook by Diana F. Marks. Westport, CT: Libraries Unlimited. Copyright © 2006.

CHAPTER 13

Astrid Lindgren and the Astrid Lindgren Memorial Award

Overview

The Astrid Lindgren Memorial Award is an international award, honoring the best writers, illustrators, and promoters of children's literature. Astrid Lindgren was the famous Swedish author, best known for writing *Pippi Longstocking*.

Astrid Lindgren was born in Vimmerby, Sweden, in 1907. She moved to Stockholm, married, and had children. Her inspiration for writing children's stories came from her daughter, who when she had pneumonia asked her mother to tell her stories. The daughter created the name Pippi Longstocking, and Astrid Lindgren invented the stories. Lindgren also worked as an editor for her publisher, eventually publishing over forty books and becoming famous the world over. Astrid Lindgren died in 2002.

The Astrid Lindgren Memorial Award was created by the Swedish government in 2002. The award is not given for a specific work but for a lifetime of achievement. A cash prize of five million Swedish crowns (about $665,000) accompanies the award. The Swedish National Council for Cultural Affairs administers the award. The winners are announced in March in Vimmerby, Sweden, Astrid Lindgren's hometown. The winners receive their awards in May in Stockholm.

Astrid Lindgren Biography

Even as a child, Astrid Lindgren loved to tell stories. However, she had not planned to become a writer, let alone a very famous one. Her daughter invented the name, Pippi Longstocking, but Astrid invented the character. Children still love her *Pippi Longstocking* books. She wrote over forty other books, and she used her fame to improve children's rights.

Astrid Anna Emilia Ericsson was born on Nas, a 500-year-old farm near Vimmerby, Sweden, to Samuel August and Hanna Jonsson Ericsson on November 14, 1907. She and her siblings, Gunnar (born 1906), Stina (born 1911), and Ingegard (born 1916), loved to roam the outdoors. The Ericsson family owned few books, and no local public library existed. Yet from an early age, Astrid loved to read. She read *Robinson Crusoe* and some American classics such as *Tom Sawyer* and *Anne of Green Gables*. She also liked to tell stories, and her friends predicted she would be a writer when she grew up.

From 1924 to 1925, Astrid was a reporter for the *Wimmerby Tidning*, a local newspaper. At age nineteen, she moved to Stockholm where she worked for the Royal Automobile Club. Astrid fell in love with the office manager, Sture Lindgren, and the two were married on April 4, 1931. They had two children, Lars and Karin.

The Swedish government became concerned about the rise of Nazism in Europe. In 1940, Astrid took a secret government job reading letters that might give away information to the Germans. The government sent her containers of letters that soldiers had written to their families and friends. Astrid censored those letters, removing information that could aid the Nazis or harm Sweden. Then the letters were sent to their destinations.

In 1941, Karin contracted pneumonia and had to be in bed for a long time. To pass the time she would ask her mother to tell her stories, and she specifically told her to make up stories about a character that Karin named Pippi Longstocking. Astrid obliged and created the character of Pippi Longstocking, a brave and strong girl who had no parents.

In March 1944, Astrid fell on some ice, injuring her ankle and leaving her temporarily unable to walk. In her inactivity, she became bored and began writing down the Pippi Longstocking stories. She sent *Pippi Longstocking* to a publisher, who rejected the work. In late 1944, she saw a notice for a writing contest sponsored by the publishing house of Raben and Sjogren. She sent in her story *The Confidences of Britt-Mari* and won second prize. The next year she sent *Pippi Longstocking* to the same publisher's contest. This time she won first prize. Raben and Sjogren published *Pippi Longstocking* soon after the contest ended. The book was immediately popular with children, though some adults objected that Pippi, an amazingly strong and strong-willed nine-year-old girl who lived with a monkey and a horse, was not a good role model for children. For this reason some adults felt that Raben and Sjogren should not have published the book. Today, however, *Pippi Longstocking* is a classic. It has been translated into more than fifty languages, and movies have been made of the book and the characters.

In 1946, Astrid Lindgren was beginning to be famous. That year she published *Pippi Goes on Board,* and in 1948, she published *Pippi in the South Seas.* In 1946, she also took a job with Raben and Sjogren. Thus, in the morning, she would write her books, and in the afternoon, she would work in the publisher's office, where she primarily chose American books to be published in Sweden. Among the books she chose were *Charlotte's Web* and *The Rabbits' Wedding.*

Around 1950, she received the Nils Holgersson Plaque, honoring Sweden's best children's book of the year, and Viking Press published *Pippi Longstocking* in the United States. Although at first the book was not popular in America, over time it became one of the standards for public libraries.

In the late 1940s, her husband Sture became ill, and he died in June 1952. Fortunately, Astrid had both the book royalties and the job at Raben and Sjogren to provide income for Karin and herself. (Her son Lars was already an adult by this time.) After Sture's death, Astrid continued writing and publishing. In the same year that he passed away, *Bill Bergson, Master Detective* was published in the United States.

Astrid received the Hans Christian Andersen Medal in 1958. She wrote *Pippi's After Christmas Party* in 1959. *Madicken,* published in Sweden in 1960, appeared as *Mischievous Meg* in United States in 1962.

Astrid retired from Raben and Sjogren in 1970, and in 1978, she received the Peace Prize of the German Book Trade. In 1983, *Ronia, the Robber's Daughter* was published in the United States. The next year Viking Press received the Mildred L. Batchelder Award for *Ronia, the Robber's Daughter.* In 1986, Lars died. In 1987, Sweden created postage stamps in her honor; each stamp was a drawing of one of the characters from her book.

By the 1980s, Astrid was quite famous. She had published a book a year for about thirty years. She had also become a spokesperson for issues such as children's rights and animal rights. The Right Livelihood Award was presented to her on December 9, 1993, before the Swedish Parliament. Also in 1993, UNESCO presented her with the International Book Award.

Astrid Lindgren died in Stockholm, Sweden, on January 28, 2002. Following her death, the Swedish government founded the Astrid Lindgren Memorial Award.

Astrid Lindgren Timeline

Date	Event
1907	Born Astrid Anna Emilia Ericsson on Nas, a farm near Vimmerby, Sweden, to Samuel August and Hanna Jonsson Ericsson on November 14
1924–1925	Was a reporter for the local paper *Wimmerby Tidning*
1931	Married Sture Lindgren on April 4
1940	Took secret government job reading letters that might give away information to the Germans
1941	Daughter Karin, ill with pneumonia; asked her mother to tell her *Pippi Longstocking* stories
1944	Slipped and fell on ice in March; was confined to bed with injured ankle; wrote down *Pippi Longstocking* stories
	Sent *Pippi Longstocking* story to publishers; it was rejected
1944	In the fall, sent story *The Confidences of Britt-Mari* to writing contest sponsored by publishing house of Raben and Sjogren; won second prize
1945	Sent *Pippi Longstocking* to writing contest sponsored by Raben and Sjogren; won first prize
1946	Wrote *Pippi Goes on Board*, worked for Raben and Sjogren publishers; chose American books to be published in Sweden
1948	Wrote *Pippi in the South Seas*
1950?	Received Nils Holgersson Plaque, honoring Sweden's best children's book of the year
1950	*Pippi Longstocking* published in United States by Viking Press
1952	*Bill Bergson, Master Detective* published in the United States; Sture died
1958	Received Hans Christian Andersen Medal
1959	Wrote *Pippi's After Christmas Party*
1960	*Madicken* published in Sweden; book appeared as *Mischievous Meg* in United States in 1962
1970	Retired as editor for Raben and Sjogren
1978	Received Peace Prize of the German book trade
1983	*Ronia, the Robber's Daughter* published in the United States
1984	Viking Press received Mildred L. Batchelder Award for *Ronia, the Robber's Daughter*
1986	Son Lars died
1987	Sweden's postage stamps created in her honor, each stamp a drawing of one of the characters from her book
1993	Received Right Livelihood Award and International Book Award
2002	Died in Stockholm, Sweden, on January 28; Swedish government created the Astrid Lindgren Memorial Award

History and Criteria of Award

Astrid Lindgren died in Stockholm, Sweden, on January 28, 2002. The Swedish government founded the Astrid Lindgren Memorial Award in the same year. The award provides the largest children's literature prize, giving five million Swedish crowns (approximately $665,000) to the winner. An international award, the Astrid Lindgren Memorial Award honors the best writers, illustrators, and promoters of children's literature. The award is not for a specific work but for a lifetime of achievement. The award's purpose is to stimulate interest in children's literature and to serve as watchdog over children's rights.

The Swedish National Council for Cultural Affairs oversees the award and has the following requirements.

1. The Council creates a jury for each year's award.

2. In December the jury decides what groups can be nominating bodies.

3. In January the jury contacts nominating bodies, close to 400 groups from many countries, and asks them to nominate individuals.

4. Each nominating body can select two candidates from its own country and two candidates from other countries.

5. The jury requires that the candidates be living.

6. The jury requires that the nominating bodies submit support materials by May.

7. During the summer, the jury organizes all the data and begins to evaluate the nominations.

8. In September the jury publishes the list of nominations.

9. From October to February, the jury members meet often and discuss nominations.

10. The jury meets for the final time in March in Vimmerby, Sweden, Astrid Lindgren's hometown. The jury decides on winners and announces the winners' names at a press conference.

11. The winners receive their awards at a public ceremony in Stockholm, Sweden, in May.

In 2003, the first author award was presented to Christine Nöstlinger of Austria. The first illustrator award was given to Maurice Sendak of the United States.

Books by Astrid Lindgren Published in the United States

Bill Bergson and the White Rose Rescue
Bill Bergson Lives Dangerously
Bill Bergson, Master Detective
Brenda Helps Grandmother
Brothers Lionheart, The
Calf for Christmas, A
Children of Noisy Village, The
Children on Troublemaker Street, The
Christmas in Noisy Village
Christmas in the Stable
Circus Child
Day Adam Got Mad, The
Dirk Lives in Holland
Dragon with Red Eyes, The
Gerda Lives in Norway
Emil and His Clever Pig
Emil and the Bad Tooth
Emil Gets into Mischief
Emil in the Soup Tureen
Emil's Little Sister
Emil's Pranks
Emil's Sticky Problem
Ghost of Skinny Jack, The
Happy Times in Noisy Village
I Don't Want to Go to Bed
I Want a Brother or Sister
I Want to Go to School Too
Kati in America
Kati in Paris
Lotta
Lotta Leaves home
Lotta on Troublemaker Street

Lotta's Bike
Lotta's Christmas Surprise
Lotta's Easter Surprise
Mardie
Mardie to the Rescue
Marko Lives in Yugoslavia
Mio, My Son
Mirabelle
Mischievous Martens, The
Mischievous Meg
Most Beloved Sister
My Nightingale Is Singing
My Swedish Cousins
My Very Own Sister
Noriko-San: Girl of Japan
Noy Lives in Thailand
Pippi Goes on Board
Pippi in the South Seas
Pippi Longstocking
Pippi's After Christmas Party
Rasmus and the Tramp
Rasmus and the Vagabond
Ronia, the Robber's Daughter
Runaway Sleigh Ride, The
Scrap and the Pirates
Seacrow Island
Sia Lives on Kilimanjaro
Simon Small Moves In
Six Bullerby Children, The
That's My Baby
Tomten, The
Tomten and the Fox, The
World's Best Karlson, The

Award Recipients

Year	Award	Author/Illustrator	Country
2005	Author	Philip Pullman	United Kingdom
	Illustrator	Ryoji Arai	Japan
2004	Author	Lygia Bojunga	Brazil
2003	Author	Christine Nöstlinger	Austria
	Illustrator	Maurice Sendak	United States

Activities

1. Astrid Lindgren was born in Sweden. Children could find flags of Sweden and other Scandinavian countries. A good Web site is: http://www.crwflags.com/fotw/flags/. They could draw and then compare and contrast the flags.

2. Astrid Lindgren was born in Sweden. Children could draw a large map of the country and indicate her place of birth and major cities. They could also add other major cities and land features. A good Web site is: http://www.worldatlas.com/webimage/countrys/europe/se.htm.

3. Children could have a Pippi Longstocking fest, reading books, watching a video, and wearing costumes.

4. In 1987, Sweden created postage stamps honoring Astrid Lindgren. Each stamp had the image of one of her characters. Children could view some of those stamps at: http://arthistory.heindorffhus.dk/frame-LiteratureAstridLindgren.htm. Children could draw large "stamps" of their favorite Lindgren character.

5. Viking Press translated and printed Lindgren's *Ronia, the Robber's Daughter*. The publisher received the Mildred L. Batchelder Award in 1984. Children could read the book and share their feelings regarding the characters via a short essay.

6. Astrid Lindgren received the Hans Christian Andersen Award in 1958. Children could write a dialogue between Lindgren and Andersen. What would the two discuss?

7. Maurice Sendak received the Astrid Lindgren Memorial Award for illustration in 2003. Children could read a biography of Sendak at: http://www.northern.edu/hastingw/sendak.htm. The site also has links to other Web sites. One of the great sites features his illustrations for *Swine Lake*. Children could read the book and then perform scenes from the book.

8. Philip Pullman was the 2005 recipient of the Astrid Lindgren Memorial Award. Children could look at his Web site: http://www.philip-pullman.com/index.asp. They could find out where he went to school. Then they could locate those spots on a large map.

9. Ryoji Arai received the 2005 Astrid Lindgren Memorial Award for illustration. Children could read his biography at the Astrid Lindgren Memorial Award site: http://www.alma.se/page.php?realm=477. Ryoji Arai was very interested in manga, the Japanese comic books that are popular with both children and adults. Children could share what they know about manga and discuss whether they like it.

10. Lygia Bojunga received the 2004 Astrid Lindgren Memorial Award. Children could visit her English Web site at: http://www.casalygiabojunga.com.br/english/. They could find out what country was her birthplace. They could find out what language is spoken in that country.

Astrid Lindgren and the Astrid Lindgren Memorial Award

Student Handout 1—Information

Who Was Astrid Lindgren?

Astrid Lindgren, even as a child, loved to tell stories. Children still love her *Pippi Longstocking* books. She wrote over forty other books, and she used her fame to improve children's rights. Astrid Anna Emilia Ericsson was born on Nas, a 500-year-old farm near Vimmerby, Sweden, on November 14, 1907. She and her three siblings loved to roam the outdoors. The Ericsson family owned few books, and no local public library existed. Yet from an early age, Astrid loved to read.

From 1924 to 1925, Astrid was a reporter for the *Wimmerby Tidning,* a local newspaper. She moved to Stockholm. Astrid fell in love with her office manager, Sture Lindgren. The two were married in 1931, and they had two children, Lars and Karin.

The Swedish government became concerned about the rise of Nazism in Europe. In 1940, Astrid took a secret government job. The government sent her containers of letters that soldiers had written to their families and friends. Astrid removed any information that could aid the Nazis or harm Sweden. Then the letters were sent to their destinations.

In 1941, Karin had pneumonia, and she had to be in bed for a long time. She told her mother to make up stories about a character that Karin named Pippi Longstocking. Astrid obliged and created the character of Pippi Longstocking, a brave and strong orphan.

Astrid in March 1944 fell on some ice. She injured her ankle and could not walk. She became bored and wrote down the Pippi Longstocking stories. In late 1944, the publishing house of Raben and Sjogren sponsored a contest. She sent in her story *The Confidences of Britt-Mari* and won second prize. The next year she sent *Pippi Longstocking* to the same contest. This time she won first prize. Raben and Sjogren published the book, and it was immediately popular with children. *Pippi Longstocking* today is a classic. It has been translated into more than fifty languages. Movies have been made about the book and the characters.

In 1946, Astrid published *Pippi Goes on Board,* and in 1948, she published *Pippi in the South Seas.* She took a job with Raben and Sjogren. In the morning, she wrote her books. In the afternoon, she worked in the publisher's office, choosing American books to be published in Sweden. Some of the books she chose were *Charlotte's Web* and *The Rabbits' Wedding.* Around 1950 she received the Nils Holgersson Plaque, honoring Sweden's best children's book of the year. Astrid received the Hans Christian Andersen Medal in 1958. In 1970, she retired from Raben and Sjogren. In 1978, she received the Peace Prize of the German Book Trade. In 1983, *Ronia, the Robber's Daughter* was published in the United States. The next year Viking Press received the Mildred L. Batchelder Award for the book. In 1987, Sweden created postage stamps in her honor; each stamp was a drawing of one of her characters.

Astrid by this time had become quite famous. She had published a book a year for about thirty years. She had become a spokesperson for issues such as children's rights and animal rights. The Right Livelihood Award was presented to her on December 9, 1993, before the Swedish Parliament. Also in 1993, UNESCO presented her with the International Book Award.

Astrid Lindgren died in Stockholm, Sweden, on January 28, 2002.

What Is the Astrid Lindgren Memorial Award?

The Astrid Lindgren Memorial Award was created by the Swedish government in 2002. The award is not given for a specific work but for a lifetime of achievement. A cash prize of five million Swedish crowns (about $665,000) accompanies the award. The Swedish National Council for Cultural Affairs administers the award. The winners are announced in March in Vimmerby, Sweden, Astrid Lindgren's hometown. The winners receive their awards in May in Stockholm, Sweden.

From *Children's Book Award Handbook* by Diana F. Marks. Westport, CT: Libraries Unlimited. Copyright © 2006.

Astrid Lindgren and the Astrid Lindgren Memorial Award

Student Handout 2—Questions

Name_____ Date_____

Investigate the life of Astrid Lindgren, and find out more about the Astrid Lindgren Memorial Award. Then answer the following questions.

1. Where and when was Astrid Lindgren born?

2. Describe her childhood.

3. What secret job did Astrid do in 1940?

4. How was *Pippi Longstocking* created?

5. Astrid Lindgren wrote books, but she also worked in an office. What did she do in the office?

6. List at least three awards Astrid received.

7. Where and when did Astrid Lindgren die?

8. What is the Astrid Lindgren Memorial Award?

9. What group chooses the award winner?

10. Where does the winner receive his or her award? Do you know what other famous awards are given in Stockholm?

Astrid Lindgren and the Astrid Lindgren Memorial Award

Student Handout 3—Winners and Flags

Name_____ Date_____

Astrid Lindgren was Swedish. The Astrid Lindgren Memorial Award honors the lifetime accomplishments of children's writers and illustrators. These writers and illustrators are from all over the world. Below is a list of the Astrid Lindgren Memorial Award winners. Pick one winner and on a sheet of paper, draw the flag of that person's country. Where can you find pictures of flags? A good place is: http://www.plcmc.org/forkids/mow/. Another good place is an almanac.

Maurice Sendak (United States) and Christine Nöstlinger (Austria) received the 2003 award.

Lygia Bojunga (Brazil) received the 2004 award.

Ryogi Arai (Japan) and Philip Pullman (United Kingdom) received the 2005 award.

Astrid Lindgren and the Astrid Lindgren Memorial Award for Literature

Student Handout 4—Postage Stamps

Name_____ Date_____

Astrid Lindgren was Swedish. The Swedish government honored Astrid by creating a series of postage stamps. Each stamp showed a character from one of her books. Now you can create a pretend postage stamp. In the empty postage stamp below, draw a picture of your favorite book character. Below the picture, write the name of the character.

CHAPTER 14

John Newbery and the
John Newbery Medal

Overview

The John Newbery Medal is probably the most coveted children's literature award in America. It honors the year's best children's book published in the United States. John Newbery became a popular and fairly wealthy bookseller, publisher, and most likely author in London. He felt that children at that time had little to read that would interest them.

John Newbery was born in England in 1713. He became the first person to publish substantial amounts of literature that appealed to children. Some experts believe he was the author of at least some of the books he sold in his shop. He died in 1767.

The John Newbery Medal, first given in 1922, recognizes the highest quality of children's literature. The Association for Library Service to Children (ALSC), a division of the American Library Association (ALA), oversees the award. The award may be given to any genre, fiction, nonfiction, or poetry. Compilations are not considered. Medal winners and honor books are announced at ALA's midwinter meeting, and the awards are presented to the authors during ALA's summer conference.

John Newbery Biography

John Newbery was one of the first publishers of books for children, and he probably wrote many of those books. However, he could not have dreamed that his name would be associated with a very prestigious American children's book award, first given in 1922. He died eight years before the American Revolutionary War began. His name is well known, but few people know much about him.

John Newbery was born in 1713, probably on July 9, in Waltham Saint Lawrence in Berkshire, England. Records indicate that he was baptized on July 19, 1713. He was the second son of Robert Newbery, a farmer. John's education was rather sporadic, and books were rare in the area and at that time. However, according to notes left by his son Francis, John read whenever he had free time. When he was sixteen, around the year 1729, he was apprenticed to William Ayres, a printer in Reading, nine miles away from Waltham Saint Lawrence. In 1737, William Carnan acquired the printing business. Newberry must have been a trusted employee. Carnan died in 1737, and he willed the printing business in equal shares to his brother, Charles Carnan, and his employee, John Newbery. In 1739, John married William's widow, Mary, and adopted her three children, John, Thomas, and

Anna-Maria. While John provided for Mary and her children, Mary made sure John was well housed and well fed. Mary, several years older than John, was Catholic; John was Protestant. The custom of the time was that girls followed the faith of their mothers and boys followed the faith of their fathers.

John called his printing business the Bible and Crown. In addition to selling books, he displayed stationery, medicines (one of which was Dr. Hooper's Female Pills) and haberdashery items, including needles, pins, and ribbons.

In March of 1740, a daughter, Mary, was born. In that same year, John toured parts of England in hopes of expanding his business. When he returned, he published two books that bore his imprint. One was *The Whole Duty of Man*, a book by Richard Allestree about piety. The other book was *Miscellaneous Works ... for the Amusement of the Fair Sex.* A son, John, was born in September of 1741, but he died at age eleven. Another son, Francis, was born on July 6, 1743.

In 1744, Newbery moved his family to London, leaving John Carnan to manage the Reading printing business. He brought his sign, the Bible and Crown, with him and set up shop near Devereux Court. He printed at least two books that would appeal to adults. Always a busy man, he began to look around him for another business opportunity. He believed that a large market for children's books existed. The growing middle class was interested in improving the lives of their children, and children's books were certainly one vehicle for achieving this improvement. He also knew that only a few adult novels, such as *Robinson Crusoe* and *Gulliver's Travels,* were available to children. Newbery, therefore, decided to produce children's books. He printed his first book for children on June 18, 1744: *A Little Pretty Pocket-Book, intended for the Instruction and Amusement of little Master Tommy and pretty Miss Polly...* The book cost 6 pence. However, for 2 pence more the purchaser could get a pincushion for a girl or a ball for a boy. These items were half red and half black. Every time the child did a good deed, a pin could be placed on the red side. A bad deed got a pin on the black side. Parents hoped more pins were on the red side than on the black side.

A Little Pretty Pocket-Book was an extremely popular book, bringing fame and some amount of fortune to Newbery. This book really changed the type and quality of juvenile literature. The small book fit comfortably in the hands of small children. Brightly colored paper decorated the cover board. The many illustrations appealed to both adults and children. It did not have a story line, however. It was really an alphabet book layered with moral exhortations. Today the book would seem to preach at children. Also in 1744, he printed *A Sett of Fifty-six Squares; with Cuts and Directions for playing them, newly invented for the Use of Children. By which alone or with very little Assistance, they may learn to Spell, Read, Write, make Figures, and cast up any common Sum in Arithmetick, before they are old enough to be sent to School, and that by Way of Amusement and Diversion.*

In 1745, he moved his shop to a more prestigious London address at 65 St. Paul's Churchyard. He called this shop Bible and Sun. He was so busy that he had to sell the Reading business. However, his shop, located in a bustling, prosperous part of London, flourished. As time went on, he continued to publish books for adults as well as books for children. In 1750, he published *Nurse Truelove's Christmas-Box: Or, The Golden Plaything for Little Children...Adorned with Thirty Cuts.* The following year he published *The Lilliputian Magazine: Or, The Young Gentleman and Lady's Golden Library, being an attempt to Mend the World, to render the society of Man More Amiable and to Establish the Plainness, Simplicity, Virtue and Wisdom of the Golden Age.* Actually, the "magazine" was only that one issue, but it was filled with stories, jokes, and games.

Newbery published newspapers and more books for adults. However, he was partial to books for children. Sometimes he would publish and sell three children's books in one year. Probably one of the most famous of Newbery's publications was *The History of Little Goody Two-Shoes; Otherwise Called Mrs. Margery Two-Shoes.*

Newbery was an excellent father and a good husband, providing for both his children and stepchildren. Francis attended both Oxford and Cambridge for around five years. He never earned a degree, but John paid all the bills. He also gave his sons and stepsons jobs in his printing business.

Newbery was both popular and generous. He often loaned money to struggling authors, including Oliver Goldsmith and Samuel Johnson. In addition, he had a very full social schedule. His friends and associates truly liked him, but they often felt he was too busy. For example, sometimes he would arrive at an event only to tell the other guests that he could not stay because he had to attend another event. Newbery continued to sell more than books and newspapers at his shop. He also sold patent medicines, including a potion called Dr. James's Fever Powder. The medicine was as profitable as the publishing/printing company was. In one of his children's books he even mentioned that a character died because he did not take Dr. James's Fever Powder.

One of the mysteries surrounding Newbery is the authorship of the books. Authors at that time were not always acknowledged. Some experts believe Oliver Goldsmith penned some of the books. Others feel that Giles and Griffith Jones wrote them. Still others believe Newbery himself wrote them, because the books seem to reflect his boisterous and humorous personality. Other experts, however, maintain that Newbery was much too busy to be writer, publisher, and bookseller.

John began to feel ill in 1767, so much so that he made his will. Dr. James (of the famous fever powder) attended him, but Newbery's health did not improve. John Newbery died on December 22, 1767, at Canonbury House, Islington. He was buried in the churchyard of Waltham Saint Lawrence, the site of his baptism. No known portrait of John Newbery exists.

John Newbery Timeline

Date	Event
1713	Born July 9; baptized July 19, in Waltham Saint Lawrence, England
1730	Apprenticed to William Ayres, printer, in Reading, England
1737	William Carnan took over printing business; Carnan died and willed property to Newbery and Charles Carnan, William's brother
1739	Married widow Mary Carnan and became stepfather to John, Thomas, and Anna-Maria
1740	Daughter Mary born in March; Newbery opened a haberdashery shop at his place of business; published *The Whole Duty of Man, Laid Down in a Plain and Familiar Way, for the Use of All, but Especially the Meanest Reader* and *Miscellaneous Works, serious and humorous; in Verse and Prose; design'd for the Amusement of the Fair Sex*; On July 9 set off on trip to advertise his business and to find new products; returned in mid-August
1741	Son John born in September; sold a shoeshine kit called a "blacking ball for shoes"
1742	Printed *Micrographica Nova: Or, a New Treatise on the Microscope and Microscopic Objects* and *Synopsis Scientiae Celestis: Or, the Knowledge of the Heavens and Earth displayed...* both by Benjamin Martin
1743	Son Francis born on July 6; printed *A Course of Lectures in Natural and Experimental Philosophy, Geography and Astronomy* by Benjamin Martin
1744	Opened a new business in London at the Bible and Crown, near Devereux Court; kept Reading business; printed *Travels of the late Charles Thompson, Esq., ...* by Charles Thompson; printed *Colloquia selecta ... Or, Select Colloquys ... adapted by Samuel Loggon* by Mathurin Cordier; printed *A Sett of Fifty-six Squares; with Cuts and Directions for playing them, newly invented for the Use of Children. By which alone or with very little Assistance, they may learn to Spell, Read, Write, make Figures, and cast up any common Sum in Arithmetick, before they are old enough to be sent to School, and that by Way of Amusement and Diversion*; published *A Little Pretty Pocket-Book, intended for the Instruction and Amusement of little Master Tommy and pretty Miss Polly...*
1745	Moved business to Bible and Sun, near St. Paul's churchyard; sold Reading business; printed *The Royal Battledore: being the first introductory Part of the Circle of the Sciences etc.* and *The Circle of the Sciences: Or, The Compendious Library* (ten volumes printed between 1745 and 1748)
1750	Published *Nurse Truelove's Christmas-Box: Or, The Golden Plaything for Little Children...Adorned with Thirty Cuts* and *The Pretty Book for Children: Or, An easy Guide to the English Tongue...* and *A Museum for young Gentlemen and Ladies (Youth): Or, a private (compleat) Tutor for little Masters and Misses* and *Alphabet Royale: ou, Guide commonde et agréable dans l'art de lire* (French version of the *Royal Battledore*)
1751	Published *The Lilliputian Magazine: Or, The Young Gentleman and Lady's Golden Library, being an attempt to Mend the World, to render the society of Man More Amiable and to Establish the Plainness, Simplicity, Virtue and Wisdom of the Golden Age*
1753	Published *An Historical Account of the Curiosities of London and Westminster in 3 parts. Part I. Contains a full Description of the Tower of London, and everything curious in and belonging to it, Part 2. Contains the History of Westminster Abbey from its foundation to the present time...Part 3. Treats of the old Cathedral of St. Paul's and the New...*
1755	Published *The New Testament adapted to the Capacities of Children, to which is added An Historical Account of the lives, Actions, Travels, Sufferings and Deaths of the Apostles and Evangelists...*

Date	Event
1756	Published *The Little Lottery Book for Children: containing a new Method of playing them into a Knowledge of the Letters, Figures, etc. Embellished with above fifty (forty) Cuts, and published with the Approbation of the Court of Common Sense.* and *A Collection of Pretty Poems, for the Amusement of Children Three Foot High, by Thomas Tagg, Esq.* and *(A Little Book of) Letters (and Cards) on the most common as well as important Occasions of Life, by Cicero, Pliny, etc. etc...for the Use of young Gentlemen and Ladies*
1757	Published *The Royal Primer: Or, An easy and pleasant Guide to the Art of Reading...*
1758	Published *Fables in Verse, for the Improvement of Young and Old, by Abraham Aesop, Esq.; to which are added Fables in Verse and Prose, with the Conversations of Birds and Beasts at their several Meetings, Routs, and Assemblies, by Woglog the (great) Giant...Illustrated with a Variety of curious Cuts, and an Account of the Lives of the Authors* and *Food for the Mind: Or, A New Riddle-Book compiled for the Use of the great and little good Boys and Girls in England, Scotland and Ireland, by John-the-Giant-Killer, Esq.* and *A Compendious History of England, from the Invasion of the Romans to the present Time. Adorned with a Map of Great Britain and Ireland, Colour'd; and embellished with Thirty-one Cuts of all the Kings and Queens, who have reign'd since the Conquest: drawn chiefly from their Statues at the Royal Exchange* and *Be Merry and Wise: Or, The Cream of the Jests and the Marrow of Maxims for the Conduct of Life; publish'd for the Use of all little good Boys and Girls, by T. Trapwit* and *(A Collection of) Pretty Poems for the Amusement of Children Six Foot High...Calculated with a Design to do good, Adorned with a Variety of Copperplate Cuts designed and engrav'd by the best Masters* and *The Holy Bible abridg'd: Or, The History of the Old and New Testament, illustrated with Notes, and Adorned with Cuts, for the Use of Children* and *Atlas Minimus: Or, A new Set of Pocket Maps of the several Empires, Kingdoms, and States of the known World...*
1759	Published *The Infant Tutor: Or, An easy Spelling-Book for little Masters and Misses...*and *Nurse Truelove's New-Year's-Gift: Or, The Book of Books for Children. Embellished with Cuts; and designed for a Present to every little Boy who would become a great Man, and ride upon a find Horse; and to every little Girl who would become a great Woman, and ride in a Lord-Mayor's gilt Coach* and *The Mosaic Creation; Or, Divine Wisdom displayed in the Works of the first six Days* and *A Pretty Book of Pictures for little Masters and Misses; or, Tommy Trip's History of Birds and Beats; with a familiar Description of each in Verse and Prose. To which is added, the History of little Tom Trip himself, of his Fog Jowler, and of Woglog, the great Giant* and *A Pretty Play-Thing for Children of all Denominations Containing, I The Alphabet in Verse for the Use of little Children II An Alphabet in Prose interspersed with proper Lessons in Life for the Use of great Children. III The Sound of the Letters explained by visible Objects, IV The Cuz's Chorus set to Music; to be sung by Children in order to teach them to join their Letters into Syllables, and pronounce them properly. The Whole embellish'd with Variety of Cuts, after the Manner of Ptolemy*
1761	Published *The Newtonian System of Philosophy, adapted to the Capacities of young Gentlemen and Ladies, and familiarized and made entertaining by Objects with which there are intimately acquainted. Being the Substance of six Lectures read to the Lilliputian Society by Tom Telescope, A.M., and collected and methodized for the Benefit of the Youth of these Kingdoms, by their old Friend, Mr. Newbery, in St. Paul's Churchyard: who has added Variety of Copper-plate Cuts, to illustrate and confirm the Doctrines advanced.* and *A New History of England, from the Invasion of Julius Caesar to the present Time. Adorned with Cuts of all the Kings and Queens who have reigned since the Norman Conquest*
1762	Published *Plutarch's Lives, abridg'd from the original Greek, illustrated with Notes and Reflections, and embellish'd with Copper-plate Prints* and *The Art of Poetry on a new Plan, illustrated with a great Variety of Examples...as may tend to form in our Youth an elegant Taste and render the Study of this Part of the Belles Lettres with rational and pleasing* (2 volumes)
1763	Published *A Compendious History of the World from the Creation to the Dissolution of the Roman Republic. Compiled for the Use of young Gentlemen and Ladies by their old Friend, Mr. Newbery* and *An History of the Lives, Actions, Travels, Sufferings and Deaths of the Apostles and Evangelists*

Date	Event
1764	Published *An History of the Lives, Actions, Travels, Sufferings and Deaths of the most eminent Martyrs and primitive Fathers of the Church* and *An History of the Life of our Lord and Saviour Jesus Christ, to which is added the Life of the blessed Virgin Mary...* and *An History of England in a Series of Letters from a Nobleman to his Son*
1765	Published *The (Renowned) History of Giles Gingerbread: a little Boy who lived upon Learning* and *The Easter Gift: Or, The Way to be (very) good. A Book much wanted* and *The Whitsuntide Gift: Or, the Way to be (very) happy: a Book necessary for all Families...* and *The Valentine('s) Gift: Or, a Plan to enable Children of all Sizes and Denominations to behave with Honour, Integrity and Humanity: very necessary in a Trading Nation* and *The Fairing: Or, (A) Golden Toy (Present) for Children, In which they may see all the Fun of the Fair, and at Home be as happy as if they were there...* and *The (Renowned) History of Little Goody Two-Shoes, otherwise called Mrs. Margery Two-Shoes...*
1767	Published *The Twelfth-Day Gift: Or, the Grand Exhibition* and *Sixpennyworth of Wit: Or, Little Stories for little Folks of all Denominations*; died on December 22; was buried in churchyard at Waltham Saint Lawrence, England
1922	First Newbery Award given

History and Criteria of Medal

Around 1920, children's books were growing in popularity. The Children's Librarian Section of the American Library Association (ALA) was searching for ways to make children's books even more popular. Frederic G. Melcher, a bookseller, publisher, and co-editor of *Publisher's Weekly*, spoke before the group on June 21, 1921. A member of ALA, he suggested that a medal be awarded annually to outstanding children's literature. He felt that the award would bring prestige to the winners and to all children's books. He stated that the objective of the award was "To encourage original creative work in the field of books for children. To emphasize to the public that contributions to the literature for children deserve similar recognition to poetry, plays, or novels. To give those librarians, who make it their life work to serve children's reading interests, an opportunity to encourage good writing in this field."

Melcher suggested that the award be named after John Newbery, an eighteenth-century English bookseller, writer, and publisher. Alice Hazeltine, the chair of the Children's Library Section, agreed. The ALA Executive Board accepted Melcher's proposal in 1922.

Melcher commissioned René Paul Chambellan, an American sculptor, to design the medal. The front of the medal depicts a man, a girl, and a boy, and on the back are engraved the award winner's name and date. The Newbery Medal's inscription states "Children's Librarians' Section." The group overseeing the Newbery Award has changed several times, but the inscription remains the same. Today the Association for Library Service to Children (ALSC) administers the award. ALSC includes both public library and school library employees.

The Newbery Committee reads hundreds of books before nominating winners. The award winners must be residents or citizens of the United States. Co-authors may be considered, and the award can be given posthumously. The committee will not consider a body of work award, and the committee should not be swayed if an author has been a past winner. The book must be published in the United States, and the text must be in English. Any genre can be considered, but compilations will not be examined. The book must not be supported by any sort of media (for example, music). The award will be given for a book published in the previous year.

From the award's inception, the committee could and did recognize other books as being meritorious. These works were called "runners-up" until 1971. Since that year, such works have been called "honor books."

In 1922, the first Newbery Medal was awarded, and five honor books were also noted. Since then the award has been given every year. At least one honor book has been recognized every year as well. The Newbery Medal was the world's first children's literature award. It has served as an excellent model for other groups and other awards. It continues to fulfill the goals set by Frederic G. Melcher.

John Newbery's Children's Publications

1744	A Little Pretty Pocket-Book, intended for the Instruction and Amusement of little Master Tommy and pretty Miss Polly...
	A Sett of Fifty-six Squares; with Cuts and Directions for playing them, newly invented for the Use of Children. By which alone or with very little Assistance, they may learn to Spell, Read, Write, make Figures, and cast up any common Sum in Arithmetick, before they are old enough to be sent to School, and that by Way of Amusement and Diversion
1745	The Royal Battledore: being the first introductory Part of the Circle of the Sciences etc.
	The Circle of the Sciences: Or, The Compendious Library (ten volumes printed between 1745 and 1748)
1750	Nurse Truelove's Christmas-Box: or, The Golden Plaything for Little Children: by which they can learn the Letters as soon as they can speak, and know how to behave so as to make every body love them. Adorned with Thirty Cuts. Price One Penny, bound and gilt
	The Pretty Book for Children: Or, An easy Guide to the English Tongue...
	A Museum for young Gentlemen and Ladies (Youth): Or, a private (compleat) Tutor for little Masters and Misses
	Alphabet Royale: ou, Guide commonde et agréable dans l'art de lire (French version of the Royal Battledore)
1751	The Lilliputian Magazine: Or, The Young Gentleman and Lady's Golden Library, being an attempt to Mend the World, to render the society of Man More Amiable and to Establish the Plainness, Simplicity, Virtue and Wisdom of the Golden Age
1753	An Historical Account of the Curiosities of London and Westminster in 3 parts. Part I. Contains a full Description of the Tower of London, and everything curious in and belonging to it, Part 2. Contains the History of Westminster Abbey from its foundation to the present time...Part 3. Treats of the old Cathedral of St. Paul's and the New...
1755	The New Testament adapted to the Capacities of Children, to which is added An Historical Account of the lives, Actions, Travels, Sufferings and Deaths of the Apostles and Evangelists...
1756	The Little Lottery Book for Children: containing a new Method of playing them into a Knowledge of the Letters, Figures, etc. Embellished with above fifty (forty) Cuts, and published with the Approbation of the Court of Common Sense
	A Collection of Pretty Poems, for the Amusement of Children Three Foot High, by Thomas Tagg, Esq.
	(A Little Book of) Letters (and Cards) on the most common as well as important Occasions of Life, by Cicero, Pliny, etc. etc...for the Use of young Gentlemen and Ladies
1757	The Royal Primer: Or, An easy and pleasant Guide to the Art of Reading...
1758	Fables in Verse, for the Improvement of Young and Old, by Abraham Aesop, Esq.; to which are added Fables in Verse and Prose, with the Conversations of Birds and Beasts at their several Meetings, Routs, and Assemblies, by Woglog the (great) Giant...Illustrated with a Variety of curious Cuts, and an Account of the Lives of the Authors
	Food for the Mind: Or, A New Riddle-Book compiled for the Use of the great and little good Boys and Girls in England, Scotland and Ireland, by John-the-Giant-Killer, Esq.
	A Compendious History of England, from the Invasion of the Romans to the present Time. Adorned with a Map of Great Britain and Ireland, Colour'd; and embellished with Thirty-one Cuts of all the Kings and Queens, who have reign'd since the Conquest: drawn chiefly from their Statues at the Royal Exchange

	Be Merry and Wise: Or, The Cream of the Jests and the Marrow of Maxims for the Conduct of Life; publish'd for the Use of all little good Boys and Girls, by T. Trapwit
	(A Collection of) Pretty Poems for the Amusement of Children Six Foot High...Calculated with a Design to do good, Adorned with a Variety of Copperplate Cuts designed and engrav'd by the best Masters
	The Holy Bible abridg'd: Or, The History of the Old and New Testament, illustrated with Notes, and Adorned with Cuts, for the Use of Children
	Atlas Minimus: Or, A new Set of Pocket Maps of the several Empires, Kingdoms, and States of the known World...
1759	*The Infant Tutor: Or, An easy Spelling-Book for little Masters and Misses...*
	Nurse Truelove's New-Year's-Gift: Or, The Book of Books for Children. Embellished with Cuts; and designed for a Present to every little Boy who would become a great Man, and ride upon a find Horse; and to every little Girl who would become a great Woman, and ride in a Lord-Mayor's gilt Coach
	The Mosaic Creation; Or, Divine Wisdom displayed in the Works of the first six Days
	A Pretty Book of Pictures for little Masters and Misses; or, Tommy Trip's History of Birds and Beats; with a familiar Description of each in Verse and Prose. To which is added, the History of little Tom Trip himself, of his Fog Jowler, and of Woglog, the great Giant
	A Pretty Play-Thing for Children of all Denominations Containing, I The Alphabet in Verse for the Use of little Children II An Alphabet in Prose interspersed with proper Lessons in Life for the Use of great Children. III The Sound of the Letters explained by visible Objects, IV The Cuz's Chorus set to Music; to be sung by Children in order to teach them to join their Letters into Syllables, and pronounce them properly. The Whole embellish'd with Variety of Cuts, after the Manner of Ptolemy
1761	*The Newtonian System of Philosophy, adapted to the Capacities of young Gentlemen and Ladies, and familiarized and made entertaining by Objects with which there are intimately acquainted. Being the Substance of six Lectures read to the Lilliputian Society by Tom Telescope, A.M., and collected and methodized for the Benefit of the Youth of these Kingdoms, by their old Friend, Mr. Newbery, in St. Paul's Churchyard: who has added Variety of Copper-plate Cuts, to illustrate and confirm the Doctrines advanced.*
	A New History of England, from the Invasion of Julius Caesar to the present Time. Adorned with Cuts of all the Kings and Queens who have reigned since the Norman Conquest
1762	*Plutarch's Lives, abridg'd from the original Greek, illustrated with Notes and Reflections, and embellish'd with Copper-plate Prints*
	The Art of Poetry on a new Plan, illustrated with a great Variety of Examples...as may tend to form in our Youth an elegant Taste and render the Study of this Part of the Belles Lettres with rational and pleasing (2 volumes)
1763	*A Compendious History of the World from the Creation to the Dissolution of the Roman Republic. Compiled for the Use of young Gentlemen and Ladies by their old Friend, Mr. Newbery*
	An History of the Lives, Actions, Travels, Sufferings and Deaths of the Apostles and Evangelists
1764	*An History of the Lives, Actions, Travels, Sufferings and Deaths of the most eminent Martyrs and primitive Fathers of the Church*
	An History of the Life of our Lord and Saviour Jesus Christ, to which is added the Life of the blessed Virgin Mary...
	An History of England in a Series of Letters from a Nobleman to his Son
1765	*The (Renowned) History of Giles Gingerbread: a little Boy who lived upon Learning*
	The Easter Gift: Or, The Way to be (very) good. A Book much wanted

	The Whitsuntide Gift: Or, the Way to be (very) happy: a Book necessary for all Families...
	The Valentine('s) Gift: Or, a Plan to enable Children of all Sizes and Denominations to behave with Honour, Integrity and Humanity: very necessary in a Trading Nation
	The Fairing: Or, (A) Golden Toy (Present) for Children, In which they may see all the Fun of the Fair, and at Home be as happy as if they were there...
	The (Renowned) History of Little Goody Two-Shoes, otherwise called Mrs. Margery Two-Shoes...
1767	*The Twelfth-Day Gift: Or, the Grand Exhibition*
	Sixpennyworth of Wit: Or, Little Stories for little Folks of all Denominations

Medal and Honor Books

Year	Award	Author/Illustrator	Title	Publisher
2006	Medal Winner	Lynne Rae Perkins	*Criss Cross*	Greenwillow Books
	Honor Books	Alan Armstrong	*Whittington*	S. D. Schindler (Random House)
		Susan Campbell Bartoletti	*Hitler Youth: Growing Up in Hitler's Shadow*	Scholastic
		Shannon Hale	*Princess Academy*	Bloomsbury Children's Books
		Jacqueline Woodson	*Show Way*	G. P. Putnam's Sons
2005	Medal Winner	Cynthia Kadohata	*Kira-Kira*	Atheneum Books for Young Readers
	Honor Books	Gennifer Choldenko	*Al Capone Does My Shirts*	G.P. Putnam's Sons
		Russell Freedman	*The Voice that Challenged a Nation: Marian Anderson and the Struggle for Equal Rights*	Clarion Books
		Gary D. Schmidt	*Lizzie Bright and the Buckminster Boy*	Clarion Books
2004	Medal Winner	Kate DiCamillo, author Timothy Basil Ering, illustrator	*The Tale of Despereaux: Being the Story of a Mouse, a Princess, Some Soup, and a Spool of Thread*	Candlewick Press
	Honor Books	Kevin Henkes	*Olive's Ocean*	Greenwillow Books
		Jim Murphy	*An American Plague: The True and Terrifying Story of the Yellow Fever Epidemic of 1793*	Clarion Books
2003	Medal Winner	Avi	*Crispin: The Cross of Lead*	Hyperion Books for Children
	Honor Books	Nancy Farmer	*The House of the Scorpion*	Atheneum
		Patricia Reilly Giff	*Pictures of Hollis Woods*	Random House/Wendy Lamb Books
		Carl Hiaasen	*Hoot*	Knopf
		Ann M. Martin	*A Corner of the Universe*	Scholastic
		Stephanie S. Tolan	*Surviving the Applewhites*	HarperCollins
2002	Medal Winner	Linda Sue Park	*A Single Shard*	Clarion Books
	Honor Books	Polly Horvath	*Everything on a Waffle*	Farrar, Straus & Giroux

Year	Award	Author/Illustrator	Title	Publisher
		Marilyn Nelson	*Carver: A Life in Poems*	Front Street
2001	Medal Winner	Richard Peck	*A Year Down Yonder*	Dial
	Honor Books	Joan Bauer	*Hope Was Here*	G.P. Putnam's Sons
		Kate DiCamillo	*Because of Winn-Dixie*	Candlewick Press
		Jack Gantos	*Joey Pigza Loses Control*	Farrar, Straus & Giroux
		Sharon Creech	*The Wanderer*	Joanna Cotler Books/HarperCollins
2000	Medal Winner	Christopher Paul Curtis	*Bud, Not Buddy*	Delacorte
	Honor Books	Audrey Couloumbis	*Getting Near to Baby*	G.P. Putnam's Sons
		Jennifer L. Holm	*Our Only May Amelia*	HarperCollins
		Tomie dePaola	*26 Fairmount Avenue*	G.P. Putnam's Sons
1999	Medal Winner	Louis Sachar	*Holes*	Frances Foster
	Honor Book	Richard Peck	*A Long Way from Chicago*	Dial
1998	Medal Winner	Karen Hesse	*Out of the Dust*	Scholastic
	Honor Books	Gail Carson Levine	*Ella Enchanted*	HarperCollins
		Patricia Reilly Giff	*Lily's Crossing*	Delacorte
		Jerry Spinelli	*Wringer*	HarperCollins
1997	Medal Winner	E. L. Konigsburg	*The View from Saturday*	Jean Karl/Atheneum
	Honor Books	Nancy Farmer	*A Girl Named Disaster*	Richard Jackson/Orchard Books
		Eloise McGraw	*Moorchild*	Margaret K. McElderry/Simon and Schuster
		Megan Whalen Turner	*The Thief*	Greenwillow/Morrow
		Ruth White	*Belle Prater's Boy*	Farrar, Straus & Giroux
1996	Medal Winner	Karen Cushman	*The Midwife's Apprentice*	Clarion
	Honor Books	Carolyn Coman	*What Jamie Saw*	Front Street
		Christopher Paul Curtis	*The Watsons Go to Birmingham—1963*	Delacorte
		Carol Fenner	*Yolanda's Genius*	Margaret K. McElderry/Simon & Schuster
		Jim Murphy	*The Great Fire*	Scholastic
1995	Medal Winner	Sharon Creech	*Walk Two Moons*	HarperCollins
	Honor Books	Karen Cushman	*Catherine, Called Birdy*	Clarion

Year	Award	Author/Illustrator	Title	Publisher
		Nancy Farmer	*The Ear, the Eye and the Arm*	Richard Jackson/Orchard Books
1994	Medal Winner	Lois Lowry	*The Giver*	Houghton
	Honor Books	Jane Leslie Conly	*Crazy Lady*	HarperCollins
		Laurence Yep	*Dragon's Gate*	HarperCollins
		Russell Freedman	*Eleanor Roosevelt: A Life of Discovery*	Clarion Books
1993	Medal Winner	Cynthia Rylant	*Missing May*	Richard Jackson/Orchard Books
	Honor Books	Bruce Brooks	*What Hearts*	A Laura Geringer Book/ HarperCollins imprint
		Patricia McKissack	*The Dark-Thirty: Southern Tales of the Supernatural*	Knopf
		Walter Dean Myers	*Somewhere in the Darkness*	Scholastic Hardcover
1992	Medal Winner	Phyllis Reynolds Naylor	*Shiloh*	Atheneum
	Honor Books	Avi	*Nothing but the Truth: A Documentary Novel*	Richard Jackson/Orchard Books
		Russell Freedman	*The Wright Brothers: How They Invented the Airplane*	Holiday House
1991	Medal Winner	Jerry Spinelli	*Maniac Magee*	Little, Brown
	Honor Book	Avi	*The True Confessions of Charlotte Doyle*	Richard Jackson/Orchard Books
1990	Medal Winner	Lois Lowry	*Number the Stars*	Houghton
	Honor Books	Janet Taylor Lisle	*Afternoon of the Elves*	Richard Jackson/Orchard Books
		Suzanne Fisher Staples	*Shabanu, Daughter of the Wind*	Knopf
		Gary Paulsen	*The Winter Room*	Richard Jackson/Orchard Books
1989	Medal Winner	Paul Fleischman	*Joyful Noise: Poems for Two Voices*	Harper
	Honor Books	Virginia Hamilton	*In the Beginning: Creation Stories from Around the World*	Harcourt
		Walter Dean Myers	*Scorpions*	Harper
1988	Medal Winner	Russell Freedman	*Lincoln: A Photobiography*	Clarion
	Honor Books	Norma Fox Mazer	*After the Rain*	Morrow
		Gary Paulsen	*Hatchet*	Bradbury

Year	Award	Author/Illustrator	Title	Publisher
1987	Medal Winner	Sid Fleischman	*The Whipping Boy*	Greenwillow
	Honor Books	Cynthia Rylant	*A Fine White Dust*	Bradbury
		Marion Dane Bauer	*On My Honor*	Clarion
		Patricia Lauber	*Volcano: The Eruption and Healing of Mount St. Helens*	Bradbury
1986	Medal Winner	Patricia MacLachlan	*Sarah, Plain and Tall*	Harper
	Honor Books	Rhoda Blumberg	*Commodore Perry in the Land of the Shogun*	Lothrop
		Gary Paulsen	*Dogsong*	Bradbury
1985	Medal Winner	Robin McKinley	*The Hero and the Crown*	Greenwillow
	Honor Books	Mavis Jukes	*Like Jake and Me*	Knopf
		Bruce Brooks	*The Moves Make the Man*	Harper
		Paula Fox	*One-Eyed Cat*	Bradbury
1984	Medal Winner	Beverly Cleary	*Dear Mr. Henshaw*	Morrow
	Honor Books	Elizabeth George Speare	*The Sign of the Beaver*	Houghton
		Cynthia Voigt	*A Solitary Blue*	Atheneum
		Kathryn Lasky	*Sugaring Time*	Macmillan
		Bill Brittain	*The Wish Giver: Three Tales of Coven Tree*	Harper
1983	Medal Winner	Cynthia Voigt	*Dicey's Song*	Atheneum
	Honor Books	Robin McKinley	*The Blue Sword*	Greenwillow
		William Steig	*Doctor De Soto*	Farrar, Straus & Giroux
		Paul Fleischman	*Graven Images*	Harper
		Jean Fritz	*Homesick: My Own Story*	Putnam
		Virginia Hamilton	*Sweet Whispers, Brother Rush*	Philomel
1982	Medal Winner	Nancy Willard	*A Visit to William Blake's Inn: Poems for Innocent and Experienced Travelers*	Harcourt
	Honor Books	Beverly Cleary	*Ramona Quimby, Age 8*	Morrow
		Aranka Siegal	*Upon the Head of the Goat: A Childhood in Hungary 1939–1944*	Farrar
1981	Medal Winner	Katherine Paterson	*Jacob Have I loved*	Crowell
	Honor Books	Jane Langton	*The Fledgling*	Harper

Year	Award	Author/Illustrator	Title	Publisher
		Madeleine L'Engle	*A Ring of Endless Light*	Farrar
1980	Medal Winner	Joan W. Blos	*A Gathering of Days: A New England Girl's Journal, 1830–1832*	Scribner
	Honor Book	David Kherdian	*The Road from Home: The Story of an Armenian Girl*	Greenwillow
1979	Medal Winner	Ellen Raskin	*The Westing Game*	Dutton
	Honor Book	Katherine Paterson	*The Great Gilly Hopkins*	Crowell
1978	Medal Winner	Katherine Paterson	*Bridge to Terabithia*	Crowell
	Honor Books	Beverly Cleary	*Ramona and Her Father*	Morrow
		Jamake Highwater	*Anpao: An American Indian Odyssey*	Lippincott
1977	Medal Winner	Mildred D. Taylor	*Roll of Thunder, Hear My Cry*	Dial
	Honor Books	William Steig	*Abel's Island*	Farrar
		Nancy Bond	*A String in the Harp*	Atheneum
1976	Medal Winner	Susan Cooper	*The Grey King*	McElderry/Atheneum
	Honor Books	Sharon Bell Mathis	*The Hundred Penny Box*	Viking
		Laurence Yep	*Dragonwings*	Harper
1975	Medal Winner	Virginia Hamilton	*M. C. Higgins, the Great*	Macmillan
	Honor Books	Ellen Raskin	*Figgs & Phantoms*	Dutton
		James Lincoln Collier and Christopher Collier	*My Brother Sam Is Dead*	Four Winds
		Elizabeth Marie Pope	*The Perilous Guard*	Houghton
		Bette Greene	*Philip Hall Likes Me, I Reckon Maybe*	Dial
1974	Medal Winner	Paula Fox	*The Slave Dancer*	Bradbury
	Honor Book	Susan Cooper	*The Dark Is Rising*	McElderry/Atheneum
1973	Medal Winner	Jean Craighead George	*Julie of the Wolves*	Harper
	Honor Books	Arnold Lobel	*Frog and Toad Together*	Harper
		Johanna Reiss	*The Upstairs Room*	Crowell
		Zilpha Keatley Snyder	*The Witches of Worm*	Atheneum
1972	Medal Winner	Robert C. O'Brien	*Mrs. Frisby and the Rats of NIMH*	Atheneum
	Honor Books	Allan W. Eckert	*Incident at Hawk's Hill*	Little, Brown

Year	Award	Author/Illustrator	Title	Publisher
		Virginia Hamilton	*The Planet of Junior Brown*	Macmillan
		Ursula K. Le Guin	*The Tombs of Atuan*	Atheneum
		Miska Miles	*Annie and the Old One*	Little, Brown
		Zilpha Keatley Snyder	*The Headless Cupid*	Atheneum
1971	Medal Winner	Betsy Byars	*Summer of the Swans*	Viking
	Honor Books	Natalie Babbitt	*Knee Knock Rise*	Farrar
		Sylvia Louise Engdahl	*Enchantress from the Stars*	Atheneum
		Scott O'Dell	*Sing Down the Moon*	Houghton
1970	Medal Winner	William H. Armstrong	*Sounder*	Harper
	Honor Books	Sulamith Ish-Kishor	*Our Eddie*	Pantheon
		Janet Gaylord Moore	*The Many Ways of Seeing: A Introduction to the Pleasures of Art*	World
		Mary Q. Steele	*Journey Outside*	Viking
1969	Medal Winner	Lloyd Alexander	*The High King*	Holt
	Honor Books	Julius Lester	*To Be a Slave*	Dial
		Isaac Bashevis Singer	*When Shlemiel Went to Warsaw and Other Stories*	Farrar
1968	Medal Winner	E. L. Konigsburg	*From the Mixed-Up Files of Mrs. Basil E. Frankweiler*	Atheneum
	Honor Books	E. L. Konigsburg	*Jennifer, Hecate, Macbeth, William McKinley, and Me, Elizabeth*	Atheneum
		Scott O'Dell	*The Black Pearl*	Houghton
		Isaac Bashevis Singer	*The Fearsome Inn*	Scribner
		Zilpha Keatley Snyder	*The Egypt Game*	Atheneum
1967	Medal Winner	Irene Hunt	*Up a Road Slowly*	Follett
	Honor Books	Scott O'Dell	*The King's Fifth*	Houghton
		Isaac Bashevis Singer	*Zlateh the Goat and Other Stories*	Harper
		Mary Hays Weik	*The Jazz Man*	Atheneum
1966	Medal Winner	Elizabeth Borton de Trevino	*I, Juan de Pareja*	Farrar

Year	Award	Author/Illustrator	Title	Publisher
	Honor Books	Lloyd Alexander	*The Black Cauldron*	Holt
		Randall Jarrell	*The Animal Family*	Pantheon
		Mary Stolz	*The Noonday Friends*	Harper
1965	Medal Winner	Maia Wojciechowska	*Shadow of a Bull*	Atheneum
	Honor Book	Irene Hunt	*Across Five Aprils*	Follett
1964	Medal Winner	Emily Neville	*It's Like This, Cat*	Harper
	Honor Books	Sterling North	*Rascal: A Memoir of a Better Era*	Dutton
		Ester Wier	*The Loner*	McKay
1963	Medal Winner	Madeleine L'Engle	*A Wrinkle in Time*	Farrar
	Honor Books	Sorche Nic Leodhas, pseudonym of Leclaire Alger	*Thistle and Thyme: Tales and Legends from Scotland*	Holt
		Olivia Coolidge	*Men of Athens*	Houghton
1962	Medal Winner	Elizabeth George Speare	*The Bronze Bow*	Houghton
	Honor Books	Edwin Tunis	*Frontier Living*	World
		Eloise Jarvis McGraw	*The Golden Goblet*	Coward
		Mary Stolz	*Belling the Tiger*	Harper
1961	Medal Winner	Scott O'Dell	*Island of the Blue Dolphins*	Houghton
	Honor Books	Gerald W. Johnson	*America Moves Forward: A History for Peter*	Morrow
		George Selden	*The Cricket in Times Square*	Farrar
1960	Medal Winner	Joseph Krumgold	*Onion John*	Crowell
	Honor Books	Jean Craighead George	*My Side of the Mountain*	Dutton
		Gerald W. Johnson	*America Is Born: A History for Peter*	Morrow
		Carol Kendall	*The Gammage Cup*	Harcourt
1959	Medal Winner	Elizabeth George Speare	*The Witch of Blackbird Pond*	Houghton
	Honor Books	Natalie Savage Carlson	*The Family Under the Bridge*	Harper
		Meindert DeJong	*Along Came a Dog*	Harper
		Francis Kalnay	*Chucaro: Wild Pony of the Pampa*	Harcourt

Year	Award	Author/Illustrator	Title	Publisher
		William O. Steele	*The Perilous Road*	Harcourt
1958	Medal Winner	Harold Keith	*Rifles for Watie*	Crowell
	Honor Books	Mari Sandoz	*The Horsecatcher*	Westminster
		Elizabeth Enright	*Gone-Away Lake*	Harcourt
		Robert Lawson	*The Great Wheel*	Viking
		Leo Gurko	*Tom Paine, Freedom's Apostle*	Crowell
1957	Medal Winner	Virginia Sorenson	*Miracles on Maple Hill*	Harcourt
	Honor Books	Fred Gipson	*Old Yeller*	Harper
		Meindert DeJong	*The House of Sixty Fathers*	Harper
		Clara Ingram Judson	*Mr. Justice Holmes*	Follett
		Dorothy Rhoads	*The Corn Grows Ripe*	Viking
		Marguerite de Angeli	*Black Fox of Lorne*	Doubleday
1956	Medal Winner	Jean Lee Latham	*Carry On, Mr. Bowditch*	Houghton
	Honor Books	Margorie Kinnan Rawlings	*The Secret River*	Scribner
		Jennie Lindquist	*The Golden Name Day*	Harper
		Katherine Shippen	*Men, Microscopes, and Living Things*	Viking
1955	Medal Winner	Meindert DeJong	*The Wheel on the School*	Harper
	Honor Books	Alice Dalgliesh	*Courage of Sarah Noble*	Scribner
		James Ullman	*Banner in the Sky*	Lippincott
1954	Medal Winner	Joseph Krumgold	*. . . And Now Miguel*	Crowell
	Honor Books	Claire Huchet Bishop	*All Alone*	Viking
		Meindert DeJong	*Shadrach*	Harper
		Meindert DeJong	*Hurry Home, Candy*	Harper
		Clara Ingram Judson	*Theodore Roosevelt, Fighting Patriot*	Follett
		Mary and Conrad Buff	*Magic Maize*	Houghton
1953	Medal Winner	Ann Nolan Clark	*Secret of the Andes*	Viking
	Honor Books	E. B. White	*Charlotte's Web*	Harper
		Eloise Jarvis McGraw	*Moccasin Trail*	Coward
		Ann Weil	*Red Sails to Capri*	Viking

Year	Award	Author/Illustrator	Title	Publisher
		Alice Dalgliesh	*The Bears on Hemlock Mountain*	Scribner
		Genevieve Foster	*Birthdays of Freedom, Volume 1*	Scribner
1952	Medal Winner	Eleanor Estes	*Ginger Pye*	Harcourt
	Honor Books	Elizabeth Baity	*Americans Before Columbus*	Viking
		Holling C. Holling	*Minn of the Mississippi*	Houghton
		Nicholas Kalashnikoff	*The Defender*	Scribner
		Julia Sauer	*The Light at Tern Rock*	Viking
		Mary and Conrad Buff	*The Apple and the Arrow*	Houghton
1951	Medal Winner	Elizabeth Yates	*Amos Fortune, Free Man*	Dutton
	Honor Books	Mabel Leigh Hunt	*Better Known as Johnny Appleseed*	Lippincott
		Jeanette Eaton	*Gandhi, Fighter Without a Sword*	Morrow
		Anne Parrish	*The Story of Appleby Capple*	Harper
1950	Medal Winner	Marguerite de Angeli	*The Door in the Wall*	Doubleday
	Honor Books	Rebecca Caudill	*Tree of Freedom*	Viking
		Catherine Coblentz	*The Blue Cat of Castle Town*	Longmans
		Rutherford Montgomery	*Kildee House*	Doubleday
		Genevieve Foster	*George Washington*	Scribner
		Walter and Marion Havighurst	*Song of the Pines: A Story of Norwegian Lumbering in Wisconsin*	Winston
1949	Medal Winner	Marguerite Henry	*King of the Wind*	Rand McNally
	Honor Books	Holling C. Holling	*Seabird*	Houghton
		Louise Rankin	*Daughter of the Mountain*	Viking
		Ruth Stiles Gannett	*My Father's Dragon*	Random House
		Arna Bontemps	*Story of the Negro*	Knopf
1948	Medal Winner	William PPne du Bois	*The Twenty-One Balloons*	Viking
	Honor Books	Claire Huchet Bishop	*Pancakes-Paris*	Viking

Year	Award	Author/Illustrator	Title	Publisher
		Carol Treffinger	*Li Lun, Lad of Courage*	Abingdon
		Catherine Besterman	*The Quaint and Curious Quest of Johnny Longfoot*	Bobbs-Merrill
		Harold Courlander	*The Cow-Tail Switch, and Other West African Stories*	Holt
		Marguerite Henry	*Misty of Chincoteague*	Rand McNally
1947	Medal Winner	Carolyn Sherwin Bailey	*Miss Hickory*	Viking
	Honor Books	Nancy Barnes	*Wonderful Year*	Messner
		Mary and Conrad Buff	*Big Tree*	Viking
		William Maxwell	*The Heavenly Tenants*	Harper
		Cyrus Fisher, pseudonym of Darwin L. Teilhet	*The Avion My Father Flew*	Appleton
		Eleanor Jewett	*The Hidden Treasure of Glaston*	Viking
1946	Medal Winner	Lois Lenski	*Strawberry Girl*	Lippincott
	Honor Books	Marguerite Henry	*Justin Morgan Had a Horse*	Rand McNally
		Florence Crannell Means	*The Moved-Outers*	Houghton
		Christine Weston	*Bhimsa, the Dancing Bear*	Scribner
		Katherine Shippen	*New Found World*	Viking
1945	Medal Winner	Robert Lawson	*Rabbit Hill*	Viking
	Honor Books	Eleanor Estes	*The Hundred Dresses*	Harcourt
		Alice Dalgliesh	*The Silver Pencil*	Scribner
		Genevieve Foster	*Abraham Lincoln's World*	Scribner
		Jeanette Eaton	*Lone Journey: The Life of Roger Williams*	Harcourt
1944	Medal Winner	Esther Forbes	*Johnny Tremain*	Houghton
	Honor Books	Laura Ingalls Wilder	*These Happy Golden Years*	Harper
		Julia Sauer	*Fog Magic*	Viking
		Eleanor Estes	*Rufus M.*	Harcourt
		Elizabeth Yates	*Mountain Born*	Coward
1943	Medal Winner	Elizabeth Janet Gray	*Adam of the Road*	Viking

Year	Award	Author/Illustrator	Title	Publisher
	Honor Books	Eleanor Estes	*The Middle Moffat*	Harcourt
		Mabel Leigh Hunt	*Have You Seen Tom Thumb?*	Lippincott
1942	Medal Winner	Walter Edmonds	*The Matchlock Gun*	Dodd
	Honor Books	Laura Ingalls Wilder	*Little Town on the Prairie*	Harper
		Genevieve Foster	*George Washington's World*	Scribner
		Lois Lenski	*Indian Captive: The Story of Mary Jemison*	Lippincott
		Eva Roe Gaggin	*Down Ryton Water*	Viking
1941	Medal Winner	Armstrong Sperry	*Call It Courage*	Macmillan
	Honor Books	Doris Gates	*Blue Willow*	Viking
		Laura Ingalls Wilder	*The Long Winter*	Harper
		Mary Jane Carr	*Young Mac of Fort Vancouver*	Crowell
		Anna Gertrude Hall	*Nansen*	Viking
1940	Medal Winner	James Daugherty	*Daniel Boone*	Viking
	Honor Books	Kate Seredy	*The Singing Tree*	Viking
		Mabel Robinson	*Runner of the Mountain Tops: The Life of Louis Agassiz*	Random House
		Laura Ingalls Wilder	*By the Shores of Silver Lake*	Harper
		Stephen W. Meader	*Boy with a Pack*	Harcourt
1939	Medal Winner	Elizabeth Enright	*Thimble Summer*	Rinehart
	Honor Books	Valenti Angelo	*Nino*	Viking
		Richard and Florence Atwater	*Mr. Popper's Penguins*	Little, Brown
		Phyllis Crawford	*Hello the Boat!*	Holt
		Jeanette Eaton	*Leader by Destiny: George Washington, Man and Patriot*	Harcourt
		Elizabeth Janet Gray	*Penn*	Viking
1938	Medal Winner	Kate Seredy	*The White Stag*	Viking
	Honor Books	James Cloyd Bowman	*Pecos Bill*	Little, Brown
		Mabel Robinson	*Bright Island*	Random House
		Laura Ingalls Wilder	*On the Banks of Plum Creek*	Harper
1937	Medal Winner	Ruth Sawyer	*Roller Skates*	Viking

Year	Award	Author/Illustrator	Title	Publisher
	Honor Books	Lois Lenski	*Phoebe Fairchild: Her Book*	Stokes
		Idwal Jones	*Whistler's Van*	Viking
		Ludwig Bemelmans	*The Golden Basket*	Viking
		Margary Bianco	*Winterbound*	Viking
		Agnes Hewes	*The Codfish Musket*	Doubleday
		Constance Rourke	*Audubon*	Harcourt
1936	Medal Winner	Carol Ryrie Brink	*Caddie Woodlawn*	Macmillan
	Honor Books	Phil Stong	*Honk, the Moose*	Dodd
		Kate Seredy	*The Good Master*	Viking
		Elizabeth Janet Gray	*Young Walter Scott*	Viking
		Armstrong Sperry	*All Sail Set: A Romance of the Flying Cloud*	Winston
1935	Medal Winner	Monica Shannon	*Dobry*	Viking
	Honor Books	Elizabeth Seeger	*Pageant of Chinese History*	Longmans
		Constance Rourke	*Davy Crockett*	Harcourt
		Hilda Von Stockum	*Day on Skates: The Story of a Dutch Picnic*	Harper
1934	Medal Winner	Cornelia Meigs	*Invincible Louisa: The Story of the Author of Little Women*	Little, Brown
	Honor Books	Caroline Snedeker	*The Forgotten Daughter*	Doubleday
		Elsie Singmaster	*Swords of Steel*	Houghton
		Wanda Gág	*ABC Bunny*	Coward
		Erik Berry, pseud (Allena Best)	*Winged Girl of Knossos*	Appleton
		Sarah Schmidt	*New Land*	McBride
		Padraic Colum	*Big Tree of Bunlahy: Stories of My Own Countryside*	Macmillan
		Agnes Hewes	*Glory of the Seas*	Knopf
		Ann Kyle	*Apprentice of Florence*	Houghton
1933	Medal Winner	Elizabeth Lewis	*Young Fu of the Upper Yangtze*	Winston
	Honor Books	Cornelia Meigs	*Swift Rivers*	Little, Brown
		Hildegarde Hoyt Swift	*The Railroad to Freedom: A Story of the Civil War*	Harcourt

Year	Award	Author/Illustrator	Title	Publisher
		Nora Burglon	*Children of the Soil: A Story of Scandinavia*	Doubleday
1932	Medal Winner	Laura Adams Armer	*Waterless Mountain*	Longmans
	Honor Books	Dorothy P. Lathrop	*The Fairy Circus*	Macmillan
		Rachel Field	*Calico Bush*	Macmillan
		Eunice Tietjens	*Boy of the South Seas*	Coward-McCann
		Eloise Lownsbery	*Out of the Flame*	Longmans
		Marjorie Allee	*Jane's Island*	Houghton
		Mary Gould Davis	*Truce of the Wolf and Other Tales of Old Italy*	Harcourt
1931	Medal Winner	Elizabeth Coatsworth	*The Cat Who Went to Heaven*	Macmillan
	Honor Books	Anne Parrish	*Floating Island*	Harper
		Alida Malkus	*The Dark Star of Itza: The Story of a Pagan Princess*	Harcourt
		Ralph Hubbard	*Queer Person*	Doubleday
		Julie Davis Adams	*Mountains Are Free*	Dutton
		Agnes Hewes	*Spice and the Devil's Cave*	Knopf
		Elizabeth Janet Gray	*Meggy MacIntosh*	Doubleday
		Herbert Best	*Garram the Hunter: A Boy of the Hill Tribes*	Doubleday
		Alice Lide and Margaret Johansen	*Ood-Le-Uk the Wanderer*	Little, Brown
1930	Medal Winner	Rachel Field	*Hitty, Her First Hundred Years*	Macmillan
	Honor Books	Jeanette Eaton	*A Daughter of the Seine: The Life of Madame Roland*	Harper
		Elizabeth Miller	*Pran of Albania*	Doubleday
		Marion Hurd McNeely	*Jumping-Off Place*	Longmans
		Ella Young	*The Tangle-Coated Horse and Other Tales*	Longmans
		Julia Davis Adams	*Vaino*	Dutton
		Hildegarde Hoyt Swift	*Little Blacknose*	Harcourt
1929	Medal Winner	Eric P. Kelly	*The Trumpeter of Krakow*	Macmillan
	Honor Books	John Bennett	*Pigtail of Ah Lee Ben Loo*	Longmans

Year	Award	Author/Illustrator	Title	Publisher
		Wanda Gág	*Millions of Cats*	Coward
		Grace Hallock	*The Boy Who Was*	Dutton
		Cornelia Meigs	*Clearing Weather*	Little, Brown
		Grace Moon	*Runaway Papoose*	Doubleday
		Elinor Whitney	*Tod of the Fens*	Macmillan
1928	Medal Winner	Dhan Gopal Mukerji	*Gay Neck, the Story of a Pigeon*	Dutton
	Honor Books	Ella Young	*The Wonder Smith and His Son*	Longmans
		Caroline Snedeker	*Downright Dencey*	Doubleday
1927	Medal Winner	Will James	*Smoky, the Cowhorse*	Scribner
	Honor Books	None awarded		
1926	Medal Winner	Arthur Bowie Chrisman	*Shen of the Sea*	Dutton
	Honor Book	Padraic Colum	*The Voyagers: Being Legends and Romances of Atlantic Discovery*	Macmillan
1925	Medal Winner	Charles Finger	*Tales from Silver Lands*	Doubleday
	Honor Books	Annie Carroll Moore	*Nicholas: A Manhattan Christmas Story*	Putnam
		Anne Parrish	*The Dream Coach*	Macmillan
1924	Medal Winner	Charles Hawes	*The Dark Frigate*	Little, Brown
	Honor Books	None awarded		
1923	Medal Winner	Hugh Lofting	*The Voyages of Doctor Dolittle*	Lippincott
	Honor Books	None awarded		
1922	Medal Winner	Hendrik Willem van Loon	*The Story of Mankind*	Liveright
	Honor Books	Charles Hawes	*The Great Quest*	Little, Brown
		Bernard Marshall	*Cedric the Forester*	Appleton
		William Bowen	*The Old Tobacco Shop: A True Account of What Befell a Little Boy in Search of Adventure*	Macmillan
		Padraic Colum	*The Golden Fleece and the Heroes Who Lived Before Achilles*	Macmillan
		Cornelia Meigs	*The Windy Hill*	Macmillan

Activities

1. The books that John Newbery published often had very long titles. Children could list short titles of well-known works and "Newbery" them. For example, *Cinderella* could become *Cinderella, or the Story of a Young Woman Who Lost a Slipper and Gained a Prince*.

2. John Newbery was a publisher. The school newspaper or yearbook publisher could speak to the children about the steps in publishing.

3. John Newbery also printed newspapers. Children could write a newspaper article about one of the Newbery winners. They could include who, what, when, why, and how.

4. The Newbery Award has been in existence since 1922. Children could compare and contrast an older award winner and a newer award winner. A Venn diagram would be a good organizational tool.

5. Newbery lived in London. Children could create a timeline of London's history.

6. John Newbery and Randolph Caldecott both lived in England, but they lived during different periods. Children could find a list of inventions and then decide which of the two would have used the article.

7. Avi won the 2003 Newbery Award for *Crispin: The Cross of Lead*. Children could visit Avi's Web site at: http://www.avi-writer.com/ and examine his variety of topics and ages. They could poll their peers and create a frequency table of his most popular books.

8. Russell Freedman was given the 2005 Newbery Honor Award for *The Voice that Challenged a Nation: Marian Anderson and the Struggle for Equal Rights*, the 1994 Newbery Honor Award for *Eleanor Roosevelt: A Life of Discovery*, the 1992 Newbery Honor Award for *The Wright Brothers: How They Invented the Airplane*, and the 1988 Newbery Medal for *Lincoln: A Photobiography*. Children could visit the Internet at: http://www.childrenslit.com/f_freedman.html and read some reviews of his many books. They could read some of his books and then write their own book reviews.

9. Children could create a frequency table of the Newbery authors and find out which author has won the most Newbery Awards.

10. Cynthia Kadohata was awarded the 2005 Newbery Medal for *Kira-Kira*. Children could visit her Web site at: http://www.kira-kira.us/ and read about the author, the book, her baby, and the author's dog. Children could compare their lives to her life.

John Newbery and the John Newbery Medal

Student Handout 1—Information

Who Was John Newbery?

John Newbery was born in 1713, probably on July 9, in Waltham Saint Lawrence in Berkshire, England. He was baptized on July 19, 1713. His father was a farmer. Books were rare and expensive back then, but John read whatever and whenever he could. At age sixteen, he was apprenticed to a printer in the town of Reading. Another printer bought the business, but he died a few years later. The printer, in his will, left the business to his brother and to John Newbery. John married Mary, the widow of the printer, and adopted her three children. The couple had three more children.

John expanded the business, and in 1944, he moved the shop to London. There he sold more than books and newspapers. He sold stationery, patent medicines, and small items like pins and ribbon. He believed that all children should be educated, but he found that few children's books had been written. He decided to produce children's books. He printed his first book for children, premiering on June 18, 1744: *A Little Pretty Pocket-Book, intended for the Instruction and Amusement of little Master Tommy and pretty Miss Polly....* The book cost 6 pence. However, for 2 pence more the buyer could get a pincushion for a girl or a ball for a boy. These items were half red and half black. Every time the child did a good deed, a pin could be placed on the red side. A bad deed got a pin on the black side. Parents hoped more pins were on the red side than on the black side.

A Little Pretty Pocket-Book was an extremely popular book, and it brought fame and fortune to John. This book really changed the type and quality of juvenile literature. The small book fit comfortably in the hands of small children. Brightly colored paper decorated the cover board. The many illustrations appealed to both adults and children. Today most children would not like the book. It was really an alphabet book with behavior rules added here and there.

He published newspapers and more books for adults. However, he liked to print books for children. Sometimes he would publish and sell three children's books in one year. Probably one of the most famous of John's publications was *The History of Little Goody Two-Shoes; Otherwise Called Mrs. Margery Two-Shoes.*

John was both popular and generous. He often loaned money to struggling authors, and he often donated to charities. He was a very busy man. His friends and family truly liked him, but they often felt he was too busy. Sometimes he would arrive at an event only to tell the other guests that he could not stay because he had to attend another event.

One mystery still surrounds John's books for children. Who wrote them? In his day, authors did not put their names on their published books. Some people believe that a famous author, Oliver Goldsmith, wrote them. Other experts think Giles and Griffith Jones, two authors who published other books, were the authors. Some book lovers feel John wrote them himself. Perhaps someday we will find the answer to this mystery.

John began to feel ill in 1767 and was so sick that he made his will. John Newbery died on December 22, 1767, at Canonbury House, Islington. He was buried in the churchyard of Waltham Saint Lawrence, the site of his baptism. No known portrait of John Newbery exists.

What Is the John Newbery Medal?

The John Newbery Medal is given every year to the best children's book published in the United States. It was the first children's award, and the first award was presented in 1922. Honor books are also named. The Association for Library Service to Children (ALSC), a division of the American Library Association, presents the award at a ceremony during its summer meeting.

From *Children's Book Award Handbook* by Diana F. Marks. Westport, CT: Libraries Unlimited. Copyright © 2006.

John Newbery and the John Newbery Medal

Student Handout 2—Questions

Name_____ Date_____

Investigate the life of John Newbery, and find out more about the John Newbery Medal. Then answer the following questions.

1. Where and when was John Newbery born?

2. How did his life change when he was sixteen years old?

3. What happened when his boss died?

4. Why do you think he moved the printing business to London?

5. Why did John start to print children's books?

6. Do you think John wrote the children's books that he published?

7. Where and when did John Newbery die?

8. When was the first John Newbery Medal given?

9. What group chooses the Newbery Medal winners?

10. Make a list of all the John Newbery Medal Books and Award Books you have read.

John Newbery and the John Newbery Medal

Student Handout 3—Creative Activity

Name_____ Date_____

John Newbery was one of the first printers to publish books for children. The titles of some of his books were quite long. For example, one book was *Nurse Truelove's New-Year's-Gift: Or, The Book of Books for Children. Embellished with Cuts; and designed for a Present to every little Boy who would become a great Man, and ride upon a fine Horse; and to every little Girl who would become a great Woman, and ride in a Lord-Mayor's gilt Coach.*

Today children's book titles tend to be short. However, the 2004 Medal recipient, Kate DiCamillo, wrote *The Tale of Despereaux: Being the Story of a Mouse, a Princess, Some Soup, and a Spool of Thread.*

Let's try to "Newbery" some book titles. For example, Linda Sue Park's *A Single Shard* could become *A Single Shard: Or, the Story of a Young Korean Orphan Who Seeks Truth and Beauty and Finds a Skill and a Family along the Way.*

Original Title	"Newbery" Title

From *Children's Book Award Handbook* by Diana F. Marks. Westport, CT: Libraries Unlimited. Copyright © 2006.

John Newbery and the John Newbery Medal

Student Handout 4—Did the Event Happen during His Lifetime?

Name_____ Date_____

John Newbery lived from 1713 to 1767. He was a publisher of children's books, and perhaps he wrote some of them. Below is a list of events. Decide if the event happened during Newbery's lifetime.

Event	Was It Before, During, or After Newbery's Lifetime?	Your Estimate as to the Year of the Event
Elizabeth I was crowned Queen of England.		
Michelangelo died in Rome.		
Buenos Aires became a city with a population of 20,000.		
Galileo identified four new moons of Jupiter.		
The clarinet was invented in Germany.		
The Polaroid camera was patented.		
Mount Vesuvius erupted and buried Pompeii.		
The basketball game was invented.		
John Montague, the fourth Earl of Sandwich, invented the sandwich.		
Marie Antoinette was born in Vienna.		
Jonathan Swift published *Gulliver's Travels*		
The Suez Canal opened.		
Johann Sebastian Bach died.		
Edmund Halley, the discoverer of Halley's Comet, died in England.		
The Oreo was first sold.		

From *Children's Book Award Handbook* by Diana F. Marks. Westport, CT: Libraries Unlimited. Copyright © 2006.

John Newbery and the John Newbery Medal

Student Handout 4—Did the Event Happen during His Lifetime?—Answers

Name_____ Date_____

John Newbery lived from 1713 to 1767. He was a publisher of children's books, and perhaps he wrote some of them. Below is a list of events. Decide if the event happened during Newbery's lifetime.

Event	Was It Before, During, or After Newbery's Lifetime?	Year of the Event
Elizabeth I was crowned Queen of England.	Before	1558
Michelangelo died in Rome.	Before	1564
Buenos Aires became a city. with a population of 20,000.	During	1750
Galileo identified four new moons of Jupiter.	Before	1610
The clarinet was invented in Germany.	Before	1690
The Polaroid camera was patented.	After	1947
Mount Vesuvius erupted and buried Pompeii.	Before	79
The basketball game was invented.	After	1892
John Montague, the fourth Earl of Sandwich, invented the sandwich.	During	1762
Marie Antoinette was born in Vienna.	During	1755
Jonathan Swift published *Gulliver's Travels*	During	1726
The Suez Canal opened.	After	1869
Johann Sebastian Bach died.	During	1750
Edmund Halley, the discoverer of Halley's Comet, died in England.	During	1742
The Oreo was first sold.	After	1912

CHAPTER 15

Scott O'Dell and the
Scott O'Dell Award for Historical Fiction

Overview

The Scott O'Dell Award for Historical Fiction honors the best historical novel written for children. Scott O'Dell wrote over twenty-five children's books, all of them historical fiction.

Scott O'Dell was born in Los Angeles in 1898. Los Angeles back then was a frontier town with horses and wagons. He enlisted during both World War I and World War II. He worked for the silent movie industry, and he wrote historical fiction for adults. In 1960, at around age sixty, he wrote *Island of the Blue Dolphins*, and his life changed. The book won the Newbery Award in 1961. He wrote almost a book a year after that. The settings varied, from a nineteenth-century California bay to a slave revolt in the eighteenth-century Virgin Islands to Cibola during the time of the conquistadors. His books *Sing Down the Moon, The Black Pearl,* and *The King's Fifth* were Newbery Honor Books. O'Dell died in 1989.

Scott O'Dell created the Scott O'Dell Award for Historical Fiction in 1982. The first award was given in 1984. The award recognizes the best historical fiction for the year previous. The O'Dell Award Committee decides upon the winner. The winner receives $5,000.

Scott O'Dell Biography

Odell Gabriel Scott was born in Los Angeles, California, on May 23, 1898, to Bennett Mason Scott and May Elizabeth Gabriel Scott. Los Angeles at the turn of the century was a pioneer town, with horse-drawn vehicles and lots of wild animals. Odell's parents told him he was related to Sir Walter Scott, the British writer. He felt that this literary connection may have been one of the reasons he became a writer.

Odell's family moved often. Their addresses included San Pedro, south of Los Angeles, and Rattlesnake Island. Their house at Rattlesnake Island was built on stilts, and high tides would bring the waves right up to the house. Scott attended a one-room elementary schoolhouse. School was easy for him, and he seldom had to study. He graduated from Long Beach Polytechnic High School, where he had been a track star. In 1918, he joined the army to fight in World War I. He was attending officer's school when the war ended, at which time he was discharged.

For a time Scott wandered from college to college. He attended Occidental College (Los Angeles, California) in 1919, the University of Wisconsin in 1920, and Stanford College from 1920 to 1921. He found that college was much harder than high school. His first job was with Palmer Photoplay Company where he critiqued movie scripts. He became more interested in the newly created silent movie industry, and he was hired first as a set dresser and then as a technical director for Paramount. Later he traveled to Rome with Metro-Goldwyn-Mayer. He was a Technicolor cameraman for the filming of the silent movie version of *Ben Hur*. He published his first book, *Representative Photoplay Analyzed,* in 1924.

Scott returned to Europe to attend the University of Rome in 1925. There he wrote a novel that was never published. He returned to the United States and became a newspaperman. A typesetter made an error and called the reporter Scott O'Dell. He liked the typo and legally changed his name. O'Dell was researching California's history when he came across the true story of Karana, a girl who survived alone for years on an island. He lived for a while on a farm in Julian, California.

O'Dell published *Woman in Spain* in 1934. He enlisted in the air force during World War II; by this time he was over forty years old. He was stationed at Shepherd Field, Texas. He was discharged at the end of the war.

In 1947, he published *Hill of the Hawk*. Six years later, in 1953, he published *Man Alone*, a book he wrote with an ex-convict, and he became the book editor for the *Los Angeles Daily News*. He continued to write for adults, selling stories to newspapers and magazines. He published *Country of the Sun: Southern California, an Informal Guide* in 1957 and *The Sea Is Red* in 1958.

A new career in writing opened up for him in 1960 when *Island of the Blue Dolphins*, a novel about Karana, was published. The book received the Newbery Award in 1961. He wrote only one more book for adults, *The Psychology of Children's Art,* published in 1967. Rhoda Kellogg was his co-author. The rest of his books were written for children. *The King's Fifth* was published in 1966, and it was a Newbery Honor Book the following year. He wrote over twenty other books for children, including two more Newbery Honor Books, *The Black Pearl* and *Sing Down the Moon*.

O'Dell received the Hans Christian Andersen Award in 1972. He continued to write, usually publishing a book a year. In 1976, he published three books: *The 290, Carlota,* and *Zia*. In that same year, he was awarded the University of Southern Mississippi Children's Collection Medallion.

In 1982, O'Dell established the Scott O'Dell Award for Historical Fiction. The first award was presented in 1984. In the same year, he published *Alexandra*. Two years later, he published *Streams to the River, River to the Sea: A Novel of Sacagawea*. That book received the Scott O'Dell Award for Historical Fiction in 1987. He wrote three other books in the late 1980's: *The Serpent Never Sleeps; Black Star, Bright Dawn;* and *My Name Is Not Angelica*.

O'Dell's children's books were all about events that happened in history. He loved researching events in the Western Hemisphere and creating stories around those events. He would research a topic for several months. Writing would then take about six months. He would rise at about 5:00 A.M. Around six o'clock he would start writing, and he would stop around noon. However, during the rest of the day, the story would brew in the back of his mind.

Scott O'Dell died on October 15, 1989. His ashes were scattered over the Pacific Ocean. His wife, Elizabeth Hall, published two more of his books, co-written with her, *Thunder Rolling in the Mountains* and *Venus among the Fishes.*

Scott O'Dell Timeline

Date	Event
1898	Born Odell Gabriel Scott in Los Angeles, California, on May 23 to Bennett Mason Scott and May Elizabeth Gabriel Scott
	Graduated from Long Beach Polytechnic High School
1918	Joined the army; at end of World War I, was discharged
1919	Attended Occidental College
1920	Attended University of Wisconsin
1920–1921	Attended Stanford University
	Technical director for Paramount
	Technicolor cameraman for Metro-Goldwyn-Mayer on filming of *Ben Hur* in Rome
1924	Published *Representative Photoplay Analyzed*
1925	Attended University of Rome Wrote first novel that was never published Returned to United States and became a newspaperman Changed his name legally based on typesetter's error Found story of Karana while researching California's history Lived on a farm in Julian, California
1934	Published *Woman in Spain*
World War II	Enlisted in the army during World War II; stationed at Shepherd Field, Texas
1947	Published *Hill of the Hawk*
1949	Married Dorsa Rattenbury
1953	Published *Man Alone*; became book editor of *Los Angeles Daily News*
1957	Published *Country of the Sun: Southern California, an Informal Guide*
1958	Published *The Sea Is Red*
1960	Published *Island of the Blue Dolphins*
1961	*Island of the Blue Dolphins* received the Newbery Award
1966	Published *The King's Fifth*
1967	Published *The Black Pearl*; co-wrote with Rhoda Kellogg *The Psychology of Children's Art*; *The King's Fifth* became a Newbery Honor Book
1968	Published *The Dark Canoe*; *The Black Pearl* became a Newbery Honor Book
1969	Published *Journey to Jericho*
1970	Published *Sing Down the Moon*
1971	*Sing Down the Moon* became a Newbery Honor Book
1972	Published *The Treasure of Topo-el-Bampo*; received the Hans Christian Andersen Award
1973	Published *The Cruise of the Arctic Dawn*
1974	Published *Child of Fire*

Date	Event
1975	Published *The Hawk That Dare Not Hunt by Day*
1976	Published *The 290* and *Carlota* and *Zia*; awarded University of Southern Mississippi Children's Collection Medallion
1978	Published *Kathleen, Please Come Home*
1979	Published *The Captive*
1980	Published *Sarah Bishop*
1981	Published *The Feathered Serpent*
1982	Published *The Spanish Smile*; created the Scott O'Dell Award for Historical Fiction
1983	Published *The Amethyst Ring* and *The Castle in the Sea*
1984	Published *Alexandra*; first Scott O'Dell Award for Historical Fiction was presented
1985	Published *The Road to Damietta*
1986	Published *Streams to the River, River to the Sea: A Novel of Sacagawea.*
1987	Published *The Serpent Never Sleeps*; received the Scott O'Dell Award for Historical Fiction for *Streams to the River, River to the Sea: A Novel of Sacagawea*
1988	Published *Black Star, Bright Down*
1989	Published *My Name Is Not Angelica*; died on October 15
1992	Published *Thunder Rolling in the Mountain* posthumously (with aid of Elizabeth Hall, wife)
1995	Published *Venus among the Fishes* (with aid of Elizabeth Hall, wife)

History and Criteria of Award

Scott O'Dell created the Scott O'Dell Award for Historical Fiction in 1982. He wanted to encourage writers to create historical fiction. He felt that children could learn from historical fiction. They would therefore be better citizens and decision makers.

The award is presented annually to the best historical novel written in the year previous. Scott O'Dell delineated several rules as to who was eligible for the award.

1. The book must be a work designated specifically for children.

2. The setting must be in the New World (the United States, Central America, South America, Mexico, or Canada).

3. It must be published in the United States.

4. The book must be published in English.

5. The author must be a citizen of the United States.

Zena Sutherland, professor emeritus of Children's Literature at the University of Chicago, was the chair of the O'Dell Award Committee from 1982 until she died in 2002. Today the committee is comprised of editors and librarians.

Scott O'Dell stipulated that the Scott O'Dell Award for Historical Fiction provide the winner with a monetary award of $5,000.

No books were deemed worthy of the award in 1982 or in 1983. The first Scott O'Dell Award for Historical Fiction was presented to Elizabeth George Speare for her book, *The Sign of the Beaver*.

Works by Scott O'Dell

Alexandra. New York: Houghton Mifflin, 1984.

Amethyst Ring, The. New York: Houghton Mifflin, 1983.

Black Pearl, The. New York: Houghton Mifflin, 1967.

Black Star, Bright Dawn. New York: Houghton Mifflin, 1988.

Captive, The. New York: Houghton Mifflin: 1979.

Carlota. New York: Houghton Mifflin, 1977.

Castle in the Sea, The. New York: Houghton Mifflin, 1983.

Child of Fire. New York: Houghton Mifflin, 1974.

Cruise of the Arctic Star. Chicago, IL: G. K. Hall, 1973.

Dark Canoe. New York: Houghton Mifflin, 1968.

Feathered Serpent, The. New York: Houghton Mifflin, 1981.

Hawk That Dare Not Hunt by Day, The. New York: Houghton Mifflin, 1975.

Hill of the Hawk. Indianapolis, IN: Bobbs-Merrill, 1947.

Island of the Blue Dolphins. New York: Houghton Mifflin, 1960.

Journey to Jericho. New York: Houghton Mifflin, 1969.

Kathleen, Please Come Home. New York: Houghton Mifflin, 1978.

King's Fifth. New York: Houghton Mifflin, 1966.

My Name Is Not Angelica. New York: Houghton Mifflin, 1989.

Psychology of Children's Art, The, with Rhoda Kellogg. New York: Random House, 1967.

Road to Damietta, The. New York: Houghton Mifflin, 1985.

Sarah Bishop. New York: Houghton Mifflin, 1980.

Serpent Never Sleeps, The. New York: Houghton Mifflin, 1987.

Sing Down the Moon. New York: Houghton Mifflin, 1970.

Spanish Smile, The. New York: Houghton Mifflin, 1982.

Streams to the River, River to the Sea: A Novel of Sacagawea. New York: Houghton Mifflin, 1986.

Thunder Rolling in the Mountains, with Elizabeth Hall. New York: Houghton Mifflin, 1992.

Treasure of Topo-el-Bampo, The. New York: Houghton Mifflin, 1972.

The 290. New York: Houghton Mifflin, 1976.

Venus among the Fishes, with Elizabeth Hall. New York: Houghton Mifflin, 1995.

Zia. New York: Houghton Mifflin, 1976.

Award Books

Year	Author	Title	Publisher
2006	Louise Erdich	*The Game of Silence*	HarperCollins
2005	A. LaFaye	*Worth*	Simon & Schuster
2004	Richard Peck	*A River Between Us*	Dial Press
2003	Shelley Pearsall	*Trouble Don't Last*	Alfred A. Knopf
2002	Mildred D. Taylor	*The Land*	Phyllis Fogelman Books
2001	Janet Taylor Lisle	*The Art of Keeping Cool*	Richard Jackson Books/Atheneum
2000	Miriam Bat-Ami	*Two Suns in the Sky*	Front Street/Cricket Books
1999	Harriette Robinet	*Forty Acres and Maybe a Mule*	Jean Fritz/Atheneum
1998	Karen Hesse	*Out of the Dust*	Scholastic
1997	Katherine Paterson	*Jip, His Story*	Lodestar/Dutton
1996	Theodore Taylor	*The Bomb*	Harcourt, Brace
1995	Graham Salisbury	*Under the Blood-Red Sun*	Delacorte
1994	Paul Fleischman	*Bull Run*	Laura Geringer/HarperCollins, 1996
1993	Michael Dorris	*Morning Girl*	Hyperion
1992	Mary Downing Hahn	*Stepping on the Cracks*	Clarion
1991	Pieter Van Raven	*A Time of Troubles*	Charles Scribner's Sons
1990	Carolyn Reeder	*Shades of Grey*	Macmillan
1989	Lyll Becerra de Jenkins	*The Honorable Prison*	Lodestar/Dutton
1988	Patricia Beatty	*Charley Skedaddle*	Morrow
1987	Scott O'Dell	*Streams to the River, River to the Sea: A Novel of Sacagawea*	Houghton Mifflin
1986	Patricia MacLachlan	*Sarah, Plain and Tall*	Harper & Row
1985	Avi	*The Fighting Ground*	Lippincott
1984	Elizabeth George Speare	*The Sign of the Beaver*	Houghton Mifflin

Activities

1. Children could research the settings of the books by Scott O'Dell. Then they could mark those locations on a large map.

2. *Island of the Blue Dolphins* was O'Dell's first children's book. Students could locate facts about the various types of dolphins and create a multimedia presentation about them.

3. A. Lafaye won the Scott O'Dell Award for Historical Fiction in 2005. Children could visit her Web site at: http://www.alafaye.com/ and learn about her pets. They could write letters about their pets to her. They could also read reviews of the award-winning book, *Worth*.

4. Paul Fleischman received the Scott O'Dell Award for Historical Fiction in 1994 for *Bull Run*. Children could present parts of the book as reader's theater. Children can visit Fleischman's Web site at: http://www.paulfleischman.net/works.htm.

5. Patricia MacLachlan received the Scott O'Dell Award for Historical Fiction in 1986 for *Sarah, Plain and Tall*. Children could visit her Web site at: http://www.harperchildrens. com/authorintro/index.asp?authorid=12425 and find out why she carries prairie dirt around with her. They could write a description of one of their favorite possessions.

6. Older children could read *The Black Pearl*, by Scott O'Dell. Then they could form groups and research pearls, pearl diving, and manta rays. Then they could make a poster and share their research.

7. Children could read *Streams to the River, River to the Sea: A Novel of Sacagawea* by Scott O'Dell. They could make a timeline of the Lewis and Clark Expedition. A good Web site is: http://www.pbs.org/lewisandclark/inside/saca.html.

8. Carolyn Reeder received the Scott O'Dell Award for Historical Fiction in 1990 for *Shades of Grey*. Children could visit her Web site at: http://www.reederbooks.com/ and see what else she has written. They could create a chart of her books and the subject matter.

9. Scott O'Dell worked in the silent movie industry for a time. Children could take a scene from one of his books or from an award-winning book and present it as a silent movie.

10. Shelley Pearsall's award-winning book, *Trouble Don't Last*, is about the Underground Railroad. Children may want to go to the Web site: http://www.nationalgeographic. com/railroad/j1.html and find out more about the Underground Railroad. They could mark major Underground Railroad routes on a large map.

Scott O'Dell and the Scott O'Dell Award for Historical Fiction

Student Handout 1—Information

Who Was Scott O'Dell?

Odell Gabriel Scott was born in Los Angeles, California, on May 23, 1898. Los Angeles then was a pioneer town, with horse-drawn vehicles and many wild animals. His parents told him he was related to Sir Walter Scott, the British writer. He felt that this literary connection might have been one of the reasons he became a writer.

His family moved often. Addresses included San Pedro, south of Los Angles, and Rattlesnake Island. Their house on Rattlesnake Island was on stilts, and high tide would bring the waves right up to the house. Scott attended a one-room elementary schoolhouse. School was easy for him, and he seldom had to study. He graduated from Long Beach Polytechnic High School, where he had been a track star. In 1918, he joined the army to fight in World War I. He was attending officer's school when the war ended. He was discharged.

Scott attended several colleges from 1920 to 1921. He found that college was much harder than high school. His first job was with Palmer Photoplay Company where he critiqued movie scripts. Then he worked for the silent movie industry. He traveled to Rome with Metro-Goldwyn-Mayer where he was a cameraman for the filming of the silent movie version of *Ben Hur*. Scott attended the University of Rome in 1925. He returned to the United States and became a newspaperman. A typesetter made an error and called the reporter Scott O'Dell. He liked the typo and legally changed his name. He published *Woman in Spain* in 1934.

Scott enlisted in the air force during World War II. By that time, he was over forty years old. He was stationed at Shepherd Field, Texas. He was discharged at the end of the war.

In 1947, he published *Hill of the Hawk*. Four years later, in 1953, he published *Man Alone*, a book he wrote with an ex-convict, and he became the book editor for the Los Angeles Daily News. He continued to write for adults, selling stories to newspapers and magazines. A new career in writing opened up for him in 1960 when *Island of the Blue Dolphins* was published. The book received the Newbery Award in 1961. *The King's Fifth* was published in 1966, and it was a Newbery Honor Book the following year. He wrote over twenty other books for children, including two more Newbery Honor Books, *The Black Pearl* and *Sing Down the Moon*. O'Dell received the Hans Christian Andersen Award in 1972. He continued to write, publishing usually a book a year. In 1976, he was awarded the University of Southern Mississippi Children's Collection Medallion.

In 1982, O'Dell established the Scott O'Dell Award for Historical Fiction. The first award was presented in 1984. In the same year, he published *Alexandra*. Two years later, he published *Streams to the River, River to the Sea: A Novel of Sacagawea*. That book received the Scott O'Dell Award for Historical Fiction in 1987. O'Dell's children's books were all about events that happened in history. He loved researching events in the Western Hemisphere and creating stories around those events. He would research a topic for several months. Writing would then take about six months. Scott O'Dell died on October 15, 1989.

What Is the Scott O'Dell Award for Historical Fiction?

Scott O'Dell created the Scott O'Dell Award for Historical Fiction in 1982. The award recognizes the best historical fiction written for children in the year previous to the award. The first award was given in 1984. The O'Dell Award Committee decides upon the winner. The book's setting must be somewhere in the Western Hemisphere. The book must be published in the United States, and it must be published in English. The winner receives $5,000.

From *Children's Book Award Handbook* by Diana F. Marks. Westport, CT: Libraries Unlimited. Copyright © 2006.

Scott O'Dell and the Scott O'Dell Award for Historical Fiction

Student Handout 2—Questions

Name_____ Date_____

Investigate the life of Scott O'Dell, and find out more about the Scott O'Dell Award for Historical Fiction. Then answer the following questions.

1. Where and when was Scott O'Dell born?

2. What was his name when he was born?

3. What was his school like?

4. What kinds of jobs did Scott have before he became a writer?

5. How did he get the name Scott O'Dell?

6. List at least three books that he wrote.

7. When did he die?

8. What is the Scott O'Dell Award for Historical Fiction?

9. List at least two rules the book committee must follow.

10. How do you think historical fiction is different from fiction?

From *Children's Book Award Handbook* by Diana F. Marks. Westport, CT: Libraries Unlimited. Copyright © 2006.

Scott O'Dell and the Scott O'Dell Award for Historical Fiction

Student Handout 3—Odd Place Out

Name_____ Date_____

Scott O'Dell created the Scott O'Dell Award for Historical Fiction. One of his rules was that the setting for award-winning books must be somewhere in the Western Hemisphere. Below you will find some riddles about places that for the most part are in the Western Hemisphere. Circle the place that does not belong with the others. On the line, state why it is "odd." Use a map to help you.

1. New York, West Virginia, Maryland, North Carolina _____

2. United States, Uruguay, Canada, Mexico _____

3. Costa Rica, Panama, Canada, Nicaragua _____

4. Missouri, Massachusetts, Rhode Island, Connecticut _____

5. Ohio, Nevada, Iowa, Utah _____

6. Brazil, Jamaica, Puerto Rico, Cuba _____

7. Toronto, Saskatchewan, Alberta, Nova Scotia _____

8. Buenos Aires, Havana, San Francisco, Chile _____

9. Delaware, Rhode Island, Connecticut, Texas _____

10. Argentina, Haiti, Bolivia, Ecuador _____

11. Gulf of Mexico, Caribbean Sea, North Sea, Pacific Ocean _____

12. Georgia, Nebraska, North Carolina, South Carolina _____

13. Alps, Andes, Rockies, Cascades _____

14. Amazon, Mississippi, Rio Grande, Atacama _____

15. Mexico City, Houston, Bismarck, São Paulo _____

Scott O'Dell and the Scott O'Dell Award for Historical Fiction

Student Handout 3—Odd Place Out—Answers

Name_____ Date_____

Note: The following are good answers. However, children could also have different but good answers.

1. Maryland—the other states have two-word names

2. Uruguay—the other countries are in North America

3. Canada—the other countries are in Central America

4. Missouri—the other states are in New England

5. Nevada— the other states have exactly four letters in their names

6. Brazil—the other places are islands

7. Toronto—the other places are provinces in Canada; Toronto is a city

8. Chile—the other places are cities

9. Texas—the other places are small states

10. Haiti—the other places are countries in South America

11. North Sea—the other bodies of water are in the Western Hemisphere

12. Nebraska—the other states are in the South

13. Alps—the other mountains are in the Western Hemisphere; the Alps are in the Eastern Hemisphere

14. Atacama—the other places are rivers; the Atacama is a desert

15. Bismarck—the other cities are big

Scott O'Dell and the Scott O'Dell Award for Historical Fiction

Student Handout 4—Dolphins

Name_____ Date_____

Scott O'Dell wrote several books for adults. However, he became famous when he published *Island of the Blue Dolphins* in 1960. The book, a Newbery Medal winner, is about a girl, Karana, marooned on an island.

After the book was published, dolphins and Scott O'Dell's name were often linked together. Let's find out what you know about dolphins. Below are some true-false statements. If the statement is true, write the word "true" after it. If the statement is false, write the word "false" after it. Then change the false sentence to a true sentence.

1. Dolphins are fish. _____

2. Some species of dolphin can grow to be 30 feet long. _____

3. Dolphins have only about ten teeth. _____

4. Dolphins may be one of the smartest animals. _____

5. Dolphins have a poor sense of smell, but they have a great sense of hearing. _____

6. Dolphins are herbivores. _____

7. Dolphins can stay under water for as long as an hour at a time. _____

8. A group of dolphins is called a herd. _____

9. Only about five types of dolphin exist. _____

10. Dolphins like to be around people. _____

Scott O'Dell and the Scott O'Dell Award for Historical Fiction

Student Handout 4—Dolphins—Answers

Name_____ Date_____

Scott O'Dell wrote several books for adults. However, he became famous when he published *Island of the Blue Dolphins* in 1960. The book, a Newbery Medal winner, is about a girl, Karana, marooned on an island.

After the book was published, dolphins and Scott O'Dell's name were often linked together. Let's find out what you know about dolphins. Below are some true-false statements. If the statement is true, write the word "true" after it. If the statement is false, write the word "false" after it. Then change the false sentence to a true sentence.

1. Dolphins are fish. False, dolphins are mammals.

2. Some species of dolphin can grow to be 30 feet long. True

3. Dolphins have only about ten teeth. False, they may have up to 250 teeth.

4. Dolphins may be one of the smartest animals. True

5. Dolphins have a poor sense of smell, but they have a great sense of hearing. True

6. Dolphins are herbivores. False, dolphins are carnivores.

7. Dolphins can stay under water for as long as an hour at a time. False, they can stay under water for about fifteen minutes at a time.

8. A group of dolphins is called a herd. False, a group is called a pod or school.

9. Only about five types of dolphin exist. False, at least thirty types exist.

10. Dolphins like to be around people. True

From *Children's Book Award Handbook* by Diana F. Marks. Westport, CT: Libraries Unlimited. Copyright © 2006.

CHAPTER 16

Edgar Allan Poe and the Edgar Award

Overview

The Edgar Awards honor the best mystery writers in many different categories. Two awards are reserved for children's books, the juvenile award and the young adult award. Edgar Allan Poe was a master at writing mystery and horror stories.

Although Edgar Allan Poe considered himself a Southerner, he was born in Boston in 1809. His father abandoned the family, and his mother died when Edgar was quite young. He was raised by the Allan family, and he took their last name as his middle name. He battled alcoholism for most of his life. He perfected the short story, created the detective genre, and penned many poems (among others, "The Raven," "The Pit and the Pendulum," and "Annabel Lee"), yet he barely made enough money to pay all the bills. He married his cousin, a thirteen-year-old, only to watch her die of tuberculosis when she was twenty-four. He died in 1849.

Mystery Writers of America, formed in 1945, sponsors the yearly Edgar Awards. Publishers, writers, and agents may submit books for consideration. The books under consideration are announced on the first Thursday in February, and the winners are announced at the annual Edgar Award banquet. The event is hosted in New York City in late April or early May. The winners receive a small bust of Edgar Allan Poe.

Edgar Allan Poe Biography

Edgar Allan Poe was a gifted writer. He created the police detective genre, and he was a master of horror stories. He wrote at least thirty-one poems, sixty-seven short stories, and two novels. He wrote countless other articles and reviews. He never wrote anything specifically for children, but children do like to read "The Raven" and some of his other works. His personal life was filled with tragedy. He battled alcoholism, and he struggled all his life to provide financially for himself and his family. He died at a young age. Many people admired his work, but few wanted to be his friend.

Edgar Poe was born on January 19, 1809, to David Poe and Eliza Arnold Hopkins Poe in Boston, Massachusetts. Eliza Poe was an accomplished English actress; David Poe became an actor so that he could be around the woman he loved. However, David drank to excess, and the couple fought often. Edgar was their second son. Henry Poe, their first son, was born in 1807. In 1810, David Poe deserted his family, and his mother gave birth to a daughter, Rosalie. In late 1811, Eliza became very ill. On December 8 of that year, Eliza died at age twenty-four from tuberculosis, and young Edgar Poe came under the care of Frances and John Allan. (Frances Allan had been acquainted with

Poe's mother.) Edgar took their last name, Allan, as his middle name. They had no children of their own. Frances loved Poe dearly, and she lavished him with attention and material goods. John, on the other hand, did not seem to care for him. John felt that Poe showed little ambition and little gratitude. John Allan and a partner owned a successful general store.

The Allan family, including Poe, moved to London, England, in 1815 to establish a branch business. Poe attended a local school for two years. Then he enrolled in Manor House, a boarding school, in Stoke Newington, England. In 1820, the branch office failed, and the family moved to Richmond, Virginia. The general store failed in 1824, and John Allan faced a risky future. However, Allan's uncle died, and suddenly the family was quite rich.

In 1825, Poe fell in love with Sarah Elmira Royster. They became secretly engaged. In February 1826, Poe entered the University of Virginia, but Allan withdrew him from the university because the young man had accumulated large debts. Poe returned to Sarah, only to find out she was going to marry another man. Two years later Poe and Allan argued violently and Poe moved to Boston. After trying to find work for seven weeks, Poe enlisted in the army. He privately published *Tamerlane and Other Poems*.

Poe excelled in the army, and he moved with his regiment to Fort Monroe, Virginia. There in the next year he became a sergeant major. He wanted to go to West Point, and he asked Allan to help him financially and politically. However, Frances Allan died on February 28, 1829. Poe knew that no one could intercede on his behalf and that John Allan would probably not help him enter West Point. Deeply distraught by the event, Poe hired a stand-in and resigned from the army on April 15. He stayed for some time with his aunt Maria Clemm and her young daughter Virginia Clemm in Baltimore, Maryland. He published *Al Aaraaf, Tamerlane, and Minor Poems*. Critics gave the book good reviews, and Poe became somewhat famous.

In 1830, Poe entered West Point Military Academy, hoping that John Allan would provide financial aid, but Allan had remarried and cut Poe out of his will. Poe argued with Allan when he realized that he would not inherit anything from Allan's estate. Poe also knew he could never be rich as a military officer. Wanting desperately to leave West Point, he began breaking many of the academy's rules. The following year he was court-martialed, and he left West Point. That year he published *Poems* in New York City, and he again stayed with the Clemm family in Baltimore. The family struggled to make ends meet, and he helped them financially

At this time Poe entered several short stories in short story contests. His "MS. Found in a Bottle" won a story contest in 1833. Two years later the *Southern Literary Messenger* hired him to be an editor at ten dollars a week, and he moved the Clemm family to Richmond. He fell in love with Virginia, and they married on May 16, 1836. She was thirteen years old, and he was twenty-seven. Just months later, in December, however, he was fired from his job because he had been drinking too much. Edgar, Virginia, and Maria then moved to New York City where he wrote the novel, *The Narrative of Arthur Gordon Pym*. The following year they moved to Philadelphia. In 1839, he became an editor at *Burton's Gentleman's Magazine*; *Burton's* published "The Fall of the House of Usher" in September.

In 1840, Poe quit his job and published *Tales of the Grotesque and Arabesque*. In November, he discovered that Burton had sold the magazine to George Rex Graham. Poe became an editor at *Graham's Magazine* at $800 a year plus four dollars per page of original Poe material published in the magazine. He published "The Murders in the Rue Morgue," the first detective story, in April. Poe's contributions to the magazine were substantial: by February 1843, the number of magazine subscriptions had jumped from 5,000 to 40,000.

In 1842, Virginia developed tuberculosis. Poe quit his job at *Graham's Magazine*, but during this period he published some of his most famous stories, including "The Mystery of Marie Roget," "The Masque of the Red Death," "The Pit and the Pendulum," and "The Tell-Tale Heart." Despite his apparent success, he was still struggling financially. A friend suggested he apply for a government job in Washington, D.C, that would have paid $1,500 a year. He arranged for an interview, but he became nervous and started to drink. He became drunk and missed the meeting.

In 1843, Poe continued to publish, writing "The Gold Bug" and "The Black Cat." The following year he moved to New York City and took a job at the *Mirror* newspaper. The year after that, he published "The Raven" in the *American Whig Review*. The poem was a huge success. Poe became a partner at *The Broadway Journal*, but the paper did not survive the year.

Poe next moved his family to Fordham, New York, in 1846. There he published "The Cask of Amontillado." Virginia died on January 30, 1847 at age twenty-four. Upon her death, Poe fell into a deep depression and wondered if he could live without her. In that same year, he wrote the essay, "Eureka" and published the poem "Ulalume."

Poe gave a lecture in Lowell, Massachusetts, in 1848. There he met and fell in love with Nancy "Annie" Richmond, but she had a husband and a daughter. Then he fell in love with Sarah Helen Whitman. He attempted suicide in Boston in November, but Sarah Helen Whitman still agreed to marry him. She broke the engagement later when she found out he had broken his promise to abstain from liquor.

In 1849, Poe published "Annabel Lee" and received an offer from an admirer to publish his own literary magazine, *The Stylus*. He became engaged to Elmira Royster Shelton, the woman he had loved so many years before, and they decided to marry on October 17. On September 27, 1849, he started a boat trip from Richmond to New York City to organize and consolidate his possessions and business arrangements. However, he was found ill and almost unconscious on a Baltimore street on October 3. For several days, he experienced fever and pain. The doctors could do little to help him. They were not even sure what had caused his illness. Edgar Allan Poe died in Washington Hospital in Baltimore on October 7, 1849. His death notice was published throughout the country. While people mourned the loss of the writer, few people seemed to miss Edgar Allan Poe the man.

The first Edgar Award for children was given in 1961 to Phyllis A. Whitney for *The Mystery of the Haunted Pool*.

Edgar Allan Poe Timeline

Date	Event
1809	Born to David Poe and Eliza Poe in Boston, Massachusetts, on January 19
1810	David Poe left family; Eliza gave birth to Rosalie on December 20
1811	Eliza died in Richmond, Virginia, on December 8; young Poe entered home of Frances and John Allan; took the name Edgar Allan Poe
1815	Moved to London, England, with Allan family
1818	Attended Manor House (boarding school) in Stoke Newington, England
1820	Returned to Richmond with Allan family in August
1825	Fell in love with Sarah Elmira Royster
1826	Entered University of Virginia in February; Allan withdrew him in December when Poe accumulated large debts
1827	Argued with Allan; moved to Boston; in May enlisted in army; published *Tamerlane and Other Poems*
1828	Moved with his regiment to Fort Monroe, Virginia
1829	Gained rank of sergeant major; Frances Allan died on February 28; Poe hired a stand-in and was discharged from the army on April 15; visited his aunt Maria Clemm and her daughter Virginia Clemm in Baltimore, Maryland; published *Al Aaraaf, Tamerlane and Minor Poems*
1830	Entered Military Academy at West Point; had argument with John Allan
1831	Was court-martialed and left West Point; published *Poems* in New York City; returned to Clemm family in Baltimore
1833	"MS. Found in a Bottle" won a story contest
1835	Took a job with *Southern Literary Messenger*; moved the Clemm family to Richmond
1836	Married Virginia Clemm (thirteen years old) on May 16; was fired from job in December because of drinking problem
1837	Moved to New York City and wrote *The Narrative of Arthur Gordon Pym*
1838	Moved to Philadelphia
1839	Became an editor at *Burton's Gentleman's Magazine*; *Burton's* published "The Fall of the House of Usher" in September
1840	Quit job and published *Tales of the Grotesque and Arabesque*; in November Burton sold magazine to George Rex Graham
1841	Took job as editor at *Graham's Magazine*; published "The Murders in the Rue Morgue" in April
1842	Learned Virginia had tuberculosis; left his job at *Graham's*; published "The Mystery of Marie Roget," "The Masque of the Red Death," "The Pit and the Pendulum," and "The Tell-Tale Heart"; tried to get a government job but became drunk and missed the meeting
1843	Wrote "The Gold Bug" and "The Black Cat"
1844	Moved to New York City; published "The Balloon Hoax"; took a job at the *Mirror* newspaper
1845	Published "The Raven" in *Evening Mirror* in January; became a partner at *The Broadway Journal*; published *Tales and The Raven and Other Poems*; *Broadway Journal* went out of business in December
1846	Moved to Fordham, New York; published "The Cask of Amontillado"

Date	Event
1847	Virginia died on January 30; wrote "Eureka"; published "Ulalume" in December
1848	Gave lecture in Lowell, Massachusetts; fell in love with Nancy "Annie" Richmond; fell in love with Sarah Helen Whitman; attempted suicide in Boston in November; became engaged to Sarah Helen Whitman; Whitman decided against marrying Poe because of his alcoholism
1849	Published "Annabel Lee"; was given a chance to create his own magazine, *The Stylus*; became engaged to Elmira Royster Shelton, his love of long ago; started on a journey to New York City on September 27 to organize his affairs; was found ill in Baltimore on October 3; died in Washington College Hospital in Baltimore on October 7

Works by Edgar Allan Poe

"Al Aaraaf," 1829

"Alone," 1830

"Angel of the Odd, - An Extravaganza, The," 1850

"Annabel Lee," 1849

"Assignation, The," 1834

"Balloon-Hoax, The," 1850

"Bells, The," 1849

"Berenice," 1835

"Black Cat, The," 1843

"Bon-Bon," 1850

"Bridal Ballad," 1837

"Business Man, The," 1850

"Cask of Amontillado, The," 1846

"City in the Sea, The," 1831

"Coliseum, The," 1833

"Colloquy of Monos and Una," 1850

"Conqueror Worm, The," 1843

"Conversation of Eiros and Charmion, The," 1850

"Criticism," 1850

"Daguerreotype, The," 1840

"Descent into the Maelstrom, A," 1841

"Devil in the Belfry, The," 1850

"Diddling—Considered As One of the Exact Sciences," 1850

"Doman of Arnheim, The," 1850

"Dream, A," 1827

"Dream within a Dream, A," 1827

"Dreamland," 1844

"Dreams," 1827

"Duc de l'Omelette, The," 1850

"Eldorado," 1849

"Eleonora," 1850

"Elizabeth," 1850

"Enigma, An," 1848

"Eulalie," 1845

"Evening Star," 1827

"Facts in the Case of M. Valdemar, The," 1845

"Fairy-Land," 1829

"Fall of the House of Usher, The," 1839

"For Annie," 1849

"Four Beasts in One—The Homo-Cameleopard," 1850

"Gold-Bug, The," 1843

"Hans Phaall," 1850

"Happiest Day, the Happiest Hour, The," 1827

"Haunted Palace, The," 1839

"Ho-Frog or the Eight Chained Ourang-Outangs," 1850

"How to Write a Blackwood Article," 1850

"Hymn," 1835

"Imp of the Perverse, The," 1850

"In Youth I Have Known One," 1827

"Island of the Fay, The," 1850

"Israfel," 1831

"Journal of Julius Rodman, The," 1840

"King Pest—A Tale Containing an Allegory," 1835

"Lake, The. To—," 1827

"Landor's Cottage—A Pendant to 'The Domain of Arnheim,' " 1850

"Landscape Garden, The," 1850

"Lenore," 1831

"Ligeia," 1838

"Lionizing," 1850

"Literary Life of Thingum Bob, Esq.—Late Editor of the Goosetherumfoodle—By Himself," 1850

"Loss of Breath—A Tale Neither In Nor Out of 'Blackwood,' 1850

"Man of the Crowd, The," 1850

"Man That Was Used Up—A Tale of the Late Bugaboo and Kickapoo Campaign, The," 1850

"Marginalia," 1844–1849

"Masque of the Red Death, The," 1842

"Mellonta Tauta," 1850

"Mesmeric Revelation," 1850

"Metzengerstein," 1850

"Morella," 1850

"Morning on the Wissahiccon," 1850

"MS. Found in a Bottle," 1833

"Murders in the Rue Morgue, The," 1841

"Mystery of Marie Roget—A Sequel to 'The Murder in the Rue Morgue,' The," 1850

"Mystification," 1850

Narrative of Arthur Gordon Pym of Nantucket, The, 1850

"Never Bet the Devil Your Head—A Tale with a Moral," 1850

"Oblong Box, The," 1850

"Oval Portrait, The," 1850

History and Criteria of Award

Edgar Allan Poe died in 1849, and the first Edgar Award devoted to juvenile mysteries was given in 1961.

The Edgar Awards honor the best mystery writers. The Mystery Writers of America organization, with offices in New York City, oversees the Edgar Awards. About twelve people who wanted to promote the mystery genre and protect the rights of the authors organized the Mystery Writers of America in 1945. They organized their first large meeting, and over fifty people attended. Some of the attendees were still in military uniform, having served in World War II.

The group felt that one way to promote the mystery genre was to create an award for the best first mystery novel. The group decided to honor their "patron saint," Edgar Allan Poe, by naming the awards after him. Peter Williams created the Edgar bust given to the winners. The first Edgar Awards were given in 1946, but no category for children existed at that time. As years passed, other award categories were added. The first time an Edgar was awarded for juvenile literature was in 1961 to Phyllis A. Whitney for her book, *The Mystery of the Haunted Pool.* The first Edgar awarded for young adult literature went to Sonia Levitin in 1989 for her book, *Incident at Loring Groves.*

The rules for eligibility for the award are simple.

1. The book must have been published in the year prior to the award.

2. The book must have been published in the United States.

3. Foreign books published in prior years will be considered only if the American publication is in the year prior to the award.

4. The best children's mystery award and the best young adult mystery could be either hardbound or paperback.

5. The best children's mystery award should appeal to children from preschool up to age twelve.

6. The best young adult mystery should appeal to people twelve and older.

7. A committee for each award reviews submissions and determines the winner.

The winners receive busts of Edgar Allan Poe.

Award Books

Year	Award	Author/Illustrator	Title	Publisher
2005	Best Juvenile	Blue Balliett and Brett Helquist	*Chasing Vermeer*	Scholastic
	Best Young Adult	Dorothy and Thomas Hoobler	*In Darkness, Death*	Philomel Books
2004	Best Juvenile	Phyllis Reynolds Naylor	*Bernie Magruder and the Bats in the Belfry*	Simon & Schuster/Atheneum
	Best Young Adult	Graham McNamee	*Acceleration*	Wendy Lamb Books
2003	Best Juvenile	Helen Ericson	*Harriet Spies Again*	Random House/Delacorte
	Best Young Adult	Daniel Parker	*The Wessex Papers, Vols. 1–3*	Avon
2002	Best Juvenile	Lillian Eige	*Dangling*	Simon & Schuster/Atheneum
	Best Young Adult	Tim Wynne-Jones	*The Boy in the Burning House*	Farrar, Straus & Giroux
2001	Best Juvenile	Frances O'Roark Dowell	*Dovey Coe*	Simon & Schuster
	Best Young Adult	Elaine Marie Alphin	*Counterfeit Son*	Harcourt
2000	Best Juvenile	Elizabeth McDavid Jones	*The Night Flyers*	Pleasant Company Publications
	Best Young Adult	Vivian Vande Velde	*Never Trust a Dead Man*	Harcourt
1999	Best Juvenile	Wendelin Van Draanen	*Sammy Keyes and the Hotel Thief*	Knopf
	Best Young Adult	Nancy Werlin	*The Killer's Cousin*	Delacorte
1998	Best Juvenile	Barbara Brooks Wallace	*Sparrows in the Scullery*	Atheneum
	Best Young Adult	Will Hobbs	*Ghost Canoe*	Morrow Junior Books
1997	Best Juvenile	Dorothy Reynolds Miller	*The Clearing*	Atheneum
	Best Young Adult	Willo Davis Roberts	*Twisted Summer*	Atheneum
1996	Best Juvenile	Nancy Springer	*Looking for Jamie Bridger*	Dial
	Best Young Adult	Rob MacGregor	*Prophecy Rock*	Simon & Schuster

Year	Award	Author/Illustrator	Title	Publisher
1995	Best Juvenile	Willo Davis Roberts	*The Absolutely True Story ... How I Visited Yellowstone Park with the Terrible Rupes*	Atheneum
	Best Young Adult	Nancy Springer	*Toughing It*	Harcourt
1994	Best Juvenile	Barbara Brooks Wallace	*The Twin in the Tavern*	Atheneum
	Best Young Adult	Joan Lowery Nixon	*The Name of the Game Was Murder*	Delacorte
1993	Best Juvenile	Eve Bunting	*Coffin on a Case!*	HarperCollins
	Best Young Adult	Chap Reaver	*A Little Bit Dead*	Delacorte
1992	Best Juvenile	Betsy Byars	*Wanted...Mud Blossom*	Delacorte
	Best Young Adult	Theodore Taylor	*The Weirdo*	Harcourt
1991	Best Juvenile	Pam Conrad	*Stonewords*	Harper & Row
	Best Young Adult	Chap Reaver	*Mote*	Delacorte
1990	Best Juvenile	No Award		
	Best Young Adult	Alane Ferguson	*Show Me the Evidence*	Bradbury
1989	Best Juvenile	Willo Davis Roberts	*Megan's Island*	Atheneum
	Best Young Adult	Sonia Levitin	*Incident at Loring Groves*	Dial
1988	Best Juvenile	Susan Shreve	*Lucy Forever and Mrs. Rosetree, Shrinks*	Henry Holt
1987	Best Juvenile	Joan Lowery Nixon	*The Other Side of Dark*	Delacorte
1986	Best Juvenile	Patricia Windsor	*The Sandman's Eyes*	Delacorte
1985	Best Juvenile	Phyllis Reynolds Naylor	*Night Cry*	Atheneum
1984	Best Juvenile	Cynthia Voigt	*The Callender Papers*	Atheneum
1983	Best Juvenile	Robbie Branscum	*The Murder of Hound Dog Bates*	Viking
1982	Best Juvenile	Norma Fox Mazer	*Taking Terri Mueller*	Avon
1981	Best Juvenile	Joan Lowery Nixon	*The Séance*	Harcourt
1980	Best Juvenile	Joan Lowery Nixon	*The Kidnapping of Christina Lattimore*	Harcourt
1979	Best Juvenile	Dana Brookins	*Alone In Wolf Hollow*	Seabury Press
1978	Best Juvenile	Eloise Jarvis McGraw	*A Really Weird Summer*	Atheneum
1977	Best Juvenile	Richard Peck	*Are You in the House Alone?*	Viking

Year	Award	Author/Illustrator	Title	Publisher
1976	Best Juvenile	Robert C. O'Brien	*Z for Zachariah*	Atheneum
1975	Best Juvenile	Jay Bennett	*The Dangling Witness*	Delacorte
1974	Best Juvenile	Jay Bennett	*The Long Black Coat*	Delacorte
1973	Best Juvenile	Robb White	*Deathwatch*	Doubleday
1972	Best Juvenile	Joan Aiken	*Nightfall*	Holt, Rinehart & Winston
1971	Best Juvenile	John Rowe Townsend	*The Intruder*	Lippincott
1970	Best Juvenile	Winfred Finlay	*Danger at Black Dyke*	S. G. Phillips
1969	Best Juvenile	Virginia Hamilton	*The House of Dies Drear*	Macmillan
1968	Best Juvenile	Gretchen Sprague	*Signpost to Terror*	Dodd, Mead
1967	Best Juvenile	Kin Platt	*Sinbad and Me*	Chilton
1966	Best Juvenile	Leon Ware	*The Mystery of 22 East*	Westminster Press
1965	Best Juvenile	Marcella Thum	*Mystery at Crane's Landing*	Dodd, Mead
1964	Best Juvenile	Phyllis A. Whitney	*Mystery of the Hidden Hand*	Westminster Press
1963	Best Juvenile	Scott Corbett	*Cutlass Island*	Little, Brown
1962	Best Juvenile	Edward Fenton	*The Phantom of Walkaway Hill*	Doubleday
1961	Best Juvenile	Phyllis A. Whitney	*The Mystery of the Haunted Pool*	Westminster Press

Activities

1. Edgar Allan Poe was born in Boston, but he also lived in Virginia, Pennsylvania, and New York. He died in Maryland. Children could locate all these states on a large map. They could also figure out why he chose to live in these places.

2. Edgar Allan Poe wrote poems, short stories, novels, essays, and a play. Children could take a poll of their peers and find out which type of literature the majority of the group prefers.

3. Children could make a frequency table of the recipients of the Edgar Awards and find out which author has received the most awards.

4. Poe was adopted by the Allan family after his mother died. Children could decide what Poe's life would have been like if his mother had lived. They could write a "biography" of his new life.

5. Phyllis Reynolds Naylor received the 2004 Best Juvenile Edgar for *Bernie Magruder and the Bats in the Belfry*. Children could visit her Web site at: http://www.ipl.org/div/kidspace/askauthor/Naylor.html. They could find out how she became a writer. They could write a short essay about their feelings about writing.

6. Willo Davis Roberts received three Edgars. Children could visit her Web site at: http://www.willodavisroberts.com/index.php. They could find out how many books she wrote. They could also read some of the letters children have written to her. They could write a letter to her.

7. Theodore Taylor received the 1992 Edgar for *The Weirdo*. Children could visit his Web site at: http://www.theodoretaylor.com/. They could find out how and for what he earned a Scott O'Dell Award for Historical Fiction. They could read the two books and decide which book they like best.

8. Wendelin Van Draanen received the 1999 Edgar for *Sammy Keyes and the Hotel Thief*. Children could try to name all the Sammy Keyes books before they go to her Web site at: http://www.randomhouse.com/kids/vandraanen/.

9. Phyllis A. Whitney received the first Edgar for children in 1961 for *The Mystery of the Haunted Pool*. She won another Edgar in 1964. She is still writing books. Children can visit her Web site at: http://www.phyllisawhitney.com/. They could read about the other types of books that she writes.

10. Kin Platt received the 1967 Edgar for *Sinbad and Me*. Kin is also a cartoonist. Children can read his *The Mask* at: http://www.lambiek.net/platt_kin.htm. Then they could create a cartoon character.

Edgar Allan Poe and the Edgar Award

Student Handout 1—Information

Who Was Edgar Allan Poe?

Edgar Allan Poe created the first detective stories, and he wrote many horror stories as well. He also wrote poems, essays, and two novels. His personal life was unusual. His writings were very popular, but he was not an easy person to like.

Edgar Poe was born on January 19, 1809, in Boston, Massachusetts. His father moved away from the family, and his mother died when he was about two years old. Frances and John Allan, wealthy acquaintances, decided to raise him, and he took their last name as his middle name. They had no children of their own. Frances loved Poe dearly. John, on the other hand, did not seem to care for him. John felt that Poe showed little ambition and little gratitude.

The family briefly moved to England and then decided to live in Virginia. Edgar attended the University of Virginia for a few months, but Allan removed the young man because he had many debts. Edgar moved to Boston and tried to find work. However, after seven weeks, he had no job and no money. He joined the army. Edgar was a good soldier, and he wanted to attend the United States Military Academy at West Point to become an officer. However, Frances died, so Poe hired a stand-in and left the army. He visited his aunt Maria Clemm and her young daughter Virginia Clemm in Baltimore, Maryland. He published *Al Aaraaf, Tamerlane and Minor Poems.* Critics gave the book good reviews, and Poe became somewhat famous.

In 1830, Poe entered West Point Military Academy, but he found out that Allan had married again and had cut Poe out of his will. Poe had an argument with Allan when Poe realized he would not inherit anything from Allan's estate. Poe also knew he could never be rich as a military officer. He wanted desperately to leave West Point. He therefore began breaking many of the academy's rules. The following year he was court-martialed, and he left West Point. He published *Poems* in New York City, and he again lived with the Clemm family in Baltimore. The family struggled to make ends meet.

Poe entered several stories in short story contests. His "MS. Found in a Bottle" won a story contest in 1833. Two years later a magazine hired him to be an editor at $10 a week, and he moved the Clemm family to Richmond. He married Virginia on May 16, 1836. She was thirteen years old, and he was twenty-seven. However, he was fired from his job in December because he had been drinking too much. For the next few years, he worked for various magazines, and the family moved often. He published many short stories, including "The Pit and the Pendulum" and "The Black Cat," and several poems, including "The Raven." His stories and poems, while scary and strange, were very popular. However, the family never seemed to have enough money. Virginia died on January 30, 1847, at age twenty-four. Poe fell into a deep depression and wondered if he could live without her.

Several years later, Edgar fell in love several times, but the relationships did not last. He continued to write and publish many stories and poems. He became engaged to a woman he had loved many years before. On September 27, 1849, he started a boat trip from Richmond to New York City to put his affairs in order. However, he was found ill and almost unconscious on a Baltimore street on October 3. For several days, he experienced fever and pain. The doctors could do little to help him. They were not even sure what had caused his illness. Edgar Allan Poe died in a hospital in Baltimore on October 7, 1849.

What Is the Edgar Award?

The Mystery Writers of America organization, founded in 1945, gives Edgar Awards every year to the best mystery books. The first Edgar Award for juvenile literature was given in 1961, and the first Edgar Award for young adult literature was awarded in 1981. The award committee considers only mystery books published in the United States. The winners receive small busts of Edgar Allan Poe.

Edgar Allan Poe and the Edgar Award

Student Handout 2—Questions

Name_____ Date_____

Investigate the life of Edgar Allan Poe, and find out more about the Edgar Award. Then answer the following questions.

1. Where and when was Edgar Allan Poe born?

2. Why did Francis and John Allan decide to raise Edgar?

3. Did Edgar graduate from college?

4. Why did Edgar join the military?

5. Edgar Allan Poe was a writer. What kinds of works did he write?

6. Why did Edgar Allan Poe have difficulty keeping jobs?

7. Where and when did Edgar Allan Poe die?

8. What group gives out the Edgar Awards?

9. What do the Edgar winners receive?

10. Edgar Allan Poe is known for his mystery stories and his horror stories. Which do you like better, mystery stories or horror stories? Why?

From *Children's Book Award Handbook* by Diana F. Marks. Westport, CT: Libraries Unlimited. Copyright © 2006.

Edgar Allan Poe and the Edgar Award

Student Handout 3—Science Activity

Name_____ Date_____

Edgar Allan Poe was one of the first authors to write mysteries. The Edgar Awards honor mystery books. In "The Gold Bug," one of Poe's stories, the hero picks up a piece of parchment along with something else that he considers valuable. Later the parchment is placed next to heat. A message appears on the parchment, and the hero solves the case.

Invisible ink was used on the parchment. You can make invisible ink, and then you can send secret messages to your friends.

You will need:

    a fine art brush

    paper

    ½ cup of any of the following liquids:

    milk

    lemon juice

    grapefruit juice

    orange juice

    sugar-water solution

    lamp with a bulb

Then do the following:

1. Dip the brush in the liquid.

2. Write a message on the paper. The message should disappear as the liquid dries.

3. To bring back the message, turn on the lamp. Warm the paper over the hot light bulb.

Edgar Allan Poe and the Edgar Award

Student Handout 4—Poe's Own Mystery

Name_____ Date_____

Many people believe that Edgar Allan Poe was the first author to write detective stories. The Edgar Award honors good mystery books. Poe's last few days would make a great mystery story. Here are some of the facts.

Edgar Allan Poe became engaged to Elmira Royster Shelton, the woman he had loved many years before. They were to marry on October 17, 1849. On September 27, 1849, Poe started a boat trip from Richmond, Virginia, to New York City to gather his personal possessions and settle his accounts. However, he was found ill and almost unconscious on a Baltimore street on October 3. For several days, he experienced fever and pain. Doctors could do little to help him. They were not even sure what had caused his illness. Edgar Allan Poe died in Washington Hospital in Baltimore on October 7, 1849.

How did he get from the ship to the city of Baltimore? Why did he leave the ship? What caused his illness? What caused his death? Experts have been trying to answer these questions for about 150 years.

You get to be a mystery writer. On other lined paper, you are to write the last chapter in Poe's life. Why did he get off the ship? Were there people who wished him harm? Was there foul play?

You will be able to introduce some new and possibly sinister characters. You could name and describe the ship. Did the weather affect Edgar? Can you add some drama? Share your story with friends.

CHAPTER 17

Michael L. Printz and the Michael L. Printz Award for Excellence in Young Adult Literature

Overview

The Michael L. Printz Award for Excellence in Young Adult Literature honors writers of excellent young adult books. Michael L. Printz was a librarian who devoted his life to his Kansas students and to young adult literature. He was active in the Young Adult Library Services Association (YALSA), a division of the American Library Association (ALA).

Born in 1937, Printz was an avid reader and lifelong learner. He was the librarian of several public schools in Kansas. He wanted his students to be independent and accomplished scholars. He created the Kansas Oral History Project, and he started an author-in-residence program at his high school. He was active in YALSA and became an expert regarding young adult literature. He retired from Topeka School District in 1994 and worked as a marketing consultant for Econo-Clad Books. He died in 1996.

The Michael L. Printz Award for Excellence in Young Adult Literature was created in 1999 and is administered by YALSA. The first award was presented in 2000. The winners are announced at the midwinter meeting of ALA, and the awards are presented at the group's summer conference.

Michael L. Printz Biography

Michael L. Printz was a librarian who believed that every young adult could and should be an engaged learner. He attracted many young adults into his library, sending them out into the world as accomplished and confident men and women.

Michael Larry Printz was born to Hazel and Floyd Printz in Clay Center, Kansas, on May 27, 1937. Floyd worked in manufacturing. The Great Depression, the Dust Bowl period, and World War II had all created a great stranglehold on the region, necessitating Floyd's absence from home much of the time to provide for his family. Hazel, however, was able to do wonders with little money, and young Michael always seemed to have few needs. Michael was an avid reader, and his books brought him great happiness. Michael graduated from Clay Center Community High School on 1955. He went to the University of Kansas for one year, and then he transferred to Washburn University of Topeka, where he majored in English and history. He graduated in 1960 and became a half-time librarian, half-time English teacher at Onaga High School in Onaga, Kansas, a town located about fifty miles northwest of Topeka.

In 1963, Printz became the librarian at Highland Park High School in Topeka. The next year he obtained his Master's degree in library science from Emporia State University. In 1969, he transferred to Topeka West High School where again he was the librarian. In his first year there, Printz established a multimedia center and encouraged staff and students to use the center to conduct research. His work earned the school a large federal grant regarding multimedia. He would also arrange "book talks" with small groups of students. During these "book talks," he would entice students to check out new book acquisitions.

Printz, intent on broadening his range of influence, became president of the Kansas Association of School Librarians in 1970. He took on the role of regional director of the American Association of School Librarians in 1972. To celebrate the nation's bicentennial in 1976, he created the Kansas Oral History Project. Students would take on significant research projects regarding a famous Kansan or an important happening in Kansas history. Sometimes these students traveled great distances to interview people and gather information for their project. Video documentaries created by these students were donated to the Kansas State Historical Society.

From 1982 to 1985, Printz served on the Young Adult Library Services Association, Best Books for Young Adults Committee, and in 1985 he became the chair of the group. During this period, people began to see him as an expert on young adult literature. He was a popular speaker and a good sounding board for publishers. Through his many meetings and workshops, he met a number of famous authors. He talked some of those authors into visiting his school and working with his students. In 1983, he created the Author-in-Residence Program. Some of the authors who participated in his program were Chris Crutcher, Hazel Rochman, and Gary Paulsen.

Printz often returned to Washburn as an adjunct professor to teach a course called "Literature for Young Adults." He was also a visiting professor at Emporia State's Graduate School of Library and Information Management.

Topeka Unified School District 501 named Michael Printz Teacher of the Year in 1988, and Gary Paulsen dedicated his book, *The Island*, to Printz. In 1993, Printz received the Grolier Foundation Award from ALA, stating that he made an "unusual contribution to the stimulation and guidance of reading by children and young people." The award included $1,000 and a 24-karat gold-framed citation. Again, he agreed to serve on the YALSA Best Books for Young Adults Committee. He never resigned from that committee.

On January 14, 1994, Printz retired from teaching and became a marketing consultant and selection specialist for Econo-Clad Books. He did not let friends and associates know that he was experiencing heart problems. Eventually he needed heart bypass surgery. Printz died on September 29, 1996, from complications arising from the heart surgery. The library in Topeka West High School was dedicated in his name.

In January of 1999, YALSA approved an award honoring writers of literature for young adults. The group decided to name the award the Michael L. Printz Award for Excellence in Young Adult Literature. That medal was awarded for the first time in 2000 to Walter Dean Myers for *Monster*.

Michael Printz was shy and self-deprecating. He had a great sense of humor and a devotion to his students. He expected great things from both himself and his students. He is truly missed by his colleagues and his former students.

Michael Larry Printz Timeline

Date	Event
1937	Born to Hazel and Floyd Printz in Clay Center, Kansas, on May 27
1955	Graduated from Clay Center Community High School; attended University of Kansas for one year before transferring to Washburn University
1960	Graduated from Washburn University of Topeka, Kansas; became a part-time librarian and part-time English teacher at Onaga High School in Kansas
1963	Became librarian at Highland Park High School in Topeka, Kansas
1964	Earned Master's degree in library science from Emporia State University (Kansas)
1969	Became librarian at Topeka West High School
1970	Became president of Kansas Association of School Librarians
1972	Became regional director of the American Association of School Librarians
1976	Started Kansas Oral History Project
1982	Served on YALSA Best Books for Young Adults Committee until 1985
1983	Created Mike Printz Author-in-Residence Program
1985	Became committee chair of YALSA Best Books for Young Adults Committee
1988	Named District Teacher of the Year for Topeka Unified School District 501; Gary Paulsen dedicated his book *The Island* to Michael
1993	Received Grolier Award from ALA; again served on YALSA Best Books for Young Adults Committee until he died
1994	Retired on January 14; worked as a consultant for Econo-Clad
1996	Died on September 29 from heart surgery complications
1999	In January the YALSA approved the Michael L. Printz Award for Excellence in Young Adult Literature
2000	The Michael L. Printz Award for Excellence in Young Adult Literature was awarded for the first time

History and Criteria of Award

Michael L. Printz was a librarian who worked in Kansas. He became an expert in young adult literature and inspired young people to become independent and responsible. He was active in the Young Adult Library Services Association (YALSA), a division of the American Library Association (ALA). Michael Printz died in 1996.

Michael Cart was the chair of the Best Young Adult Book Award Feasibility Task Force of YALSA. His group drafted the rules and regulations for an award for young adult literature and searched for a name for the award. Cart always felt it should be named after Michael L. Printz, but he did not want to unduly influence the group. At some point, a movement to honor the memory of Michael L. Printz began. Cart enthusiastically supported the name, and the Michael L. Printz Award for Excellence in Young Adult Literature became a reality. The YALSA board approved the award, its rules and procedures in January 1999. The first medal was awarded in 2000.

The rules regarding the Michael L. Printz Award for Excellence in Young Adult Literature are very broad. The reader audience is between the ages of twelve and eighteen. Fiction, nonfiction, anthology, and poetry are all possibilities for awards. The book may be published in another country, but it must also be published in the United States. Co-authors are considered, and the medal may be awarded posthumously. The book must not depend on another media form, and the book must have been published in the year before the award is given. The committee will not base its decision on popularity or controversy, nor will it choose books based on other books by the same authors. Finally, as many as four honor books may also be listed.

Medal and Honor Books

Year	Award	Author/Illustrator	Title	Publisher
2006	Medal Book	John Green	*Looking for Alaska*	Dutton Books
	Honor Books	Margo Lanagan	*Black Juice*	EOS (HarperCollins)
		Markus Zusak	*I Am the Messenger*	Alfred A. Knopf
		Elizabeth Partridge	*John Lennon: All I Want Is the Truth, a Photographic Biography*	Viking
		Marilyn Nelson	*A Wreath for Emmett Till*	Houghton Mifflin
2005	Medal Book	Meg Rosoff	*How I Live Now*	Wendy Lamb Books
	Honor Books	Kenneth Oppel	*Airborn*	HarperCollins
		Allan Stratton	*Chandra's Secrets*	Annick Press
		Gary D. Schmidt	*Lizzie Bright and the Buckminster Boy*	Clarion Books
2004	Medal Book	Angela Johnson	*The First Part Last*	Simon & Schuster Books for Young Readers
	Honor Books	Jennifer Donnelly	*A Northern Light*	Harcourt
		Helen Frost	*Keesha's House*	Farrar, Straus and Giroux
		K. L. Going	*Fat Kid Rules the World*	G. P. Putnam's Sons/Penguin Young Readers Group
		Carolyn Mackler	*Earth, My Butt and Other Big Round Things*	Candlewick Press
2003	Medal Book	Aidan Chambers	*Postcards from No Man's Land*	Dutton Books
	Honor Books	Nancy Farmer	*The House of the Scorpion*	Atheneum Books for Young Readers
		Garret Freymann-Weyr	*My Heartbeat*	Houghton Mifflin
		Jack Gantos	*Hole in My Life*	Farrar, Straus & Giroux
2002	Medal Book	An Na	*A Step from Heaven*	Front Street
	Honor Books	Peter Dickinson	*Ropemaker*	Delacorte Press
		Jan Greenberg	*Heart to Heart: New Poems Inspired by Twentieth-Century Art*	Abrams
		Chris Lynch	*Freewill*	HarperCollins
		Virginia Euwer Wolff	*True Believer*	Atheneum
2001	Medal Book	David Almond	*Kit's Wilderness*	Delacorte Press

Year	Award	Author/Illustrator	Title	Publisher
	Honor Books	Carolyn Coman	*Many Stones*	Front Street
		Carol Plum-Ucci	*The Body of Christopher Creed*	Harcourt, Brace
		Louise Rennison	*Angus, Thongs, and Full Frontal Snogging*	HarperCollins
		Terry Trueman	*Stuck in Neutral*	HarperCollins
2000	Medal Book	Walter Dean Myers	*Monster*	HarperCollins
	Honor Books	David Almond	*Skellig*	Delacorte Press
		Laurie Halse Anderson	*Speak*	Farrar, Straus & Giroux
		Ellen Wittlinger	*Hard Love*	Simon & Schuster Books for Young Readers

Activities

1. Michael L. Printz lived in Kansas. Students could research the state and make up a board game regarding products, geography, history, famous Kansans, or cultural events.

2. Printz grew up during the Great Depression. Students could research the Great Depression and produce a timeline of the period. An excellent Web site is at the Library of Congress: http://memory.loc.gov/ammem/fsowhome.html.

3. Printz also grew up during the Dust Bowl. Young adolescents could research the Dust Bowl to discover the causes of the catastrophe. They could find out if the Dust Bowl could happen again. A good Web site is: http://www.usd.edu/anth/epa/dust.html.

4. Printz created an oral history project. Students interviewed someone who had lived through a significant event. Then they presented their findings in an assembly. Young adults could create their own oral history projects. A good model can be found at: http://www.nps.gov/hstr/ohp_index_1.htm.

5. Meg Rosoff received the 2005 Michael L. Printz Award for Excellence in Young Adult Literature for *How I Live Now*. Young adults could read about her at: http://www.randomhouse.com/teachers/authors/results.pperl?authorid=58449. They could compare their lives to her life. A Venn diagram may be helpful.

6. Aiden Chambers received the 2003 Printz Award for *Postcards from No Man's Land*. Chambers is British, and at one time he was a monk. Children could read his biography at: http://www.aidanchambers.co.uk/. They could find out why he became a writer.

7. David Almond received the Printz Award in 2001 for *Kit's Wilderness*. His *Skellig* was an honor book in 2000. Like Aiden Chambers, David Almond is British. Children could look at this Web site at: http://www.randomhouse.com/features/davidalmond/. Students could read books from both authors and compare/contrast them.

8. Allan Stratton's *Chandra's Secrets* was a 2005 honor book. Stratton is Canadian. Children could learn about him at: http://www.allanstratton.com/strattonmain3.html. His book is about AIDS and Africa. Students might want to read the book and then find out more about AIDS. They could share their research by making a slide show.

9. Jennifer Donnelly's *A Northern Light* was a 2004 honor book. Donnelly's books often take place in past times. Children could view her Web site at: http://www.jenniferdonnelly.com/. Students could take an event in their lives and change the setting/time to a different place long ago.

10. Printz established a visiting author program at his high school. Students could find out if a local author could work with them.

Michael L. Printz and the Michael L. Printz Award for Excellence in Young Adult Literature

Student Handout 1—Information

Who Was Michael L. Printz?

Michael Larry Printz was a librarian who believed that every young adult could and should be an engaged learner. He was born in Clay Center, Kansas, on May 27, 1937. The Great Depression, the Dust Bowl period, and World War II made life tough. Michael's father had to be away from home much of the time to provide for his family. His mother, however, did wonders with little money, and young Michael never lacked. Michael graduated from Clay Center Community High School in 1955. He went to the University of Kansas for one year, and then he transferred to Washburn University of Topeka. He majored in English and history. He graduated in 1960 and became a half-time librarian, half-time English teacher at Onaga High School in Onaga, Kansas.

In 1963, Michael became the librarian at Highland Park High School in Topeka. The next year he earned his Master's degree in library science from Emporia State University. In 1969, he transferred to Topeka West High School where again he was the librarian. In his first year there, Printz established a multimedia center. His work earned the school a large federal grant regarding multimedia. He would also arrange "book talks" with small groups of students to entice teenagers to check out new books.

In 1970, Michael became president of the Kansas Association of School Librarians. He became the regional director of the American Association of School Librarians in 1972. In 1976, he created the Kansas Oral History Project. Students conducted significant research projects regarding a famous Kansan or an important event in Kansas history. Sometimes these students traveled great distances to interview people and gather information for their project.

From 1982 to 1985, Printz served on the Young Adult Library Services Association (YALSA) Best Books for Young Adults Committee, and in 1985 he became the chair of the group. During this period, people began to see him as an expert on young adult literature. He was a popular speaker and a good sounding board for publishers. He met a number of famous authors. He talked some of those authors into visiting his school and working with his students. In 1983, he created the Author-in-Residence Program. Some of the authors who participated in his program were Chris Crutcher, Hazel Rochman, and Gary Paulsen.

Michael often returned to Washburn as an adjunct professor to teach a course called "Literature for Young Adults." He was also a visiting professor at Emporia State's Graduate School of Library and Information Management.

Topeka Unified School District 501 named Michael Printz Teacher of the Year in 1988; and Gary Paulsen dedicated his book, *The Island*, to him. In 1993, Michael received the Grolier Foundation Award, $1,000 and a 24-karat gold-framed citation, from ALA. Again, he agreed to serve on the YALSA Best Books for Young Adults Committee. In 1994, he retired from teaching and became a marketing consultant and selection specialist for Econo-Clad Books. He did not let friends know he was having heart problems. Eventually he needed heart bypass surgery. Michael Printz died on September 29, 1996, from heart surgery complications. The library in Topeka West High School was dedicated in his name.

What Is the Michael L. Printz Award for Excellence in Young Adult Literature?

The Michael L. Printz Award for Excellence in Young Adult Literature, created in 1999, yearly honors the best literature for teenagers. The first award was presented in 2000. YALSA administers the award. The winner and honor books are announced at the midwinter meeting of ALA, and the awards are presented at the group's summer conference.

Michael L. Printz and the Michael L. Printz Award for Excellence in Young Adult Literature

Student Handout 2—Questions

Name_____ Date_____

Investigate the life of Michael L. Printz, and find out more about the Michael L. Printz Award for Excellence in Young Adult Literature. Then answer the following questions.

1. Where and when was Michael L. Printz born?

2. What three historical events made life challenging for young Michael?

3. Where did Michael become a librarian?

4. What was the Kansas Oral History Project?

5. What was the Author-in-Residence Program?

6. List three of Michael's leadership roles in the American Library Association or the American Association of School Librarians.

7. When did Michael die?

8. What is the Michael L. Printz Award for Excellence in Young Adult Literature?

9. Who decides the award winners?

10. How is the Michael L. Printz Award for Excellence in Young Adult Literature different from the Margaret A. Edwards Award?

Michael L. Printz and the Michael L. Printz Award for Excellence in Young Adult Literature

Student Handout 3—Geography and Literature Connection

Name_____ Date_____

Michael L. Printz lived all his life in Kansas. Where were the authors of the Printz Award books and honor books born? Use the Internet and other resources to find out where the following authors were born. Then mark those locations on a map of North America.

Author	Place of Birth
Angela Johnson	
Meg Rosoff	
Walter Dean Myers	
Kenneth Oppel	
Allan Stratton	
Garrett Freyman	
Virginia Euwer Wolff	
Helen Frost	
Jack Gantos	
Carolyn Coman	

Michael L. Printz and the Michael L. Printz Award for Excellence in Young Adult Literature

Student Handout 3—Geography and Literature Connection —Answers

Name_____ Date_____

Michael L. Printz lived all his life in Kansas. Where were the authors of the Printz Award books and honor books born? Use the Internet and other resources to find out where the following authors were born. Then mark those locations on a map of North America.

Author	Place of Birth
Angela Johnson	Tuskegee, Alabama
Meg Rosoff	Boston, Massachusetts
Walter Dean Myers	Martinsburg, West Virginia
Kenneth Oppel	British Columbia
Allan Stratton	Ontario
Garrett Freyman	New York City
Virginia Euwer Wolff	Portland, Oregon
Helen Frost	Brookings, South Dakota
Jack Gantos	Mount Pleasant, Pennsylvania
Carolyn Coman	Chicago, Illinois

From *Children's Book Award Handbook* by Diana F. Marks. Westport, CT: Libraries Unlimited. Copyright © 2006.

Michael L. Printz and the Michael L. Printz Award for Excellence in Young Adult Literature

Student Handout 4—Book Talk Project

Name_____ Date_____

Michael L. Printz enticed his students to read more and better books by creating book talks. He would bring together a small group of students and then show them several good books. He would share enough of the plot so that students would take the books out of the library.

You will create a book talk to try to get a fellow student to read your book.

1. Choose a book you really like.

2. Describe the setting and the main characters.

3. Summarize the book, but do not describe the ending.

4. Tell students why this book is worthwhile.

5. See if students decide to read your book!

CHAPTER 18

Robert F. Sibert and the
Robert F. Sibert Informational Book Award

Overview

The Robert F. Sibert Informational Book Award is given annually to the author of an outstanding nonfiction book. Honor books may also be announced. Robert F. Sibert was a bookbinder.

Robert F. Sibert was born in Jacksonville, Illinois, in 1915. He was the son of L. D. Sibert. L. D. Sibert and a brother-in-law created a bookbinding business. The business flourished. Robert F. Sibert, after serving in the military during World War II, made the bookbinding business even more successful. He had a passion for good books and good intuition when it came to children's literature. Eventually, the company was renamed Bound to Stay Bound Books, Inc. Robert F. Sibert's son, Robert L. Sibert, became the company president in 1992. Robert L. Sibert felt an award should be created to honor nonfiction writers. The award was not originally to be named after his father. However, the Association for Library Service to Children (ALSC) committee for the award felt that his father, because of his contributions to children's literature and his philanthropic activities, should be remembered through this award. Robert F. Sibert died in 1998.

The Association for Library Service to Children administers the Robert F. Sibert Informational Book Award, first presented in 2001. The committee may examine any kind of nonfiction book except poetry and folktales. The writer must be an American citizen or live in the United States. The publisher must also be an American enterprise. The names of the winners are announced at the midwinter meeting of the American Library Association (ALA), and the awards are presented to the authors during ALA's summer conference.

Robert F. Sibert Biography

Many children's literature awards have been named after authors or librarians. However, Robert F. Sibert was neither. He was a bookbinder, a businessman who had a good nose for good children's literature, a family man, and a philanthropist.

Robert Frederic Sibert was born on January 20, 1915, in Jacksonville, Illinois. He was the only child of Lawrence DeWitt (L. D.) and Jessie Irene (Duncan) Sibert. His childhood was happy. When Robert was five years old, his father and his uncle, William Suhy, created the New Method Book Bindery. Robert attended Jacksonville High School. He was involved in many activities, including the tennis team and student council. He played the saxophone in the band, and he was on the basketball team. He also worked at the bookbindery after school. He set type, made cases, and created a card inventory system. Employees remember him bouncing a basketball on his way to work.

He graduated from high school in 1932 and entered Illinois College in the fall of the same year. He graduated from college in 1936 and became a full-time employee in the bindery. He became treasurer of the company in 1937, and he made a very creative change to the warehouse. Observing the employees of the warehouse, he noted that they were walking great distances to gather books from various locations. He suggested the employees wear roller-skates. The skates enabled the workers to move faster and with more ease.

After the United States joined the Allies in 1941, Robert enlisted in the army. He attended Quartermaster School in Camp Lee, Virginia, and had further training at Fort Bliss, Texas. Then he was transferred to France. He found himself in Germany at the end of the fighting and was at Buchenwald when the concentration camp was liberated. Next he was assigned to duty in Japan. However, by the time his ship arrived in Japan, that arena of the fighting had ended. At the end of his military duty in 1946, he had achieved the rank of captain in the quartermaster corps.

Robert returned home where he again worked for the New Method Book Bindery. He and his father bought out William Suhy's portion of the company. He was traveling to various libraries, and in 1946, he attended the Louisiana Library Association meeting. There he met Jessica Boatner, a librarian. Jessica had also joined the army during World War II. She had served in the Women's Army Corps as a cryptographer in the Philippines and New Guinea. After the war, she returned to the Vermilion Parish Library in Louisiana. Robert and Jessica fell in love, and they married on August 20, 1946.

Robert and Jessica both worked hard for the company, but they also decided to become parents. Their first child, Barbara, was born in 1948; and their second daughter, Martha Frances, followed in 1950. Katherine Anne was born in 1952, and Robert L. Sibert arrived in 1956.

Robert F. continued to work very hard for the New Method Book Bindery. When he was not traveling as a salesman, he was completing paperwork at the office. In 1959, he became president of the Library Binding Institute, a trade association that his father had helped create in 1935. Also in that year, they moved the company to a much bigger facility.

The company continued to prosper, and in 1962, L. D. retired as president and became Chairman of the board. Robert F. became president and general manager. In January 1970, the Siberts changed the company name to Bound to Stay Bound Books, Inc.

In 1972 Jessie, Robert's mother, died. Robert L. Sibert, the youngest offspring of Robert and Jessica, joined the firm in 1978. In September of the following year L. D. died. Still the company prospered, changing with time but always producing quality bindings. They were one of the first binding companies to embrace technology. For example, the Siberts saw the value of the MARC system, and they were one of the first binders to create a CD-ROM of their products.

In 1992, Robert F. Sibert became chairman of the board, and Robert L. Sibert became president. Around 1995 Robert L. Sibert began the process of creating an information book award. In February of 1998, Robert F. Sibert died. The Robert F. Sibert Informational Book Award was created in 2001.

The Siberts and their company, Bound to Stay Bound Books, Inc., have always been actively involved with the ALA. At almost every ALA meeting, the company would give out souvenirs to attendees. The first souvenir, produced in 1938, was a small replica of Ferdinand the Bull. Walt Disney signed one of those replicas and returned it to L. D. Several years later Robert gave another souvenir to Shirley Temple.

The Sibert family has always been very generous. In 1983, they created the Bound to Stay Bound Books Foundation. Many of their books have been donated to the Jacksonville Library and the Jacksonville Public Schools. In 1984, they created the Bound to Stay Bound Books Scholarship Program with ALA. The scholarships are awarded to people who plan to obtain advanced library degrees and then work in libraries. In addition, they have contributed to Illinois College and many other local and international aid agencies.

Interestingly, the warehouse employees at Bound to Stay Bound Books, Inc. still wear roller skates.

Robert F. Sibert Timeline

Date	Event
1915	Born Robert Frederic Sibert in Jacksonville, Illinois, to Lawrence DeWitt (L. D.) Sibert and Jessie Irene Duncan on January 20
1920	L. D. Sibert and William Suhy (brothers-in-law) founded New Method Book Bindery
1929	Attended Jacksonville High School and worked at bindery (Employees remember him bouncing a basketball on his way to work)
1932	Graduated from high school and entered Illinois College
1936	Graduated from Illinois College
1937	Suggested some employees wear skates; became treasurer
1941–1946	Performed military duty during World War II
1946	Met Jessica Boatner; married August 20
1948	Daughter Barbara was born
1950	Daughter Martha Frances was born
1952	Daughter Kathryn Anne was born
1956	Son Robert L. was born
1959	Became President of LBI; moved company to a new facility
1962	L. D. retired as president and became chairman of the board; Robert became president and general manager
1970	In January changed company name to Bound to Stay Bound Books, Inc.
1972	Jessie (mother) died in September
1978	Robert L. Sibert joined the firm
1979	L. D. (father) died
1992	Robert F. Sibert became chairman; Robert L. Sibert became president
1998	Died in February
2001	Robert F. Sibert Informational Book Award presented for the first time

History and Criteria of Award

The Robert F. Sibert Informational Book Award is named after Robert F. Sibert, the second president of Bound to Stay Bound Books, Inc. However, the award's present name was not what it started out to be.

In 1995, Robert L. Sibert, son of Robert F. Sibert and president of Bound to Stay Bound Books, Inc., felt that an award for children's informational literature should exist. He began talking to Susan Roman, then executive director of the Association for Library Service to Children (ALSC). She agreed that such an award was a good idea. The award proposal gained momentum, and the ALSC board appointed a committee to draw up the rules.

Robert L. Sibert originally wanted to call the award the Benjamin Franklin Award because Benjamin Franklin was a printer and publisher. Franklin is also considered the father of public libraries. However, the Publishers Marketing Association, a trade association for independent book publishers, already sponsored an award by that name. Then Thomas Jefferson's name was suggested, because he was an avid reader and collector of books. However, the Virginia Library Association's Children's and Young Adult Round Table presents yearly the Jefferson Cup to children's literature about America's history. Therefore, the name Thomas Jefferson could not be used.

Robert L. Sibert then asked that the committee decide on the award name. The members suggested that the award be named after his father, Robert F. Sibert, because his father had done so much for children's literature. He and his company had sponsored scholarships for people who wished to pursue graduate degrees in library sciences. He had also created standards for bookbinding. The family had been very generous to various libraries and school districts. At first, the younger Sibert felt that the name was self-serving. Eventually, however, Susan Roman and members of the committee convinced him that the award name was deserved. The decision was made, and the award was named after his father.

A photograph of Robert F. Sibert was sent to an artist, who forwarded a medal design to Medallic Art, a company that sculpted and cast the medal. The medals were then made. Bound to Stay Bound Books, Inc. funds the cost of the medals and the administrative and committee expenses.

The rules regarding the award are broad. The award-winning books must be published in English. Any type of informational book will be considered, but poetry and folktales will not. The author must be either an American citizen or a resident of the United States. The book must also be published in the United States. The award is presented to a book published in the previous year. For example, the 2005 Robert F. Sibert Informational Award was presented to the author of a book published in 2004. The names of the winners are announced at the midwinter meeting of the American Library Association (ALA), and the awards are presented to the authors during ALA's summer conference.

Interestingly, Robert L. Sibert has no input as to who will be honored with the medal. In an interview on March 15, 2005, he stated: "I enter the office pool for my dad's award just like everyone else. I have my favorites when it comes to the Newberys, the Caldecotts and the Siberts, but I have no inside information."

Medal and Honor Books

Year	Award	Author/Illustrator	Title	Publisher
2006	Medal Book	Sally M. Walker	*Secrets of a Civil Submarine: Solving the Mysteries of the H. L. Hunley*	Carolrhoda Books
	Honor Book	Susan Campbell Bartoletti	*Hitler Youth: Growing Up in Hitler's Shadow*	Scholastic
2005	Medal Book	Russell Freedman	*The Voice that Challenged a Nation: Marian Anderson and the Struggle for Equal Rights*	Clarion Books/Houghton Mifflin
	Honor Books	Barbara Kerley, author Brian Selznick, illustrator	*Walt Whitman: Words for America*	Scholastic
		Sy Montgomery, author Nic Bishop, photographer	*The Tarantula Scientist*	Houghton Mifflin
		James Rumford, author Anna Sixkiller Huckaby, translator into Cherokee	*Sequoyah: The Cherokee Man Who Gave His People Writing*	Houghton Mifflin
2004	Medal Book	Jim Murphy	*An American Plague: The True and Terrifying Story of the Yellow Fever Epidemic of 1793*	Clarion Books/Houghton Mifflin
	Honor Book	Vicki Cobb, author Julia Gorton, illustrator	*I Face the Wind*	HarperCollins
2003	Medal Book	James Cross Giblin	*The Life and Death of Adolf Hitler*	Clarion
	Honor Books	Karen Blumenthal	*Six Days in October: The Stock Market Crash of 1929*	Atheneum
		Jack Gantos	*Hole in My Life*	Farrar, Straus & Giroux
		Jan Greenberg and Sandra Jordan, authors Robert Andrew Parker, illustrator	*Action Jackson*	Roaring Brook Press/Millbrook Press
		Pam Muñoz Ryan, author Brian Selznick, illustrator	*When Marian Sang*	Scholastic
2002	Medal Book	Susan Campbell Bartoletti	*Black Potatoes: The Story of the Great Irish Famine*	Houghton Mifflin
	Honor Books	Andrea Warren	*Surviving Hitler: A Boy in the Nazi Death Camps*	HarperCollins

Year	Award	Author/Illustrator	Title	Publisher
		Jan Greenberg and Sandra Jordan	*Vincent van Gogh*	Delacorte Press
		Lynn Curlee	*Brooklyn Bridge*	Simon & Schuster/Atheneum Books for Young Readers
2001	Medal Book	Marc Aronson	*Sir Walter Raleigh and the Quest for El Dorado*	Clarion Books
	Honor Books	Joan Dash, author Dusan Petricic, illustrator	*The Longitude Prize*	Frances Foster Books/Farrar, Straus & Giroux
		Jim Murphy	*Blizzard! The Storm that Changed America*	Scholastic
		Sophie Webb	*My Season with Penguins: An Antarctic Journal*	Houghton Mifflin
		Judd Winick	*Pedro and Me: Friendship, Loss, and What I Learned*	Henry Holt

Activities

1. Robert F. Sibert lived in Illinois. Children could research the state and make a board game filled with facts.

2. Robert F. Sibert was a bookbinder. Perhaps a local bookbindery could provide a tour.

3. The Sibert Award is for works of nonfiction. Children could poll their peers and see how many prefer to read poetry, fiction, or nonfiction. They could present their results by making a pie chart.

4. Some employees at Sibert's warehouse wear roller skates. The children could roller skate for a charity or for money to buy more library books.

5. Jim Murphy received the Robert F. Sibert Informational Book Award in 2004 for his book *An American Plague: The True and Terrifying Story of the Yellow Fever Epidemic of 1793*. His *Blizzard! The Storm that Changed America* was a 2001 honor book. Children could visit his site at: http://www.jimmurphybooks.com/. They could answer his question of the week.

6. Barbara Kerley's *Walt Whitman: Words for America* was a 2005 honor book. Children could visit her Web site at: http://www.barbarakerley.com/ and then link to a site where they can view Walt Whitman's notebooks. They could find some of his poems, memorize them, and conduct a poetry recital.

7. Sy Montgomery, author, and Nic Bishop, photographer, won a 2005 honor award for *The Tarantula Scientist*. Children could read an excerpt from the book at: http://www.authorwire.com/s/s_excerpt.html. They could also make their own book about nature and include some photographs.

8. Vicki Cobb's *I Face the Wind* was a 2004 honor book. Children could check out her Web site at: http://www.vickicobb.com/. She offers many experiments that children can conduct.

9. Robert F. Sibert was a binder. That means that he took existing books and made the covers stronger. Children could compare a bound book with a paperback book and find the strengths and weaknesses of both.

10. Jan Greenberg and Sandra Jordan wrote *Action Jackson*, a 2003 honor book. The book is about the artist, Jackson Pollock. Children could visit Greenberg's site at: http://mowrites4kids.drury.edu/authors/greenberg/. They could also view many of Pollock's works at: http://www.ibiblio.org/wm/paint/auth/pollock/. Then they could make their own versions of a Jackson Pollock work of art.

Robert F. Sibert and the Robert F. Sibert Informational Book Award

Student Handout 1—Information

Who Was Robert F. Sibert?

Many children's literature awards have been named after authors or librarians. However, Robert F. Sibert was neither. He was a bookbinder, a businessman who had a good nose for good children's literature, a family man, and a philanthropist.

Robert Frederic Sibert was born on January 20, 1915, in Jacksonville, Illinois. When Robert was five years old, his father and his uncle created the New Method Book Bindery. Robert attended Jacksonville High School. He was involved in many activities, including the tennis team and student council. He played saxophone in the band, and he was on the basketball team. He also worked at the bookbindery after school. Employees remember him bouncing the basketball on his way to work.

He graduated from high school in 1932 and from Illinois College in 1936. He became a full-time employee in the bindery, and he was named the company treasurer in 1937. Observing the employees of the warehouse, he found they were walking great distances to gather books from various locations. He suggested that the employees wear roller skates. The skates enabled the workers to move faster and with greater ease.

After the United States entered World War II in 1941, Robert enlisted in the army. He found himself in Germany and then in Japan. At the end of his military duty in 1946, he was a captain in the quartermaster corps. He returned home and again worked for the New Method Book Bindery. He and his father bought out his uncle's portion of the company. In 1946, he attended the Louisiana Library Association meeting. There he met Jessica Boatner, a librarian. Robert and Jessica fell in love, and they married in 1946. They had four children.

Robert F. continued to work very hard for the New Method Book Bindery. In 1959, he became president of the Library Binding Institute, a trade association that his father had helped create in 1935. Also in that year, they moved the company to a larger facility. In 1962, Robert's father retired as president and became chairman of the board. Robert F. became president and general manager. In January 1970, the Siberts changed the company name to Bound to Stay Bound Books, Inc.

Robert L. Sibert, the youngest child of Jessica and Robert F., joined the company in 1978. The company prospered, changing with time but always producing quality bindings. They were one of the first binding companies to embrace technology, and they created a CD-ROM of their products. In 1992, Robert F. Sibert became chairman of the board, and Robert L. Sibert became president. In February of 1998 Robert F. Sibert died. The warehouse employees at Bound to Stay Bound Books, Inc. still wear roller-skates.

What Is the Robert F. Sibert Informational Book Award?

The Robert F. Sibert Informational Book Award, first presented in 2001, is given annually to the author of an outstanding nonfiction book. Honor books may also be announced. Robert L. Sibert felt an award should be created to honor nonfiction writers. The award was not originally to be named after his father. However, the Association for Library Service to Children (ALSC) award committee, a division of the American Library Association (ALA), felt his father should be remembered.

The award committee may consider any nonfiction book except poetry and folktales. The writer must be an American citizen or live in the United States. The publisher must also be an American enterprise. The names of the winners are announced at the midwinter meeting of the American Library Association, and the awards are presented to the authors during ALA's summer conference.

From Children's Book Award Handbook by Diana F. Marks. Westport, CT: Libraries Unlimited. Copyright © 2006.

Robert F. Sibert and the Robert F. Sibert Informational Book Award

Student Handout 2—Questions

Name_____ Date_____

Learn about the life of Robert F. Sibert, and find out more about the Robert F. Sibert Informational Book Award. Then answer the following questions.

1. Where and when was Robert F. Sibert born?

2. List three facts about his childhood.

3. What company did his father and uncle create?

4. What interesting change did Robert F. Sibert make in the warehouse?

5. What happened to Robert during World War II?

6. Was Bound to Stay Bound Books, Inc. successful? How do you know?

7. When did Robert F. Sibert die?

8. What is the Robert F. Sibert Informational Book Award?

9. Why do you think the award committee will not consider poetry books?

10. Do you read more fiction or nonfiction? Why?

Robert F. Sibert and the Robert F. Sibert Informational Book Award

Student Handout 3—Bookbinding

Name_____ Date_____

Robert F. Sibert was a bookbinder; his company assembled books. You can make a simple book and then write in it.

You will need:

    3 sheets of white copy paper

    1 sheet of colored construction paper slightly larger than the white copy paper

    a ruler

    a pencil

    a hole punch

    2 pieces of yarn, each about 15 inches long

    markers, paints or crayons

Do the following:

1. Fold the three sheets of white paper together from short side to short side. You have just created the pages in your book. The three folded sheets make twelve book pages.

2. Fold the colored construction paper from short side to short side. This will be the book's cover.

3. Place the pages of your book inside the cover.

4. Open up your book to the center pages.

5. Use the ruler and pencil to make a mark 1 inch from the top and another mark 2 inches from the top.

6. Use the ruler and pencil to make a mark 1 inch from the bottom and another mark 2 inches from the bottom.

7. Use the hole punch to punch holes at the four marks.

8. Thread a piece of yarn about 1 foot long through the top two holes and tie the yarn together outside of the cover.

9. Thread a piece of yarn about 1 foot long through the top two holes and tie the yarn together outside of the cover.

10. Now your book is done. Feel free to decorate the cover by using markers, paints, or crayons.

Robert F. Sibert and the Robert F. Sibert Informational Book Award

Student Handout 4—Fiction and Nonfiction

Name_____ Date_____

The Robert F. Sibert Informational Book Award is given to nonfiction books. Some of the award or honor books are biographies, and some of the books describe historical events. Several discuss scientific topics.

Can you figure out from a book title whether it is fiction or nonfiction? Below are the names of some books. After the title, tell whether you think the book is fiction or nonfiction.

Volcano: The Eruption and Healing of Mount St. Helens _____

Six Days in October: The Stock Market Crash of 1929 _____

Crispin: The Cross of Lead _____

Sequoyah: The Cherokee Man Who Gave His People Writing _____

Action Jackson _____

A Single Shard _____

A Year Down Yonder _____

Brooklyn Bridge _____

Walk Two Moons _____

Walt Whitman: Words for America _____

Lincoln: A Photobiography _____

Number the Stars _____

I Face the Wind _____

Pedro and Me: Friendship, Loss, and What I Learned _____

Dear Mr. Henshaw _____

From *Children's Book Award Handbook* by Diana F. Marks. Westport, CT: Libraries Unlimited. Copyright © 2006.

Robert F. Sibert and the Robert F. Sibert Informational Book Award

Student Handout 4—Fiction and Nonfiction—Answers

Name_____ Date_____

The Robert F. Sibert Informational Book Award is given to nonfiction books. Some of the award or honor books are biographies, and some of the books describe historical events. Several discuss scientific topics.

Can you figure out from a book title whether it is fiction or nonfiction? Below are the names of some books. After the title, tell whether you think the book is fiction or nonfiction.

Volcano: The Eruption and Healing of Mount St. Helens Nonfiction

Six Days in October: The Stock Market Crash of 1929 Nonfiction

Crispin: The Cross of Lead Fiction

Sequoyah: The Cherokee Man Who Gave His People Writing Nonfiction

Action Jackson Nonfiction

A Single Shard Fiction

A Year Down Yonder Fiction

Brooklyn Bridge Nonfiction

Walk Two Moons Fiction

Walt Whitman: Words for America Nonfiction

Lincoln: A Photobiography Nonfiction

Number the Stars Fiction

I Face the Wind Nonfiction

Pedro and Me: Friendship, Loss, and What I Learned Nonfiction

Dear Mr. Henshaw Fiction

CHAPTER 19

Sydney Taylor and the Sydney Taylor Book Award

Overview

The Sydney Taylor Book Award honors the best Jewish writers and illustrators every year. Sydney Taylor was a writer, best known for her *All-of-a-Kind Family* books.

Sydney Taylor was born in 1904 in New York City. The daughters of immigrants, she and her sisters grew up in a happy but not affluent home. She married Ralph Taylor in 1925. She wrote down her childhood experiences, but she put the stories away. Her husband submitted the stories to a contest, and her first book, *All-of-a-Kind Family*, was published in 1951. She wrote other books, including more *All-of-a-Kind* books about her childhood and family, before she died in 1978.

Ralph Taylor created the Sydney Taylor Book Award in his wife's memory in 1978. The Association of Jewish Libraries administers the award. The Sydney Taylor Book Award Committee seeks books that portray Jewish experiences accurately, that set high standards for writing and/or illustration, and that urge children to read on. Two categories have been formed, one for older readers and one for young readers. Occasionally, a body-of-work award is given to an individual whose entire works have enriched the lives of children. The award is announced through a January press release and is presented at the association's annual meeting, usually held in the summer.

Sydney Taylor Biography

Sydney Taylor was born with neither the name Sydney nor Taylor. She did not plan to be a writer, but she became a famous writer, chronicling the lives of Jews in the early part of the twentieth century. She would probably be amazed to know that a children's literature award honoring Jewish writers and illustrators is named after her.

Sarah Brenner was born on October 30, 1904, to Cecilia (Marowitz) and Morris Brenner in New York City. Cecilia and Morris had immigrated to America from Europe, had established a home on the Lower East Side of New York City, and had kept their Jewish heritage. Sarah was their third child. Ella had been born in 1900, and Henrietta made an appearance in 1902.

Life on the Lower East Side was difficult. Sarah's father owned and operated a store, while her mother cared for house and children (increased by Charlotte in 1907, Gertrude in 1908, Irving in 1912, and Jerry in 1919). Both of Sarah's parents were very religious, and the Sabbath and holy days were strictly observed. Sarah was not as religious as her parents.

Around 1920, Sarah changed her name to Sydney and joined the Young People's Socialist League. There she met Ralph Taylor, and they were married on July 11, 1925. Later the couple became less politically active, and Ralph became the president of the company Caswell-Massey. Sydney pursued a life in the arts. From 1925 to 1929 she performed with the Lenox Hill Players, and from 1930 to 1935, she danced with the Martha Graham Dance Studio.

In 1935, Sydney gave birth to a daughter, Joanne. Sydney devoted her time and energy to Joanne and would often share stories of her childhood with her daughter. Joanne, an avid reader, complained that all the books she read had non-Jewish protagonists. Sydney studied the literature and agreed with her daughter. She therefore began to tell Joanne more stories of her childhood. Her daughter and husband found them to be very interesting and encouraged her to write them down. She did put the stories onto paper, but she filed them away. Meanwhile, she became a counselor at Cejwin Camps, Point Jervis, New York.

Sydney's husband sent her stories to Follett, a publishing company that was sponsoring a contest for "distinguished contribution to children's literature." Follett published her book, *All-of-a-Kind Family*, in 1951. The book was filled with tender and humorous stories about her family. It won the 1952 Jewish Book Council Award and was so successful that readers asked for more. Other books followed, including *More All-of-a-Kind Family* (1954), *All-of-a-Kind Family Uptown* (1957), and *All-of-a-Kind Family Downtown* (1972).

Sydney also wrote books about subjects other than her family, including *Now That You Are Eight* (1963) and *The Dog Who Came to Dinner* (1966). In 1962, she won the Junior Book Award Certificate from Boy's Club of America for *Mr. Barney's Beard*.

Sydney Taylor died in New York City on February 12, 1978. Her husband created the Sydney Taylor Book Award that same year.

Taylor's *All-of-a-Kind Family* books are still being printed. They give non-Jewish readers an accurate account of the celebration of Jewish holidays and also portray life in the 1920s in New York City. The characters, like those in books by Laura Ingalls Wilder, are intelligent, loving, resourceful, and responsible.

Sydney Taylor Timeline

Date	Event
1904	Born Sarah Brenner to Cecilia (Marowitz) and Morris Brenner in New York City, on October 30; two sisters (Ella, born 1900, and Henrietta, born 1902) welcomed her
1907	Sister Charlotte born
1908	Sister Gertrude born
1912	Brother Irving born
1919	Brother Jerry born
ca. 1920	Changed her first name to Sydney
early 1920s	Joined the Young People's Socialist League
1925	Married Ralph Taylor on July 11; actress with Lenox Hill Players until 1929
1930	Dancer with Martha Graham Dance Studio until 1935
1935	Gave birth to daughter Joanne
1942	Became a counselor at Cejwin Camps, Point Jervis, New York
1951	Published *All-of-a-Kind Family*; won Follett Award for *All-of-a-Kind Family*
1952	Won Jewish Book Council Award for *All-of-a-Kind Family*
1953	Contributed to *The Holiday Story Book*, published by Crowell
1954	Published *More All-of-a-Kind Family*
1957	Published *All-of-a-Kind Family Uptown*
1961	Published *Mr. Barney's Beard*
1962	Won Junior Book Award Certificate from Boys' Club of America for *Mr. Barney's Beard*
1963	Published *Now That You Are Eight*
1966	Published *The Dog Who Came to Dinner* and *A Papa Like Everyone Else*
1972	Published *All-of-a-Kind Family Downtown*
1978	Published *Ella of All-of-a-Kind Family*; Sydney Taylor Body-of-Work Award created; died in New York City on February 12
1979	Awarded Sydney Taylor Body-of-Work Award posthumously
1980	Published posthumously *Danny Loves a Holiday*

History and Criteria of Award

Sydney Taylor became a published writer when her husband, Ralph Taylor, submitted her collection of stories, *All-of-a-Kind Family,* to a publisher's manuscript contest. She published ten books in all.

The Sydney Taylor Award, administered by the Association of Jewish Libraries (AJL), was created by her husband in her memory. The award honors the best Jewish writers and illustrators. In 1969, the AJL gave an award, the Shirley Kravitz Award, to *The Endless Steppe* by Esther Hautzig. It was the AJL's first award for a children's book, and the award was made by its School and Center Division. That group continued to give awards on a yearly basis. In 1971, the AJL decided that it would, on occasion, give a body-of-work award to honor an author whose life's work has enriched the lives of children. In 1975, the AJL moved its awards into the AJL Awards Program. Ralph Taylor, with the consent of Rita Frischer, then chair and coordinator of the Children's Book Award Committee, created the Sydney Taylor Body-of-Work Award in 1978.

In 1981, the AJL created an award for older readers and an award for younger readers. Four years later, the entire AJL program for children's book awards was named after Sydney Taylor. The winning books of the two groups receive gold emblems to be added to the covers. Honor books, which may also be awarded, receive silver emblems.

The Sydney Taylor Book Award Committee, made up of a group of Judaica librarians (also members of the Association of Jewish Libraries) reads the books submitted. The books may be published anywhere in the world, and the authors can be foreign. The books must be in English or translated into English. Until 2005, the award winner's copyright year coincided with the year of the award. For example, the 2003 award was given to a book published in 2003. However, in 2005, the Sydney Taylor Book Award Committee decided to align the date of the award with the dates of other awards. In other words, the award is given to a book published the year before. No award was given in 2005. The winners are announced in a press release in January. The cash awards and certificates are presented at the association's annual June meeting.

The Sydney Taylor Book Award winner usually appeals to a broad spectrum of readers and must accurately portray some aspect of Jewish life. The cover and/or illustrations must attract the reader and contribute to the story's message. Sydney Taylor Honor Books generally have a slightly narrower focus. An AJL Notable Children's Book of Jewish Content may have an even more narrow audience. However, all represent good writing and authentic Jewish experiences.

Works by Sydney Taylor

All-of-a-Kind Family. New York: Follett, 1951.

All-of-a-Kind Family Downtown. New York: Follett, 1972.

All-of-a-Kind Family Uptown. New York: Follett, 1957.

Danny Loves a Holiday. New York: E. P. Dutton, 1980.

Dog Who Came to Dinner, The. New York: Follett, 1966.

Ella of All-of-a-Kind Family. New York: E. P. Dutton, 1978.

More All-of-a-Kind Family. New York: Follett, 1954.

Mr. Barney's Beard. New York: Follett, 1961.

Now That You Are Eight. New York: Follett, 1963.

Papa Like Everyone Else, A. New York: Follett, 1966.

Award Books and Recipients

Year	Award	Title	Author/Illustrator	Publisher
2006	Younger Reader	*Sholom's Treasure: How Sholom Aleichem Became a Writer*	Erica Silverman, author Mordicai Gerstein, illustrator	Farrar, Straus & Giroux
	Older Reader	*Confessions of a Closet Catholic*	Sarah Darer Littman	Dutton
2004	Younger Reader	None		
	Older Reader	*Real Time*	Pnina Moed Kass	Clarion
	Body-of-Work Award		Eric A. Kimmel	
2003	Younger Reader	*Bagels from Benny*	Aubrey Davis, author Dusan Petricic, illustrator	Kids Can Press
	Older Reader	*Who Was the Woman Who Wore the Hat?*	Nancy Patz	Dutton
2002	Younger Reader	*Chicken Soup by Heart*	Esther Hershenhorn, author Rosanne Litzinger, illustrator	Simon & Schuster
	Older Reader	*Hana's Suitcase*	Karen Levine	Second Story Press; U.S. publisher Albert Whitman & Company
	Body-of-Work Award		Judyth Groner and Madeline Wikler, founders of Kar-Ben Copies Publishers	
2001	Younger Reader	*Rivka's First Thanksgiving*	Elsa Okon Rael, author Maryann Kovaski, illustrator	Market K. McElderry/Simon & Schuster
	Older Reader	*Sigmund Freud: Pioneer of the Mind*	Catherine Reef	Clarion
2000	Younger Reader	*Gershon's Monster*	Eric A. Kimmel, author Jon J. Muth, Illistrator	Scholastic
	Older Reader	*The Key Is Lost*	Ida Vos, author Terese Edelstein, translator	HarperCollins
1999	Younger Reader	*The Peddler's Gift*	Maxine Rose Schur, author Kimberly Bulcken Root, illustrator	Dial Books for Young Readers

Year	Award	Title	Author/Illustrator	Publisher
	Older Reader	*Speed of Light*	Sybil Rosen	Atheneum Books for Young readers/Anne Schwartz Book
1998	Younger Reader	*Nine Spoons*	Marci Stillerman, author Pesach Gerber, illustrator	HaChai Publishers
	Older Reader	*Stones in Water*	Donna Jo Napoli	Dutton
1997	Younger Reader	*When Zaydeh Danced on Eldridge Street*	Elsa Okon Rael, author Marjorie Priceman, illustrator	Simon & Schuster
	Older Reader	*The Mysterious Visitor: Stories of the Prophet Elijah*	Nina Jaffe, author Elivia Savadier, illustrator	Scholastic
	Body-of-Work Award		Barbara Diamond Goldin	
1996	Younger Reader	*Shalom, Haver: Goodbye, Friend*	Barbara Sofer	Kar-Ben Copies
	Older Reader	*When I Left My Village*	Maxine Rose Schur, author Brian Pinkney, illustrator	Dial Books
1995	Younger Reader	*Star of Fear, Star of Hope*	Jo Hoestlandt, author Johanna Kang, illustrator	Walker & Company
	Older Reader	*Dancing on the Bridge of Avignon*	Ida Vos, author Terese Edelstein and Inez Schmidt, translators	Houghton Mifflin
1994	Younger Reader	*The Always Prayer Shawl*	Sheldon Oberman	Boyds Mills Press
	Older Reader	*The Shadow Children*	Steven Schnur, author Herbert Tauss, illustrator	Morrow Junior Books
1993	Younger Reader	*The Uninvited Guest*	Nina Jaffe, author Elivia Savadier, illustrator	Scholastic
	Older Reader	*Sworn Enemies*	Carol Matas	Bantam Doubleday Dell
1992	Younger Reader	*Something from Nothing*	Phoebe Gilman	North Winds Press/Scholastic Canada
	Older Reader	*Letters from Rifka*	Karen Hesse	Henry Holt
1991	Younger Reader	*Cakes and Miracles: A Purim Tale*	Barbara Diamond Goldin, author Erika Weihs, illustrator	Viking Press
		Daddy's Chair	Sandy Lanton, author Shelly O. Haas, illustrator	Kar-Ben Copies

Year	Award	Title	Author/Illustrator	Publisher
	Older Reader	*The Diamond Tree: Jewish Tales from Around the World*	Howard Schwartz and Barbara Rush, authors Uri Shulevitz, illustrator	HarperCollins
1990	Younger Reader	*The Chanukah Guest*	Eric A. Kimmel, author Giora Carmi, illustrator	Holiday House
	Older Reader	*My Grandmother's Stories*	Adèle Geras, author Jael Jordan, illustrator	Alfred A. Knopf
1989	Younger Reader	*Berchick*	Esther Silverstein Blanc, author Tennessee Dixon, illustrator	Volcano Press
	Older Reader	*Number the Stars*	Lois Lowry	Houghton Mifflin
1988	Younger Reader	*The Keeping Quilt*	Patricia Polacco	Simon & Schuster
	Older Reader	*The Devil's Arithmetic*	Jane Yolen	Viking Kestrel
	Body-of-Work Award		Yaffa Ganz	
1987	Younger Reader	*The Number on My Grandfather's Arm*	David Adler, author Rose Eichenbaum, photographer	UAHC
	Older Reader	*The Return*	Sonia Levitin	Atheneum
1986	Younger Reader	*Joseph Who Loved the Sabbath*	Marilyn Hirsch, author Devis Grebu, illustrator	Viking Kestrel
	Older Reader	*Beyond the High White Wall*	Nancy Pitt	Charles Scribner's Sons
1985	Younger Reader	*Brothers*	Florence Freedman, author Robert Andrew Parker, illustrator	Harper & Row
	Older Reader	*Ike and Mama and the Seven Surprises*	Carol Snyder	Lothrop, Lee & Shepard
1984	Younger Reader	*Mrs. Moskowitz and the Sabbath Candlesticks*	Amy Schwartz	Jewish Publication Society
	Older Reader	*The Island on Bird Street*	Uri Orlev	Houghton Mifflin
	Body-of-Work Award		Miriam Chalkin	
1983	Younger Reader	*Bubby, Me, and Memories*	Barbara Pomerantz, author Leon Lurie, photographer	UAHC
	Older Reader	*In the Mouth of the Wolf*	Rose Zar	Jewish Publication Society
1982	Younger Reader	*The Castle on Hester Street*	Linda Heiler	Jewish Publication Society

Year	Award	Title	Author/Illustrator	Publisher
	Older Reader	*Call Me Ruth*	Marilyn Sachs	Doubleday
1981	Younger Reader	*Yussel's Prayer*	Barbara Cohen, author Michael J. Deraney, illustrator	Lothrop, Lee & Shepard
	Older Reader	*The Night Journey*	Kathryn Lasky	Frederick Warne
1980	Award	*A Russian Farewell*	Leonard Everett Fisher	Four Winds Press
	Body-of-Work Award		Barbara Cohen and Sadie Rose Wellerstein	
1979	Award	*Ike and Mama and the Block Wedding*	Carol Snyder	Coward, McCann & Geoghegan
	Body-of-Work Award		Marilyn Hirsch	
1978	Award	*The Devil in Vienna*	Doris Orgel	Dial
	Body-of-Work Award		Sydney Taylor	
1977	Award	*Exit from Home*	Anita Heyman	Crown
1976	Award	*Never to Forget*	Milton Meltzer	Harper & Row
1975	Award	*Waiting for Mama*	Marietta Moskin	Coward, McCann & Geoghegan
1974		*No award given*		
1973	Award	*Uncle Misha's Partisans*	Yuri Suhl	Four Winds
1972	Body-of-Work Award		Molly Cone	
1971	Body-of-Work Award		Isaac Bashevis Singer	
1970	Award	*The Year*	Suzanne Lange	S. G. Phillips
1969	Award	*Our Eddie*	Sulamith Ish-Kishor	Pantheon
1968	Award	*The Endless Steppe*	Esther Hautzig	Crowell

Activities

1. Sydney's name at birth was Sarah. She changed her name when she was a young adult. Children might want to change their first names. They could list their new names.

2. Sydney Taylor's parents were immigrants. Perhaps a family new to the community would like to talk to the children about their experiences.

3. Sydney's All-of-a-Kind series is based on events in her own life. Children could read at least two of the books and then decide which character they like best. They could pretend to be that character and present information to their peers.

4. Children could compare All-of-a-Kind characters with the Laura Ingalls Wilder characters. They could also compare them to the characters in *Little Women*. A Venn diagram could be very useful.

5. Karen Hesse was the recipient of the 1992 Award for Older Readers. Her book, *Letters from Rifka*, is loosely based on a relative's immigration to America and her experiences at Ellis Island. Children could examine Hesse's biography at: http://www.edupaperback.org/showauth.cfm?authid=56. Children could also participate in a virtual tour of Ellis Island at: http://teacher.scholastic.com/activities/immigration/tour/.

6. Aubrey Davis wrote *Bagels from Benny*. The book received the 2003 Sydney Taylor Book Award for Younger Readers. Children could learn about Davis at: http://www.writersunion.ca/d/davis.htm. Then they could eat bagels.

7. Eric A. Kimmel has received the Sydney Taylor Book Award several times. Children could view his books at: http://www.childrenslit.com/f_kimmel.html. He has worked with many different illustrators. Children could decide which illustrating style best appeals to them.

8. Amy Schwartz received the 1984 Younger Reader Award for *Mrs. Moskowitz and the Sabbath Candlesticks*. She also received the 2004 Charlotte Zolotow Award for *What James Likes Best*. Children could read about her at: http://www.soemadison.wisc.edu/ccbc/authors/experts/schwartz.asp. Then they could read both books and other books by her. Which do they like best?

9. Children could make a frequency table to find out which author or illustrator has received the most awards.

10. Children could read *Rivka's First Thanksgiving* (2001 Younger Reader Award) at Thanksgiving.

Sydney Taylor and the Sydney Taylor Book Award

Student Handout 1—Information

Who Was Sydney Taylor?

Sydney Taylor was born with neither the name Sydney nor Taylor. She did not plan to be a writer, but she became famous, describing the lives of Jews in the early part of the twentieth century. Sarah Brenner was born on October 30, 1904, in New York City. Her parents had immigrated to America from Europe, had established a home on the Lower East Side of New York City, and had kept their Jewish heritage. Sarah was their third child.

Life on the Lower East Side was difficult. Sarah's father owned and operated a store, while her mother cared for house and children, increased by three more. Both of Sarah's parents were very religious, and the Sabbath and holy days were strictly observed. Sarah was not as religious as her parents.

Around 1920, Sarah changed her name to Sydney and joined the Young People's Socialist League. There she met Ralph Taylor, and they were married in 1925. Later, Ralph became the president of the company Caswell-Massey. Sydney pursued a life in the arts. From 1925 to 1929, she performed with the Lenox Hill Players, and from 1930 to 1935, she danced with the Martha Graham Dance Studio.

In 1935, Sydney gave birth to a daughter, Joanne. Sydney devoted her time and energy to Joanne and would often share stories of her childhood with her daughter. Her daughter, an avid reader, complained that all the books she read had non-Jewish characters. Sydney studied the literature and agreed with her daughter. She began to tell Joanne stories of her childhood. Her daughter and husband found them to be very interesting and encouraged her to write them down. She did put the stories onto paper, but she filed them away. She became a counselor at Cejwin Camps, Point Jervis, New York.

Sydney's husband sent her stories to Follett, a publishing company that was sponsoring a contest for "distinguished contribution to children's literature." Follett published her book, *All-of-a-Kind Family*, in 1951. The book was filled with tender and humorous stories about her family. The book won the 1952 Jewish Book Council Award and was so successful that readers asked for more. Other books followed, including *More All-of-a-Kind Family* (1954), *All-of-a-Kind Family Uptown* (1957), and *All-of-a-Kind Family Downtown* (1972).

Sydney also wrote books about subjects other than her family. She wrote *Now That You Are Eight* (1963), *The Dog Who Came to Dinner* (1966), and others. In 1962, she won the Junior Book Award Certificate from Boy's Club of America for *Mr. Barney's Beard*.

Sydney Taylor died in New York City on February 12, 1978.

Taylor's *All-of-a-Kind Family* books are still being printed. They give non-Jewish readers an accurate account of the celebration of Jewish holidays and also portray life in the 1920s in New York City. The characters are intelligent, loving, resourceful, and responsible.

What Is the Sydney Taylor Book Award?

Ralph Taylor created the Sydney Taylor Book Award in his wife's memory in 1978. The Association of Jewish Libraries administers the award. The Sydney Taylor Book Award Committee seeks books that accurately portray Jewish experiences, that set high standards for writing and/or illustration, and that urge children to read on. Two categories have been formed, one for older readers and one for young readers. Occasionally, a body-of-work award is given to an individual whose entire works have enriched the lives of children. The award is announced through a January press release and is presented at the association's annual meeting, usually held in the summer.

From Children's Book Award Handbook by Diana F. Marks. Westport, CT: Libraries Unlimited. Copyright © 2006.

Sydney Taylor and the Sydney Taylor Book Award

Student Handout 2—Questions

Name_____ Date_____

Investigate the life of Sydney Taylor, and find out more about the Sydney Taylor Book Award. Then answer the following questions.

1. Where and when was Sydney Taylor born?

2. What was her name when she was born?

3. Describe her childhood.

4. Why did she begin to write down the events of her childhood?

5. How and why was her first book published?

6. List at least three books that she wrote.

7. When and where did Sydney Taylor die?

8. What is the Sydney Taylor Book Award?

9. Who created the award?

10. What are the three award categories?

Sydney Taylor and the Sydney Taylor Book Award

Student Handout 3—Dreidel Game with a Twist

Name_____ Date_____

The Sydney Taylor Book Award honors the best Jewish writers and illustrators every year. Sydney Taylor was Jewish.

Every year at Hanukkah Jewish children play the dreidel game. The dreidel is a kind of four-sided top. A different Hebrew letter is on each side. On one side is the letter נ (nun); on another side is ה (hay); on a third side is ג (gimmel); and on the fourth side is ש (shin). Together the four symbols create an acronym for "a great miracle happened here."

Usually four to six children play the game at one time. The players all have the same amount of tokens. Rocks, coins, and pieces of candy can be used as tokens. Each player places one token into the pot. Each player spins the dreidel.

If it stops on nun, the player gets or loses nothing.

If it stops on hay, the player gets half the pot.

If it lands on gimmel, the player gets the whole pot.

If it lands on shin, the player adds a token to the pot.

When the pot is empty, everyone places a token into the pot. The game goes on.

Let's play the dreidel game but with a twist. You are going to combine the game with information about books and authors.

1. Find a dreidel. You could also make a dreidel out of clay.

2. Make a list of questions about books and authors. You could ask who was the author of a particular book. Or you could ask a question about a main character of a particular book. Or you could ask questions about Sydney Taylor.

3. Then you could start the game by asking one of your questions.

4. If the player answers the question correctly, then the player spins the dreidel and finds the outcome.

5. If the player does not answer the question correctly, he or she does not spin the dreidel.

You are combining knowledge with tradition and a bit of luck. Have fun!

Sydney Taylor and the Sydney Taylor Book Award

Student Handout 4—Diorama Project

Name_____ Date_____

The Sydney Taylor Book Award honors the best Jewish writers and illustrators every year. Sydney Taylor was a writer, best known for her *All-of-a-Kind Family* books. She drew on her experiences growing up when she wrote her *All-of-a-Kind Family* books. The characters in the books are her parents, sisters, brother, other family members, and friends.

The characters in her book, like those in books by Laura Ingalls Wilder, are intelligent, loving, resourceful, and responsible. We want to read books with great characters, and we want to share with others the good books we have found. One way to share is to make a diorama, a three-dimensional scene from a book.

You will be making a diorama of a scene from a book you really like. You will need:

a good book

a pencil

drawing paper

a shoe box or other box about that size

various types of craft material (for example, pipe cleaners, fabric, different types of paper, clay, leaves, small rocks)

paints, crayons or markers

scissors

glue

To make the diorama:

1. Decide on a scene from the good book.

2. Sketch out the scene on the drawing paper.

3. Decide how to make the scene three-dimensional.

4. Place the box on its side. The box will be the frame of the scene.

5. Cover the bottom of the box (the background of the scene).

6. Make the characters and their possessions out of the craft items.

7. Place the characters and items in the diorama.

8. When you are happy, glue everything in.

9. Label the box with the name of the book, the scene, and your name.

10. Place your diorama on display.

CHAPTER 20

E. B. White and the
E. B. White Read Aloud Award

Overview

The E. B. White Read Aloud Award is given annually to the best read aloud book of the year. The Association of Booksellers for Children (ABC) sponsors the award. E. B. White wrote for adults for many years. However, he is most famous as the author of three children's stories: *Stuart Little*, *Charlotte's Web*, and *The Trumpet of the Swan*.

E. B. White was born in 1899 in Mount Vernon, New York. He wrote essays for the *New Yorker* and *Harper's* for many years. He also penned many books, including *Every Day Is Saturday* and *The Points of My Compass*. In 1937, he moved his family to a farm in Maine and through his writings, he amused and inspired readers through the Great Depression and World War II. White had entertained family members with tales of a small mouse born to humans. He decided to develop those stories into a book, and *Stuart Little* was published in 1945. His two other famous children's books followed. He, together with William Strunk, Jr., also wrote the classic handbook on writing style, *Elements of Style*, published in 1956. E. B. White died in 1985.

The Association of Booksellers for Children presented the first E. B. White Read Aloud Award in 2004. The award-winning books represent the best of read aloud books. The award can honor either a chapter book or a picture book. ABC member stores nominate books for the award. Next, a committee of ABC members, chaired by a member of the ABC Board, selects one book to receive the award. The name of the award-winning book is announced on May 1, and the author/illustrator accepts the crystal award at the ABC annual dinner.

E. B. White Biography

E. B. White published many books and essays, and he wrote for the *New Yorker* for many years. He wrote simply and often humorously about his daily life, comforting those who were struggling through the Great Depression and World War II. However, he is most famous for writing three children's books: *Stuart Little*, *Charlotte's Web*, and *The Trumpet of the Swan*.

Elwin Brooks White was born on July 11, 1899, to Samuel Tilly White and Jessie Hart White in Mount Vernon, New York. En, as he was called then, had five older siblings—Marion, Clara, Albert, Stanley, and Lillian. His father was a businessman. En loved the out of doors, and he was shy. He did not always like school, particularly when he had to talk before the class. He enjoyed looking up words in the dictionary, and early on he knew he wanted to be a writer. In June of 1911, his first published piece, "A Winter Walk," appeared in *St. Nicholas Magazine,* and he received a silver badge.

En graduated from Mount Vernon High School in 1917. In April of that year, the United States had entered World War I. That summer he became a Farm Cadet, harvesting crops for farmers who were fighting in the war. In the fall he attended Cornell University where he wrote for the *Cornell Daily Sun.* There he received the nickname Andy. His classmates named him after Cornell's president, Andrew W. White.

Andy registered for the draft on September 2, 1918. However, the army had plenty of soldiers, and he could stay in college, although many other students did join the war effort. At Cornell he enlisted in the Student Army Training Corps. For a while, the *Cornell Daily Sun*, lacking sufficient student staff, stopped publication. Andy missed seeing his name in print, and he also missed the camaraderie of his reporter friends. At the conclusion of World War I, Andy became chief editor of the *Cornell Daily Sun.* He was also the president of his fraternity. He honed his writing skills by heeding the advice of several professors, including William Strunk, Jr., Martin Sampson, and Bristow Adams.

In 1921, Andy graduated from Cornell University and became a reporter in New York City. However, he was not very successful. He quit the reporting job, loaded up Hotspur, his Model T Ford, and traveled west with a good friend, Howard Cushman. When they ran out of money, they worked. Sometimes local newspapers printed Andy's stories. In the fall of 1922, he took a job at the *Seattle Times* newspaper. There he wrote a column about his experiences and opinions. However, the newspaper had to reduce staff, and White was again unemployed. At this point he worked for several months on a trading ship.

White returned to New York in 1924 where he worked for an advertising firm. However, he was unhappy with a job whose sole purpose was to convince people to buy products. At this time, he also published some poems in a New York–based magazine called the *Conning Tower,* and in 1925, the *New Yorker*, a new magazine, published one of his essays. The readers loved his writing. The magazine continued to publish more of his work, and in 1927 he was hired full-time at the *New Yorker.* Two years later, on November 13, 1929, he married Katherine Angell, an editor at the *New Yorker.* Katherine had two children, Nancy and Roger, from a previous marriage. In that same year he published *The Lady Is Cold*, a collection of poems.

Their son, Joel McCoun White, was born on December 21, 1930. E. B. White's father died in 1935, and his mother died in the following year. White quit the *New Yorker* in 1937 and moved the family to a farm near North Brooklin, Maine. There he wrote a monthly column for *Harper's* called "One Man's Meat." In 1943, during World War II, he returned to New York and the *New Yorker.*

One night White had a dream about a mouse born to human parents. He amused Joel and various relatives with many stories about this mouse, Stuart. He finally decided to organize those stories, and in 1945 he published *Stuart Little.* The book immediately won the hearts of children. By this time, White had lived on a farm for a number of years. Aware that pigs were regarded with contempt, he began to think about a children's book that would include a pig. He also began researching spiders. The result was *Charlotte's Web,* which was published in 1952 and became a 1953 Newbery Honor Book. He published *Elements of Style* with William Strunk, Jr., his professor at Cornell, in 1956. He persuaded Katherine to retire from editing in 1961, and she devoted her time to gardening and writing about gardening. In 1963, just days after President Kennedy was assassinated, White was presented the Presidential Medal of Freedom. In 1970, he published *The Trumpet of the Swan,* for which he received the Laura Ingalls Wilder Award. Katherine died from heart failure on July 20, 1977. In 1978 White received a Pulitzer Prize Special Citation for his contributions to literature.

Children eagerly awaited another White book to arrive on the shelves, but White published little after 1978. He died on October 1, 1985, in North Brooklin, Maine. The first E. B. White Read Aloud Award was given to Judy Schachner for *Skippyjon Jones* in 2004.

E. B. White Timeline

Date	Event
1899	Born Elwin Brooks White on July 11 to Samuel Tilly White and Jessie Hart White in Mount Vernon, New York
1911	In June published "A Winter Walk" in *St. Nicholas Magazine* and received a silver badge
1917	Graduated from Mount Vernon High School; that summer became a Farm Cadet, harvesting crops for farmers who were fighting in World War I; attended Cornell University; wrote for *Cornell Daily Sun*; received nickname "Andy"
1918	Registered for draft on September 2; at Cornell enlisted in Student Army Training Corps
1919	Became chief editor of *Cornell Daily Sun*; elected president of fraternity; received instruction by William Strunk, Jr., Martin Sampson, and Bristow Adams
1921	Graduated from Cornell University; took a reporting job in New York City; quit reporting job; traveled west with Howard Cushman
1922	In fall took a job at *Seattle Times* newspaper
1924	Returned to New York; worked for advertising firm; published some poems in the *Conning Tower*
1925	One of his essays published by the *New Yorker* in April
1927	Was hired full-time at the *New Yorker*
1929	Married Katherine Sergeant Angell on November 13; published *The Lady Is Cold*
1930	Son Joel McCoun White born on December 21
1935	Father died
1936	Mother died
1937	Quit the *New Yorker* and moved family to a North Brooklin, Maine, farm
1938	Wrote a column for *Harper's* called "One Man's Meat"
1943	Returned to New York and the *New Yorker*
1945	Published *Stuart Little*
1952	Published *Charlotte's Web*
1953	Received Newbery Honor Book Award for *Charlotte's Web*
1956	Published *Elements of Style* with William Strunk, Jr.
1961	Persuaded Katherine to retire
1963	Received Presidential Medal of Freedom
1970	Published *The Trumpet of the Swan;* was presented Laura Ingalls Wilder Award
1977	Katherine died July 20
1978	Received Pulitzer Prize Special Citation
1985	Died October 1 in North Brooklin, Maine
2004	First E. B. White Read Aloud Award given to Judy Schachner for *Skippyjon Jones*

History and Criteria of Award

E. B. White wrote many books and essays. However, he is most well known for his three famous children's books: *Stuart Little*, *Charlotte's Web*, and *The Trumpet of the Swan*. White died in 1985.

The Association of Booksellers for Children (ABC) was formed in 1985. For a number of years, the group created the ABC Choices Awards. However, the list was becoming a burden to its members. The ABC board decided to create an award honoring just one book. This book would be a perfect fit to their literacy campaign, "The Most Important 20 Minutes of Your Day … Read with a Child." The board decided to name the award after an author, and E. B. White's name was a natural. The group felt that White's works stood as models for read aloud books. The first award was presented in 2004 to Judy Schachner for *Skippyjon Jones*.

Member stores can nominate books for the award, and they may nominate more than one book. Member stores encourage their employees to suggest titles. The book may be either a chapter book or a picture book. The nominated books should be the titles that the employees suggest when a patron asks for book suggestions.

The nominations are forwarded to a committee of ABC members. The committee is chaired by an ABC board member. The committee then decides who will receive the award.

The award recipient receives a crystal book engraved with the medal, the book title, his or her name, and the date.

Books by E. B. White

Alice through the Cellophane. New York: The John Day Company, 1933.

Another Ho Hum: More Newsbreaks from "The New Yorker." New York: Farrar & Rinehart, 1932.

Charlotte's Web. New York: Harper & Brothers, 1952.

E. B. White Reader, An. Edited by William W. Watt and Robert W. Bradford. New York: Harper & Row, 1966.

Elements of Style, The. By William Strunk, Jr. With Revisions, an Introduction, and a New Chapter on Writing by E. B. White. New York: Macmillan, 1959.

Essays of E. B. White. New York: Harper & Row, 1977.

Every Day Is Saturday. New York: Harper & Brothers, 1934.

Farewell to Model T. By Lee Strout White [pseudonym for Richard Lee Strout and E. B. White]. New York: G. P. Putnam's Sons, 1936.

Fox of Peapack and other Poems, The. New York: Harper & Brothers, 1938.

Here Is New York. New York: Harper & Brothers, 1949.

Ho Hum: Newsbreaks from "The New Yorker." New York: Farrar & Rinehart, 1931.

Is Sex Necessary? Or Why You Feel the Way You Do. By James Thurber and E. B. White. New York: Harper & Brothers, 1929.

Lady Is Cold. New York: Harper & Brothers, 1929.

Letters of E. B. White. New York: Harper & Row, 1970.

One Man's Meat. New York: Harper & Brothers, 1942.

Poems and Sketches of E. B. White. New York: Harper & Row, 1981.

Points of My Compass, The. New York: Harper & Row, 1962.

Quo Vadimus? Or the Case for the Bicycle. New York: Harper & Brothers, 1939.

Second Tree from the Corner, The. New York: Harper & Brothers, 1954.

Stuart Little. New York: Harper & Brothers, 1945.

Subtreasury of American Humor, A. Edited by E. B. White and Katharine S. White. New York: Coward-McCann, 1941.

Trumpet of the Swan, The. New York: Harper & Row, 1970.

Wild Flag, The. Boston: Houghton Mifflin, 1946.

Award Books

Year	Author/Illustrator	Title	Publisher
2005	Judy Sierra, author Marc Brown, illustrator	*Wild About Books*	Alfred A. Knopf
2004	Judy Schachner	*Skippyjon Jones*	Dutton Children's Books

Activities

1. At one time E. B. White was a newspaper reporter. Children could take a chapter from one of his books and turn it into a newspaper story.

2. E. B. White wrote many essays. Children could write a persuasive essay about a topic of their choice.

3. E. B. White wrote three children's books: *Stuart Little*, *Charlotte's Web*, and *The Trumpet of the Swan*. Children could poll their classmates and find out which one was most popular.

4. E. B. White seldom used his full, real name. He had various nicknames at different points of his life. Children could interview peers who have nicknames and find out how those nicknames were acquired.

5. Since White was at one time a reporter, children could interview a reporter, possibly even from the high school newspaper.

6. The E. B. White Read Aloud Award honors read aloud books. Children could visit other grades or other groups and read aloud their favorite books.

7. Judith Schachner wrote *Skippyjon Jones*, the 2004 E. B. White Award book. Children could visit her Web site at: http://www.judithbyronschachner.com/index.htm. They could find out which author helped her become a published artist/author. They could then make a list of Lloyd Alexander books and check off the ones they have read.

8. Marc Brown illustrated *Wild about Books*. Children could visit his Web site at: http://www.twbookmark.com/authors/26/224/. They could find the name of a famous aardvark Brown created.

9. Judy Sierra received the 2005 E. B. White Award for writing *Wild About Books*. Children could visit her Web site at: http://www.judysierra.net/. They could find out what her occupation was before she became a writer. Children could interview several adults and see if these people had occupations other than the ones they have now.

10. E. B. White feared speaking in school. He was afraid he would have to give a speech or presentation. Children should be comfortable speaking before their peers. Children could make a picture of White and write down five facts about his life. Then they could present their research to the rest of the class.

E. B. White and the E. B. White Read Aloud Award

Student Handout 1—Information

Who Was E. B. White?

Elwin Brooks White was born on July 11, 1899, in Mount Vernon, New York. En, as he was called, was shy and enjoyed being outdoors. He dreaded speaking before others in school. He enjoyed looking up words in the dictionary, and early on he knew he wanted to be a writer. In June of 1911, his first published piece, "A Winter Walk," appeared in *St. Nicholas Magazine,* and he received a silver badge.

En graduated from Mount Vernon High School in 1917. In April of that year, the United States had entered World War I. That summer he became a Farm Cadet, harvesting crops for farmers who were fighting in the war. In the fall, he attended Cornell University where he wrote for the *Cornell Daily Sun*. There he received the nickname Andy. His classmates named him after Cornell's president, Andrew W. White.

In 1921, he graduated from Cornell University and became a reporter in New York City. However, he was not very successful. He quit the reporting job, loaded up Hotspur, his Model T Ford, and traveled west with a friend. When they ran out of money, they worked. Sometimes local newspapers printed his stories.

White returned to New York in 1924 where he worked for an advertising firm. However, he was unhappy that his job was to convince people to buy products. the *New Yorker*, a new magazine in 1925, published one of his essays. The readers loved his writing. The magazine continued to publish more of his work, and in 1927 he was hired full-time at the *New Yorker*. Two years later, on November 13, 1929, he married Katherine Angell.

Their son, Joel McCoun White, was born on December 21, 1930. White quit the *New Yorker* in 1937 and moved the family to a farm near North Brooklin, Maine. There he wrote a monthly column for *Harper's* called "One Man's Meat." In 1943, during World War II, he returned to New York and the *New Yorker*.

One night White had a dream about a mouse born to human parents. He amused Joel and relatives with many stories about this mouse, Stuart. He finally decided to organize those stories, and in 1945, he published *Stuart Little.* The book immediately won the hearts of children. White, by this time, had lived on a farm for a number of years. He began to think about a children's book that included pigs. He also began researching spiders. In 1952, he published *Charlotte's Web,* a 1953 Newbery Honor Book. On December 6, 1963, just days after President Kennedy was assassinated, White was presented the Presidential Medal of Freedom. In 1970, he published *The Trumpet of the Swan* and received the Laura Ingalls Wilder Award. In 1978, White received a Pulitzer Prize Special Citation for his contributions to literature.

E. B. White died on October 1, 1985, in North Brooklin, Maine.

What Is the E. B. White Read Aloud Award?

Every year the Association of Booksellers for Children (ABC) presents the E. B. White Read Aloud Award to the best book to be read aloud to children. The book's story and illustrations exemplify their literacy campaign, "The Most Important 20 Minutes of Your Day Read with a Child." ABC members and employees can nominate books, and a committee of ABC members picks the winning book.

The award winner receives a crystal book engraved with the medal, the book title, his or her name, and the date.

E. B. White and the E. B. White Read Aloud Award

Student Handout 2—Questions

Name_____ Date_____

Investigate the life of E. B. White, and find out more about the E. B. White Read Aloud Award. Then answer the following questions.

1. Where and when was E. B. White born?

2. Did he enjoy school?

3. Why was E. B. White a farmer in 1917?

4. E. B. White worked for a magazine for many years. What was the name of the magazine?

5. Why do you think he moved his family from New York City to a farm in Maine?

6. What three famous children's books did he write?

7. Where and when did E. B. White die?

8. What awards did E. B. White earn?

9. List three facts about the E. B. White Read Aloud Award.

10. Why do you think read aloud books help children?

E. B. White and the E. B. White Read Aloud Award

Student Handout 3—Creative Activity

Name_____ Date_____

E. B. White wrote *Stuart Little*, published in 1945. Stuart Little, a mouse, was two inches tall. Stuart's parents were people. Stuart's father made Stuart a bed out of four clothespins and a cigarette box.

What else would have to be constructed specially for Stuart? In the space below, draw a picture of an item that would have to be made small enough for Stuart.

E. B. White and the E. B. White Read Aloud Award

Student Handout 4—Research Activity

Name_____ Date_____

E. B. White wrote three children's books: *Stuart Little*, *Charlotte's Web*, and *The Trumpet of the Swan*. All three books were about animals. See how much you know about animals. Fill in the chart below. Animals are listed in the left column. See if you know the name of the mother, father, baby, and group.

Animal	Mother	Father	Baby	Group Name
Example: Swan	Pen	Cob	Cygnet	Bevy
Pig				
Mouse				
Duck				
Goose				
Rabbit				
Goat				
Turkey				
Penguin				
Lion				
Deer				
Seal				
Sheep				
Grasshopper				
Tiger				
Wallaby				

E. B. White and the E. B. White Read Aloud Award

Student Handout 4—Research Activity—Answers

E. B. White wrote three children's books: *Stuart Little*, *Charlotte's Web*, and *The Trumpet of the Swan*. All three books were about animals. See how much you know about animals. Fill in the chart below. Animals are listed in the left column. See if you know the name of the mother, father, baby, and group.

Animal	Mother	Father	Baby	Group Name
Example: Swan	Pen	Cob	Cygnet	Bevy
Pig	Sow	Boar	Piglet	Litter
Mouse	Doe	Buck	Pup, Kitten	Horde
Duck	Duck	Drake	Duckling	Flock, Brace
Goose	Goose	Gander	Gosling	Flock, Gaggle
Rabbit	Doe	Buck	Bunny	Colony
Goat	Doe, Nanny	Billy, Buck	Kid	Herd, Tribe
Turkey	Hen	Tom	Poult	Rafter
Penguin	Female	Male	Chick	Rookery
Lion	Lioness	Lion	Cub	Pride
Deer	Doe	Stag, Buck	Fawn	Herd
Seal	Cow	Bull	Pup	Harem, Pod, Rookery
Sheep	Ewe, Doe	Buck, Ram	Lamb	Flock
Grasshopper	Female	Male	Nymph	Swarm
Tiger	Tigress	Tiger	Whelp, Cub	Ambush
Wallaby	Jill	Jack	Joey	Mob

CHAPTER 21

Laura Ingalls Wilder and the Laura Ingalls Wilder Award

Overview

The Laura Ingalls Wilder Award is given every two years to an author or illustrator whose collective works have contributed to children's literature. Laura Ingalls Wilder was an author best known for her children's books about the American pioneer era.

Laura Ingalls was born in 1867 near Pepin, Wisconsin. She and her family moved several times, often establishing farms on the American prairie. She was a teacher before she married Almanzo Wilder in 1885. They also moved several times before they settled down in Rocky Ridge, Missouri. She published her first book, *Little House in the Big Woods,* in 1932. She wrote more books, and her book, *Little House on the Prairie,* was the inspiration of a television series. Laura Ingalls Wilder died in 1957.

The Association for Library Service to Children (ALSC) a division of the American Library Association (ALA) created the award in the 1950s. Laura herself was given the first award in 1954. Other award winners include Russell Freedman and Laurence Yep. The name of the winner is announced at the midwinter meeting of the ALA, and the awards are presented to the winners during ALA's summer conference.

Laura Ingalls Wilder Biography

The life of Laura Ingalls Wilder was often exciting and at times dangerous. Her book series recorded daily pioneer life, helping succeeding generations to understand the difficulties of such a life and to appreciate their own lives. She published her first book when she was sixty-four years old. Her stories were even made into a television series. Her books won many awards, and the Laura Ingalls Wilder Award honors those authors and illustrators who have enriched the lives of children around the world.

Laura Elizabeth Ingalls was born on February 7, 1867, near Pepin, Wisconsin. Her father, Charles Phillip Ingalls, was a farmer. Her mother, Caroline Quiner, had been born in Minnesota. Another daughter, Mary, was born earlier, on January 10, 1865. Laura's parents, forever known to the world as Ma and Pa, scratched out a living in the Minnesota woods. Charles hunted local game, and they farmed what they could. However, longing for an easier life, they packed all their belongings in a Conestoga wagon and moved to Kansas in 1869. Laura's sister, Carrie, was born there on August 3,

1869. They unknowingly farmed on Osage land. Although the Osage Indians were paid by the government to move further west, the Ingalls family returned to Wisconsin in 1874.

Again, in 1874 they packed up and moved to a farm near Walnut Grove, Minnesota. At first, the family lived in a dugout and Charles planted wheat. Laura attended school for the first time. Unfortunately, swarms of grasshoppers devoured the wheat crop for two years in a row. Charles had to leave his family to become a harvester in eastern Minnesota and would return periodically with enough money to keep the family going. In 1875, a son, Charles Frederick, was born, but he died just nine months later.

In 1876, the family decided to move to Burr Oak, Iowa, to help some friends run a hotel. The children also worked in the hotel, but here Laura was able to go back to school. Baby Grace was born on May 23, 1877. However, in that same year the family moved back to Walnut Grove. While the Ingalls family experienced great hardships, they were a loving and supportive group. Laura remembered that her father would often play his violin to help his children fall asleep.

In 1879, an unknown disease, possibly scarlet fever, struck all the members of the family. Everyone survived, but Mary lost her sight. Difficult times again fell on the family, and Charles was having a hard time supporting his family. However, in 1879 he found a job in De Smet, Dakota Territory, earning fifty dollars a month as the railroad timekeeper and paymaster. He went to De Smet first and found lodging. The family followed by train (Laura's first train ride). The Ingalls family was considered one of the most important families in the town because they had been there a winter before so many other families arrived. The family added to their income by renting sleeping space on the floor and by providing meals at twenty-five cents per person.

The winter of 1880 brought one blizzard after another. During one storm, Laura and Carrie almost lost their way from school to their home. At first, Charles and other employees could keep the tracks clear, and trains could bring supplies. However, in January trains stopped arriving there, as a result of which food and supplies became dangerously low. Two men volunteered to travel about twenty miles to a homesteader who could provide them with wheat. Although they almost got lost in another prairie blizzard, they returned to town with plenty of wheat. One of those men was Almanzo Wilder.

The Ingalls family decided to send Mary to a special school for the blind in Iowa. Laura helped provide the funds by making shirts. At age fifteen, she took on a teaching job in a community twelve miles from home. She had only a few students, and one of her students was older than she was. She boarded with a family that she did not like. However, every weekend Almanzo Wilder would take her back to her home; at the beginning of the workweek, he would bring her back to school. Almanzo, who preferred the name Manly, was ten years older than Laura, and at first Laura considered him to be more of a friend. However, after she returned to De Smet and took another teaching job, she continued to go on buggy rides with him. She also worked for a seamstress on the weekends. Laura was reluctant to marry Manly because then she would have to stop teaching. Married women in that region at that time could not be teachers.

On August 25, 1885, Laura and Manly were married. Their early life on the farm was difficult. She learned to run machinery and do heavy work. In 1886, a hailstorm destroyed their crops. Their daughter Rose was born on December 5, 1886. A drought and dry winds destroyed the next year's crops. Their hay and barn burned. In 1888, both Laura and Almanzo contracted diphtheria. Rose went to live with relatives while her parents recuperated. Almanzo's health never completely returned.

Their bad luck continued. Drought destroyed the following year's crops. A baby son, never named, died a few days after birth. The kitchen caught fire when Rose was placing hay sticks into the stove. She suffered only minor burns, but the house was destroyed. During the spring of 1890, the Wilders went to Spring Family, Minnesota, to live with his family.

In 1894, the Wilder family went to Westville, Florida, hoping the warmer weather would be better for Manly. However, Laura became ill. They returned to De Smet. There Manly worked as a carpenter and Laura as a seamstress. Then they moved to Mansfield, Missouri, deep in the Ozark Mountains. They bought a farm and called it Rocky Ridge. They fixed up the log cabin, planted crops, and established an orchard. They got by selling firewood, chickens, and eggs. The railroad came through, bringing industries and new people to the area. Manly became a drayman, and at last they were financially comfortable. Rose went to school. Laura was so successful with her chickens that she became known as an expert on farm life. She wrote for the *Missouri Ruralist* from 1912 to 1920. She also wrote articles for *McCall's* and the *Country Gentleman*. She entertained her daughter with the delightful and warm memories of her childhood.

Rose Wilder moved to California in 1908 and became a journalist. During World War I, she was a reporter in Europe, writing articles that made her a famous woman. In 1923, she moved back to her family's farm and encouraged her mother to write about pioneer life. Laura wrote an autobiography, and she called it *Pioneer Girl*. She sent it to an editor, who suggested that she tell just about her childhood. She followed his suggestions and also changed the title to *Little House in the Big Woods*. Harper and Brothers published the book in 1932. Encouraged, she continued to write about her life and the life of her husband. In 1933, *Farmer Boy* was published, followed by *Little House on the Prairie* in 1935; *On the Banks of Plum Creek* in 1938; *By the Shores of Silver Lake* in 1939; *The Long Winter* in 1940; *Little Town on the Prairie* in 1941; and *These Happy Golden Years* in 1943. Helen Sewell was her illustrator for all of these books.

Manly died on October 23, 1949, but Laura stayed at Rocky Ridge. Children around the world loved her books, and she became famous. Her books won several Newbery Honor Awards. They were reissued in 1962 with a new illustrator, Garth Williams. The Laura Ingalls Wilder Award, created in 1954, celebrates authors and illustrators whose bodies of works have enriched the lives of children. Garth Williams designed the Laura Ingalls Wilder Medal. Laura herself was the first recipient of the award. She died on February 10, 1957. Three of her books, *On the Way Home*, *The First Four Years*, and *West from Home*, were published posthumously.

Laura's works continue to be influential. Her books appeared in paperback form in 1971. Laura's life and writings became the springboard for a television series, *Little House on the Prairie*, that aired from 1974 to 1983. New generations of children continually discover and devour her books. Finally, the Laura Ingalls Wilder Award still honors good authors and illustrators and excellent children's books.

Laura Ingalls Wilder Timeline

Date	Event
1867	Born Laura Elizabeth Ingalls on February 7, near Pepin, Wisconsin, to Caroline and Charles Ingalls; an older sister, Mary welcomed the baby
1869	Family moved to Kansas; sister Carrie born August 3
1871	Family returned to Pepin, Wisconsin
1874	Family moved to Walnut Grove, Minnesota
1875	Charles Frederick (Freddie) born
1876	Freddie died at age nine months; family moved to Burr Oak, Iowa, to help run a hotel
1877	Sister Grace born on May 23; family moved back to Walnut Grove
1879	Unknown disease struck family, causing Mary to become blind; family moved to railroad camp (De Smet) Silver Lake in Dakota Territory; Almanzo Wilder, Laura's future husband, filed homestead claim
1884	Laura took a teaching job
1885	Married Almanzo (Manly) Wilder on August 25
1886	Daughter Rose born December 5
1888	Laura and Manly contracted diphtheria in spring
1889	Son born and died in August; house burned down
1890	Moved to Spring Valley, Minnesota, to be with Manly's family
1894	Moved to Westville, Florida, then back to De Smet and then to Mansfield, Missouri
1902	Charles Ingalls died in De Smet on June 8
1908	Rose moved to San Francisco, California
1909	Rose married Gillette Lane
1912	Laura named Home Editor of the *Missouri Ruralist* until 1920
1915	Traveled to California to see Rose
1924	Caroline Ingalls died in De Smet on April 20
1925	Published "My Ozark Kitchen" in January 17 issue of *Country Gentlemen*
1930	At age sixty-three wrote first book
1932	*Little House in the Big Wood* published by Harper and Brothers; illustrator was Helen Sewell
1933	Published *Farmer Boy*
1935	Published *Little House on the Prairie*
1937	Published *On the Banks of Plum Creek*
1938	*On the Banks of Plum Creek* given Newbery Honor Book Award
1939	Published *By the Shores of Silver Lake*
1940	Published *The Long Winter*; *By the Shores of Silver Lake* given Newbery Honor Book Award
1941	Published *Little Town on the Prairie*; *The Long Winter* given Newbery Honor Book Award
1942	*Little Town on the Prairie* presented Newbery Honor Book Award

Date	Event
1943	Published *These Happy Golden Years*
1944	*These Happy Golden Years* given Newbery Honor Book Award
1949	Manly's death at Rocky Ridge Farm on October 23
1953	Laura's books reissued with a new illustrator, Garth Williams
1954	Laura Ingalls Wilder Award created; the first award given to Laura
1957	Laura's death at Mansfield, Missouri, on February 10
1962	*On the Way Home* published posthumously
1971	*The First Four Years* published posthumously; Laura's books premiered in paperback form
1974	*West from Home* published posthumously
1974	Television series *Little House on the Prairie* aired until 1983

History and Criteria of Award

Laura Ingalls Wilder won many awards, including five Newbery Honor Awards. In the 1950s, the Association for Library Service to Children, a division of the American Library Association (ALA), created an award in honor of Laura.

The Laura Ingalls Wilder Award is given to an author or illustrator whose collective body of work has contributed to children's literature. The books must be published in the United States. The writer or illustrator must have created more than one work, and the works must have been obtainable by children at least ten years prior to the award. The award may be given posthumously, but the bulk of the work must have been done within twenty-five years of the award. Co-authors or co-illustrators may be considered.

The award committee should be knowledgeable regarding the writer's or illustrator's entire body of work. The work may be nominated because it is exceptional in comparison to similar works or because it is unique and new.

The first Laura Ingalls Wilder Award was actually given to Laura. From 1960 to 1980, the award was given every five years. From 1980 to 2001, it was awarded every three years. From 2001 to the present, it has been awarded every two years. The winners are made known at the ALA midwinter meeting, and they receive their awards at the ALA Annual Conference in June.

The Laura Ingalls Wilder Medal is made of bronze. Garth Williams, the illustrator of her books when they were reissued in 1953, created the original medal.

Works by Laura Ingalls Wilder

(Unless noted, all books, New York: Harper & Brothers)

By the Shores of Silver Lake, 1939

Farmer Boy, 1933

Little House in the Big Woods, 1932

Little House on the Prairie, 1935

Little Town on the Prairie, 1941

The Long Winter, 1940

On the Banks of Plum Creek, 1937

On the Way Home, New York: Harper & Row, 1962

The First Four Years, New York: Harper & Row, 1971

These Happy Golden Years, 1943

West from Home, New York: Harper & Row, 1974

Award Recipients

Year	Author
2005	Laurence Yep
2003	Eric Carle
2001	Milton Meltzer
1998	Russell Freedman
1995	Virginia Hamilton
1992	Marcia Brown
1989	Elizabeth George Speare
1986	Jean Fritz
1983	Maurice Sendak
1980	Theodor S. Geisel (Dr. Seuss)
1975	Beverly Cleary
1970	E. B. White
1965	Ruth Sawyer
1960	Clara Ingram Judson
1954	Laura Ingalls Wilder

Activities

1. On a large map children could mark all the spots where Laura Ingalls Wilder lived.

2. The Ingalls family moved to the Dakota Territory. Children could find out when the Dakota Territory became states.

3. Laura's sister Mary became blind in 1879. Children could learn more about Braille. An excellent Web site about Braille is: http://www.afb.org/braillebug/.

4. Many inventions made their appearance during Laura's life. Children could make two parallel timelines, one of her life and one of inventions.

5. Laura's father often played his violin for the children. The string teacher or a student proficient in string instruments could demonstrate the instrument.

6. Laura's books have been in publication since 1932. Several generations have grown up reading the series. Children could poll different age groups to see which of her books were their favorites.

7. The Laura Ingalls Wilder books and the Sydney Taylor books have some similarities. In both books, the characters are good role models, and the family unit is strong and loving. Children could read one of each series and then compare and contrast the main characters.

8. The book *Little House in the Big Woods* described many of the activities a pioneer family had to perform to survive. It talked about making bullets, smoking meat, salting fish, and gathering honey. Children could interview people who still carry out those activities.

9. Laura, her sisters, and her mother made quilts from scraps of cloth. Children could make paper quilts.

10. Eric Carle was given the Laura Ingalls Wilder Medal in 2003. Children could visit his Web site at: http://www.eric-carle.com/ and read his biography.

11. Beverly Cleary received the 1975 Laura Ingalls Wilder Medal. Children could visit her Web site at: http://www.beverlycleary.com/index.html. They could take various quizzes about the characters in Cleary's books.

12. Ruth Sawyer, the 1965 recipient of the Laura Ingalls Wilder Medal, was a pseudonym. Children could research her life to find her real name and the name of her famous son-in-law. Hint: http://www.stkate.edu/library/spcoll/ruthsaw.html.

13. Clara Ingram Judson, the 1960 recipient of the Laura Ingalls Wilder Medal, was a prolific writer. Children could read and react to one of her Mary Jane books at: http://library.beau.org/gutenberg/1/5/9/5/15954/15954-h/15954-h.htm.

14. Children could find out which of the Laura Ingalls Wilder Medal winners are still living. Then they could make birthday cards for them.

15. Marcia Brown, the 1992 Laura Ingalls Wilder Medal recipient, has won many other awards as well. Children could visit a Web site of her illustrations at: http://library.albany.edu/speccoll/findaids/marciaimages.htm. There they could see an illustration from "The Steadfast Tin Soldier," a tale by Hans Christian Andersen.

Laura Ingalls Wilder and the Laura Ingalls Wilder Award

Student Handout 1—Information

Who Was Laura Ingalls Wilder?

Laura Ingalls Wilder published her first book when she was sixty-four years old. Her books tell the story of her life on the American frontier.

Laura Elizabeth Ingalls was born on February 7, 1867, near Pepin, Wisconsin. Her parents, her sisters, and she moved several times, each time trying to survive as farmers. In 1879, the family was struck by a disease, probably scarlet fever. The disease caused Laura's sister Mary to become blind. The family worked together to send Mary to a school for the blind in Iowa. Eventually, Laura became a teacher, and some of her salary helped pay Mary's expenses. However, Laura had to quit teaching when she married Almanzo (Manly) Wilder.

Laura and Almanzo also moved several times, finally settling at Rocky Ridge in Missouri. They farmed and raised chickens and tended an orchard. Almanzo also worked as a drayman, driving a horse that pulled heavy loads. There they raised their daughter, Rose, and Laura wrote articles for local newspapers and magazines. Rose grew up and became a writer. She encouraged her mother to write down her childhood adventures. *Little House in the Big Woods* was published in 1932. More of her books were published, and she received five Newbery Honor Book Awards. Her books are still popular today, and her work inspired a television series.

Laura Ingalls Wilder died on February 10, 1957.

What Is the Laura Ingalls Wilder Award?

The Laura Ingalls Wilder Award honors lifetime achievement for writers and illustrators of children's literature. The books must be published in the United States. The writer or illustrator must have created more than one work, and the works must have been available to children at least ten years prior to the award. The Association for Library Service to Children (ALSC) a division of the American Library Association (ALA) created the award in the 1950s. Laura herself received the first award in 1954. At first, the award was given every five years. Then it was given every three years. Now it is given every two years. The name of the winner is announced at the midwinter meeting of the ALA, and the awards are presented to the winners during ALA's summer conference.

From *Children's Book Award Handbook* by Diana F. Marks. Westport, CT: Libraries Unlimited. Copyright © 2006.

Laura Ingalls Wilder and the Laura Ingalls Wilder Award

Student Handout 2—Questions

Name_____ Date_____

Investigate the life of Laura Ingalls Wilder, and find out more about the Laura Ingalls Wilder Award. Then answer the following questions.

1. Where and when was Laura Ingalls Wilder born?

2. Why did her family move often?

3. What happened to her sister Mary?

4. What job did Laura have before she got married?

5. Where did Laura and Almanzo finally settle down? How did they make a living?

6. At what age did Laura Ingalls Wilder publish her first book? Why did she write her first book?

7. When did Laura Ingalls Wilder die?

8. List three facts about the Laura Ingalls Wilder Award.

9. How is the Laura Ingalls Wilder Award different from either the Newbery Medal or the Caldecott Medal?

10. Could J. K. Rowling ever receive the Laura Ingalls Wilder Award?

Laura Ingalls Wilder and the Laura Ingalls Wilder Award

Student Handout 3—Making Butter

Name_____ Date_____

Laura Ingalls Wilder grew up on the American frontier. She and her family raised their own animals, harvested their own crops, and prepared their own food. They dried fruits, made preserves, smoked meats, baked bread, and made butter. Usually you buy butter at the grocery store, but today you are going to make butter. Then you get to taste it!

Butter (makes about 1 cup butter, enough for about 18 children)

Materials

6 very clean small jars with lids

6 very clean marbles

1 pint heavy cream

salt (optional)

crackers

plastic knives

Procedure

1. Place a marble in each jar.

2. Pour some cream into each jar.

3. Screw the jar lids on tightly.

4. Begin to shake the jars. You can see and hear the marbles bounce around in each jar.

5. After about ten minutes, you will not be able to hear the marble hit the sides of the jar. The cream has become unsweetened whipped cream.

6. Continue to shake the jars.

7. After a few more minutes, the solid butter will begin to separate from the liquid.

8. Continue to shake until the butter has settled.

9. Carefully drain off the liquid and remove the marbles.

10. Add a bit of salt if you want.

11. Use the plastic knife to spread some butter on a cracker.

12. Eat and enjoy!

From *Children's Book Award Handbook* by Diana F. Marks. Westport, CT: Libraries Unlimited. Copyright © 2006.

Laura Ingalls Wilder and the Laura Ingalls Wilder Award

Student Handout 4—Research

Name_____ Date_____

Many famous writers have received the Laura Ingalls Wilder Award. Below is a table of the winners and the dates. Can you provide a book title for each of the winners? If you cannot think of a title, do some research. Find a title and add it to the list. You will be amazed as to how many books many of these authors wrote.

Year	Author	Book Title
2005	Laurence Yep	
2003	Eric Carle	
2001	Milton Meltzer	
1998	Russell Freedman	
1995	Virginia Hamilton	
1992	Marcia Brown	
1989	Elizabeth George Speare	
1986	Jean Fritz	
1983	Maurice Sendak	
1980	Theodor S. Geisel (Dr. Seuss)	
1975	Beverly Cleary	
1970	E. B. White	
1965	Ruth Sawyer	
1960	Clara Ingram Judson	
1954	Laura Ingalls Wilder	

CHAPTER 22

Charlotte Zolotow and the Charlotte Zolotow Award

Overview

The Charlotte Zolotow Award is given annually to the best writer of a children's picture book. Charlotte Zolotow has written over seventy children's picture books, and she has served as an editor for many more books.

Charlotte Shapiro was born in 1915 in Norfolk, Virginia. She knew at an early age that she wanted to be a writer. She graduated in 1936 from the University of Wisconsin on a writing scholarship and married Maurice Zolotow. They moved to New York City, and she became an assistant editor at Harper's. She published her first book, *The Park Book*, in 1944. For decades she published at least one children's picture book a year. Her books have been illustrated by many artists, including Margaret Bloy Graham, Maurice Sendak, Garth Williams, Anita Lobel, and William Pene du Bois. She also maintained her editing job at Harper's, and in 1982, she received her own imprint. Zolotow edited the works of many famous authors, including Lee Bennett Hopkins, Patricia Maclachlan, Paul Zindel, and Laurence Yep.

The Charlotte Zolotow Award, first presented in 1998, is administered by the Cooperative Children's Book Center of the University of Wisconsin-Madison. In addition to the winning title, up to three honor books and up to ten highly commended books can be designated. The name of the winner is announced in January; the winner receives the cash prize of $1,000 and a bronze medallion at a ceremony in the spring.

Charlotte Zolotow Biography

Charlotte Zolotow has balanced two careers, writing and editing. She has written over seventy children's books, and she has edited many more. She knows what children like to read, and she knows how to write simply but eloquently.

Charlotte Shapiro was born on June 26, 1915, to Louis J. Shapiro and Ella Bernstein Shapiro in Norfolk, Virginia. A sister, Dorothy, had been born six years before. The beautiful Ella Bernstein Shapiro loved to dress well. She was very active in a number of Jewish charities, and she was a strong advocate for women's rights. She marched for women's suffrage. Charlotte idolized her father. Louis Shapiro was a lawyer and ran an antique reproduction business. Unfortunately, he was not a very good executive, and their financial situation was often precarious. Her family moved often to seek better monetary situations. They lived in Detroit, Michigan, Brookline, Massachusetts, and New York City. Even within an area, they often moved to several addresses. Charlotte therefore often switched schools. She felt different from her peers. She wore thick glasses in second grade, and she had to have braces on her teeth. She was also diagnosed with scoliosis and had to wear a stiff back brace. Because she was shy and reserved, she had few friends. However, she loved to read and draw. From an early age, she knew she wanted to be a writer.

From 1933 to 1936 Charlotte attended the University of Wisconsin, where she studied literature. There she met Maurice Zolotow, a writer. They were married in 1938.

The couple moved to New York City, and they lived in a small apartment off Washington Park. Maurice was a literary agent. Charlotte was able to work for the legendary Ursula Norstrom, editor of Harper's children's book department. Charlotte was hired as an editorial assistant and became the editor of the children's division at Harper, serving until 1944. An admirer of Margaret Wise Brown, renowned author of *Goodnight Moon,* she suggested to Norstrom that Brown write a children's book about events that happen on a typical day in Washington Park. Charlotte did not understand that editors did not suggest topics to writers, let alone writers as famous as Brown. Norstrom asked her to outline the idea in more detail. Norstrom liked the idea but suggested that Charlotte herself write the book. *The Park Book*, illustrated by H. A. Rey, was published in 1944.

In 1945, Charlotte gave birth to a son, Stephen. She began to publish more books, including *But Not Billy.* In 1952, a daughter Ellen was born. She continued to publish books, including *The Magic Word* and *The City Boy and the Country Horse.* In 1953, her *The Storm Book*, illustrated by Margaret Bloy Graham, was a Caldecott Honor Book.

In 1969, Charlotte divorced Maurice Zolotow. He died in 1991.

From 1957 to 1984, Charlotte Zolotow published at least one book and sometimes as many as three books a year. Some of those books were *If It Weren't for You, A Father Like That,* and *William's Doll.* She also continued to work as a children's book editor. From 1962 to 1976, Charlotte was senior editor in the children's division of Harper's. Her *Mr. Rabbit and the Lovely Present*, published in 1962, won the illustrator, Maurice Sendak, a Caldecott Honor Book Award in 1963. In 1973, she edited *An Overpraised Season: Ten Stories of Youth*

In 1976, Charlotte became editorial director of Harper Junior Books. In 1981, she became vice president of Harper and Row. In 1982, she was given her own imprint, Charlotte Zolotow Books. After 1984, Charlotte's pace slowed but did not stop. The University of Minnesota gave her the Kerlan Award in 1986 for her contributions to children's literature. In 1987, she took the title of editorial consultant to Harper Junior Books. The University of Mississippi honored her in 1990 with the Silver Medallion, noting her body of work. The American Library Association in 1991 recognized her literary accomplishments in a resolution.

Charlotte Zolotow continues to publish books. *Who Is Ben?* appeared in 1997, and *Seasons* was published in 2002.

The first Charlotte Zolotow Award was given in Madison, Wisconsin, on October 1, 1998.

Charlotte Zolotow has stated that she is inspired by events that happened in the lives of her children and their friends. She also remembers happenings in her own life. She writes from the child's perspective, and her books are both compassionate and realistic.

Charlotte Zolotow Timeline

Date	Event
1915	Born Charlotte Shapiro to Louis J. Shapiro and Ella Bernstein Shapiro in Norfolk, Virginia, on June 26; a sister, Dorothy, had been born six years prior
	Moved to Detroit, Michigan
	Moved to Brookline, Massachusetts
	Moved to New York City
1933–1936	Attended University of Wisconsin
1938	Married Maurice Zolotow, writer
	Worked for Ursula Norstrom, editor of Harper's children's book department as editorial assistant
1938–1944	Was senior editor of children's division at Harper until 1944
1944	Published *The Park Book*, illustrated by H. A. Rey
1945	Son Stephen was born
1947	Published *But Not Billy*
1952	Daughter Ellen born; published *The Storm Book* and *The Magic Word* and *Indian, Indian* and *The City Boy and the Country Horse*
1953	Her *The Storm Book*, illustrated by Margaret Bloy Graham, was a Caldecott Honor Book; published *The Quiet Mother and the Noisy Little Boy*
1955	Published *One Step, Two…*
1957	Published *Over and Over* and *Not a Little Monkey*
1958	Published *Do You Know What I'll Do?* and *Sleepy Book* and *The Night When Mother Was Away*
1959	Published *The Bunny Who Found Easter*
1960	Published *Big Brother* and *In My Garden* and *The Little Black Puppy*
1961	Published *The Three Funny Friends* and *The Man with the Purple Eyes*
1962	Published *When the Wind Stops* and *Mr. Rabbit and the Lovely Present* and *Aren't You Glad?*; was again senior editor in children's division at Harper until 1976
1963	Published *A Tiger Named Thomas* and *The Sky Was Blue* and *The Quarreling Book* and *The White Marble* and *Aren't You Glad?*; her *Mr. Rabbit and the Lovely Present*, illustrated by Maurice Sendak, was a Caldecott Honor Book
1964	Published *A Rose, a Bridge, and a Wild Black Horse* and *The Poodle Who Barked at the Wind* and *I Have a Horse of My Own*
1965	Published *Someday* and *When I Have a Little Girl* and *Flocks of Birds*
1966	Published *If It Weren't for You* and *Big Sister and Little Sister* and *I Want to Be Little*
1967	Published *I Want to Be Little* and *When I Have a Son* and *All That Sunlight* and *Summer Is…*
1968	Published *My Friend John* and *The New Friend*
1969	Divorced Maurice Zolotow; published *A Week in Yani's World* and *Some Things Go Together* and *The Hating Book*

Date	Event
1970	Published *River Winding* and *A Week in Latef's World: India* and *Where I Begin*
1971	Published *You and Me* and *A Father Like That* and *Wake Up and Goodnight*
1972	Published *The Beautiful Christmas Tree* and *The Old Dog* and *Hold My Hand* and *William's Doll*
1973	Published *Janey*; edited *An Overpraised Season: Ten Stories of Youth*
1974	Published *My Grandson Lew*
1975	Published *The Unfriendly Book*
1976	Published *May I Visit?* and *It's Not Fair;* became editorial director of Harper Junior Books
1978	Published *Someone New*
1980	Published *Say It!* and *If You Listen*
1981	Became vice president of Harper and Row
1982	Was given her own imprint at Harper; published *The Song*
1984	Published *I Know a Lady*
1986	Published *Timothy Too!;* edited *Early Sorrow: Ten Stories of Youth*; received University of Minnesota's Kerlan Award
1987	Published *Everything Glistens and Everything Sings: New and Selected Poems*
1988	Published *Something Is Going to Happen*
1990	Received University of Mississippi's Sliver Medallion
1991	Honored by American Library Association; published *The Summer Night*; Maurice Zolotow died
1992	Published *This Quiet Lady* and *The Seashore Book*
1993	Published *Peter and the Pigeons* and *Snippets: A Gathering of Poems, Pictures, and Possibilities* and *The Moon Was the Best*
1997	Published *Who Is Ben?*
1998	The first Charlotte Zolotow Award given in Madison, at the University of Wisconsin on October 1
2002	Published *Seasons*

History and Criteria of Award

The Charlotte Zolotow Award has been given every year since 1998 to a writer of a children's picture book.

Charlotte Zolotow felt that picture book writers were slighted. The Caldecott Medal honors illustrators of picture books, and the Newbery Medal honors writers of chapter books. She was upset that some picture book writers, including Margaret Wise Brown, never received any awards.

The University of Wisconsin-Madison houses the Cooperative Children's Book Center (CCBC), the School of Education children's library. Ginny Moore Cruse, the director of the CCBC, knew Charlotte Zolotow. As an alumnus of the University of Wisconsin, Charlotte had contributed a number of her manuscripts to CCBC. Cruse felt that Zolotow should be honored in some way. Cruse and Kathleen T. Horning, the coordinator of Special Collections at CCBC, began to dialogue. The two and John Uselman, the University of Wisconsin's Development Director, traveled to New York and met with Susan Katz, an editor of HarperCollins's children's book department. HarperCollins also felt that Charlotte Zolotow should be honored. The Charlotte Zolotow Award was created, and HarperCollins provided the initial funding.

The CCBC administers the award. A committee composed of members of the Friends of the CCBC, Inc. and staff members examine eligible books and determine the winners.

The following rules determine the committee's work:

1. The book must be written with children up to age seven in mind.

2. The book must be originally published in English.

3. The book must be published in the United States.

4. The book must be published in the year prior to the award year.

5. The book may be fiction, nonfiction, or folklore.

6. Easy Readers are not eligible.

7. Books written by Charlotte Zolotow are not eligible.

8. In addition to the award-winning book, the committee may name up to three honor books and up to ten highly commended books.

The author of the winning book receives a bronze medallion and a cash prize of $1,000. Authors of honor books are given plaques.

Works by Charlotte Zolotow

All That Sunlight. New York: Harper, 1967.

Aren't You Glad? New York: Lothrop, 1963.

Beautiful Christmas Tree, The. New York: Parnassus, 1972.

Big Brother. New York: Harper, 1960.

Big Sister and Little Sister. New York: Harper, 1966.

Bunny Who Found Easter, The. New York: Parnassus, 1959.

But Not Billy. New York: Harper Brothers, 1947.

City Boy and the Country Horse, The. (Pseudonym Charlotte Bookman). New York: Treasure Books, 1952.

Do You Know What I'll Do? New York: Harper, 1958.

Early Sorrow: Ten Stories of Youth. New York: Harper, 1986.

Everything Glistens and Everything Sings: New and Selected Poems. New York: Harcourt, 1987.

Father Like That, A. New York: Harper, 1971.

Flocks of Birds. New York: Abelyard-Schuman, 1965.

Hating Book, The. New York: Harper, 1969.

Hold My Hand. New York: Harper, 1972.

If It Weren't for You. New York: Harper, 1966.

If You Listen. New York: Harper, 1980.

I Have a Horse of My Own. New York: Abelyard-Schuman, 1964.

I Know a Lady. New York: Greenwillow, 1984.

Indian, Indian. New York: Simon & Schuster, 1952.

In My Garden. New York: Lothrop, 1960.

It's Not Fair. New York: Harper, 1976.

I Want to Be Little. New York: Abelyard-Schuman, 1966. Second edition, retitled: *I Like to Be Little.* New York: Crowell, 1987.

Janey. New York: Harper, 1973.

Little Black Puppy, The. New York: Golden Press, 1960.

Magic Word, The. New York: Wonder Books, 1952.

Man with the Purple Eyes, The. New York: Abelyard-Schuman, 1961.

May I Visit? New York: Harper, 1976.

Moon Was the Best, The. New York: Greenwillow, 1993.

Mr. Rabbit and the Lovely Present. New York: Harper, 1962.

My Friend John. New York: Harper, 1968.

My Grandson Lew. New York: Harper, 1974.

New Friend, The. New York: Abelyard-Schuman, 1968.

The Night When Mother Was Away. New York: Lothrop, 1958; republished as *Summer Night, The.* New York: Harper, 1974.

Not a Little Monkey. New York: Lothrop, 1957.

Old Dog, The. (Pseudonym Sarah Abbott). New York: Coward-McCann, 1972.

One Step, Two . . . New York: Lothrop, 1955.

Over and Over. New York: Harper, 1957.

Overpraised Season, An: Ten Stories of Youth. New York: Harper, 1973.

Park Book, The. New York: Harper, 1944.

Peter and the Pigeons. New York: Greenwillow, 1993.

Poodle Who Barked at the Wind, The. New York: Lothrop, 1964.

Quarreling Book, The. New York: Harper, 1963.

Quiet Lady, This. New York: Greenwillow, 1992.

Quiet Mother and the Noisy Little Boy, The. New York: Lothrop, 1953.

River Winding. New York: Abelyard-Schuman, 1970.

Rose, a Bridge, and a Wild Black Horse, A. New York: Harper, 1964.

Say It! New York: Greenwillow, 1980.

Seashore Book, The. New York: HarperCollins, 1992.

Seasons. New York: HarperCollins, 2002.

Sky Was Blue, The. New York: Harper, 1963.

Sleepy Book. New York: Lothrop, 1958.

Snippets: A Gathering of Poems, Pictures, and Possibilities. New York: HarperCollins, 1993.

Someday. New York: Harper, 1965.

Some Things Go Together. New York: Abelyard-Schuman, 1969.

Something Is Going to Happen. New York: Harper, 1988.

Song, The. New York: Greenwillow, 1982.

Storm Book, The. New York: Harper, 1952.

Summer Is . . . New York: Abelyard-Schuman, 1967.

Summer Night, The. New York: Harper, 1974.

Three Funny Friends, The. New York: Harper, 1961.

Tiger Called Thomas, A. New York: Lothrop, 1963.

Timothy Too! New York: Houghton, 1986.

Unfriendly Book, The. New York: Harper, 1975.

Wake Up and Goodnight. New York: Harper, 1971.

Week in Lateef's World, A: India. New York: Crowell-Collier, 1970.

Week in Yani's World, A: Greece. New York: Macmillan, 1969.

When I Have a Little Girl. New York: Harper, 1965.

When I Have a Son. New York: Harper, 1967.

When the Wind Stops. New York: Abelyard-Schuman, 1962.

Where I Begin. Coward-McCann, 1970.

White Marble, The. New York: Abelyard-Schuman, 1963.

Who Is Ben? New York: HarperCollins, 1997.

William's Doll. New York: Harper, 1972.

You and Me. New York: Macmillan, 1971.

Award, Honor, and Highly Commended Books

Year	Award	Author/Illustrator	Title	Publisher
2006	Winner	Mary Ann Rodman, author E. B. Lewis, illustrator	*My Best Friend*	Viking
	Honor Books	Patricia C. McKissack and Onawumi Jean Moss, authors Krysten Brooker, illustrator	*Precious and the Boo Hag*	Anne Schwartz Book/Atheneum
		Jon J. Muth	*Zen Shorts*	Scholastic
	Highly Commended Books	Leslie Patricelli	*Binky*	Candlewick Press
		Sandy Turner	*Cool Cat, Hot Dog*	Atheneum
		Norton Juster, author Chris Raschka, illustrator	*The Hello, Goodbye Window*	Michael di Capua/Hyperion
		Mo Willems	*Leonardo the Terrible Monster*	Hyperion
		Stephen Michael King	*Mutt Dog!*	U. S. edition: Harcourt
		Elivia Savadier	*No Haircut Today!*	Neal Porter/Roaring Brook Press
		Bob Graham	*Oscar's Half Birthday*	U. S. edition: Candlewick Press
		Mara Berman, author Nick Maland, illustrator	*Snip, Snap! What's That?*	U. S. edition: Greenwillow Books/HarperCollins
		William Bee	*Whatever*	U. S. edition: Candlewick Press
2005	Winner	Kevin Henkes	*Kitten's First Full Moon*	Greenwillow Books/HarperCollins
	Honor Books	Lauren Thompson, author Stephen Savage, illustrator	*Polar Bear Night*	Scholastic
		Mo Willems	*Knuffle Bunny: A Cautionary Tale*	Hyperion
		Jacqueline Woodson, author E. B. Lewis, illustrator	*Coming on Home Soon*	Putnam
	Highly Commended Books	Karen Beaumont, author Jennifer Plecas, illustrator	*Baby Danced the Polka*	Dial
		Caralyn Buehner, author Mark Buehner, illustrator	*Superdog: The Heart of a Hero*	HarperCollins

Year	Award	Author/Illustrator	Title	Publisher
		Alan Durant, author Debi Gliori, illustrator	*Always and Forever*	Harcourt
		Olivier Dunrea	*BooBoo*	Houghton Mifflin
		Karen English, author Javaka Steptoe, illustrator	*Hot Day on Abbott Avenue*	Clarion
		Mary Ann Hoberman, author Jane Dyer, illustrator	*Whose Garden Is It?*	Harcourt
		Dave Horowitz	*A Monkey Among Us*	HarperCollins
		Patricia and Emily MacLachlan, authors Dan Yaccarino, illustrator	*Bittle*	Joanna Cotler Books/HarperCollins
		Carole Lexa Schaefer, author Stacey Dressen-McQueen, illustrator	*The Biggest Soap*	Melanie Kroupa/Farrar, Straus & Giroux
2004	Winner	Amy Schwartz	*What James Likes Best*	Richard Jackson/Atheneum
	Honor Books	John Coy, author Carolyn Fisher, illustrator	*Two Old Potatoes and Me*	Alfred A. Knopf
		Rebecca O'Connell, author Ken Wilson-Max, illustrator	*The Baby Goes Beep*	Deborah Brodie/Roaring Book Press
		Won-Ldy Paye and Margaret H. Lippert, authors Julie Paschkis, illustrator	*Mrs. Chicken and the Hungry Crocodile*	Henry Holt
		James Rumford	*Calabash Cat and His Amazing Journey*	Houghton Mifflin
		George Shannon, author Laura Dronzek, illustrator	*Tippy-Toe Chick, Go!*	Greenwillow Books/HarperCollins
	Highly Commended Books	Kate Banks, author Tomek Bogacki, illustrator	*Mama's Coming Home*	Frances Foster Books/Farrar, Straus & Giroux
		Deborah Chandra and Madeleine Comora, authors Brock Cole, illustrator	*George Washington's Teeth*	Farrar, Straus & Giroux
		Denise Fleming	*Buster*	Henry Holt
		Jeron Ashford Frame, author R. Gregory Christie, illustrator	*Yesterday I Had the Blues*	Tricycle Press

Year	Award	Author/Illustrator	Title	Publisher
		Steve Jenkins and Robin Page	*What Do You Do with a Tail Like This?*	Houghton Mifflin
		Naomi Shihab Nye, author Nancy Carlson, illustrator	*Baby Radar*	Greenwillow Books/HarperCollins
		Lynne Rae Perkins	*Snow Music*	Greenwillow Books/HarperCollins
		Andrea U'ren	*Mary Smith*	Farrar, Straus & Giroux
		Mo Willems	*Don't Let the Pigeon Drive the Bus*	Hyperion
2003	Winner	Holly Keller	*Farfallina & Marcel*	Greenwillow Books/HarperCollins
	Honor Book	Susan Marie Swanson, author Christine Davenier, illustrator	*The First Thing My Mama Told Me*	Harcourt
	Highly Commended Books	Nancy Andrews-Goebel, author David Diaz, illustrator	*The Pot That Juan Built*	Lee & Low
		Kate Banks, author Georg Hallensleben, illustrator	*Close Your Eyes*	Frances Foster Books/Farrar, Straus & Giroux
		Kevin Henkes	*Owen's Marshmallow Chick*	Greenwillow Books/HarperCollins
		Juan Felipe Herrera, author Anita de Lucio-Brock, illustrator	*Grandma and Me at the Flea*	Children's Book Press
		Kate and Jim McMullan	*I Stink!*	Joanna Cotler Books/HarperCollins
		Jean Davies Okimoto and Elaine M. Aoki, authors Meilo So, illustrator	*The White Swan Express: A Story about Adoption*	Clarion
		Alice Schertle, author Barbara Lavallee, illustrator	*All You Need for a Snowman*	Silver Whistle/Harcourt
		David Shannon	*Duck on a Bike*	Blue Sky Press/Scholastic
		Karma Wilson, author Jane Chapman, illustrator	*Bear Snores On*	Margaret K. McElderry Books
		Janet S. Wong, author Margaret Chodos-Irvine, illustrator	*Apple Pie Fourth of July*	Harcourt
2002	Winner	Margaret Willey, author Heather Solomon, illustrator	*Clever Beatrice*	Atheneum

Year	Award	Author/Illustrator	Title	Publisher
	Honor Book	Emily Jenkins	*Five Creatures*	Frances Foster Books/Farrar, Straus & Giroux
	Highly Commended Books	Lenore Look, author Yumi Leo, illustrator	*Henry's First Moon Birthday*	Anne Schwartz/Atheneum
		Margaret Read MacDonald, author Tim Coffey, illustrator	*Mabela the Clever*	Albert Whitman
		Marisabina Russo	*Come Back, Hannah*	Greenwillow Books/HarperCollins
		Catherine Stock	*Gugu's House*	Clarion
		Janet S. Wong, author John Wallace, illustrator	*Grump*	Margaret K. McElderry Books
2001	Winner	Kate Banks, author Georg Hallensleben, illustrator	*The Night Worker*	Frances Foster Books/Farrar, Straus & Giroux
	Honor Book	Christopher Myers	*Wings*	Scholastic
	Highly Commended Books	Peggy Christian, author Barbara Hirsch Lember, illustrator	*If You Find a Rock*	Harcourt
		Doreen Cronin, author Betsy Lewin, illustrator	*Click, Clack, Moo: Cows That Type*	Simon & Schuster
		Joy Harjo, author Paul Lee, illustrator	*The Good Luck Cat*	Harcourt
		Kimiko Kajikawa, author Yumi Heo, illustrator	*Yoshi's Feast*	Melanie Kroupa/ DK Ink
		Sandra L. Pinkney, author Myles C. Pinkney, photographer	*Shades of Black: A Celebration of Our Children*	Scholastic
		Nancy Van Laan, author Susan Gaber, illustrator	*When Winter Comes*	Anne Schwartz/Atheneum
2000	Winner	Molly Bang	*When Sophie Gets Angry—Really, Really Angry…*	Blue Sky/Scholastic
	Honor Books	Cari Best, author Gieselle Potter, illustrator	*Three Cheers for Catherine the Great!*	Melanie Kroupa/ DK Ink
		Jules Feiffer	*Bark, George*	Michael di Capua/HarperCollins
	Highly Commended Books	Baba Wagué Diakité	*The Hatseller and the Monkeys*	Scholastic
		Kristine O'Connell George, author June Otani, illustrator	*Little Dog Poems*	Clarion

Year	Award	Author/Illustrator	Title	Publisher
		Joan Bransfield Graham, author Nancy Davis, illustrator	*Flicker Flash*	Houghton Mifflin
		Elizabeth Fitzgerald Howard, author Nina Crews, illustrator	*When Will Sarah Come?*	Greenwillow
		Amy Schwartz	*How to Catch an Elephant*	DK Ink
		Joyce Carol Thomas, author Nneka Bennett, illustrator	*You Are My Perfect Baby*	Harper Growing Tree/HarperCollins
		Andrea Zimmerman and David Clemesha	*Trashy Town*	HarperCollins
1999	Winner	Uri Shulevitz	*Snow*	Farrar, Straus & Giroux
	Honor Books	Holly Meade	*John Willy and Freddy McGee*	Marshall Cavendish
		William Steig	*Pete's a Pizza*	Michael di Capua/HarperCollins
	Highly Commended Books	Denise Fleming	*Mama Cat Has Three Kittens*	Henry Holt
		Kevin Henkes, author Dan Yaccarino, illustrator	*Circle Dogs*	Greenwillow
		Bill T. Jones and Susan Kuklin, authors Susan Kuklin, photographer	*Dance*	Hyperion
		Lynn Reiser	*Little Clam*	Greenwillow
		Stephanie Stuve-Bodeen, author Christy Hale, illustrator	*Elizabeti's Doll*	Lee & Low
1998	Winner	Vera B. Williams	*Lucky Song*	Greenwillow
	Honor Book	Keiko Kasza	*Don't Laugh, Joe!*	Putnam
	Highly Commended Books	Marion Dane Bauer, author JoEllen MacAllister Stammen, illustrator	*If You Were Born a Kitten*	Simon & Schuster
		Elisha Cooper	*Country Fair*	Greenwillow
		Denise Fleming	*Time to Sleep*	Henry Holt
		Patricia C. McKissack, author Floyd Cooper, illustrator	*Ma Dear's Aprons*	Anne Schwartz/Atheneum
		Bernard Waber	*Bearsie Bear and the Surprise Sleepover Party*	Houghton Mifflin
		Rosemary Wells	*Bunny Cakes*	Dial

Activities

1. Charlotte Zolotow was born in Virginia, lived in Michigan, Massachusetts, and New York, and attended college in Wisconsin. Children could mark those locations on a big map.

2. Charlotte was a writer and an editor. Children could interview a teacher or volunteer who edits others' writing. They could learn about editing marks and how the writer and editor converse.

3. One of Charlotte Zolotow's favorite writers was Margaret Wise Brown, the author of *Goodnight Moon*. Children could visit Brown's Web site at: http://www. margaretwisebrown.com/. Then they could read either *Goodnight Moon* or *Runaway Bunny*.

4. Children could obtain some Zolotow books and look at the illustrating styles. Some of her illustrators were Maurice Sendak, Garth Williams, H. A. Rey, and Anita Lobel. Children could vote on their favorite illustrator for a Zolotow book.

5. In 1982, Charlotte Zolotow was given her own imprint at Harper. Children could pretend they each have their own imprint. What kind of books would they print?

6. Jacqueline Woodson's *Coming on Home Soon* is a 2005 honor book. Children could look at her Web site at: http://www.jacquelinewoodson.com/. They could research her favorite food. Then they could make paper pizza bookmarks.

7. Baba Wagué Diakité's book, *The Hatseller and the Monkeys,* was a highly commended book in 2000. Children can read a summary at: http://www.rambles.net/diakite_ hats.html. They could compare and contrast it to *Caps for Sale*.

8. Christopher Myers wrote *Wings*, a 2001 honor book. Children could visit his Web site at: http://www.rif.org/art/illustrators/myers.mspx. They could find out if he is related to Walter Dean Myers.

9. Molly Bang's *When Sophie Gets Angry—Really, Really Angry...*received the Charlotte Zolotow Award in 2000. Children could visit her Web site at: http://www. mollybang.com/index.html and find out who the original Sophie was. Each child could write down what he or she does when anger comes along.

10. Dave Horowitz wrote *A Monkey Among Us*, a 2005 highly commended book. Children could see his works at: http://www.horowitzdave.com/. They can find out what instrument he plays. They could find out who in their school plays the drums and watch that person in action.

Charlotte Zolotow and the Charlotte Zolotow Award

Student Handout 1—Information

Who Is Charlotte Zolotow?

Charlotte Zolotow has written over seventy children's picture books, and she has served as an editor for many more books.

Charlotte Shapiro was born on June 26, 1915, in Norfolk, Virginia. She knew at an early age that she wanted to be a writer. She graduated from the University of Wisconsin in 1936 on a writing scholarship. She married Maurice Zolotow. They moved to New York City, and she became an assistant editor at Harper's. She suggested to her boss that a children's book about a park would be a good book. Her boss said that Charlotte should write the book. She published her first book, *The Park Book*, in 1944. For decades she published at least one children's picture book a year. Her books have been illustrated by many artists, including Margaret Bloy Graham, Maurice Sendak, Garth Williams, Anita Lobel, and William Pene du Bois. She also kept her editing job at Harper's and received her own imprint in 1982. Zolotow edited the works of many famous authors, including Lee Bennett Hopkins, Patricia Maclachlan, Paul Zindel, and Laurence Yep.

What Is the Charlotte Zolotow Award?

The Charlotte Zolotow Award is given annually to the best writer of a children's picture book. The award, first presented in 1998, is managed by the Cooperative Children's Book Center of the University of Wisconsin-Madison. The winning book must originally be published in English, and the book must have originally been published in the United States. In addition to the winning title, up to three honor books and up to ten highly commended books can be listed. The name of the winner is announced in January, and the winner receives the cash prize of $1,000 and a bronze medallion at a ceremony in the spring. Authors of honor books are given plaques.

Charlotte Zolotow and the Charlotte Zolotow Award

Student Handout 2—Questions

Name_____ Date_____

Investigate the life of Charlotte Zolotow, and find out more about the Charlotte Zolotow Award. Then answer the following questions.

1. Where and when was Charlotte Zolotow born?

2. What was her first job after graduating college? Where did she work?

3. How did Charlotte become a writer?

4. Charlotte Zolotow was both a writer and an editor. What does an editor do?

5. Would you rather be a writer or an editor?

6. You write a great deal, at least in school. Who are your editors?

7. List three facts about the Charlotte Zolotow Award.

8. Pick another children's literature award. How is the Charlotte Zolotow Award like the award you picked?

9. How is the Charlotte Zolotow Award different from the award you picked?

10. Read several books written by Charlotte Zolotow. Which one was your favorite? Why?

Charlotte Zolotow and the Charlotte Zolotow Award

Student Handout 3—Picture Books

Name_____ Date_____

Charlotte Zolotow wrote more than seventy picture books. She did not illustrate her picture books. Famous illustrators, including Maurice Sendak, Margaret Bloy Graham, and H. A. Rey, provided the artwork for her books. Several of the artists won Caldecott Honor Book Awards.

The Charlotte Zolotow Award is given every year to the best writer of a children's picture book.

What do you know about picture books? Did you know there are rules? Select three picture books, perhaps books written by Charlotte Zolotow. Perhaps you could choose Charlotte Zolotow Award-winning books. Spread them out and look at them carefully. Read the words and look at the pictures.

Do you see anything that is the same in all three books? Write down what you found out in the spaces below.

Charlotte Zolotow and the Charlotte Zolotow Award

Student Handout 4—Parade of Picture Books

Name_____ Date_____

Charlotte Zolotow has written more than seventy picture books. The Charlotte Zolotow Award is given every year to the best writer of a children's picture book.

Let's have a parade of picture books. You will need:

a favorite picture book

a large piece of paper

a pencil

crayons, markers or paint

Let's get ready.

1. Pick out one of your favorite picture books. It could be a book written by Charlotte Zolotow. It could be a Charlotte Zolotow Award book. It could be another award-winning book.

2. Find your favorite part of the story.

3. Now draw a scene that describes that story on a large piece of paper.

4. Add lots of color and detail to the picture.

5. When everyone is done, you will hold your poster in front of you and line up.

6. Then everyone can walk in a parade of picture books.

7. Maybe another class could watch your parade of picture books.

8. Do you see another poster of a book that looks really interesting to you?

CHAPTER 23

Other Children's Literature Awards

Many other children's book awards exist. Some of them are quite broad. For instance, the Jefferson Cup, presented by the Virginia Library Association's Children's and Young Adult Round Table, is presented to outstanding biographies, historical fiction, or American history books. Some of the awards are specialized. For example, in 1974 the National Council for Social Studies created the Carter G. Woodson Book Award, recognizing outstanding social science books that portray ethnicity in the United States. Another specialized award is the Phoenix Award. Created in 1985 by the Children's Literature Association, the Phoenix Award honors books that were published in English twenty years prior to the award and did not receive any major awards at the time of publication.

Many organizations provide lists of outstanding books. Since 1996, the Association for Library Service to Children has published a yearly list of Notable Children's Books. The National Science Teachers Association and the Children's Book Council annually print a list of Outstanding Science Trade Books for Students K–12. The International Reading Association (IRA) has since 1975 given the IRA Children's Book Awards to exemplary authors who have published one or two children's or young adults' books.

Many states support their own awards. The Minnesota Humanities Commission created the Minnesota Book Awards in 1988. More than 900 Minnesota writers and illustrators have been honored. The Rhode Island Children's Book Award was founded in 1990 by the Rhode Island Chapter of the IRA the Rhode Island Library Association (RILA), and the Rhode Island Educational Media Association (RIEMA) under the sponsorship of the Rhode Island Office of Library and Information Services (OLIS). Children vote for their favorite books in the Iowa Children's Choice Awards, created by the Iowa Association of School Librarians and first presented in 1980.

Countries other than the United States sponsor their own awards. Children's Book Council of Australia Awards are given to Australian writers. Five categories of awards are currently presented, and the award was first conferred in 1946. New Zealand founded the New Zealand Children's Book Awards in 1945. The Young Adult Services Interest Group of the Canadian Library Association coordinates the Young Adult Canadian Book Award, first presented in 1981.

Two awards deserve special mention, the Golden Kite Award and the Boston Globe-Horn Book Award.

341

The Golden Kite Award

The Society of Children's Book Writers and Illustrators sponsors the Golden Kite Award. The award is the only children's literature award determined by authors and illustrators. Currently, four awards are presented annually: fiction, nonfiction, picture book text, and picture book illustration. An honor book can be awarded in each category as well. Finally, the group presents a certificate of acknowledgment to the author of the book that receives the picture book illustration award.

The Society of Children's Book Writers and Illustrators was created in 1971 in Los Angeles, California, and the first Golden Kite Awards were presented for books published in 1973. Presently, over 19,000 members in over seventy regions provide support to each other, as well as librarians, educators, and publishers.

The rules regarding the Golden Kite Award are fairly basic.

1. The books must be written or illustrated by members of the Society of Children's Book Writers and Illustrators.

2. Co-authors must also be members of the group.

3. Every book written by a member of the group is eligible.

4. Anthologies and translations are not considered for the award.

5. The books must be submitted by mid-December of the year of publication.

6. The winners are announced by March of the following year.

7. The winning recipients are given a Gold Kite statuette.

8. The honor book recipients are given an Honor Book plaque.

9. The Society of Children's Book Writers and Illustrators also sponsors the Sid Fleischman Humor Award, honoring witty books. The award was first presented to Sid Fleischman in 2002.

Award and Honor Books

Year	Category	Award	Author/Illustrator	Title	Publisher
2004	Fiction	Award Book	Christopher Paul Curtis	*Bucking the Sarge*	Wendy Lamb Books
		Honor Book	Steve Lyon	*The Gift Moves*	Houghton Mifflin
	Nonfiction	Award Book	Michael L. Cooper	*Dust to Eat: Drought and Depression in the 1930s*	Clarion
		Honor Book	Judith Bloom Fradin and Dennis Brindell Fradin	*The Power of One: Daisy Bates and the Little Rock Nine*	Clarion
	Picture Book Text	Award Book	Deborah Hopkinson	*Apples to Oregon*	Atheneum
		Honor Book	Pamela S. Turner	*Hachiko: The True story of a Loyal Dog*	Houghton Mifflin
	Picture Book Illustration	Award Book	Jean Cassels	*The Mysterious Collection of Dr. David Harleyson*	Walker & Co.
		Honor Book	Loren Long (author Walt Whitman)	*When I Heard the Learn'd Astronomer*	Simon & Schuster
2003	Fiction	Award Book	Jerry Spinelli	*Milkweed*	Alfred A. Knopf/Random House
		Honor Book	Donna Jo Napoli	*Breath*	Atheneum/Simon & Schuster
	Nonfiction	Award Book	Robert Byrd	*Leonardo: Beautiful Dreamer*	Dutton/Penguin
		Honor Book	Carmen Bredeson	*After the Last Dog Died: The True-Life, Hair-Raising Adventure of Douglas Mawson and His 1911-1914 Antarctic Expedition*	National Geographic
	Picture Book Text	Award Book	Amy Timberlake	*The Dirty Cowboy*	Farrar, Straus & Giroux
		Honor Book	Jacqueline Briggs Martin	*On Sand Island*	Houghton Mifflin
	Picture Book Illustration	Award Book	Loren Long (author Angela Johnson)	*I Dream of Trains*	Simon & Schuster

Year	Category	Award	Author/Illustrator	Title	Publisher
		Honor Book	Yuyi Morales	*Just a Minute*	Chronicle
2002	Fiction	Award Book	JaVra Placide	*Fresh Girl*	Wendy Lamb Books
		Honor Book	Jessie Haas	*Shaper*	Greenwillow
	Nonfiction	Award Book	Elizabeth Partridge	*This Land Was Made for You and Me: The Life and Songs of Woody Guthrie*	Viking
		Honor Book	Beverly Gherman	*Ansel Adams: America's Photographer*	Little, Brown
	Picture Book Text	Award Book	Sarah Wilson	*George Hogglesberry, Grade School Alien*	Tricycle Press
		Honor Book	Barbara Joose	*Stars in the Darkness*	Chronicle Books
	Picture Book Illustration	Award Book	Maria Frazee (author Linda Smith)	*Mrs. Biddlebox*	HarperCollins
		Honor Book	Ponder Goembel (author Lisa Wheeler)	*Sailor Moo, Cow at Sea*	Atheneum
2001	Fiction	Award Book	Virginia Euwer Wolff	*True Believer*	Atheneum
		Honor Book	Kelly Easton	*The Life History of a Star*	McElderry
	Nonfiction	Award Book	Susan Campbell Bartoletti	*Black Potatoes: The Story of the Great Irish Famine*	Houghton Mifflin
		Honor Book	Judith St. George	*John and Abigail Adams: An American Love Story*	Holiday House
	Picture Book Text	Award Book	J. Patrick Lewis	*The Shoe Tree of Chagrin*	Creative Editions
		Honor Book	Deborah Hopkinson	*Bluebird Summer*	Greenwillow
	Picture Book Illustration	Award Book	Beth Krommes (author Jacqueline Briggs Martin)	*The Lamp, the Ice and the Boat Called Fish*	Houghton Mifflin
		Honor Book	Lauren String (author Linda Ashman)	*Castles, Caves and Honeycombs*	Harcourt

Year	Category	Award	Author/Illustrator	Title	Publisher
2000	Fiction	Award Book	Kathleen Karr	*The Boxer*	Farrar, Straus & Giroux
		Honor Book	Patricia Reilly Giff	*Nory Ryan's Song*	Delacorte Press
	Nonfiction	Award Book	Ellen Levine	*Darkness over Denmark*	Holiday House
		Honor Book	Susan Goldman Rubin	*Fireflies in the Dark: The Story of Freidl Dicker-Brandeis and the Children of Terezin*	Holiday House
	Picture Book Text	Award Book	Jane Kurtz	*River Friendly, River Wild*	Simon & Schuster
		Honor Book	Marie Bradby	*Momma, Where Are You From?*	Orchard Books
	Picture Book Illustration	Award Book	David Shannon	*The Rain Came Down*	Blue Sky Press
		Honor Book	Kristen Balouch	*The King and the Three Thieves*	Viking
1999	Fiction	Award Book	Laurie Halse Anderson	*Speak*	Farrar, Straus & Giroux
		Honor Book	Christopher Paul Curtis	*Bud, Not Buddy*	Delacorte Press
	Nonfiction	Award Book	Marianne J. Dyson	*Space Station Science: Life in Free Fall*	Scholastic
		Honor Book	Elizabeth Cody Kimmel	*Ice Story: Shackleton's Lost Expedition*	Clarion
	Picture Book Text	Award Book	Deborah Hopkinson	*A Band of Angels*	Atheneum
		Honor Book	David Adler	*The Babe and I*	Harcourt, Brace
	Picture Book Illustration	Award Book	Amy Walrod	*The Little Red Hen (Makes a Pizza)*	Dutton
		Honor Book	Tim Coffey	*Red Berry Wook*	Albert Whitman & Co.
1998	Fiction	Award Book	Joan Bauer	*Rules of the Road*	Putnam
		Honor Book	Paul Fleischman	*Whirligig*	Henry Holt
	Nonfiction	Award Book	Russell Freedman	*Martha Graham: A Dancer's Life*	Clarion

Year	Category	Award	Author/Illustrator	Title	Publisher
		Honor Book	Elizabeth Partridge	*Restless Spirit: The Life and Work of Dorothea Lange*	Viking
	Picture Book Text	Award Book	Kristine O'Connell George	*Old Elm Speaks: Tree Poems*	Clarion
		Honor Book	Laura McGee Kvasnosky	*Zelda and Ivy*	Candlewick
	Picture Book Illustration	Award Book	Uri Shulevitz	*Snow*	Farrar, Straus & Giroux
		Honor Book	Laura McGee Kvasnosky	*Zelda and Ivy*	Candlewick
1997	Fiction	Award Book	Donna Jo Napoli	*Stones in Water*	Dutton
		Honor Book	Paul Fleischman	*Seedfolks*	HarperCollins
	Nonfiction	Award Book	Arlene Schulman	*Carmine's Story: A Book about a Boy Living with AIDS*	Lerner
		Honor Book	Norman H. Finkelstein	*With Heroic Truth: The Life of Edward R. Murrow*	Clarion
	Picture Book Text	Award Book	Marguerite W. Davol	*The Paper Dragon*	Atheneum
		Honor Book	Eve Bunting	*December*	Harcourt, Brace
	Picture Book Illustration	Award Book	Robert Sabuda	*The Paper Dragon*	Atheneum
		Honor Book	Janet Stevens	*To Market, to Market*	Harcourt, Brace
1996	Fiction	Award Book	Eloise McGraw	*The Moorchild*	McElderry
		Honor Book	Karen Hesse	*The Music of the Dolphins*	Scholastic
	Nonfiction	Award Book	Peg Kehret	*Small Steps: The Year I Got Polio*	Albert Whitman & Co.
		Honor Book	Susan Campbell Bartoletti	*Growing Up in Coal Country*	Houghton Mifflin
	Picture Book Text	Award Book	Diane Stanley	*Saving Sweetness*	Putnam
		Honor Book	Elizabeth Friedrich	*Leah's Pony*	Boyds Mills Press
	Picture Book Illustration	Award Book	Holly Berry	*Market Day*	HarperCollins/ JC

Year	Category	Award	Author/Illustrator	Title	Publisher
		Honor Book	Jerry Pinkney	*Minty: A Story of Young Harriet Tubman*	Dial
1995	Fiction	Award Book	Christopher Paul Curtis	*The Watsons Go to Birmingham—1963*	Delacorte
		Honor Book	Lee Bennett Hopkins	*Been to Yesterdays*	Boyds Mills Press
	Nonfiction	Award Book	Natalie S. Bober	*Abigail Adams*	Atheneum
		Honor Book	Walter Dean Myers	*One More River to Cross*	Harcourt, Brace
	Picture Book Illustration	Award Book	Dennis Nolan and Lauren Mills	*Fairy Wings*	Little, Brown
		Honor Book	Aki Sogabe	*The Loyal Cat*	Browndeer Press
1994	Fiction	Award Book	Karen Cushman	*Catherine, Called Birdy*	Clarion
		Honor Book	Nancy Farmer	*The Ear, the Eye and the Arm*	Orchard
	Nonfiction	Award Book	Russell Freedman	*Kids at Work: Lewis Hine and the Crusade against Child Labor*	Clarion
		Honor Book	Laurie Lawlor	*Shadow Catcher: The Life and Work of Edward S. Curtis*	Walker & Co.
	Picture Book Illustration	Award Book	Keith Baker	*Big Fat Hen*	Harcourt, Brace
		Honor Book	Robert Sabuda	*The Christmas Alphabet*	Orchard
1993	Fiction	Award Book	Virginia Euwer Wolff	*Make Lemonade*	Henry Holt
		Honor Book	Patrice Kindl	*Owl in Love*	Houghton Mifflin
	Nonfiction	Award Book	Russell Freedman	*Eleanor Roosevelt: A Life of Discovery*	Clarion
		Honor Book	Kathleen Krull	*Lives of the Musicians: Good Times, Bad Times, (And What the Neighbors Thought)*	Harcourt
	Picture Book Illustration	Award Book	Kevin Hawkes	*By the Light of the Halloween Moon*	Lothrop
		Honor Book	William Joyce	*Santa Calls*	HarperCollins/ LG

Year	Category	Award	Author/Illustrator	Title	Publisher
1992	Fiction	Award Book	Mary E. Lyons	*Letters from a Slave Girl*	Scribners
		Honor Book	Jennifer Armstrong	*Steal Away*	Orchard
	Nofiction	Award Book	Jim Murphy	*The Long Road to Gettysburg*	Clarion
		Honor Book	Russell Freedman	*An Indian Winter*	Holiday House
	Picture Book Illustration	Award Book	Patricia Polacco	*Chicken Sunday*	Philomel
		Honor Book	Trina Schart Hyman	*The Fortune Tellers*	Dutton
1991	Fiction	Award Book	Jean Thesman	*The Raincatchers*	Houghton Mifflin
		Honor Book	Paul Fleischman	*The Borning Room*	HarperCollins/ CZ
	Nonfiction	Award Book	Russell Freedman	*The Wright Brothers: How They Invented the Airplane*	Holiday House
		Honor Book	Walter Dean Myers	*Now Is Your Time!*	HarperCollins
	Picture Book Illustration	Award Book	Barbara Lavallee	*Mama, Do You Love Me?*	Chronicle
		Honor Book	Brian Pinkney	*Where Does the Trail Lead?*	Simon & Schuster
1990	Fiction	Award Book	Avi	*The True Confessions of Charlotte Doyle*	Orchard/RJ
		Honor Book	Bruce Brooks	*Everywhere*	HarperCollins
	Nonfiction	Award Book	Jim Murphy	*The Boy's War*	Clarion
		Honor Book	Russell Freedman	*Franklin Delano Roosevelt*	Clarion
	Picture Book Illustration	Award Book	Jerry Pinkney	*Home Place*	Macmillan
		Honor Book	Dennis Nolan	*Dinosaur Dream*	Macmillan
1989	Fiction	Award Book	Kristiana Gregory	*Jenny of the Tetons*	Gulliver/HBJ
		Honor Book	Linda Crew	*Children of the River*	Delacorte
	Nonfiction	Award Book	Judith St. George	*Panama Canal: Gateway to the World*	Putnam

Year	Category	Award	Author/Illustrator	Title	Publisher
		Honor Book	Bill Peet	*Bill Peet: An Autobiography*	Houghton Mifflin
	Picture Book Illustration	Award Book	Richard Jesse Watson	*Tom Thumb*	Harcourt
		Honor Book	Bill Peet	*Bill Peet: An Autobiography*	Houghton Mifflin
1988	Fiction	Award Book	George Ella Lyon	*Borrowed Children*	Orchard
		Honor Book	Pamela F. Service	*The Reluctant God*	Atheneum
	Nonfiction	Award Book	James Cross Giblin	*Let There Be Light*	Crowell
		Honor Book	Russell Freedman	*Buffalo Hunt*	Holiday
	Picture Book Illustration	Award Book	Susan Jeffers	*Forest of Dreams*	Dial
		Honor Book	Trina Schart Hyman	*Canterbury Tales*	Lothrop
1987	Fiction	Award Book	Lois Lowry	*Rabble Starkey*	Houghton Mifflin
		Honor Book	Janet Taylor Lisle	*The Great Dimpole Oak*	Orchard
	Nonfiction	Award Book	Rhoda Blumberg	*Incredible Journey of Lewis and Clark*	Lothrop
		Honor Book	Russell Freedman	*Lincoln: A Photobiography*	Clarion
	Picture Book Illustration	Award Book	Arnold Lobel	*The Devil and Mother Crump*	Harper
		Honor Book	Tomie dePaola	*What the Mailman Brought*	Putnam
1986	Fiction	Award Book	Margaret Rostkowski	*After the Dancing Days*	Harper
		Honor Book	Lynn Hall	*The Solitary*	Scribners
	Nonfiction	Award Book	Milton Meltzer	*Poverty in America*	Morrow
		Honor Book	Diane Stanley	*Peter the Great*	Four Winds
	Picture Book Illustration	Award Book	Suse MacDonald	*Alphabatics*	Bradbury
		Honor Book	Charles Mikolaycak	*Juma and the Magic Jinn*	Lothrop
1985	Fiction	Award Book	Patricia MacLachlan	*Sarah, Plain and Tall*	Harper

Year	Category	Award	Author/Illustrator	Title	Publisher
		Honor Book	Pam Conrad	*Prairie Songs*	Harper
	Nonfiction	Award Book	Rhoda Blumberg	*Commodore Perry in the Land of the Shogun*	Lothrop
		Honor Book	Judith St. George	*The Mount Rushmore Story*	Putnam
	Picture Book Illustration	Award Book	Barbara Helen Berger	*The Donkey's Dream*	Philomel
1984	Fiction	Award Book	Belinda Hermence	*Tancy*	Clarion
		Honor Book	Ellen Howard	*Circle of Giving*	Atheneum
	Nonfiction	Award Book	James Cross Giblin	*Walls: Defense throughout History*	Little, Brown
		Honor Book	Joanna Cole	*How You Were Born*	Morrow
	Picture Book Illustration	Award Book	Don Wood	*Little Red Riding Hood*	Harcourt
1983	Fiction	Award Book	Gloria Skurzynski	*The Tempering*	Clarion
		Honor Book	Paul Fleischman	*The Path of the Pale Horse*	Harper
	Nonfiction	Award Book	Helen Roney Sattler	*The Illustrated Dinosaur Dictionary*	Lothrop
		Honor Book	Caroline Arnold	*Pets without Homes*	Clarion
	Picture Book Illustration	Award Book	Trina Schart Hyman	*Little Red Riding Hood*	Holiday
1982	Fiction	Award Book	Beverly Cleary	*Ralph S. Mouse*	Morrow
		Honor Book	Mel Glenn	*Class Dismissed*	Clarion
	Nonfiction	Award Book	James Cross Giblin	*Chimney Sweeps*	Crowell
		Honor Book	Judith St. George	*The Brooklyn Bridge*	Putnam
	Picture Book Illustration	Award Book	Tomie dePaola	*Giorgio's Village*	Putnam
1981	Fiction	Award Book	M. E. Kerr	*Little, Little*	Harper

Year	Category	Award	Author/Illustrator	Title	Publisher
		Honor Book	Nancy Willard	*A Visit to William Blake's Inn: Poems for Innocent and Experienced Travelers*	Harcourt
	Nonfiction	Award Book	Elizabeth Helfman	*Blissymbolics*	Lodestar
		Honor Book	Helen Roney Sattler	*Dinosaurs of North America*	Lothrop
1980	Fiction	Award Book	Patricia MacLachlan	*Arthur, for the Very First Time*	Harper
		Honor Book	Paul Fleischman	*The Half-a-Moon Inn*	Harper
	Nonfiction	Award Book	Dorothy Hinshaw Patent	*The Lives of Spiders*	Holiday
		Honor Book	Sue Alexander	*Finding Your First Job*	Dutton
1979	Fiction	Award Book	Carole S. Adler	*The Magic of the Glits*	Macmillan
		Honor Book	Mary Calhoun	*Cross-Country Cat*	Morrow
	Nonfiction	Award Book	Arnold Madison	*Runaway Teens*	Elsevier/Nelson
		Honor Book	Robert McClung	*America's Endangered Birds*	Morrow
1978	Fiction	Award Book	Stella Pevsner	*And You Give Me a Pain, Elaine*	Seabury
		Honor Book	Doris Orgel	*The Devil in Vienna*	Dial
	Nonfiction	Award Book	Phyllis Reynolds Naylor	*How I Came to Be a Writer*	Atheneum
		Honor Book	Gloria Skurzynski	*Bionic Parts for People*	Four Winds
1977	Fiction	Award Book	Bernice Rabe	*The Girl Who Had No Name*	Dutton
		Honor Book	Marion Dane Bauer	*Foster Child*	Seabury
	Nonfiction	Award Book	Robert McClung	*Peeper, First Voice of Spring*	Morrow
		Honor Book	Dorothy Hinshaw Patent	*Evolution Goes on Everyday*	Holiday
1976		Award Book	Eve Bunting	*One More Flight*	Warne
		Honor Books	Florence Parry Heide	*Growing Anyway Up*	Lippincott

Year	Category	Award	Author/Illustrator	Title	Publisher
			Jane Yolen	*The Moon Ribbon*	Crowell
1975		Award Book	Carol Farley	*The Garden Is Doing Fine*	Atheneum
		Honor Books	Jane Yolen	*The Transfigured Hart*	Crowell
			Bernice Rabe	*Naomi*	Nelson
1974		Award Book	Jane Yolen	*The Girl Who Cried Flowers*	Crowell
		Honor Books	Myra Cohen Livingston	*The Way Things Are*	Atheneum
			Sheila Cole	*Meaning Well*	Watts
1973		Award Book	Bette Green	*Summer of My German Soldier*	Dial
		Honor Books	Patricia Beatty	*Red Rock over the River*	Morrow
			Sid Fleischman	*McBroom the Rainmaker*	Grossett

Sid Fleischman Humor Award

Year	Author	Title	Publisher
2004	Gennifer Choldenko	*Al Capone Does My Shirts*	G. P. Putnam's Sons
2003	Lisa Yee	*Millicent Min, Girl Genius*	Arthur A. Levine Books
2002	Sid Fleischman		

Boston Globe-Horn Book Award

The *Horn Book* was created in 1924 by Bertha Mahony to announce publication of children's literature. The organization publishes two periodicals. The *Horn Book Magazine* is a bimonthly magazine that contains articles regarding children's literature. The *Horn Book Guide*, printed twice a year, summarizes and reviews more than 2000 newly published books. The organization also sponsors the Boston Globe-Horn Book Awards.

The Boston Globe-Horn Book Awards, honoring "excellence in literature for children and young adults," were first presented in 1967. Like so many other awards, the rules are easy to understand and follow.

1. Books must be published in the United States.

2. Authors and illustrators may be citizens of countries other than the United States.

3. Presently, three categories—fiction and poetry, nonfiction, and picture book—exist. Prior to 1976, only fiction and picture book categories provided awards.

4. Presently, one winner and two honor books may be awarded in each category. Prior to 1987, more than two honor books could be listed.

5. Books must be published between June 1 of the year before the award and May 31 of the year of the award. For example, the 2005 award-winning books were published between June 1, 2004 and May 31, 2005.

6. Winners are announced in June of the year of the award.

7. The winners receive their awards at a ceremony in September or October at the Boston Atheneum in Boston, Massachusetts.

8. The award winners receive an engraved silver bowl and a cash prize.

9. Honor book awardees receive an engraved silver plate.

Award and Honor Books

Year	Category	Award	Author/Illustrator	Title	Publisher
2005	Fiction	Award Book	Neal Shusterman	*The Schwa Was Here*	Dutton
		Honor Books	Judith Clarke	*Kalpana's Dream*	Front Street
			Marilyn Nelson, author Philippe Lardy, illustrator	*A Wreath for Emmett Till*	Houghton
	Nonfiction	Award Book	Phillip Hoose	*The Race to Save the Lord God Bird*	Kroupa/Farrar
		Honor Books	James Cross Giblin	*Good Brother, Bad Brother: The Story of Edwin Booth and John Wilkes Booth*	Clarion
			Michael Rosen, author Quentin Blake, illustrator	*Michael Rosen's Sad Book*	Candlewick
	Picture Book	Award Book	Mini Grey	*Traction Man Is Here!*	Knopf
		Honor Books	Emily Jenkins, author Pierre Pratt, illustrator	*That New Animal*	Foster/Farrar
			Norton Juster, author Chris Raschka, illustrator	*The Hello, Goodbye Window*	Michael di Capua/ Hyperion
2004	Fiction	Award Book	David Almond	*The Fire-Eaters*	Delacorte
		Honor Books	Cynthia Rylant	*God Went to Beauty School*	HarperTempest

Year	Category	Award	Author/Illustrator	Title	Publisher
			Jonathan Stroud	*The Amulet of Samarkand: The Bartimaeus Trilogy*	Hyperion
	Nonfiction	Award Book	Jim Murphy	*An American Plague: The True and Terrifying Story of the Yellow Fever Epidemic of 1793*	Clarion
		Honor Books	Nicola Davies, author James Croft, illustrator	*Surprising Sharks*	Candlewick
			Bea Uusma Schyffert	*The Man Who Went to the Far Side of the Moon: The Story of Apollo 11 Astronaut Michael Collins*	Chronicle
	Picture Book	Award Book	Mordicai Gerstein	*The Man Who Walked between the Towers*	Roaring Brook
		Honor Books	Anthony Browne	*The Shape Game*	Farrar
			Lynne Rae Perkins	*Snow Music*	Greenwillow
2003	Fiction	Award Book	Anne Fine, author Penny Dale, illustrator	*The Jamie and Angus Stories*	Candlewick
		Honor Books	M. T. Anderson	*Feed*	Candlewick
			Jacqueline Woodson	*Locomotion*	Putnam
	Nonfiction	Award Book	Maira Kalman	*Fireboat: The Heroic Adventures of the John J. Harvey*	Putnam
		Honor Books	Wendie C. Old, author Robert Andrew Parker	*To Fly: The Story of the Wright Brothers*	Clarion
			Nathaniel Philbrick	*Revenge of the Whale: The True Story of the Whaleship Essex*	Putnam
	Picture Book	Award Book	Phyllis Root, author Helen Oxenbury, illustrator	*Big Momma Makes the World*	Candlewick

Year	Category	Award	Author/Illustrator	Title	Publisher
		Honor Books	Barbara McClintock	*Dahlia*	Foster/Farrar
			Walter Dean Myers, author Christopher Myers, illustrator	*Blues Journey*	Holiday
2002	Fiction	Award Book	Graham Salisbury	*Lord of the Deep*	Delacorte
		Honor Books	Hilary McKay	*Saffy's Angel*	McElderry
			Vera B. Williams	*Amber Was Brave, Essie Was Smart*	Greenwillow
	Nonfiction	Award Book	Elizabeth Partridge	*This Land Was Made for You and Me: The Life and Songs of Woody Guthrie*	Viking
		Honor Books	M. T. Anderson, author Kevin Hawkes, illustrator	*Handel, Who Knew What He Liked*	Candlewick
			Bonnie Christensen	*Woody Guthrie: Poet of the People*	Knopf
	Picture Book	Award Book	Bob Graham	*"Let's Get a Pup!" Said Kate*	Candlewick
		Honor Books	Kate McMullan, author Jim McMullan, illustrator	*I Stink!*	Cotler/Harper
			Monika Bang-Campbell, author Molly Bang, illustrator	*Little Rat Sets Sail*	Harcourt
2001	Fiction	Award Book	Marilyn Nelson	*Carver: A Life in Poems*	Front Street
		Honor Books	Polly Horvath	*Everything on a Waffle*	Farrar
			Adèle Geras	*Troy*	Harcourt
	Nonfiction	Award Book	Joan Dash, author Dusan Petricic, illustrator	*The Longitude Prize*	Foster/Farrar
		Honor Books	Carol Otis Hurst, author James Stevenson, illustrator	*Rocks in His Head*	Greenwillow

Year	Category	Award	Author/Illustrator	Title	Publisher
			Don Brown	*Uncommon Traveler: Mary Kingsley in Africa*	Houghton
	Picture Book	Award Book	Cynthia DeFelice, author Robert Andrew Parker	*Cold Feet*	DK Ink
		Honor Books	Emily Jenkins, author Tomel Bogacki, illustrator	*Five Creatures*	Foster/Farrar
			Marc Simont	*The Stray Dog*	HarperCollins
2000	Fiction	Award Book	Franny Billingsley	*The Folk Keeper*	Atheneum
		Honor Books	Susan Cooper	*King of Shadows*	McElderry
			Walter Dean Myers	*145th Street: Short Stories*	Delacorte
	Nonfiction	Award Book	Marc Aronson	*Sir Walter Raleigh and the Quest for El Dorado*	Clarion
		Honor Books	Alan Govenar, editor Shane W. Evans, illustrator	*Osceola: Memories of a Sharecropper's Daughter*	Jump at the Sun/Hyperion
			Albert Marrin	*Sitting Bull and His World*	Dutton
	Picture Book	Award Book	D. B. Johnson	*Henry Hikes to Fitchburg*	Houghton
		Honor Books	Brock Cole	*Buttons*	Farrar
			Gabrielle Vincent	*a day, a dog*	Front Street
1999	Fiction	Award Book	Louis Sachar	*Holes*	Foster/Farrar
		Honor Books	Polly Horvath	*The Trolls*	Farrar
			Walter Dean Myers, author Christopher Myers, illustrator	*Monster*	HarperCollins
	Nonfiction	Award Book	Steve Jenkins	*The Top of the World: Climbing Mount Everest*	Houghton

Year	Category	Award	Author/Illustrator	Title	Publisher
		Honor Books	Jennifer Armstrong	*Shipwreck at the Bottom of the World: The Extraordinary True Story of Shackleton and the Endurance*	Crown
			Aliki	*William Shakespeare & the Globe*	HarperCollins
	Picture Book	Award Book	Joy Cowley, author Nic Bishop, photographer	*Red-Eyed Tree Frog*	Scholastic
		Honor Books	Bill T. Jones and Susan Kuklin, authors Susan Kuklin, photographer	*Dance*	Hyperion
			Edward Lear, author James Marshall, illustrator	*The Owl and the Pussycat*	Michael di Capua/ HarperCollins
	Special Citation		Peter Sis	*Tibet Through the Red Box*	Foster/Farrar
1998	Fiction	Award Book	Francisco Jimenez	*The Circuit: Stories from the Life of a Migrant Child*	University of New Mexico Press
		Honor Books	Jane Leslie Conly	*While No One Was Watching*	Holt
			Kimberly Willis Holt	*My Louisiana Sky*	Holt
	Nonfiction	Award Book	Leon Walter Tillage, author Susan L. Roth, illustrator	*Leon's Story*	Farrar
		Honor Books	Russell Freedman	*Martha Graham: A Dancer's Life*	Clarion
			Jan Greenberg and Sandra Jordan	*Chuck Close Up Close*	DK Ink
	Picture Book	Award Book	Kate Banks, author Georg Hallensleben, illustrator	*And If the Moon Could Talk*	Foster/Farrar
		Honor Books	Betsy Hearne, author Bethanne Andersen, illustrator	*Seven Brave Women*	Greenwillow
			James Stevenson	*Popcorn: Poems*	Greenwillow

Year	Category	Award	Author/Illustrator	Title	Publisher
1997	Fiction	Award Book	Kazumi Yumoto, author Cathy Hirano, translator	*The Friends*	Farrar
		Honor Books	Patricia Reilly Giff	*Lily's Crossing*	Delacourt
			Walter Dean Myers, author Christopher Myers, illustrator	*Harlem*	Scholastic
	Nonfiction	Award Book	Walter Wick	*A Drop of Water: A Book of Science and Wonder*	Scholastic
		Honor Books	David A. Adler, author Terry Widener, illustrator	*Lou Gehrig: The Luckiest Man*	Gulliver/Harcourt
			Diane Stanley	*Leonardo da Vinci*	Morrow
	Picture Book	Award Book	Brian Pinkney	*The Adventures of Sparrowboy*	Simon
		Honor Books	G. Brian Karas	*Home on the Bayou: A Cowboy's Story*	Simon
			Kate Lied, author Lisa Campbell Ernst, illustrator	*Potato: A Tale from the Great Depression*	National Geographic
1996	Fiction	Award Book	Avi, author Brian Floca, illustrator	*Poppy*	Jackson/Orchard
		Honor Books	Eloise McGraw	*The Moorchild*	McElderry
			Ruth White	*Belle Prater's Boy*	Farrar
	Nonfiction	Award Book	Andrea Warren	*Orphan Train Rider: One Boy's True Story*	Houghton
		Honor Books	Joseph Bruchac, author Murv Jacob, illustrator	*The Boy Who Lived with the Bears: And Other Iroquois Stories*	Harper
			Bonnie and Arthur Geisert	*Haystack*	Houghton
	Picture Book	Award Book	Amy Hest, author Jill Barton, illustrator	*In the Rain with Baby Duck*	Candlewick

Year	Category	Award	Author/Illustrator	Title	Publisher
		Honor Books	Caralyn Buehner, author Mark Buehner, illustrator	*Fanny's Dream*	Dial
			Lynne Rae Perkins	*Home Lovely*	Greenwillow
1995	Fiction	Award Book	Tim Wynne-Jones	*Some of the Kinder Planets*	Kroupa/Orchard
		Honor Books	Janet Hickman	*Jericho*	Greenwillow
			Theresa Nelson	*Earthshine*	Jackson/Orchard
	Nonfiction	Award Book	Natalie S. Bober	*Abigail Adams: Witness to a Revolution*	Atheneum
		Honor Books	Robie H. Harris, author Michael Emberley, illustrator	*It's Perfectly Normal: Changing Bodies, Growing Up, Sex, and Sexual Health*	Candlewick
			Jim Murphy	*The Great Fire*	Scholastic
	Picture Book	Award Book	Julius Lester, author Jerry Pinkney, illustrator	*John Henry*	Dial
		Honor Book	Anne Isaacs, author Paul O. Zelinsky, illustrator	*Swamp Angel*	Dutton
1994	Fiction	Award Book	Vera Williams	*Scooter*	Greenwillow
		Honor Books	Anne Fine	*Flour Babies*	Little
			Paula Fox	*Western Wind*	Orchard
	Nonfiction	Award Book	Russell Freedman	*Eleanor Roosevelt: A Life of Discovery*	Clarion
		Honor Books	Albert Marrin	*Unconditional Surrender: U. S. Grant and the Civil War*	Atheneum
			Constance Levy, author Robert Sabuda, illustrator	*A Tree Place and Other Poems*	McElderry
	Picture Book	Award Book	Allen Say	*Grandfather's Journey*	Houghton
		Honor Books	Kevin Henkes	*Owen*	Greenwillow

Year	Category	Award	Author/Illustrator	Title	Publisher
			Peter Sis	*A Small Tall Tale from the Far Far North*	Knopf
1993	Fiction	Award Book	James Berry	*Ajeemah and His Son*	Harper
		Honor Book	Lois Lowry	*The Giver*	Houghton
	Nonfiction	Award Book	Patricia C. and Fredrick McKissack	*Sojourner Truth: Ain't I a Woman?*	Scholastic
		Honor Book	Kathleen Krull, author Kathryn Hewitt, illustrator	*Lives of the Musicians: Good Times, Bad Times (And What the Neighbors Thought)*	Harcourt
	Picture Book	Award Book	Lloyd Alexander, author Trina Schart Hyman	*The Fortune Tellers*	Dutton
		Honor Books	Peter Sis	*Komodo!*	Greenwillow
			Gerald McDermott	*Raven: A Trickster Tale from the Pacific Northwest*	Harcourt
1992	Fiction	Award Book	Cynthia Rylant	*Missing May*	Jackson/Orchard
		Honor Books	Avi	*Nothing but the Truth*	Jackson/Orchard
			Walter Dean Myers	*Somewhere in the Darkness*	Scholastic
	Nonfiction	Award Book	Pat Cummings	*Talking with Artists*	Bradbury
		Honor Books	Lois Ehlert	*Red Leaf, Yellow Leaf*	Harcourt
			Laura Rankin	*The Handmade Alphabet*	Dial
	Picture Book	Award Book	Ed Young	*Seven Blind Mice*	Philomel
		Honor Book	Denise Fleming	*In the Tall, Tall Grass*	Holt
1991	Fiction	Award Book	Avi	*The True Confessions of Charlotte Doyle*	Orchard
		Honor Books	Martha Brooks	*Paradise Café and Other Stories*	Joy Street
			Brenda Seabrooke	*Judy Scuppernong*	Cobblehill

Year	Category	Award	Author/Illustrator	Title	Publisher
	Nonfiction	Award Book	Cynthia Rylant, author Barry Moser, illustrator	*Appalachia: The Voices of Sleeping Birds*	Harcourt
		Honor Books	Russell Freedman	*The Wright Brothers: How They Invented the Airplane*	Holiday House
			Diane Stanley and Peter Vennema, authors Diane Stanley, illustrator	*Good Queen Bess: The Story of Elizabeth I of England*	Four Winds
	Picture Book	Award Book	Katherine Paterson, author Leo and Diane Dillon, illustrators	*The Tale of the Mandarin Ducks*	Lodestar
		Honor Books	Ann Jonas	*Aardvarks, Disembark!*	Greenwillow
			Petra Mathers	*Sophie and Lou*	Harper
1990	Fiction	Award Book	Jerry Spinelli	*Maniac Magee*	Little, Brown
		Honor Books	Paul Fleischman	*Saturnalia*	Harper
			Pam Conrad	*Stonewords*	Harpers
	Nonfiction	Award Book	Jean Fritz	*The Great Little Madison*	Putnam
		Honor Book	Ron and Nancy Goor, authors Ron Goor, photographer	*Insect Metamorphosis: From Egg to Adult*	Atheneum
	Picture Book	Award Book	Ed Young, translator and illustrator	*Lon Po Po: A Red-Riding Hood Story from China*	Philomel
		Honor Book	Bill Martin, Jr. and John Archambault, authors Lois Ehlert, illustrator	*Chicka Chicka Boom Boom*	Simon
	Special Citation		Nancy Ekholm Burkert	*Valentine and Orson*	Farrar
1989	Fiction	Award Book	Paula Fox	*The Village by the Sea*	Orchard
		Honor Books	Peter Dickinson	*Eva*	Delacorte
			William Mayne	*Gideon Ahoy!*	Delacorte

Year	Category	Award	Author/Illustrator	Title	Publisher
	Nonfiction	Award Book	David Macaulay	*The Way Things Work*	Houghton
		Honor Books	Laurence Yep	*The Rainbow People*	Harper
			Philip M. Isaacson	*Round Buildings, Square Buildings, & Buildings That Wiggle Like a Fish*	Knopf
	Picture Book	Award Book	Rosemary Wells	*Shy Charles*	Dial
		Honor Books	Barbara Cooney	*Island Boy*	Viking
			Julie Vivas, illustrator	*The Nativity*	Gulliver/Harcourt
1988	Fiction	Award Book	Mildred D. Taylor, author Max Ginsburg, illustrator	*The Friendship*	Dial
		Honor Books	Berlie Doherty	*Granny Was a Buffer Girl*	Orchard
			Paul Fleischman, author Eric Beddows, illustrator	*Joyful Noise: Poems for Two Voices*	Harper/Zolotow
			Margaret Mahy	*Memory*	McElderry
	Nonfiction	Award Book	Virginia Hamilton	*Anthony Burns: The Defeat and Triumph of a Fugitive Slave*	Knopf
		Honor Books	John Chiasson	*African Journey*	Bradbury
			Jean Little	*Little by Little: A Writer's Education*	Viking
	Picture Book	Award Book	Dianne Snyder, author Allen Say, illustrator	*The Boy of the Three-Year Nap*	Houghton
		Honor Books	Jeannie Baker	*Where the Forest Meets the Sea*	Greenwillow
			Vera B. Williams, author Jennifer Williams and Vera B. Williams, illustrators	*Stringbean's Trip to the Shining Sea*	Greenwillow
1987	Fiction	Award Book	Lois Lowry	*Rabble Starkey*	Houghton

Year	Category	Award	Author/Illustrator	Title	Publisher
		Honor Books	Helen V. Griffith, author James Stevenson, illustrator	*Georgia Music*	Greenwillow
			Janni Howker	*Isaac Campion*	Greenwillow
	Nonfiction	Award Book	Marcia Sewall	*The Pilgrims of Plimoth*	Atheneum
		Honor Books	Sheila Kitzinger, author Lennart Nilsson, photographer	*Being Born*	Grosset and Dunlap
			Joanna Cole, author Bruce Degan, illustrator	*The Magic Schoolbus at the Waterworks*	Scholastic
			John Hartford	*Steamboat in a Cornfield*	Crown
	Picture Book	Award Book	John Steptoe	*Mufaro's Beautiful Daughters*	Lothrop
		Honor Books	Judith Hendershot, author Thomas B. Allen, illustrator	*In Coal Country*	Knopf
			Vera B. Williams	*Cherries and Cherry Pits*	Greenwillow
			Joan W. Blos, author Stephen Gammell, illustrator	*Old Henry*	Morrow
1986	Fiction	Award Book	Zibby Oneal	*In Summer Light*	Viking
		Honor Books	Pam Conrad	*Prairie Songs*	Harper
			Diana Wynne Jones	*Howl's Moving Castle*	Greenwillow
	Nonfiction	Award Book	Peggy Thomson	*Auks, Rocks, and the Odd Dinosaur: Inside Stories from the Smithsonian's Museum of Natural History*	Crowell
		Honor Books	Brent Ashabranner, author Paul Conklin, photographer	*Dark Harvest: Migrant Farmworkers in America*	Dodd
			James C. Giblin	*The Truth about Santa Claus*	Crowell

Year	Category	Award	Author/Illustrator	Title	Publisher
	Picture Book	Award Book	Molly Bang	*The Paper Crane*	Greenwillow
		Honor Books	Anthony Browne	*Gorilla*	Knopf
			Ann Jonas	*The Trek*	Greenwillow
			Chris Van Allsburg	*The Polar Express*	Houghton
1985	Fiction	Award Book	Bruce Brooks	*The Moves Make the Man*	Harper
		Honor Books	Dick King-Smith, author Mary Rayner, illustrator	*The Gallant Pig*	Crown
			Margaret Mahy	*The Changeover: A Supernatural Romance*	Atheneum/ McElderry
	Nonfiction	Award Book	Rhoda Blumberg	*Commodore Perry in the Land of the Shogun*	Lothrop
		Honor Books		*Boy*	Farrar
			Albert Marin	*1812: The War Nobody Won*	Atheneum
	Picture Book	Award Book	Thacher Hurd	*Mama Don't Allow*	Harper
		Honor Books	Mavis Jukes, author Lloyd Bloom, illustrator	*Like Jake and Me*	Knopf
			David M. Schwartz, author Stephen Kellogg, illustrator	*How Much Is a Million?*	Lothrop
		Honor Book	Chris Van Allsburg	*The Mysteries of Harris Burdick*	Houghton
	Special Citation		Tana Hoban	*1, 2, 3*	Greenwillow
1984	Fiction	Award Book	Patricia Wrightson	*A Little Fear*	Atheneum/ McElderry
		Honor Books	Diana Wynne Jones	*Archer's Goon*	Greenwillow
			Patricia MacLachlan	*Unclaimed Treasures*	Harper
			Cynthia Voigt	*A Solitary Blue*	Atheneum
	Nonfiction	Award Book	Jean Fritz, author Ed Young, illustrator	*The Double Life of Pocahontas*	Putnam

Year	Category	Award	Author/Illustrator	Title	Publisher
		Honor Books	Polly Schoyer Brooks	*Queen Eleanor: Independent Spirit of the Medieval World: A Biography of Eleanor of Aquitaine*	Lippincott
			Russell Freedman	*Children of the Wild West*	Clarion
			David and Charlotte Yue	*The Tipi: A Center of Native American Life*	Knopf
	Picture Book	Award Book	Warwick Hutton	*Jonah and the Great Fish*	Atheneum/ McElderry
		Honor Books	Molly Bang	*Dawn*	Morrow
			Kate Duke	*The Guinea Pig ABC*	Dutton
			Arnold Lobel, author Anita Lobel, illustrator	*The Rose in My Garden*	Greenwillow
1983	Fiction	Award Book	Virginia Hamilton	*Sweet Whispers, Brother Rush*	Philomel
		Honor Books	Jean Fritz, author Margot Tomes, illustrator	*Homesick: My Own Story*	Putnam
			Rosemary Sutcliff	*The Road to Camlann*	Dutton
			Cynthia Voigt	*Dicey's Song*	Atheneum
	Nonfiction	Award Book	Daniel S. Davis	*Behind Barbed Wire: The Imprisonment of Japanese Americans During World War II*	Dutton
		Honor Books	Toshi Maruki	*Hiroshima No Pika*	Lothrop
			Milton Meltzer	*The Jewish Americans: A History in Their Own Words*	Crowell
	Picture Book	Award Book	Vera B. Williams	*A Chair for My Mother*	Greenwillow
		Honor Books	Helme Heine	*Friends*	Atheneum/ McElderry

Year	Category	Award	Author/Illustrator	Title	Publisher
			Ai-Ling Louie, author Ed Young, illustrator	*Yeh-Shen: A Cinderella Story from China*	Philomel
			William Steig	*Doctor De Soto*	Farrar
1982	Fiction	Award Book	Ruth Park	*Playing Beatie Bow*	Atheneum
		Honor Books	Nancy Bond	*The Voyage Begun*	Atheneum
			Ann Schlee	*Ask Me No Questions*	Holt
			Robert Westall	*The Scarecrows*	Greenwillow
	Nonfiction	Award Book	Aranka Siegal	*Upon the Head of the Goat: A Childhood in Hungary 1939–1944*	Farrar
		Honor Books	John Nance	*Lobo of the Tasaday*	Pantheon
			Helen Roney Sattler, author Anthony Rao, illustrator	*Dinosaurs of North America*	Lothrop
	Picture Book	Award Book	Nancy Willard, author Alice and Martin Provensen, illustrators	*A Visit to William Blake's Inn: Poems for Innocent and Experienced Travelers*	Harcourt
		Honor Book	Tomie dePaola	*The Friendly Beasts: An Old English Christmas Carol*	Putnam
1981	Fiction	Award Book	Lynn Hall	*The Leaving*	Scribners
		Honor Books	Robert Burch	*Ida Early Comes Over the Mountain*	Viking
			Leon Garfield	*Footsteps*	Delacorte
	Nonfiction	Award Book	Kathryn Lasky, author Christopher G. Knight, photographer	*The Weaver's Gift*	Warne
		Honor Books	Betty English	*You Can't Be Timid with a Trumpet: Notes from the Orchestra*	Lothrop

Year	Category	Award	Author/Illustrator	Title	Publisher
			James Howe, author Mal Warshaw, photographer	*The Hospital Book*	Crown
			Lila Perl	*Junk Food, Fast Food, Health Food: What America Eats and Why*	Clarion
	Picture Book	Award Book	Maurice Sendak	*Outside Over There*	Harper
		Honor Books	Olaf Baker, author Stephen Gammell, illustrator	*Where the Buffaloes Begin*	Warne
			Arnold Lobel, author Anita Lobel, illustrator	*On Market Street*	Greenwillow
			Chris Van Allsburg	*Jumanji*	Houghton
1980	Fiction	Award Book	Andrew Davies	*Conrad's War*	Crown
		Honor Books	Betsy Byars	*The Night Swimmers*	Delacorte
			Clive King	*Me and My Million*	Crowell
			Jan Slepian	*The Alfred Summer*	Macmillan
	Nonfiction	Award Book	Mario Salvadori, author Saralinda Hooker and Christopher Ragus, illustrators	*Building: The Fight Against Gravity*	Atheneum/ McElderry
		Honor Books	Eloise Greenfield, author Jerry Pinkney, illustrator	*Childtimes: A Three-Generation Memoir*	Crowell
			Jean Fritz, author Stephen Gammell, illustrator	*Stonewall*	Putnam
			William Jaspersohn, author Chuck Eckart, illustrator	*How the Forest Grew*	Greenwillow
	Picture Book	Award Book	Chris Van Allsburg	*The Garden of Abdul Gasazi*	Houghton
		Honor Book	Molly Bang	*The Gray Lady and the Strawberry Snatcher*	Greenwillow

Year	Category	Award	Author/Illustrator	Title	Publisher
		Honor Book	John Chase Bowden, author Marc Brown, illustrator	*Why the Tides Ebb and Flow*	Houghton
	Special Citation		Graham Oakley	*Graham Oakley's Magical Changes*	Atheneum
1979	Fiction	Award Book	Sid Fleischman	*Humbug Mountain*	Atlantic
		Honor Books	Sue Ellen Bridgers	*All Together Now*	Knopf
			Cecil Bødker	*Silas and Ben-Godik*	Delacorte
	Nonfiction	Award Book	David Kherdian	*The Road from Home: The Story of an Armenian Girl*	Greenwillow
		Honor Books	Richard Snow, author David Plowden, photographer	*The Iron Road: A Portrait of American Railroading*	Four Winds
			Margot Zemach	*Self-Portrait: Margot Zemach*	Addison
			Martin Sandler	*The Story of American Photography: An Illustrated History for Young People*	Little
	Picture Book	Award Book	Raymond Briggs	*The Snowman*	Random
		Honor Books	Mary Calhoun, author Erik Ingraham, illustrator	*Cross-Country Cat*	Morrow
			Rachel Isadora	*Ben's Trumpet*	Greenwillow
1978	Fiction	Award Book	Ellen Raskin	*The Westing Game*	Dutton
		Honor Books	Beverly Cleary	*Ramona and Her Father*	Morrow
			Jamake Highwater	*Anpao: An American Indian Odyssey*	Lippincott
			Myron Levoy	*Alan and Naomi*	Harper
	Nonfiction	Award Book	Ilse Koehn	*Mischling, Second Degree*	Greenwillow

Year	Category	Award	Author/Illustrator	Title	Publisher
		Honor Books	Betty Baker	*Settlers and Strangers: Native Americans of the Desert Southwest and History as They Saw It*	Macmillan
			David Macaulay	*Castle*	Houghton
	Picture Book	Award Book	Mitsumasa Anno	*Anno's Journey*	Collins-World
		Honor Books	Philippe Dumas	*The Story of Edward*	Parents
			Patricia Lee Gauch, author Trina Schart Hyman, illustrator	*On to Widecombe Fair*	Putnam
			Collette O'Hare, author Jenny Rodwell, illustrator	*What Do You Feed Your Donkey On? Rhymes from a Belfast Childhood*	Collins-World
1977	Fiction	Award Book	Laurence Yep	*Child of the Owl*	Harper
		Honor Books	Rosemary Sutcliff	*Blood Feud*	Dutton
			Mildred Taylor	*Roll of Thunder, Hear My Cry*	Dial
			Robert Westall	*The Machine Gunners*	Greenwillow
	Nonfiction	Award Book	Peter Dickinson	*Chance, Luck and Destiny*	Atlantic
		Honor Books	Betty Ann Kevles	*Watching the Wild Apes*	Dutton
			Lucille Recht Penner	*The Colonial Cookbook*	Hastings
			Lucille Schulberg Warner	*From Slave to Abolitionist*	Dial
	Picture Book	Award Book	Wallace Tripp	*Granfa' Grig Had a Pig and Other Rhymes Without Reason from Mother Goose*	Little
		Honor Books	Mitsumasa Anno	*Anno's Counting Book*	Crowell
			Margaret Musgrove, author Leo and Diane Dillon, illustrators	*Ashanti to Zulu: African Traditions*	Dial

Year	Category	Award	Author/Illustrator	Title	Publisher
			William Steig	*The Amazing Bone*	Farrar
	Special Citation		Jorg Mueller	*The Changing City and the Changing Countryside*	Atheneum/ McElderry
1976	Fiction	Award Book	Jill Paton Walsh	*Unleaving*	Farrar
		Honor Books	Nancy Bond	*A String in the Harp*	Atheneum/ McElderry
			Mollie Hunter	*A Stranger Came Ashore*	Harper
			Laurence Yep	*Dragonwings*	Harper
	Nonfiction	Award Book	Alfred Tamarin and Shirley Glubok	*Voyaging to Cathay: Americans in the China Trade*	Viking
		Honor Books	Jean Fritz, author Trina Schart Hyman, illustrator	*Will You Sign Here, John Hancock?*	Coward
			Milton Meltzer	*Never to Forget: The Jews of the Holocaust*	Harper
			David Macaulay	*Pyramid*	Houghton
	Picture Book	Award Book	Remy Charlip and Jerry Joyner	*Thirteen*	Parents
		Honor Books	Byrd Baylor, author Peter Parnall, illustrator	*The Desert Is Theirs*	Scribners
			Chris Conover	*Six Little Ducks*	Crowell
			Lorenz Graham, author Leo and Diane Dillon, illustrators	*Song of the Boat*	Crowell
1975	Fiction	Award Book	T. Degens	*Transport 7-41-R*	Viking
		Honor Book	Sharon Bell Mathis, author Leo and Diane Dillon, illustrators	*The Hundred Penny Box*	Viking
	Picture Book	Award Book	Mitsumasa Anno	*Anno's Alphabet*	Crowell
		Honor Books	Eloise Greenfield, author John Steptoe, illustrator	*She Come Bringing Me That Little Baby Girl*	Lippincott

Year	Category	Award	Author/Illustrator	Title	Publisher
			Ann McGovern, author Nola Langner, illustrator	*Scram Kid!*	Viking
			Emilie Warren McLeod, author David McPhail, illustrator	*The Bear's Bicycle*	Atlantic
1974	Fiction	Award Book	Virginia Hamilton	*M. C. Higgins, the Great*	Macmillan
		Honor Books	Jean Fritz, author Margot Tomes, illustrator	*And Then What Happened, Paul Revere?*	Coward
			Jane Gardam	*The Summer after the Funeral*	Macmillan
			Doris Buchanan Smith	*Tough Chauncey*	Morrow
	Picture Book	Award Book	Muriel Feelings, author Tom Feelings, illustrator	*Jambo Means Hello*	Dial
		Honor Books	Marcia Brown	*All Butterflies*	Scribners
			Robert Kraus, author Jose Aruego and Ariane Dewey, illustrators	*Herman the Helper*	Windmill
			William Kurelek	*A Prairie Boy's Winter*	Houghton
1973	Fiction	Award Book	Susan Cooper	*The Dark Is Rising*	Atheneum
		Honor Books	Lloyd Alexander	*The Cat Who Wished to Be a Man*	Dutton
			Mabel Esther Allan	*An Island in a Green Sea*	Atheneum
			Emma Smith	*No Way of Telling*	Atheneum/ McElderry
	Picture Book	Award Book	Howard Pyle, author Trina Schart Hyman, illustrator	*King Stork*	Little
		Honor Books	Gerald McDermott	*The Magic Tree*	Holt
			Ellen Raskin	*Who, Said Sue, Said Whoo?*	Atheneum

Year	Category	Award	Author/Illustrator	Title	Publisher
			Lynd Ward	*The Silver Pony*	Houghton
1972	Fiction	Award Book	Rosemary Sutcliff	*Tristan and Iseult*	Dutton
	Picture Book	Award Book	John Burningham	*Mr. Grumpy's Outing*	Holt
1971	Fiction	Award Book	Eleanor Cameron	*A Room Made of Windows*	Atlantic
		Honor Books	Hester Burton	*Beyond the Weir Bridge*	Crowell
			Olivia Coolidge	*Come by Here*	Houghton
			Robert C. O'Brien	*Mrs. Frisby and the Rats of NIMH*	Atheneum
	Picture Book	Award Book	Kazue Mizumara	*If I Built a Village…*	Crowell
		Honor Books	Janina Domanska	*If All the Seas Were One Sea*	Macmillan
			William Sleator, author Blair Lent, illustrator	*The Angry Moon*	Atlantic
			Bernard Waber	*A Firefly Named Torchy*	Houghton
1970	Fiction	Award Book	John Rowe Townsend	*The Intruder*	Lippincott
		Honor Book	Vera and Bill Cleaver	*Where the Lilies Bloom*	Lippincott
	Picture Book	Award Book	Ezra Jack Keats	*Hi, Cat!*	Macmillan
		Honor Book	Gail Haley	*A Story, A Story*	Atheneum
1969	Fiction	Award Book	Ursula K. Le Guin	*A Wizard of Earthsea*	Parnassus
		Honor Books	K. M. Peyton	*Flambards*	World
			Elizabeth Borton de Trevino	*Turi's Poppa*	Farrar
			Paul Zindel	*The Pigman*	Harper
	Picture Book	Award Book	John S. Goodall	*The Adventures of Paddy Pork*	Harcourt
		Honor Books	Ann Atwood	*New Moon Cove*	Scribners
			Edna Mitchell Preston, author Clement Hurd, illustrator	*Monkey in the Jungle*	Viking

Year	Category	Award	Author/Illustrator	Title	Publisher
			Brinton Turkle	*Thy Friend, Obadiah*	Viking
1968	Fiction	Award Book	John Lawson	*The Spring Rider*	Crowell
		Honor Books	E. M. Almedingen	*Young Mark*	Farrar
			Audrey White Beyer	*Dark Venture*	Knopf
			Leon Garfield	*Smith*	Pantheon
			Esther Hautzig	*The Endless Steppe*	Crowell
	Picture Book	Award Book	Arlene Mosel, author Blair Lent, illustrator	*Tikki Tikki Tembo*	Holt
		Honor Books	Bernarda Bryson	*Gilgamesh: Man's First Story*	Holt
			Pat Hutchins	*Rosie's Walk*	Macmillan
			Brothers Grimm, authors Adrienne Adams, illustrator	*Jorinda and Joringel*	Scribners
			Elizabeth Johnson, author Trina Schart Hyman, illustrator	*All in Free but Janey*	Little
1967	Fiction	Award Book	Erik Christian Haugaard	*The Little Fishes*	Houghton
	Picture Book	Award Book	Peter Spier	*London Bridge Is Falling Down*	Doubleday

Bibliography

Alter, Judy. *Laura Ingalls Wilder: Pioneer and Author*. Chanhassen, MN: The Child's World, 2004.

Anderson, Dorothy J. "Mildred L. Batchelder: 1901–1998." *Journal of Youth Services in Libraries* 12, No. 3 (Spring 1999): 7–8.

Anderson, Dorothy Jean. "Mildred L. Batchelder: A Study in Leadership." Ph.D. diss., Texas Woman's University, 1981.

"Astrid Lindgren" [accessed June 26, 2005] from en.wikipedia.org/wiki/Astrid_Lindgren.

"Astrid Lindgren (1907–2002)" [accessed June 26, 2005] from www.kirjasto.sci.fi/alindgr.htm. "The Astrid Lindgren Memorial Award" [accessed June 26, 2005] from www.alma.se/page. php?setlanguage=EN.

Balderrama, Sandra Rios. E-mail to author, November 3, 2004.

Balderrama, Sandra Rios. Telephone conversation with author, February 28, 2005.

Bankston, John. *Michael L. Printz and the Story of the Michael L. Printz Award*. Bear, DEL: Mitchell Lane Publishers, 2004.

Bankston, John. *Randolph J. Caldecott and the Story of the Caldecott Medal*. Hockessin, DEL: Mitchell Lane Publishers, 2004.

Belpré, Pura. *Firefly Summer*. Houston, TX: Piñata Books, 1996.

"Belpré, Pura." In *Fourth Book of Junior Authors and Illustrators*, updated 1999. [database online] [August 16, 2004] from vnweb.hwwilsonweb.com.

Billington, Elizabeth T., editor. *The Randolph Caldecott Treasury*. New York: Frederick Warne & Co., 1978.

"Biographical Sketch of Jane Addams" [accessed June 25, 2005] from www.uic.edu/ jaddams/hull/ja_bio.html.

"Caldecott Medal Home Page" [accessed June 26, 2005] from www.ala.org/ala/alsc/ awardsscholarships/literaryawds/caldecottmedal/caldecottmedal.htm.

Carter, Betty. "Who Is Margaret Edwards and What Is This Award Being Given in Her Honor?" *The ALAN Review* (Spring 1992): 45–48.

"The Charlotte Zolotow Award" [accessed June 25, 2005] from www.soemadison. wisc.edu/ccbc/books/zolotow.asp.

Collins, David R. *To the Point: A Story about E. B. White*. Minneapolis, MN: Carolrhoda Books, 1989.

"The Complete Works of Edgar Allan Poe" [June 26, 2005] from eserver.org/books/poe/.

"Coretta Scott King Book Award" [accessed June 26, 2005] from www.ala.org/ala/emiert/ corettascottkingbookawards/corettascott.htm.

Cummins, June. "Sydney Taylor: A Centenary Celebration." *The Horn Book Magazine* 82 (March/April 2005): 230–234.

"Dolphin" [accessed August 14, 2005] from http://en.wikipedia.org/wiki/Dolphin.

"Dr. Seuss" [accessed June 25, 2005] from en.wikipedia.org/wiki/Dr._Seuss <http://en.wikipedia. org/wiki/Dr._Seuss> .

"Dr. Seuss's Biography" [accessed June 25, 2005] from www.nea.org/readacross/resources/seussbiography.html.

"Edgar Allan Poe" [accessed January 8, 2005] from vnweb.hwwilsonweb.com.

"The Edgars and Other MWA Awards" [accessed June 26, 2005] from www.mysterywriters.org/pages/awards/index.htm.

Elledge, Scott. *E. B. White: A Biography*. New York: W. W. Norton & Co., 1984.

Engel, Dean, and Florence B. Freedman. *Ezra Jack Keats: A Biography with Illustrations*. New York: Silver Moon Press, 1995.

Engen, Rodney. *Kate Greenaway: A Biography*. New York: Schocken Books, 1981.

Engen, Rodney. K. *Randolph Caldecott: "Lord of the Nursery."* London: Bloomsbury Books, 1988.

Estes, Glenn, editor. *American Writers for Children Since 1960: Fiction*. Detroit, MI: A Bruccoli Clark Book (Gale Research Co.), 1986.

Estrin, Heidi. E-mail to author, May 9, 2005.

Estrin, Heidi. E-mail to author, May 22, 2005.

Estrin, Heidi. E-mail to author, August 23, 2005.

Gaines, Ann Graham. *Dr. Seuss: A Real-Life Reader Biography*. Bear, DEL: Mitchell Lane Publishers, 2002.

Gillespie, John T., and Corinne J. Naden. *The Newbery Companion: Booktalk and Related Materials for Newbery Medal and Honor Books*. Englewood, CO: Libraries Unlimited, 2001.

"The Golden Kite Award" [accessed July 25, 2005] from http://www.scbwi.org/awards.htm.

Gonzalez, Mario M. Facsimile to author, November 16, 2004.

Gonzalez, Mario M. Telephone conversation with author, November 16, 2004.

Griffith, Susan C., and Donna Barkman. "Imagining Peace and Social Justice." *Book Links* 14, No. 4 (March 2005): 59–63.

Hancock, Marjorie R. "Happy Birthday, Hans Christian Andersen!" *Book Links* 14, No. 4 (March 2005): 6–9.

"Hans Christian Andersen Award" [accessed June 26, 2005] from www.ibby.org/index.php?id=273.

"Hans Christian Andersen Award" [accessed June 26, 2005] from http://en.wikipedia.org/wiki/Hans_Christian_Andersen_Award.

"Hans Christian Andersen: Fairy Tales and Stories" [accessed June 26, 2005] from hca.gilead.org.il/.

Harvey, Bonnie Carman. *Jane Addams: Nobel Prize Winner and Founder of Hull House*. Berkeley Heights, NJ: Enslow Publishers, 1999.

Hopkins, Lee Bennett. *Books Are by People*. New York: Citation Press, 1969.

Hopkins, Lee Bennett. *More Books by More People*. New York: Citation Press, 1974.

"The Horn Book" [accessed July 25, 2005] from http://www.hbook.com/publications/guide/default.asp

Hurwitz, Johanna. *Astrid Lindgren: Storyteller to the World*. New York: Viking Kestrel, 1989.

Irish, Anne. E-mail to author, June 27, 2005.

Irish, Anne. Telephone call to author, July 14, 2005.

"Jane Addams" [accessed June 25, 2005] from www.lkwdpl.org/wihohio/adda-jan.htm.

"Jane Addams Children's Book Award" [accessed June 25, 2005] from home.igc.org/~japa/jacba/index_jacba.html.

Jerome, Richard. "Dream Keeper." *People Weekly* 49, No. 24 (June 22, 1998): pp. 46–49.

"The Kate Greenaway Medal" [accessed June 26, 2005] from www.carnegiegreenaway.org.uk/green/green.html.

Kemp, James F. "Kate Greenaway." In *Contemporary Authors Online.* New York: Gale, 2003 [database online] [accessed January 1, 2005].

Kent, Zachary. *Edgar Allan Poe: Tragic Poet and Master of Mystery.* Berkeley Heights, NJ: Enslow Publishers, 2001.

Kovacs, Deborah, and James Preller. *Meet the Authors and Illustrators: 60 Creators of Favorite Children's Books Talk about Their Work.* New York: Scholastic Professional Books, 1991.

Lapides, Linda F. "Margaret Alexander Edwards, 1902–1988." *Journal of Youth Services in Libraries* 15, No. 4 (Summer 2002): 44–49.

"Laura Ingalls Wilder Frontier Girl" [accessed June 25, 2005] from webpages.marshall.edu/~irby1/laura/frames.html.

"Laura Ingalls Wilder Historic Home and Museum" [accessed June 25, 2005] from www.lauraingallswilderhome.com/.

"The Laura Ingalls Wilder Medal" [accessed June 25, 2005] from www.ala.org/ala/alsc/awardsscholarships/literaryawds/wildermedal/wildermedal.htm.

"Lee Bennett Hopkins" [accessed June 26, 2005] from www.harperchildrens.com/catalog/author_xml.asp?authorid=12232.

"Lee Bennett Hopkins Poetry Award" [accessed June 26, 2005] from www.pabook.libraries.psu.edu/activities/hopkins/.

"Margaret A. Edwards Award" [accessed June 25, 2005] from www.ala.org/ala/yalsa/booklistsawards/margaretaedwards/margaretedwards.htm.

"The Michael L. Printz Award for Excellence in Young Adult Literature" [accessed June 26, 2005] from www.ala.org/ala/yalsa/booklistsawards/printzaward/Printz,_Michael_L__Award.htm.

"The Mildred L. Batchelder Award" [accessed June 26, 2005] from www.ala.org/ala/alsc/awardsscholarships/literaryawds/batchelderaward/batchelderaward.htm.

Morgan, Judith, and Neil Morgan. *Dr. Seuss and Mr. Geisel: A Biography.* New York: Random House, 1995.

"Mrs. Coretta Scott King, Human Rights Activist and Leader." [accessed June 27, 2005] from http://www.thekingcenter.org/csk/bio.html.

Newbery, John. *A Little Pretty Pocket-Book (A Facsimile with an Introductory Essay and Bibliography by M. F. Thwaite).* New York: Harcourt, Brace & World, 1966.

"The Official Charlotte Zolotow Web Site" [accessed June 25, 2005] from www.charlottezolotow.com/.

Petterchak, Janice. *"Books that Stand the Test of Time": The Story of Bound to Stay Bound Books, 1920–1998.* Jacksonville, IL: Bound to Stay Bound Books, 1997.

Pope, Deborah. E-mail to author, February 7, 2005.

"A Printz of a Man" [accessed June 26, 2005] from www.ala.org/ala/yalsa/booklistsawards/printzaward/aprintzofaman/printzman.htm.

"The Pura Belpré Award" [accessed June 26, 2005] from www.ala.org/ala/alsc/awardsscholarships/literaryawds/belpremedal/belprmedal.html.

"Pura Belpré Papers" [accessed June 27, 2005] from www.centropr.org/lib-arc/belpre2.html.

"Robert F. Sibert Informational Award." [accessed June 25, 2005] from www.ala.org/ala/alsc/awardsscholarships/literaryawds/sibertmedal/Sibert_Medal.htm.

Roberts, Russell. *John Newbery and the Story of the Newbery Medal.* Hockessin, DEL: Mitchell Lane Publishers, 2004.

Roman, Susan. E-mail to author, May 31, 2005.

Roman, Susan. E-mail to author, April 1, 2005.

"Scott O'Dell" [accessed June 26, 2005] from www.scottodell.com/.

Sibert, Bob. E-mail to author, April 1, 2005.

Silvey, Anita, Editor. *The Essential Guide to Children's Books and Their Creators.* New York: Houghton Mifflin, 2002.

Smith, Henrietta M. *The Coretta Scott King Awards Book, 1970–1999.* Chicago, IL: ALA Editions, 1999.

Strong, Amy. *Lee Bennett Hopkins: A Children's Poet.* New York: Scholastic, 2003.

Sutherland, Zena. "Mildred L. Batchelder, 1901–1998." *The Horn Book* 76, No. 1 (January/February 1999): 100–102.

"Sydney (Brenner) Taylor." In *Contemporary Authors Online.* Gale, 2003 [database online] [accessed February 2, 2005] from web7.infotrac.galegroup.com/itw/infomark/395/894/59881495w7/purl=rcl_CA_0_H.

"Sydney Taylor." In *Junior Authors Electronic,* updated 1999. [database online] [accessed February 2, 2005] from vnweb.hwwilsonweb.com.

"Sydney Taylor Book Awards." in Association of Jewish Libraries Web site [accessed June 25, 2005] from www.jewishlibraries.org.

"Theodor Seuss Geisel Award" [accessed June 25, 2005] from www.ala.org/ala/alsc/awardsscholarships/literaryawds/drseussaward/DrSeussAward.htm.

Townsend, John Rowe. *John Newbery and His Books: Trade and Plumb-Cake for Ever, Huzza!* Metuchen, NJ: Scarecrow Press, 1994.

Ward, S. (Stasia). *Meet E. B. White.* New York: Rosen Publishing Group, 2001.

Weidt, Maryann N. *Oh, the Places He Went: A Story about Dr. Seuss—Theodor Seuss Geisel.* Minneapolis, MN: Carolrhoda Books, 1994.

"Welcome to the Newbery Medal Home Page!" [accessed June 27, 2005] from http://www.ala.org/ala/alsc/awardsscholarships/literaryawds/newberymedal/newberymedal.htm.

"Welcome to the World of Ezra Jack Keats…" [accessed June 25, 2005] from www.ezra-jack-keats.org/.

"Who Was Sydney Taylor?" Association of Jewish Libraries Web site [pdf file] [accessed June 25, 2005] from www.jewishlibraries.org.

Wilder, Laura Ingalls. *Little House in the Big Woods.* New York: Harper & Row, 1953.

Wilder, Laura Ingalls. *Little Town on the Prairie.* New York: Harper & Row, 1953.

Index

About the Author

DIANA F. MARKS is a teacher of gifted elementary students for the Council Rock School District in Bucks County, PA. She has been a teacher for over 25 years.